ARCHAEOLOGY AND THE
INDIGENOUS PEOPLES OF THE MARITIMES

ARCHAEOLOGY AND THE INDIGENOUS PEOPLES OF THE MARITIMES

Michael Deal

MEMORIAL UNIVERSITY PRESS

© 2023 Michael Deal

All rights reserved. No part of this publication may be reproduced, stored in a retrieval system, or transmitted in any form or by any means, without the prior written consent of the publisher.

Library and Archives Canada Cataloguing in Publication
Title: Archaeology and the Indigenous peoples of the Maritimes / Michael Deal.
Names: Deal, Michael, 1952- author.
Series: Social and economic studies (St. John's, N.L.) ; no. 94.
Description: Series statement: Social and economic studies ; 94 | Includes bibliographical references and index.
Identifiers: Canadiana (print) 20230566693 | Canadiana (ebook) 20230566723 | ISBN 9781990445118 (softcover) | ISBN 9781990445132 (PDF) | ISBN 9781990445125 (EPUB)
Subjects: LCSH: Indigenous peoples—Maritime Provinces—History. | LCSH: Maritime Provinces—Antiquities. | LCSH: Prehistoric peoples—Maritime Provinces. | LCSH: Antiquities, Prehistoric—Maritime Provinces. | LCSH: Excavations (Archaeology)—Maritime Provinces. | CSH: First Nations—Maritime Provinces—Antiquities.
Classification: LCC E78.M28 D43 2023 | DDC 971.5/0109009—dc23

Cover images: Michael Deal
Cover design: Alison Carr
Copy editing: Richard Tallman
Page design and typesetting: Alison Carr

Published by Memorial University Press
Memorial University of Newfoundland
PO Box 4200
St. John's, NL A1C 5S7
www.memorialuniversitypress.ca

Printed in Canada   29 28 27 26 25 24 23   1 2 3 4 5 6 7 8

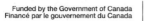

CONTENTS

vi	|	*List of Tables*
vi	|	*List of Vignettes*
vii	|	*List of Figures*
xiii	|	*Acknowledgements*
xvii	|	*A Comment on Terminology*
xix	|	*Foreword by Roger Lewis*
1	|	1 Traditional Context
21	|	2 Practising Archaeology in the Maritimes
63	|	3 The Why and How Questions
97	|	4 Peopling a New Land
129	|	5 The Long Ago People
185	|	6 The Clay Pot People
247	|	7 The Prophecy
279	|	*References Cited*
343	|	*Index*

LIST OF TABLES

| 4 | 1. Chronological Periods for Archaeology in the Maritimes.
| 77 | 2. Petersen and Sanger (1991) Ceramic Period Subdivisions and Temporal Equivalents.
| 114 | 3. Selected Palaeo Projectile Points from Small Collections and Isolated Finds.

LIST OF VIGNETTES

| 26 | 1. The First Museums.
| 33 | 2. George Patterson and the Archaeology of Merigomish.
| 42 | 3. A Stone Age Village at Bocabec.
| 69 | 4. Methods in Maritimes Archaeology.
| 76 | 5. Building a Timeline for the Maritimes.
| 101 | 6. Retreat of the Great Glacier.
| 110 | 7. Debert/Belmont Complex.
| 123 | 8. Late Palaeo Sites.
| 142 | 9. Gaspereau Lake.
| 162 | 10. Cow Point.
| 176 | 11. Mud Lake Stream.
| 201 | 12. Augustine and McKinlay.
| 211 | 13. Beginnings of a Rock Art Tradition.
| 224 | 14. Davidson Cove Quarry and Workshop.
| 241 | 15. St. Croix Village.
| 271 | 16. Wampum Use on the Maritime Peninsula.

LIST OF FIGURES

11 | **Figure 1**. Excavation and gabion placement at the Ministers Island Site, 1978.

23 | **Figure 2:** Effects of coastal erosion in the Bay of Fundy and Minas Basin.

25 | **Figure 3:** New Brunswick naturalists: Abraham Gesner and George Matthew.

27 | **Figure 4:** New Brunswick Natural History Museum, 1906–1932.

28 | **Figure 5:** Harry Piers (curator, Nova Scotia Provincial Museum) with Henry and Susan Sack, Fox Point Road, near Hubbards, Lunenburg County, 1935.

32 | **Figure 6:** Roger Lewis at Frostfish Cove, the location of the first organized archaeological excavation in the Maritimes.

34 | **Figure 7:** Reverend George Patterson, Nova Scotia's first archaeologist.

35 | **Figure 8:** George Patterson cabinet card illustrating artifacts from his fieldwork at Merigomish.

41 | **Figure 9:** Natural History Society of New Brunswick campsite at Bocabec, 1883, based on a watercolour sketch by Bessie Whitney.

43 | **Figure 10:** Top: George Matthew's profile and ground plan of an excavated feature at the Bocabec site, New Brunswick. Bottom: Bocabec beach today.

46 | **Figure 11:** Early professional archaeologists: William J. Wintemberg and Harlan I. Smith.

47 | **Figure 12:** Harlan I. Smith excavation at Merigomish shell midden, Nova Scotia, 1914.

48 | **Figure 13:** Warren K. Moorehead and "The Force" at their camp on the flat below Grand Falls, NB, 1914.

50 | **Figure 14:** Carved slate anthropomorphic figurine collected by folklorist MacEdward Leach, at an old campsite on the Clyde River, Nova Scotia.

52 | **Figure 15:** John Erskine photograph of the Debert Palaeo site, July 1962.

66 | **Figure 16:** Illustration of lithic and ground stone tool terminology.

67 | **Figure 17**: Illustration of pottery terminology.

85 | **Figure 18:** Mi'kmaw *wikhikon*: Notice of direction map, warning of a Peskotomuhkatiyik war party.

88 | **Figure 19:** Hoffman's seasonal round subsistence model for the Mi'kmaq.

94 | **Figure 20:** Clam Cove 2004, illustrating on-site hand screening of shell midden sediments.

98 | **Figure 21:** Palaeo period sites on a map by Dominic Lacroix representing the North Atlantic coast shorelines at 9,000 ^{14}C yrs BP.

100 | **Figure 22:** Glacial maximum on east coast ca. 18,000 ^{14}C yrs BP, indicating the Goldthwait Sea.

111 | **Figure 23:** A visit to the Belmont site, 1990. Background, left to right: Stephen Davis, Laird Niven, Mike Sanders, David Keenlyside; Front: Helen Kristmanson, Valery Monahan, Aaron Butt, and Stephen Powell.

111 | **Figure 24:** Selected Palaeo tools from the Debert site: (A) graver (engraving tool), (B) uniface (scraper), (C–D) fully fluted, eared projectile points, (E–F) bifacial knives.

115 | **Figure 25:** Palaeo projectile point styles discussed in the text: (A) fully fluted style, Kingsclear, New Brunswick, (B) fully fluted, eared style, Quaco Head, New Brunswick, (C) single fluted style, Melanson, Nova Scotia, (D) non-fluted, parallel flaked style, Windsor, Nova Scotia, (E) triangular style, Savage Harbour, Prince Edward Island.

118 | **Figure 26:** Pirate Cove visit, October 1983, with complete biface *in situ*.

125 | **Figure 27:** Michelle McCarthy at the Jones site, Prince Edward Island, 2001.

130 | **Figure 28:** Selected Archaic period sites on a map by Dominic Lacroix representing the North Atlantic coast shoreline around 6,000 ^{14}C yrs BP.

133 | **Figure 29:** Archaic period artifacts recovered off Digby Neck, Nova Scotia: (left) slate ulu from three nautical miles (five km) offshore from Sandy Cove; (right) stemmed slate knife from 15 nautical miles (28 km) offshore.

141 | **Figure 30:** Selected Archaic artifacts from the Maritimes.

143 | **Figure 31:** Archaic assemblages from the Gaspereau Lake site.

146 | **Figure 32:** Late Archaic Gerrish site artifacts.

151 | **Figure 33:** Late Archaic slate bayonets from Union, Maine, with textile etching.

154 | **Figure 34:** Selected artifacts from the Turner Farm site.

155 | **Figure 35:** Selected artifacts from the Beausejour Beach site, near Sackville, New Brunswick.

157 | **Figure 36:** Late Archaic artifacts from Portland Point, Saint John.

160 | **Figure 37:** Portable stone artwork, Late Archaic and Woodland.

161 | **Figure 38:** Late Archaic ground slate implements.

169 | **Figure 39:** Three views of a Transitional Archaic ¾ grooved maul (or axe) from Melanson, Nova Scotia.

170 | **Figure 40:** Selection of Transitional Archaic artifacts from the Boswell and Wilkins sites 2011–2016.

171 | **Figure 41:** Stepped excavation 2014 showing John Campbell and Erin McKee collecting and recording samples for paleoethnobotanical and paleoenvironmental study. Excavating in the background are Josh McLearn and Jodi Howe.

172 | **Figure 42:** Boswell Site north wall profile of Unit 55 with stratigraphic levels.

175	**Figure 43:** Steatite bowl recovered by Moses H. Perley at Oromocto Lake in 1896.
176	**Figure 44:** Mud Lake Stream site in foreground, southwestern New Brunswick.
177	**Figure 45:** Stemmed projectile points from Mud Lake Stream.
178	**Figure 46:** Feature 1, Mud Lake Stream.
186	**Figure 47:** Selected Woodland period sites on the Maritime Peninsula.
187	**Figure 48:** Vinette-like vessel from Boucher site, Vermont.
190	**Figure 49:** Red Bank Complex sites.
191	**Figure 50:** Tozer site artifact assemblage: copper awl, gorget fragment, and cache blades.
193	**Figure 51:** Lithic artifacts recovered from Feature 20, Mud Lake Stream.
201	**Figure 52:** Blocked-end tubular pipe from the Augustine mound.
202	**Figure 53:** Excavation at the deeply stratified Oxbow site, Red Bank, New Brunswick.
204	**Figure 54:** Pottery vessel rim from the Diggity site, featuring pseudo-scallop shell design elements, associated with the Middle Woodland period.
205	**Figure 55:** Dentate stamped vessel found by divers on the Kennebecasis River.
205	**Figure 56:** Pottery rim sherd collected by D. London at Ring Island, Maquapit Lake, New Brunswick, 1900.
207	**Figure 57:** Early Middle Woodland contracting stem projectile point cache, surface collected by Jim Legge at Gaspereau Lake, Nova Scotia.
207	**Figure 58:** Middle Woodland corner-notched projectile points from Clam Cove, Scots Bay, Nova Scotia.
217	**Figure 59:** Selection of bone and tooth artifacts from the Maritimes.

222 | **Figure 60:** Hammer's chart on the relationship between quartz-based lithics.

225 | **Figure 61:** Site map of Davidson Cove lithic workshop, 2003, with insert of a Late Woodland side-notched projectile point recovered at the site in 1988.

228 | **Figure 62:** Map indicating the approximate locations of major lithic and copper source areas mentioned in text, with arrows showing possible distribution routes of North Mountain and Minas Basin lithics.

229 | **Figure 63:** Lithic cores (i.e., blocks of raw material) from Scots Bay (NS) and Washademoak Lake (NB) as displayed in the Great Hall, Queen's College, Memorial University, 2009.

237 | **Figure 64:** Nash and Miller economic mosaic model for the precontact Mi'kmaq.

238 | **Figure 65:** Stephen Davis contiguous habitat model for St. Margaret's Bay, Nova Scotia.

242 | **Figure 66:** Artist's conception of life at a Woodland period spring–summer campsite.

243 | **Figure 67:** Selected Woodland period lithic artifacts from the St. Croix site excavations (1989–90, 1993, 2012).

248 | **Figure 68:** Selected Contact period sites from the Maritimes.

250 | **Figure 69:** L'Anse aux Meadows National Historic Site, with insert of reconstructed Norse dwelling.

252 | **Figure 70:** Petroglyph of Mi'kmaw sailing vessel, McGowan Lake, Nova Scotia.

254 | **Figure 71:** Aerial photograph of Burnt Bone Beach (BfDd-08), Gaspereau Lake, Nova Scotia, with insert of trade beads recovered at the site.

255 | **Figure 72:** Small copper pot from BlCx-1 site, Northport, Nova Scotia.

258 | **Figure 73:** Port Royal Habitation excavation 1938–39 by Charles Coatsworth Pinkney and modern reconstruction.

259 | **Figure 74:** C.W. Jeffrey's iconic vision of the Order of Good Cheer procession, with Mi'kmaw guests seated to the left.

264 | **Figure 75:** Botanical border (left side) from Samuel de Champlain's 1612 Map of New France.

264 | **Figure 76:** Botanical border (right side) from Samuel de Champlain's 1612 Map of New France.

272 | **Figure 77:** Wabanaki Confederacy wampum belt facsimile made following the specifications of Panawahpskek (Penobscot) elder Newell Lyon.

ACKNOWLEDGEMENTS

I FEEL VERY FORTUNATE to have known many of the archaeologists who helped forge our current understanding of precontact history in the Maritimes. When I was growing up in the Annapolis Valley, Nova Scotia, I dreamed of becoming an archaeologist, but my sights were set on a career in the eastern Mediterranean. I knew very little about the ancestral Mi'kmaq or French Acadians who occupied this area centuries before. My introduction to the topic came when I was a teenager in the mid-1960s. One of my brothers had a schoolteacher named John Erskine, who was a trained botanist, but also an avocational archaeologist. I was taken to meet this man and was impressed by his openness and enthusiasm. Before leaving for graduate school at Simon Fraser University in 1975, I tried to visit John and his wife Rachel. I discovered that John had had a stroke not long before my visit, from which he never recovered. After his death, Rachel gave me most of his notes and slides and a manuscript that he was working on at the time of his stroke. These things were put aside while I focused on my graduate work.

When I completed my PhD in 1982, Chris Turnbull (Archaeological Services, Fredericton) offered me a position with Archaeological Services as a contract archaeologist. This connection eventually led to a one-year teaching stint at Saint Mary's University in 1985, while Steve Davis was on sabbatical leave. The following year, I moved my family to Newfoundland for another. one-year visiting professor position at Memorial University, which fortunately turned into a permanent job. From that point on, my archaeological focus remained mainly on the Maritimes and I began training graduate students who wanted to work in the area. I even returned to John's manuscript, which I edited and submitted to the Nova Scotia Museum for publication (Erskine 1998). I think that John's book is an excellent example of archaeological practice in Nova Scotia for the 1950s.

Throughout my years at Memorial many colleagues have provided me with offprints of published papers and unpublished documents, as well as photographs and slides, and kept me apprised of regional developments. Chris Turnbull and other colleagues at Archaeological Services have kept me abreast of research in New Brunswick, including Pat Allen, Albert Ferguson, Vinnie Bourgeois, and Brent Suttie. Kevin Leonard (Archaeoconsulting) has been a correspondent on Maritimes archaeology and paleoethnobotany for many years. David Keenlyside (Canadian Museum of Civilization/History) shared information on his work in Prince Edward Island. In Nova Scotia, I have worked closely with archaeologists at the provincial museum, including Brian Preston, David Christianson, Steve Powell, and Catherine Cottreau-Robins, and with Rob Ferguson and Birgitta Wallace at the Atlantic office of Parks Canada. Jack Colwell, Head of the Department of Geology at Acadia in the early 1990s, graciously offered me a visiting professorship in his department in 1992, which made for a memorable sabbatical year and opened up several new research opportunities. Since 2011 I have worked closely with Heather MacLeod-Leslie (Mi'kmaq Rights Initiative) on the Boswell site excavation.

I would also like to thank university colleagues who have shared materials related to their research, including the late Jim Tuck (Memorial University), Steve Davis (Saint Mary's University), Ron Nash (St. Francis Xavier University), David Black (University of New Brunswick), Dorothy Godfrey-Smith (Dalhousie University), David Sanger and Bonnie Newsom (University of Maine), Bruce Bourque (Maine State Museum), Arthur Spiess (Maine Historic Preservation Commission), and the late Jim Petersen (University of

Vermont). Several former graduate students worked closely with me on projects in the Maritimes, and a few have continued to work in the region. They include Doug Rutherford, Helen Kristmanson, Brent Murphy, Michelle MacCarthy, Dawn Laybolt, Scott Buchannan, Paul McEachen, Ben Pentz, Sara Halwas, Catherine Jalbert, Roger Lewis, Heather MacLeod-Leslie, Kora Staplefeldt, Kelly-Anne Pike, Cameron Milner, Adrian Morrison, John Campbell, Bryn Tapper, and Emma Lewis-Sing.

I would like to thank the two anonymous reviewers of the latest version of this book for their many useful comments and suggestions for revisions. I would also like to acknowledge my research assistant in 2001, Stephanie Synard, who began the initial compilation of cited references and researched websites for the original online version of this work, and my research assistant in 2014, Alison Harris, who helped with editing the first printed version of this book. My wife Jane has graciously helped with the editing of this latest version. Bryn Tapper has helped immensely with improving the illustrations. Finally, I would like to thank my editor at Memorial University Press, Fiona Polack, for keeping me on track with the extensive revisions made to the submitted version of this book. The final product is all the better for it. I gladly accept responsibility for any errors in fact or judgement that you may read below.

Michael Deal
July 2023
St. John's

A COMMENT ON TERMINOLOGY

IN RECENT DECADES Canadian archaeologists have tried to distance themselves from many of the colonialist attitudes of past generations. One way of doing this is by adopting appropriate terminology when writing about Indigenous peoples. This is not always easy, as some terms are considered inappropriate by some Indigenous communities, but not by others. Gregory Younging (2018, chap. 6) provides a useful overview of acceptable and unacceptable terms, yet he stresses that the language surrounding Indigenous peoples continues to evolve. I have tried to adopt his suggestions in this book. However, I do continue to use the term "artifact," which is a fundamental concept throughout the world that is used to refer to any human-made object in the past or present. The term "Indian" is a little more difficult, as it was used in many Canadian place names and is still used by some government agencies (e.g., "Indian status and the Indian Register" with Indigenous Services Canada). Where possible, I avoid the term "Indian" and use the term "Palaeo" in place of the more common "Palaeoindian" in my archaeological chronology. Some derogatory place names in the Maritimes have been replaced (e.g., Savage Island, near Fredericton, has been officially changed to Eqpahak Island), but others still exist.

Indigenous archaeological sites are perceived here as "Indigenous cultural places" (after Newsom et al. 2021, 7). I acknowledge that Indigenous oral traditions and traditional knowledge are the property of the Indigenous

A COMMENT ON TERMINOLOGY

peoples (and storytellers) they come from. When I refer to oral traditions or traditional knowledge in this volume, I am generally discussing how other people have used the information. In the few cases where I quote short passages from specific stories (e.g., from Rand 1894), I am careful to identify the original informant.

FOREWORD
by Roger J. Lewis

AS CURATOR OF MI'KMAQ CULTURAL HERITAGE at the Nova Scotia Museum of Natural History, I have witnessed an increasing embrace, recognition, and appreciation of Mi'kmaw knowledge and experiences in the formulation of the Mi'kmaw narrative. This reflects the growing ability of academia to work with Indigenous groups to ensure their voices are heard.

As a result of my early years of study under Mike Deal, I developed a deep appreciation of a bottom-up style of research methodology to better understand the culture of my people. Archaeological research has also opened challenging opportunities for others to better appreciate the complexity of Mi'kmaw culture in the Atlantic region.

Mike Deal has proposed that the main objective of his publication is to bring up to date the archaeological evidence relating to Indigenous history in the Maritimes prior to contact with Europeans. This is very important. It is also important to work with First Nations people as collaborators and to include, as he specifies, a diversity of perspectives. It is imperative that the studies of First Nations people be interdisciplinary.

After many years of learning, listening, and conversing with elders who have since passed to the spirit world, I have determined that language is the key to cultural memory. Language is theory and how that language is understood, interpreted, and applied is the methodology.

This is not a revolutionary approach, but I believe that anthropological and even archaeological research requires that we become equal participants and collaborators, and that communities' participation be encouraged.

There must be better cooperation between First Nations and social scientists. Studies of Indigenous knowledge are challenging not only because of difficulties in cross-cultural communication and understanding but also because of their inevitable political dimensions.

This publication serves to help narrow those gaps for future young Mi'kmaw scholars and academics. It also forms a valuable addition to the existing body of knowledge and will serve as a great resource to both Indigenous and non-Indigenous readers in the Atlantic Region.

1

TRADITIONAL CONTEXT

Introduction

THE MAIN OBJECTIVE OF THIS BOOK is to update the archaeological evidence relating to Indigenous history in the Maritimes prior to contact with Europeans. Precontact history deals with the people (individuals and communities), their daily lives (lifeways), and events (where they can be perceived) and major shifts in their existence indicated by archaeological evidence. A major source of evidence for how people lived in precontact times is through the interpretation of material culture from archaeological survey and excavation. In addition, paleoenvironmental research allows for a reconstruction of past climate and landscapes. The writings of early explorers and missionaries, and ethnographies from the nineteenth and twentieth centuries help to fill in the many gaps in our understanding of past lifeways. While the precontact peoples of the Maritimes left no formal written history in the Western sense, their surviving oral traditions and artwork are imbued with historical meaning that can be directly related to archaeological research (see Chapter 3), and together with the material and documentary evidence from archaeology are important elements of modern Indigenous heritage.

Since the last major update of precontact archaeological evidence relating specifically to the Maritimes (Deal and Blair 1991), the amount of literature on the topic has more than doubled. Besides updating the existing evidence, this book includes an extensive review of the history of archaeological research in the region and a consideration of modern Indigenous concerns with archaeology. Important related topics and examples of significant projects are highlighted using vignettes, or sidebars, that provide details that would otherwise interrupt the flow of a chapter.

While the setting for this volume is the Canadian Maritimes (New Brunswick, Nova Scotia, and Prince Edward Island), it is impossible to discuss this region without frequent mention of the adjacent areas of Quebec (i.e., the Gaspé and Magdalen Islands) and the state of Maine (east of the Kennebec River drainage). This expanded area, referred to by archaeologists as the Maritime Peninsula, better reflects Indigenous territorial geography within the region. Archaeologists often attempt to identify geographical boundaries between precontact peoples within and between regions using variations in projectile point styles or the presence/absence of specific tool forms (Robinson 1996). These boundaries often are vaguely conceived since we cannot be certain how people in the past organized themselves on the landscape. When European explorers and fishermen arrived in what is today the Maritimes, they found that it was occupied by three distinct Algonquian peoples: the Mi'kmaq, Wolastoqiyik (Maliseet), and Peskotomuhkatiyik (Passamaquoddy). The physical boundaries between Indigenous peoples in the region were unstable due to recurrent epidemics and many decades of conflict triggered by the European presence in the region (Prins and McBride 2007, 6). For example, Prins (1986) argues that, in the seventeenth and eighteenth centuries, both the Mi'kmaq and Wolastoqiyik exploited the resources on both sides of the St. Lawrence as far upriver as Quebec City, that is, outside of their "traditional territories." By at least the late seventeenth century, Mi'kmaw territory even extended eastward onto the island of Newfoundland (Sable and Francis 2012, 19).

The Indigenous peoples of the region would have hunted, gathered, and fished according to the seasons. In the authoritative Smithsonian volume on the Indigenous peoples of the Northeast, the historic Wolastoqiyik

1: TRADITIONAL CONTEXT

and Peskotomuhkatiyik are described as very closely related peoples who differed primarily in their economic adaptation; the former characterized as inland hunters and the latter as sea-mammal hunters (Erickson 1978a, 123; also, Patterson 2009, 30), although today this distinction seems overly simplistic. In the same volume, the historic Mi'kmaq are depicted as generalized hunter-gatherers (Bock 1978, 109; Patterson 2009, 30). These peoples formed part of a larger confederation, the Wabanaki Confederacy (translated as "People of the First Light" or "Dawnland"), which also included the Panawahpskek (Penobscot) of Maine and the Western Abenaki of New Hampshire, Vermont, and parts of Massachusetts. According to Frederick Wiseman (2006, 1–2), Wabanaki oral history keepers often divide their history into three great epochs, which relate to the far past, close history, and living memory. The far past concerns the beginning of the world and early human adaptation, and so is closest to the theme of this book. Close history concerns the socio-political relations among the current First Nations and therefore overlaps with the ethnohistoric record. Living memory concerns the Indigenous peoples of today.

Many of the strictly archaeological terms used in this book are defined in Chapter 3. To be consistent with the archaeological literature I will be using a standard terminology for precontact developmental periods, namely, Palaeo, Archaic, and Woodland (Table 1). Mi'kmaw archaeologist Roger Lewis (2006a) worked with members of the Nova Scotia Mi'kmaw community to develop a historical timeline that accommodates the standard archaeological terminology yet is more attuned to Mi'kmaw perceptions. In the resulting timeline, the Palaeo population becomes the Sa'qewe'k L'nuk (Ancient people). The people of the Early and Middle Archaic become the Mu Awsami Saqiwe'k (Not so Ancient People), while those of the Late and Transitional Archaic are the Mu Awsami Kejikawe'k L'nuk (Not So Recent People). The Woodland people become the Kejikawe'k L'nuk (Recent People). Finally, the people of early European contact up to today become the Kiskukewe'k L'nuk (Today's People). During the Jemseg Project (see below), Karen Perley, with the Tobique First Nation and Archaeological Services, New Brunswick, suggested the following Wolastoqwey terms for the major developmental periods: *Wisoki Pihce* (very long ago) for Palaeo, *Pihce* (long ago) for Archaic, and *Pihcesis* (not too long ago) for the Woodland period (Blair 2004a, 137). Corresponding terminology for the Peskotomuhkatiyik was selected from the *Passamaquoddy–Maliseet Dictionary* (Francis and Leavitt 2008) for the 2012 N'tolonapemk exhibit at the Abbe Museum. *Kancoqi* ("very old, ancient") refers to the Palaeo, *Kaneyawiw* ("archaic") to the Archaic, *Qahqolunsqey* ("clay pot") to the Woodland, and *Astuwi* ("coming in contact with each other") to the Contact period (Soctomah et al. 2012). Since it does not seem appropriate to use one of these Indigenous systems over another for the entire region, I have selected one English equivalent term from each group that I hope will suffice, namely "Ancient," "Long Ago," and "Clay Pot" peoples.

Table 1. Chronological Periods for Archaeology in the Maritimes.

Period	Date Range
Federal*	AD 1867 -
British Colonial	AD 1763–1867
French Colonial	AD 1604–1763
Contact	AD 1497–1604
Late Woodland (Ceramic)	1000–500 ^{14}C yrs BP
Middle Woodland (Ceramic)	2000–1000 ^{14}C yrs BP
Early Woodland (Ceramic)	3000–2000 ^{14}C yrs BP
Transitional (Terminal) Archaic	4000–3000 ^{14}C yrs BP
Late Archaic	5000–4000 ^{14}C yrs BP
Middle Archaic	6000–5000 ^{14}C yrs BP
Early Archaic	8000–6000 ^{14}C yrs BP
Late Palaeo	10,000–8000 ^{14}C yrs BP
Early Palaeo	12,000–10,000 ^{14}C yrs BP

*Prince Edward Island joined Confederation with Canada in 1873.

Indigenous Voices in Archaeology

Over the last three decades, the development of Indigenous archaeology has prompted many non-Indigenous archaeologists to rethink how they deal with the archaeological record. As Sonja Atalay (2006, 280) points out, the discipline of archaeology was built around and relies on Western knowledge systems and methodologies that privilege the "material, scientific, and observable world over the spiritual, experimental, and unquantifiable aspects of archaeological sites, ancient people, and artifacts." In precontact times, Indigenous peoples were the stewards of their own cultural resources and history but, by the late nineteenth century, this role was co-opted by archaeologists and anthropologists (Atalay 2006, 281).

While traditional knowledge of plant and animal use has been important to archaeological interpretation for decades (e.g., Deal 2008a; Murphy and Black 1996), archaeologists generally are guilty of ignoring Indigenous reconstructions of their precontact history that are based on oral tradition and traditional practices (McGhee 1977). This attitude has been changing slowly. Archaeologists are beginning to adopt theoretical approaches, such as landscape ethnoecology (Johnson and Hunn 2010), which value oral traditions, traditional knowledge, place names, and sacred landscapes, and incorporate them in their interpretations of archaeological phenomena. Some Indigenous archaeologists seek to develop approaches that put "connections between contemporary Indigenous peoples and their ancestral heritage at the center of archaeological inquiry and heritage stewardship" (Newsom et al. 2021, 10). Atalay (2006, 301) suggests a collaborative model that uses the best of both approaches. One such approach is the Toqwa'tu'kl Kjijitaqnn/Integrative Science Program at Cape Breton University, which attempts to integrate Mi'kmaw and Western knowledge systems (Bartlett 2011; Julien et al. 2008, 52). This program embraces the differences between a Mi'kmaw world view based on spirituality, living knowledge, duty, and wholeness with a Western world view that is secular, book-based, and compartmentalizes knowledge (Bartlett 2011, 181; Bartlett et al. 2012). Paulette Steeves (2015, 74) also discusses the differences and similarities between Western science and Indigenous science (traditional ecological knowledge) and points out that "the discussion of Western and Indigenous archaeologies is an area of dialogue where divergent histories, epistemologies, ideologies, and philosophies are shared to inform the past, present, and future of the field." A guiding principle of the Cape Breton approach is "two-eyed seeing," where one eye sees with the strengths of Indigenous knowledge and the other sees with the strengths of Western knowledge (Bartlett 2011, 182). This is best achieved through a collaboration between archaeologists and Indigenous knowledge holders (e.g., Blair et al. 2014; Lelièvre et al. 2020, 2022; Lewis and Sable 2014).

In the 1990s the Canadian Archaeological Association developed a "Statement of Principles for Ethical Conduct Pertaining to Aboriginal Peoples" in consultation with First Nations peoples across the country (Nicholson et al. 1996). This statement explicitly recognizes the link between modern First Nations and past populations. The basic principles include dialogue, Indigenous involvement, sacred sites and places, and communication and interpretation. Dialogue recognizes that Indigenous peoples are concerned with the protection and management of archaeological resources, and that they should have a voice in how archaeological research is conducted on Indigenous lands. With respect to this statement, archaeologists were encouraged to seek input from local Indigenous communities into their research plans and permit applications. Today, research archaeologists are encouraged to involve local communities from the planning stage. The notion of stewardship of precontact resources could also be addressed here since both parties have an interest in preventing the looting of sites and illicit sale of artifacts. Indigenous involvement entails the development of partnerships between archaeologists and Indigenous peoples and communities, and the recruitment and training of Indigenous students. The principle of sacred sites and places recognizes the spiritual bond between Indigenous peoples and special places and features on the landscape, and the burial sites of ancestors. The complex issue of the reburial of excavated Indigenous human remains and repatriation of archived archaeological collections falls under this principle. Finally, communication and interpretation concern alternate and more complete ways of interpreting the archaeological record and the archaeologist's responsibility to inform Indigenous peoples of the progress and results of their research.

Since 2017 the Board of Directors of the Canadian Archaeological Association (CAA) has adopted two new ethical statements. One statement holds that authors must obtain documented permission from descendant communities to present human remains in any CAA media. A second statement endorses and adopts the United Nations Declaration on the Rights of Indigenous Peoples and the Truth and Reconciliation Commission of Canada "Calls to Action," which acknowledge that archaeological sites and artifacts are the cultural and intellectual property of Indigenous peoples, and that free, prior, and informed consent of the relevant Indigenous communities must be sought before their archaeological heritage can be investigated, protected, curated, and presented. The CAA also endorsed, in principle, private member's Bill C-391, which calls for the development of a national strategy for the repatriation of Indigenous cultural property. The primary purpose of the bill is to lend support to Indigenous nations across Canada who are seeking to repatriate cultural materials being held by institutions in other countries. The bill was prompted by efforts of the Mi'kmaq from the Millbrook First Nation in Nova Scotia to achieve the return of a nineteenth-century chief's outfit from Museum Victoria, Australia (Phillips 2011). After five years of discussion, the CAA has posted a revised statement of principles on its website (CAA 2022). The new statement upholds the original principles and more explicitly recognizes archaeology's role in colonization and the need for reconciliation with Indigenous peoples.

The following case studies, drawn from the experiences of archaeologists and Indigenous peoples on the Maritime Peninsula, relate to the CAA principles of stewardship, partnership, sacred sites, and Indigenous land and resource rights and title.

Indigenous Title

The basic premise for all Indigenous rights and title is that Indigenous societies occupied, used, and controlled lands and resources in what is now Canada prior to non-Indigenous colonization (Aronson 1997, 32). Indigenous land rights include the objective of self-government, language, culture, hunting, fishing, forestry, and use and management of natural resources (Jamal 2006). Case studies on recent Indigenous title disputes demonstrate that traditional ties to the land and resources have not been relinquished. In fact, the eighteenth-century treaties with First Nations in the Maritimes stressed peace and friendship, and not the surrender and control of lands and resources (Aronson 1997, 33).

A 1999 Supreme Court of Canada decision upheld Mi'kmaw leader and activist Donald Marshall Jr.'s rights to fish eels out of season, without a licence and with an "illegal" net. When several communities began to fish lobster out of season, clashes with non-Indigenous fishermen led to a moratorium. Mi'kmaq at Burnt Church/Esgenoôpetitj, New Brunswick, and Indian Brook, Nova Scotia, held out and continued to defy fishery officials (King 2014). The Supreme Court was forced to clarify its original decision and ruled that the government would still be able to regulate all fishing for the purposes of conservation. The dispute was finally resolved in 2002 by an agreement in which the Band Council in Burnt Church/Esgenoôpetitj agreed to abide by the federal government rules and regulations in return for fishing boats, licences, quotas in all regional fisheries, and research money (King 2014, 10). While the federal government treated the dispute as primarily a fisheries regulation matter, according to Sarah King (2011, 2014), for the local Mi'kmaq it also concerned issues of sovereignty, conservation, and identity. The serious dispute between Mi'kmaw and non-Indigenous fishers in southwestern Nova Scotia in the fall of 2020 involved similar issues over treaty rights and a "moderate livelihood" lobster fishery (MacDonald 2020).

The Peskotomuhkatiyik in New Brunswick experienced a population decline to the point where they were no longer recognized as a First Nation under Canada's Indian Act. However, a small population (about 300 people) are still scattered around Charlotte County. In 1998, they elected a new chief. In 2012, they made a formal request to the federal government for the return of lost reserves at St. Croix and Canoose, and they continue to pursue ownership rights for parts of present-day St. Andrews (i.e., the ancestral village of *Qonasqamkuk* and associated burial ground). In 2016, they received a promise from the Minister of Indigenous and Northern Affairs that the department would pursue recognition of the Peskotomuhkati Nation and acknowledgement of their elected chief (PNS 2020). Since 2018, the Peskotomuhkatiyik have been in ongoing negotiations with the federal and provincial governments and are seeking recognition for the Peskotomuhkati Nation on both sides of the Canada/US border. In February 2018, Ottawa purchased a 1,011-hectare parcel of land near the St. Croix River, at Scotch Ridge (between Saint Stephen and Canoose Flowage) that includes a historic hunting lodge and a large collection of Indigenous artifacts acquired over time by the previous owners, and turned it over to the Peskotomuhkati people (Smith 2020).

In a landmark out-of-court settlement between the state of Maine and the Peskotomuhkati and Panawahpskwei peoples in 1980, a foundation was laid for resolving land issues between the two parties (Pawling and Mitchell 2008). The settlement recognized the Penobscot River as part of the Panawahpskwei reservation and an Indigenous trust was established to help improve river quality, principally by purchasing and removing two lower-river hydropower dams, thereby restoring the sea-run fisheries of the river (Kolodny 2021). According to Maria Girouard (2012), while the agreement allowed the two Indigenous peoples to move away from poverty and dependence on the state, misunderstandings created by the wording of the original agreement have also led to numerous costly lawsuits over land and resource issues. Notably, in 2012, the state of Maine produced a directive asserting that the state had exclusive authority and control over the Penobscot River, which "threatened the Penobscot (Panawahpskwei) Nation's territorial sovereignty, its shared ecological stewardship of the river, and access to its major food resource" (Kolodny 2021). This began a six-year legal battle between the Penobscot Nation and the state of Maine. Testimony by Bruce Bourque, the curator of the Maine State Museum, on behalf of the state, offered archaeological evidence that he believed questioned the Indigenous assertion of continuous occupation on the river. Ultimately, the issue was resolved by new legislation that protects the sustenance fishery and upholds the Panawahpskwei claim (Kolodny 2021). While Bourque offered evidence against the Panawahpskwei claim, archaeological research is often used to confirm Indigenous land rights, through the documentation of land and resource use over time (e.g., Deal 2002; Kristmanson 2008).

Stewardship

As mentioned above, stewardship concerns the protection and preservation of archaeological resources and their documentation. Both First Nations and archaeologists have an obligation in this regard. Archaeologists spend much of their time in the field trying to identify and assess sites that are endangered due to natural processes, such as coastal erosion, or cultural practices, such as farming or the construction of buildings. A significant example of site protection is the work of Albert Ferguson at Ministers Island, Passamaquoddy Bay (Ferguson and Turnbull 1980). An assessment of the area indicated that this important habitation and shell midden (refuse deposit) site was eroding at an alarming rate. The New Brunswick government provided funds for the construction of an artificial breakwater to prevent further erosion. The beach in front of the site was cleared of driftwood and the outer one metre of the site was excavated. This resulted in a straight beach face, against which a wall of gabion wire cages filled with rock was built to protect the site (Figure 1). In Nova Scotia the Minas Basin and adjacent Bay of Fundy shores also are heavily impacted by coastal erosion (Simonson 1978, Figure 2).

Helen Kristmanson's work with the Fort Folly Mi'kmaq at Dorchester illustrates an example of Indigenous stewardship (1997, 29) of an

1: TRADITIONAL CONTEXT

Figure 1: Excavation and gabion placement at the Ministers Island site, 1978. Courtesy of the Government of New Brunswick.

archaeological site. The Fort Folly Mi'kmaq obtained funding from the Access to Archaeology and Pathways programs for an excavation at the historic Mi'kmaw site at Beaumont, where ancestors of many community members had lived. This funding allowed them to hire a professional archaeologist and support a two-year excavation program. Ultimately, the Mi'kmaq managed the project and took responsibility for housing the materials recovered from the excavation.

The Assembly of Nova Scotia Mi'kmaq Chiefs (Maw-lukutijik Saqmaq) has developed a strategic plan that outlines their resolve to strengthen their capacity to manage their own heritage, language, culture, and archaeology (ANSMC 2015). They have also produced their own statements of principles on the treatment of Mi'kmaw ancestral human remains and archaeological resources (ANSMC 2016a, b). The Archaeology Research Division of the Mi'kmaq Rights Initiative has been heavily involved with the monitoring of archaeological sites and the protection of archaeological resources and burials. They have also produced an archaeology newsletter, *KMKNO Archaeology: From the Ground Up*, and KMKNO's "From the Ground Up" podcast, which addresses issues in Nova Scotia archaeology. For more than a decade, they have been monitoring the effects of coastal erosion on burial sites on the Bras D'Or Lakes (Pottie 2019). So far, a soft-shell covering made from coconut-fibre mats and logs has been found to be the most effective method of preservation.

Partnership

Partnerships (or collaborations) are an increasingly important vehicle for reconciling Western and Indigenous approaches to archaeology in the region. An important collaboration between the Metepenagiag Mi'kmaw Nation (formerly Red Bank) of New Brunswick and provincial archaeologists led to a series of archaeological projects beginning with the excavations of the Augustine Burial Mound (1975–77) and the Oxbow site (1978–84; Augustine et al. 2006). This collaboration has continued in other forms (e.g., Blair et al. 2014), and includes the release of the film *Metepenagiag: The Village of Thirty Centuries* (1996) and opening of the Metepenagiag Heritage Park (2007). In 2006 the community signed a memorandum of understanding with the University of New Brunswick, which has resulted in a reanalysis of the archaeological record of Metepenagiag (Blair and Rooney 2022, 129).

When a precontact site at Jemseg Crossing, New Brunswick, was threatened by the construction of a highway bridge over the Jemseg River in 1996, Susan Blair was contracted on behalf of Archaeological Services to conduct a salvage excavation at the site. This was the first time a heritage impact assessment led to the mitigation of a major archaeological site in New Brunswick (Turnbull 2003, ix). A partnership was developed through the formation of a Wolastoqwey advisory committee that passed on information to Wolastoqwey communities, provided a workforce for the project, and appointed Pat Polchies as project manager (Blair 2004a; Blair and

Perley 2013). Excavations were halted with the discovery of a possible burial feature and the government of New Brunswick decided to relocate the bridge. A major outcome of this experience was the establishment of a permanent committee (the Maliseet Advisory Committee on Archaeology), with members from each Wolastoqwey First Nation, which meets regularly with archaeologists to co-operate on cultural heritage matters of mutual interest (Paul 2016).

The Peskotomuhkati began a collaboration with the University of Maine at Farmington in 2000–01 on the excavation of the N'tolonapemk site, on Meddybemps Lake (UMF/AFC 2002, 6). The site had been used as a salvage yard in military surplus (1940s–90s), which produced hazardous and highly toxic waste that led to serious contamination. The US Environmental Protection Agency began clean-up in 1996 and under the National Preservation Act (1966) an uncontaminated portion of the site was cleared for excavation. It was one of the largest ever excavation projects in Maine (over 220 m^2). The results were presented in a major exhibition at the Abbe Museum in 2012–14 (Socomah et al. 2012). The Abbe Museum and the Acadia National Park entered a partnership with the Wabanaki Nations in Maine in 2017 aimed at the co-management of research on Wabanaki archaeology. An Archaeology Advisory Committee was established, consisting of more than 10 Indigenous archaeologists and anthropologists and several non-Indigenous archaeologists with experience in collaborative research. The goal of this committee "is to develop guiding principles, priorities, best practices, and protocols to re-envision archaeological research, collections management, and interpretation, not only at the Abbe but across the Wabanaki homeland" (Abbe Museum 2017).

Sanger and others (2006) report on a collaborative project to study Peskotomuhkati place names, which integrated local community knowledge with the methodologies of history and archaeology. The project was designed to complement the Passamaquoddy–Maliseet Dictionary Project (Francis and Leavitt 2008). The archaeological component involved gathering oral history information at late precontact archaeological sites, in which community members were shown locations on maps or taken to sites and their memories recorded. The project provided 400 new place names, some with attached oral history, and an interactive digital map that provided spoken versions of place names and English translations (Sanger et al. 2006, 325). In 2010, a partnership of the Confederacy of Mainland Mi'kmaq, Mi'kmaq Association of Cultural Studies, Mi'kma'ki All Points Services, Saint Mary's University, the Nova Scotia Museum, and Parks Canada launched the Ta'n Weji-sqalia'tiek Mi'kmaw Place Names Digital Atlas and Website Project. The atlas includes about 1,500 place names collected through interviews with Mi'kmaw elders and other knowledge holders, as well as historical documents and dictionaries (Mi'kmaw Atlas 2019). As with the Peskotomuhkati maps, the Mi'kmaw Atlas provides both Mi'kmaw and English versions of the place names and spoken pronunciation.

There are also examples of collaborations between archaeologists and Indigenous organizations in Nova Scotia and Prince Edward Island. In 2006, the Mi'kmaq Confederacy of Prince Edward Island formed a partnership with David Keenlyside (then with the Canadian Museum of History) and Helen Kristmanson (then with Parks Canada) to survey the actively eroding shoreline of Georges Island, Malpeque Bay (Kristmanson 2019). This work led to the discovery of the previously unrecorded Pitawelkek shell midden site (CdCw-5) on the southern shore of Georges Island. Between 2007 and 2016 this site was visited several times for testing and limited excavation. The work consisted of small community-based projects to recognize the site's "status as a culturally, spiritually, and environmentally significant place to the Mi'kmaq First Nations of Prince Edward Island" (Kristmanson 2019, 6). Seven AMS radiocarbon dates, including one from charred food residue on a pottery sherd, place the use of the site around 700–800 AD, although some artifacts suggest a longer period of occupation. The site is like other coastal Middle to Late Woodland sites on Prince Edward Island (e.g., Keenlyside 1980a; Pearson 1966), with a marine procurement focus on seal, walrus, and fish, along with oysters and clams, and a mainly spring and summer period of use (see Chapter 6).

In Nova Scotia, the author has worked closely with the Mi'kmaq Rights Initiative, the Nova Scotia Museum, and Acadia University since 2011 on the excavation of the important Transitional Archaic Boswell site (Deal et al. 2022). Michelle Lelièvre collaborated with the Pictou Landing First Nation for her dissertation research at Maligomish Island, and more recently with the Millbrook and Sipekne'katik First Nations on the Chignecto Peninsula (Lelièvre 2012, 2017a, 2017b; Lelièvre et al. 2020). Matthew Betts (2019, 14–18) describes how the E'se'get Archaeological Project built a foundation for community involvement in the archaeological research at Port Joli Harbour. This took the form of communication with the Acadia First Nation, followed by data-sharing, presentations, and site tours and the inclusion of Mi'kmaw youth in archaeology.

Sacred Sites

One of the most sensitive and complex issues confronting Indigenous peoples and archaeologists across North America is that of the disturbance and reburial of human remains. As archaeology became more scientific during the 1960s, new techniques were being applied to the study of archaeologically recovered human remains in all parts of the world. The Canadian Association of Physical Anthropologists recognized specific categories of information that can be collected from human skeletal remains (Cybulski et al. 1979; also see CMC 1992). In a regional context these included the study of physical characteristics, such as stature and body build and how these varied among different populations; genetic elements, which could indicate the degree of relatedness between past and present populations; demographic factors, which help define a population in terms of age groups, sex ratios, and birth and death rates; pathological characteristics, which tell us about the diseases and accidents that afflicted past populations; and the treatment of the dead, which reflects the spiritual life and social organization of past populations. Indigenous peoples expressed their belief that such studies are disrespectful to their deceased ancestors and another form of discrimination (Lippert 1997). In the early 1970s,

Indigenous political power was increasing and there was a concerted backlash against the practices of physical anthropology (Powell et al. 1982).

Newsom (2017, 32) writes that Wabanaki peoples have been expressing their concerns over the protection of burial spaces since the late eighteenth century. Protests over the excavation of Indigenous burials in the Maritimes began in 1970 with the excavation of the 3,800-year-old (Archaic) cemetery at Cow Point, New Brunswick (Anonymous 1970a–d). In 1983, protests brought a stop to the excavation at Ste. Anne's Point, Fredericton (Christie Boyle, personal communication, 1986). Ultimately, government agencies relented and the repatriation and reburial of precontact skeletal remains began in earnest. In Nova Scotia, skeletal remains excavated at Bear River in 1959 (Erskine 1959; Erickson 1978, 1985) were repatriated and reburied in 1984 (Densmore 1984). In Prince Edward Island, Indigenous skeletal remains were eroded from a beach face at Blooming Point after a storm in 1959 (Armstrong 1991). These remains were kept in storage until they were analyzed and repatriated in 1992 (Jerkic 1992). Coastal erosion was also responsible for the exposure of a burial at Skull Island, in Shediac Bay. In this case, a salvage operation was sanctioned by the executive of the Union of New Brunswick Indians with the condition that the bones be returned for reburial after analysis (Leonard 1996, 220–21). A traditional burial for these remains was conducted by the Fort Folly First Nation at Beaumont on July 16, 1994. One other prominent case in New Brunswick was the excavation of the 2,000-year-old (Early Woodland) burial mound at Red Bank in the 1970s, which was mentioned above (Turnbull 1976, 1978). This work was conducted with the full support and involvement of local Mi'kmaq when the site was in danger of being destroyed by a gravel pit operation. The skeletal materials from this site were reburied in two separate events in the 1980s. A second burial mound was salvaged at White's Lake in Nova Scotia, after it had been inadvertently bulldozed during the construction of a subdivision (Davis 1991a). The site location was purchased by the provincial government and the single cremation was reburied at the site after analysis (Jerkic 1988).

In 1995, the museums of New Brunswick made a coordinated return of all remaining Indigenous burial remains (Allen and Orechia 1995). A special ceremony was held in Fredericton on 1 June of that year, at which spiritual leaders received the bones for reburial. Nova Scotia has also repatriated all precontact skeletal remains, and in 1999 an important "Memorandum of Understanding" was signed by Mi'kmaw leaders and government agencies, which recognized the sacred nature of all Indigenous burial sites and the need for consultation before any burials are considered for excavation (UNSI 2000). The message here for archaeologists is that conducting biological research is a privilege, not a right, and that all human remains should be treated with respect (Lippert 1997).

During an inventory of collections at the Department of Archaeology, Memorial University, in 2011, several boxes of human remains were discovered that had been sent to Memorial for identification in the early 1970s by the RCMP. They were recovered from graves that were abutting a sand pit in Old Mission Point, New Brunswick. A bulldozer had disturbed several graves and the human remains and a few artifacts were collected by the RCMP. Unfortunately, the boxes were placed in storage and not opened again for nearly four decades. Old Mission Point was an important precontact community (Turnbull 1974a), but it was also a seventeenth-century Recollect and Jesuit missionary settlement. Since the age and ethnic affiliation of the individuals was uncertain, permission was granted by the Listiguj Mi'gmaq Government Council for the study of these remains, including both physical examination of the remains and DNA analysis. A Memorial University graduate student, Kelly Anne Pike (2013), identified all the human remains as Indigenous in ancestry, one dating to the Early Woodland period, but the majority coming from the Late Woodland and Early Historic periods. Both male and female adults and several young juvenile individuals were included in the burials. Once the analysis was completed the remains were repatriated in 2014. A single DNA sample from one of the Old Mission Point individuals was later used in a study that looked at the initial divergence of ancestral North Americans from their East Asian ancestors (Raghavan et al. 2015).

How This Book Is Organized

For the most part, this book concerns research conducted since the late 1950s, after the development of the radiocarbon dating technique that allowed archaeologists to develop more accurate cultural chronologies (timelines). However, earlier work is included whenever possible. Chapter 2 puts the book into historical perspective. The history of archaeology in this region is divided into three developmental stages, with the first two being disrupted by the two world wars of the twentieth century. Three vignettes are included: the first illustrates the connection between the early naturalists and the establishment of regional museums; the second introduces the work of the first recognized archaeologist in the region, George Patterson; and the third presents our best example of archaeological fieldwork in the nineteenth century, namely, George Matthew's excavations at Bocabec, New Brunswick, in 1883.

Chapter 3 introduces the reader to the development of theory and method in the archaeology of the Maritimes. Theory is always the driver of methodological change in archaeology and can be envisioned by the notions of "thinking" and "doing." You must think over a problem first, and then develop the techniques to address it, like "How do I excavate a deep site without having the excavation walls collapse?" One solution is to do step trenching, which allows you to dig deeper units in the centre of your excavation and shallower ones as you move to the periphery (Drewett 2000). Vignettes are used to elaborate on the topic: the first is a glossary of important terms that can be referred to at any time for guidance and the second outlines how modern archaeologists in the region deal with the age of sites and artifacts they discover. This chapter also includes a discussion of Indigenous records of history, as a counterbalance to the ethnohistoric literature.

The next three chapters focus on the three recognized developmental phases of the precontact era relating to the Palaeo (Ancient), Archaic (Long Ago), and Woodland (Clay Pot) peoples. Chapter 4 considers who the first inhabitants of the region were, where they came from, and what the area was like when they arrived. The three vignettes feature an Indigenous story of the retreat of the "Great Glacier" that opened the region to the ancient people, a look at the earliest known archaeological site in the region, and a group of contemporary sites that appear to represent a transition to the following developmental phase. Chapter 5 explores the technological changes and population expansion associated with the Archaic (Long Ago) peoples. Two vignettes introduce important archaeological sites representing the early-middle and later phases of this period (i.e., the Gaspereau Lake site, Nova Scotia, and Mud Lake Stream site, New Brunswick). Chapter 6 introduces the final precontact developmental phase associated with the Woodland (Clay Pot) peoples. Four vignettes introduce two early archaeological sites from the period (i.e., Port Medway, Nova Scotia, and the Augustine Mound, New Brunswick), another site representing the Middle-Late Woodland (St. Croix, Nova Scotia), and a Late Woodland stone tool quarrying site (Davidson Cove, Nova Scotia). Chapter 7 introduces the first European explorers, exploiters, and settlers to the region and the effect of their presence on Indigenous culture. A glimpse of the earliest interactions between the first French Acadian settlers at Port Royal, Nova Scotia, and the local Mi'kmaq is viewed through the establishment of the "Order of Good Cheer." Without the help of the local Mi'kmaq, the early Acadian communities might not have survived. This chapter ends with a retrospective look at the precontact period and how precontact cultures changed as they encountered neighbouring Indigenous peoples and, finally, the European colonial forces.

2

PRACTISING ARCHAEOLOGY IN THE MARITIMES

> *These collections of oyster and clam shells mixed with bones of fish, birds, and mammals, have not yet been studied with the care they deserve. They are **the collection of ages**, and would well reward a thorough investigation.* (Gilpin 1874, 227)

J. BERNARD GILPIN'S "collection of ages" referred to the numerous precontact shell midden deposits found around the coasts of the Maritimes, yet we can easily extend this expression to all precontact cultural deposits in the region. These deposits began to receive serious scrutiny by local naturalists towards the end of the nineteenth century. However, European interest in Indigenous material culture began as soon as contact was made. Several early European explorers brought captives, and sometimes willing passengers, and their material culture back to Europe (Dickason 1997; Foreman 1943; Quinn 1981), and many Indigenous artifacts ended up in European cabinets of curiosity and museum collections (Feest 1995; Loren 2008, 19). European visitors and early settlers had a poor understanding of the time depth of Indigenous occupations of the Americas. The Indigenous peoples claimed that they had been here since "time immemorial," that is, since before the events of their oral traditions (i.e., at least predating the retreat of glacial ice; see Chapter 4). Eventually, most scholars agreed that the Indigenous peoples were indeed the original inhabitants of the region, and that they descended from northeastern Asian populations that had migrated across a land bridge to Alaska during the last ice age. Once it was established that the earth was much older than the 4,000-plus years argued by Biblical scholars, it was also possible to speculate on how long ago the original migrations might have taken place. Later, professional archaeologists used a relative dating method based on changing fads in pottery decoration and projectile point styles to date sites, until the development of the radiocarbon dating technique in the late 1940s gave archaeologists everywhere a new appreciation for the chronological relationships of precontact cultures.

Bruce Trigger (1989, 69) notes that in North America, before the late eighteenth century, few collections of artifacts had been recovered from precontact sites, and rock carvings and paintings were generally considered to be made by modern Indigenous peoples. From the period of initial colonial settlement of the Maritime Peninsula in the early seventeenth century until the early nineteenth century, a few local private collections had been amassed. As is the case today, some collections were merely a few artifacts discovered by farmers while plowing a field or digging a cellar. Other collectors were more driven and would visit and illegally dig up many sites. In his 1841 account on the New Brunswick Wolastoqiyik and Mi'kmaq and their settlements, Moses Perley reported that the archaeological site at Meductic was a popular source of stone tools for local collectors (Hamilton and Spray 1977, 84). Today, this site is governed by provincial law (see below). Some of the materials from early accumulations have been incorporated into provincial collections, but much of the information on where they were found has been lost. These old private collections, as well as archaeological materials collected before modern excavation and conservation standards were developed, and materials collected as supplemental to specific projects (i.e., legacy collections, such as sediment samples, field notebooks, and photographs), constitute a serious curatorial problem for museums today (e.g., Knoll and

Figure 2: Effects of coastal erosion in the Bay of Fundy and Minas Basin. Top: Shoreline erosion at Longspell, Kingsport, Nova Scotia. When this photograph was taken in 1988, the backyards of the cottages on the right had been diminished by about 15 metres in the preceding half-century. Bottom: The Davidson Cove lithic workshop site is exposed to violent winter storm surges that overturn trees and erode the edge of the site. In this photograph an overturned tree exposes a dense midden of lithic debris from stone tool manufacture. Photographs by Michael Deal.

Huckell 2019). There is a trend towards the formal involvement of Indigenous peoples in the long-term management of archaeological collections in North America. For example, the Penobscot (Penawapskewi) Nation and the University of Maine signed a memorandum of understanding concerning the shared management of, and research on, Penobscot cultural heritage (Penobscot-UM 2018). Legacy collections held at the University of Maine that resulted from archaeological contract work for dams on the Penobscot River continue to be useful for studying the long-term effects of climate change in the region (St. Amand et al. 2020, 8289–90).

History of Research

The history of archaeological research for the Maritimes is outlined below in three stages, namely, the Naturalist Period (1800 to 1912), the Early Professional Period (1913 to 1959), and the Modern Professional Period (1960 to present). The first two stages are characterized by small surges of research separated by long periods of relative inactivity. David Sanger (1979b, 12) attributes the slow growth of archaeological research in the Maritimes and Maine primarily to the economic state of the region, where it has always been difficult to justify the expense of archaeological fieldwork. Other factors that inhibit fieldwork are the difficult terrain, variable climate, and the poor preservation of archaeological materials due to acidic soils. Currently, much of the fieldwork is being done by contracting firms (see below). Funding for research also is an ongoing concern, as very little support is generated within the region. The Maritimes offer few opportunities for graduate training, the only dedicated graduate program being the one at the University of New Brunswick. Much of the graduate work has been conducted by students coming from outside the region, including from universities in Ontario and Newfoundland and Labrador.

Naturalist Period (1800–1912)

In the Maritimes, Harry Piers (1915) referred to the few researchers in natural history during the early part of the nineteenth century as "pioneer

Figure 3: New Brunswick naturalists: Abraham Gesner and George Matthew (Squires 1945, 8, 12).

naturalists." These were generally financially secure white men who had time to devote to a wide range of academic pursuits, which often included geology, zoology, botany, ethnology, and archaeology. One of the "pioneering" figures of this period was Abraham Gesner (Figure 3). Gesner was primarily interested in geology, but he also built a collection of precontact artifacts. In fact, he was responsible for the first official public display of precontact material culture at Gesner's Museum of Natural History in 1842, which eventually formed the core of the precontact collection of the New Brunswick Museum (see Vignette 1). These materials had been acquired in Nova Scotia and New Brunswick, beginning as early as 1831. Dr. James Robb also incorporated numerous "Indian relics," mostly from the Maquapit Lake–Grand Lake Thoroughfare, in the natural history museum he established at the University of New Brunswick in the late nineteenth century (Bailey 1923). Many of these relics were described in a paper by Loring W. Bailey (1887).

Vignette 1: The First Museums

In New Brunswick and Nova Scotia, large collections of archaeological materials were gradually amassed by provincial museums through the acquisition of smaller private collections. These collections helped to sustain an interest in Indigenous lifeways and are now an important resource for the development of local and regional cultural timelines. The Gesner Museum of Natural History, which was established in 1842 in Saint John, New Brunswick, was the first officially sanctioned museum in Canada (Webster 1945, 5). The original museum was housed in the Mechanics' Institute building on Carlton Street and consisted of six glazed cases containing marine animals and plants, fishes, reptiles, birds, mammals, rocks, minerals, fossils, and archaeological specimens (Key 1973, 105–07; Miller and Buhay 2007; Squires 1945, 7–9). An admission fee was requested, and guests were provided with a catalogue listing the 2,173 specimens on display (GMNH 1842), of which specimens #2156–2169 were listed as "Indian relics." Specimens #2156–2157 were materials from a burial from the Oromocto River area that included beads, fur clothing, and French axes. Specimen #2158 was a copper kettle of French manufacture. The beads, clothing, and axes were donated by Henry T. Partlow. The position of the kettle on the list suggests that it also was donated by Mr. Partlow. Taken together, these items appear to represent a collection from a Contact period copper kettle burial (see Chapter 7). Specimen #2159 was the nearly complete soapstone bowl from Oromocto Lake, which was donated by Moses H. Perley. Specimens #2160–2161 were stone axes donated by a Dr. McCulloch and M.H. Perley. The former is most likely Dr. Thomas McCulloch, who excavated a large burial mound at Campbell's Point, at the entrance of Tatamagouche Harbour in 1833 (see below). Specimens #2162–2163 were stone gouges donated by William Jack and a Mr. Jones. The remainder of the specimens included groups of spear points, arrowheads, and a pipe.

The Gesner Museum was a short-lived enterprise and eventually the collection was donated to the Mechanics' Institute. Hence, they were established as the Mechanics' Institute Museum, which operated until 1890. At that time, the collection was sold to the New Brunswick Natural History Society for the token sum of $200. The Natural History Society was inaugurated in 1862 by a group of dedicated and enthusiastic individuals (Connolly 1977). One of the contributors to the original Gesner Museum, Moses Perley, was the first vice-president of the Society, while another contributor, William Jack, was a later president (1869–1880). The Society built up a comprehensive collection of Indigenous artifacts and handicrafts, chiefly through the efforts of G.F. Matthew, W.F. Ganong, S. Kain, and W. MacIntosh. Between 1882 and 1914, the Society published a bulletin, which contained several articles on artifacts contributed by these researchers. William MacIntosh became the first curator of the Natural History Society in 1907, when the combined collections were moved to the Finn Building on 72 Union Street, Saint John (Figure 4).

Figure 4: New Brunswick Natural History Museum, 1906–32 (Squires 1945, 13).

Prominent members of the Nova Scotian Institute of Science were instrumental in the founding of the Nova Scotia Provincial Museum. The museum was established in 1868 and situated in a room of slightly less than 200 m² in the newly built Provincial Post Office (Piers 1915: lxxix). The original exhibit consisted of natural history collections moved from the defunct Halifax Mechanics' Institute and other collections that were prepared for the 1867 Paris International Exhibition. Reverend Dr. David Honeyman was appointed the first curator in 1868 and he was followed by Harry Piers from 1899 to 1940 (Figure 5).

Figure 5: Harry Piers (curator, Nova Scotia Provincial Museum) with Henry and Susan Sack, Fox Point Road, near Hubbards, Lunenburg County, 1935. Photograph by Constance Fairbanks Piers.

> The Provincial Museum became a repository of a wide variety of natural history collections and included precontact materials. For example, in 1910 the museum received 352 "anthropological specimens," which included many stone tools, a set of 331 impressions of Mi'kmaw petroglyphs from Queen's County, made by George Creed, and articles of Mi'kmaw clothing (Piers 1911: 205–10).

Indigenous material culture is mentioned often in Gesner's writings. In his volume on Nova Scotia mineralogy, he reports that a skeleton of a hunter and his implements had been recovered at the gypsum quarries near Windsor, Nova Scotia, and were preserved in a museum at nearby King's College (Gesner 1836, 82). Unfortunately, the human remains were later destroyed in a fire at the College (Garlie 1992, 19). In a later report, on the geology of Prince Edward Island, he describes a collection of artifacts organized by Alexander Leslie from the Souris area, which included stone axes, projectile points, crude pottery, and barbed fish bones (Gesner 1847, 7). According to Gesner, the arrowheads were made from feldspar, agate, hornstone, and jasper. The feldspar was said to be identical to that found on arrowheads in Labrador and may refer to the metacherts from Ramah Bay (also see Black 2008), while the agate was said to be like that from the Bay of Fundy area. Gesner suggests that the materials were brought in from those places, since they did not occur naturally on the island. David Black (2008) notes that Gesner may be the first of the naturalists to recognize that Indigenous people in the region transported raw materials over long distances. In the same report, Gesner (1847, 9–10) also reports precontact shell middens in the Rustico area and an extensive shell midden site on the south side of Malpeque Bay. While Gesner was obviously interested in Indigenous material culture, he did not seem to be concerned with the preservation of archaeological sites. He suggests that the shells from the middens, when burned, ground, and mixed with peat, made valuable compost for farming (Gesner 1847, 20).

Two American institutions that had a major impact on the development of archaeology in the Northeast were the Smithsonian Institution (founded 1846) and the Robert S. Peabody Museum of Harvard (founded 1866) (Willey and Sabloff 1980, 41). The Smithsonian has two arms, the Bureau of American Ethnology, and the National Museum (both founded in 1879). Morlot's reports on the excavations of Danish shell middens published by the Smithsonian (1861, 1863) greatly influenced early naturalists on the Maritime Peninsula, and some of the earliest fieldwork in the region was conducted by archaeologists affiliated with the Smithsonian (see below). Harlan I. Smith worked as an assistant at the Peabody Museum at Harvard in his early career (1891-93), and later became the first archaeologist hired by the National Museum in Ottawa (Leechman 1942, 114). Charles Willoughby worked at the Peabody Museum of Harvard University from 1894 to 1928 and served as director, 1915-1928 (Hooton 1943, 235). Over his career, he excavated at many sites in Maine and had a lasting influence on Maine archaeology. Douglas Byers was director of the Peabody from 1938 to 1968. In the 1930s he continued the Peabody research in northern Maine and extended it into the Maritimes after World War II. Byers was also involved in the founding of the American Archaeological Society (SAA) and Massachusetts Archaeological Society (MAS) and served as SAA president (1947-48) and editor of their journal *American Antiquity* (1938-47) (MacNeish 1979, 709).

The earliest systematic excavations of precontact sites in the Maritimes were conducted by local naturalist groups. Two important naturalist societies were incorporated in 1862, namely, the Nova Scotian Institute of Science and the Natural History Society of New Brunswick (Connolly 1977). The first reported excavation was undertaken by a group from the Nova Scotian Institute of Science on 11 June 1863, at a large shell midden at Frostfish Cove, near French Village, in St. Margaret's Bay, followed by a similar excursion to Cole Harbour the following year (Ambrose 1867; Gilpin 1874; Gossip 1867; Jones 1864). A return trip to St. Margaret's Bay was planned for 1870 but had to be cancelled (Fergusson 1963, 18). Interest in shell middens was stimulated by the publication of an English translation of Morlot's review of advances in European archaeology, including quite sophisticated analyses of Danish shell middens (or *kjoekkenmoeddinger*), which came to serve as a guide for North American explorations (Morlot 1861). It is probably no coincidence that the term *kjoekkenmoeddings* was already being used for Nova Scotia shell middens by J.M. Jones (president, Institute of Natural Sciences) three years later (Jones 1864). Morlot's paper had a profound influence on early work on shell middens in New England (e.g., Rau 1865; Wyman 1868). Bourque (2002, 150) suggests that a second paper by Morlot (1863) entitled "An Introductory Lecture to the Study of High Antiquity" probably had an even greater impact on archaeology in the Northeast. It stressed the similarity between geology and archaeology and promoted the use of the scientific method in the latter. This extraordinary paper also discusses the usefulness of ethnographic analogy, understanding the association of artifacts, the position in which objects are found (i.e., provenience, as distinct from provenance), and the relationship of superposition (i.e., soil layers) and chronology (Morlot 1863). Prior to Morlot, many scientists had believed that the North American shell middens were natural deposits, and as early as the seventeenth century, settlers were excavating the middens to make lime (Trigger 1986, xi). This practice continued in parts of Nova Scotia until late in the twentieth century, even though it was widely known that the shell deposits were cultural. Farmers in the Tatamagouche area even used special scoop attachments to tractors for mining local middens (Deal 1996).

Early Fieldwork in Nova Scotia
The Frostfish Cove midden excavation was typical of the period (Figure 6). The midden was composed primarily of quahog (*Mercenaria mercenaria*) and soft-shell clam (*Mya arenaria*), with smaller amounts of scallop (*Phocapecten magellanicus*), boatshell (*Crepidula fornicata*), and blue mussel (*Mytilus edulis*). It covered an area of about 322 m^2 and was over 50 cm deep. According to Jones (1864, 370), it consisted of a "layer of compact shells, perfect and imperfect, in which lie bones of animals and birds, flint and quartz arrow and spear heads, large and small teeth, and broken pieces of

very roughly made pottery, bearing evident traces of attempt at ornament." At the bottom of the midden, Jones also noted fire-altered stones and charcoal, and a distinct layer of black soil about 5 cm thick, overlaying a layer of sand of about the same thickness. David Sanger (1987, 115) reports that layers of gravel and beach sand and charcoal-stained floors are often associated with house deposits, so it is quite possible that this group encountered a precontact dwelling. The excavators also identified faunal elements of moose (*Alces alces*), black bear (*Ursus americana*), beaver (*Castor canadensis*), and porcupine (*Erethizon dorsatum*), and noted the presence of several unidentified bird species and two or three species of fish. The latter included opercular spines of haddock (*Melanogrammus aeglefinu*).

In Piers's (1915, cvi) biographies of the most prominent naturalists from Nova Scotia, only the Rev. George Patterson is described as an archaeologist (see Vignette 2). Patterson had written an important history of Pictou County (1877), which included detailed information on his archaeological

Figure 6: Roger Lewis at Frostfish Cove, the location of the first organized archaeological excavation in the Maritimes. Photograph by Michael Deal, 2005.

explorations of shell middens in Merigomish Harbour. He joined the Nova Scotian Institute of Science in 1878, and later published a paper on a collection of stone tools that he had donated to Dalhousie University (Patterson 1890; see also Patterson 1883). The famous Canadian geologist, John Dawson, even gave a description of "pre-historic man" in his work on the Maritimes (1878, 41–46, and Supplement, 18–19). His own collection included materials from what appears to be a Contact period burial from Merigomish Harbour (Dawson 1878, 45–46). Other Nova Scotian naturalists of this period focused on specific classes of material culture or attempted to describe large collections. A few reports concerned pottery (DesBrisay 1879; Honeyman 1879) or stone tools and quarry sites (Duns 1880; Miller 1887). Piers (1890, 1895) was developing a classification system for the artifact collections in Nova Scotia.

Vignette 2: George Patterson and the Archaeology of Merigomish

Over his career George Patterson reinvented himself several times, as a journalist, bibliographer, authority on church doctrine, church administrator, and local historian (Dunlop 1984; Gilpin 1898; Figure 7). It was later in life that he turned to folklore and archaeology. He was born in 1824 to a prominent Pictou family. At the time, Pictou was the second largest community in Nova Scotia. After graduating from Pictou Academy, he studied briefly with the famous ornithologist, Dr. Thomas McCulloch, at Dalhousie College, before moving to Edinburgh to train as a Presbyterian minister. After his ordination in 1849, he spent the next 27 years at the Salem Presbyterian Church at Green Hill, near Pictou. During his years at Green Hill, he pursued his interests in theological biography, Nova Scotia history, and archaeology. His 1877 publication, *History of Pictou County*, is generally considered the most scholarly of the nineteenth-century Nova Scotia county histories.

Patterson's archaeological work began in 1874 in Merigomish Harbour and was first reported in his *History of Pictou County*. Donald McGregor, a

Figure 7: Reverend George Patterson, Nova Scotia's first archaeologist. *Proceedings of the Nova Scotia Institute of Science* 1898–99, 4.

farmer on Big Island, had uncovered human remains and stone tools while ploughing a field on his property. According to Patterson, "The spot is small, not more than eight to ten feet in diameter, and as soon as the ground is turned, it will at once be distinguished from the surrounding soil, being a black mould, containing fragments of bone, so decayed that they can be crushed between the fingers" (Patterson 1877, 30). The site had been thoroughly disturbed before his visit, so that it was not possible to associate human bones and artifacts. This site came to be known as the "old cemetery" and is ascribed to the precontact period by the presence of pottery and native copper knives, and other similarities to the Late Woodland burial excavated by Kevin Leonard (1996), less than 200 km up the coast at Shediac, New Brunswick. There is also evidence of cremation with some of the burials. Sometime in the 1880s, Patterson had cabinet cards prepared in New Glasgow to illustrate some significant finds from this site. One card depicts three bone objects, identified by Patterson as fish spearheads and a pipe bowl made from grey soapstone. A second card depicts 11 copper objects from the old cemetery, including five that are identified as knives.

Figure 8: George Patterson cabinet card illustrating artifacts from his fieldwork at Merigomish: 1–2. bone points; 3. stone pipe fragment; 4. serrated bone harpoon head. Courtesy Nova Scotia Museum.

Another important observation in *History of Pictou County* is the significance of Mi'kmaw place names for illustrating their use of the land (Patterson 1877: 31–32). Surviving place names either indicate physical features of the landscape or important resource locations. When these are mapped over a large area, they give additional insights into possible precontact land use. In a later paper he discusses the skilled workmanship involved in the production of artifacts and how archaeologists have benefited from talking to Indigenous craftsmen that still made these tools (Patterson 1890, 240).

Perhaps the most important legacy of George Patterson's work was drawing attention to the rich precontact resources of the Merigomish area. He identified four sites, including the old cemetery and three shell middens. Harlon I. Smith and William Wintemberg (Archaeology Division, Geological Survey of Canada) revisited the area just before the outbreak of World War I and identified 15 additional shell midden sites (Smith and Wintemberg 1929, 3). According to Smith (1929, 1), Merigomish Harbour had the largest un-looted shell middens in the Maritimes and provided the best opportunity for developing a regional chronology. Smith was the last archaeologist to work with the Patterson collection at Dalhousie in 1914 and he left us a photograph of selected artifacts (1929, 168, Plate XX). Smith's work was the most extensive in the area. He re-excavated the old cemetery and tested several middens. The shell middens tend to be in sheltered areas, near shellfish beds, and are primarily composed of hard-shell clam, or quahog, and eastern oyster. He concludes that the people of Merigomish Harbour were precontact Mi'kmaq and noted that many of the implements recovered were still being used by the local Mi'kmaq in 1914. In his 1929 final report, he states that through this work "the most complete and detailed data yet obtained regarding the archaeology of any place in Nova Scotia were acquired" (Smith 1929, 3).

Archaeological work at Merigomish did not actually begin with Patterson, but with his fellow Pictou Academy graduate, and eminent Canadian geologist, Sir William Dawson. In his 1868 edition of *Acadian Geology*, Dawson added a chapter on "prehistoric man," in which he describes an early historic Mi'kmaw artifact cache from Merigomish Harbour. The cache contained a corroded mass of iron blades, daggers, and an awl, along with beads and traces of basketry or matting, all wrapped in beaver skins. The location of this site is uncertain, but it is probably close to the historic Mi'kmaw cemetery, a few kilometres west of the precontact cemetery. Dawson learned of Patterson's work in time for his later supplement to *Acadian Geology*, in which he included a drawing of a barbed harpoon head from the cemetery at Merigomish (Dawson 1878, 19).

By 1878, George Patterson had joined the Nova Scotia Institute of Science. In 1883, he published the first overview of the antiquities of Nova Scotia in the Annual Report of the Board of Regents of the Smithsonian Institution. In this report, he noted that shell midden sites are common along the shores of Nova Scotia, but that mounds, or earthworks, are rarely found (Patterson 1883, 673). One exception was Dr. Thomas McCulloch's excavation 50 years earlier of a large burial mound at Campbell's Point, at the entrance of Tatamagouche Harbour. Now, the artifacts are missing, unfortunately, and the site has since been levelled and developed, although McCulloch may have given some of the artifacts to Abraham Gesner for his museum. A second mound was excavated at Kempt, Yarmouth County, by Dr. Joseph Bond. He describes this mound as 10 feet (3 m) long, 5 feet (1.5 m) wide, and 4 feet (1.2 m) high. Forty very well-made projectile points were recovered, but no human remains.

Patterson also discusses the important lithic workshop area at Bachman's Island, Lunenburg County. He states that "on the north side of the island . . . have been found large quantities of flakes and splinters of stone and arrowheads in various states of preparation . . . the amount of splinters and hammer stones, etc., plainly shows what had been going on" (Patterson 1883, 675). He suggests that the flakes are not from local lithics but are sourced from the rich deposits along the Bay of Fundy side of North Mountain. He also suggests that the native copper specimens he had seen in collections from Lunenburg and Pictou counties probably also were collected from the trap rocks of the Bay of Fundy.

In 1890, Patterson published his final paper on Nova Scotia archaeology. In it he describes his archaeological work of the last 15 years and his artifact collection, which he was donating to Dalhousie College (Figure 8). He states:

> During the last few years I have embraced any opportunities afforded me of collecting relics of the Stone Age of Nova Scotia and have now concluded that the purposes of such a collection will be best served by presenting it to Dalhousie College, to

> form part of the Museum of that institution. In handing it over,
> I desire through the N.S. Institute of Science, to place on record
> any points of interest noted in my explorations or suggested by
> the articles discovered. (Patterson 1890, 231)

The paper begins with another look at his work at the old cemetery in Merigomish Harbour, but he also mentions numerous shell middens and other sites he had visited or heard about around Nova Scotia. This is followed by a description of some of the more interesting artifacts in his collection that he classed according to the system used for the Archaeological Collection of the Smithsonian Institution, which was prepared for the 1886 Centennial Exhibition. According to the Dalhousie University calendar in 1891–92, the museum consisted of three donated collections: the Thomas McCulloch ornithological collection, the Honeyman geological collection, and the Patterson Collection of 288 Indigenous artifacts, of which 250 are from Nova Scotian sites. Besides the artifacts listed earlier, the collection included a gorget (neck ornament) from Green Hill, a pottery decorating tool, three walrus ivory flakers for sharpening chipped stone tools, and a whale bone wedge. Sometime in the 1920s, the museum was packed up and put into storage. The last year that the Patterson Collection appears in the calendar is 1946–47. Arrangements were made to turn it over to the provincial museum in 1953 (McNeill 1960) but it disappeared until a small part of the original collection was recently donated to the museum (Catherine Cottreau-Robins, personal communication, Nov. 2021).

Early Fieldwork in New Brunswick

The first archaeological excavations in New Brunswick were conducted by Spencer F. Baird, a zoologist associated with the Smithsonian Institution. Baird investigated several shell midden sites in Charlotte County between 1868 and 1872, while on vacation or conducting fisheries-related research. These sites were in Passamaquoddy Bay, including Oak Bay, St. Andrews, Digdeguash, Pocologan, Frye's Island, the Bliss Islands, and

2: PRACTISING ARCHAEOLOGY IN THE MARITIMES

Grand Manan. Black (1995, 6) notes that Baird's (1882) report includes a detailed description of the stratigraphy of the Simpson's Farm shell midden in Oak Bay. Stratigraphy refers to the depositional layers of sediment within a site and their study (Fladmark 1978, 161). Like most shell midden excavations of the nineteenth century, there was no attempt to associate the various layers he describes with cultural change over time (Trigger 1986, xv). Most of Baird's work was done in 1869 while visiting his friend, the ornithologist George A. Boardman. Although at first reluctant, Boardman was eventually drawn into Baird's shell midden explorations. In a letter to Baird, he refers to the problem of coastal erosion on precontact coastal sites: "I am glad you came when you did to see the heaps for it will not be very long before most of them will be washed away. The gales last fall probably destroyed dozens of them about the coast" (Boardman 1903, 189–90). James Fowler (1870, 389) also suggests that the lack of shell midden sites on the northeastern coasts of New Brunswick were due to the effects of coastal erosion.

The Natural History Society of New Brunswick began archaeological research in earnest in the 1880s, through a series of summer camps sponsored by the Society. The best-known project is the 1883 Bocabec Village excavation, which was reported on by George Matthew (see Vignette 3). However, the 1893 summer camp at French Lake is probably more typical of these outings:

> In August the party, numbering about twenty-three, proceeded to French Lake, some by sail boat and some by steamer to McGowan's wharf, and thence by carriage to Lakeville Corner. Tents were erected and ten days were spent studying the surrounding country. Excursions were made in all directions, and very satisfactory results were obtained in archaeology and botany. The party secured many specimens of implements and weapons of the unknown people who, in the Pre-historic period, dwelt in that section of the province, and the additions thus

made to the museum furnish good material for students of this most interesting subject. (Kain 1894, 67)

The period from 1909 to 1913 was the most active for the Society, when research was focused on the Lakes region of central New Brunswick. A limited amount of site survey and testing was done in the region during the late nineteenth century (Bailey 1883, 1887; Kain 1901, 1905; Matthew 1896, 1900; Matthew and Kain 1905). According to McIntosh (1911, 363), the Society quadrupled its precontact collection between 1909 and 1911, which was accomplished through more extensive fieldwork and donations of a few large private collections (McIntosh 1909, 1914). Several important sites were identified at this time on Eqpahak Island, at Jemseg, Indian Point, and at French, Maquapit, Grand, and Swan lakes (McTavish and Dickison 2007, 81). The Portebello River also was identified by McIntosh (1911, 363) as an area of high Indigenous traffic, but only temporary camps, based on the abundance of lithics (stone tools) and lack of pottery collected. The survey was continued in 1913 along the Saint John River between Fredericton and French Village, and sites were visited at Eqpahak Island, McDonald's Point, and Indian Point (McIntosh 1913). Comparatively little fieldwork on the east coast of New Brunswick was accomplished during this period. A Contact period copper kettle burial (see Chapter 7) was reported in the Tabusintac area (Smith 1886), and W.L. Goodwin (1892) produced a brief report on precontact sites in the Cape Tormentine area, including a possible lithic quarry on Jourmain Island.

William Ganong was interested in the precontact period of New Brunswick but he focused his research on the location of sites and portage routes (1899, 1913a, 1913b, 1914), and on possible precontact rock art — petroglyphs (1904). His 1899 monograph on historic sites in New Brunswick included the first detailed inventory of precontact sites, along with observations on why specific sites were chosen. Ganong's study was ahead of its time, as he combined information from archaeological fieldwork with surviving Indigenous place names and oral history.

The most ambitious archaeological project undertaken by the naturalists of the New Brunswick Natural History Society occurred in 1883, when a summer camp was organized to investigate the botany, zoology, and archaeology of the Bocabec River area of Passamaquoddy Bay (Figure 9). The archaeological activities focused on a largely undisturbed shell midden site (BgDr-25) at Phil's Beach, near the mouth of the river. Bruce Trigger (1986, xv) refers to George Matthew's (1884) report on this fieldwork as the most remarkable publication on a Northeastern shell midden from the late nineteenth century. Matthew's analysis of the site and its remains includes many astute archaeological interpretations concerning the choice of location, form of dwelling, on-site activity areas, sources of raw materials for tools, animal and plant foods utilized, and site occupation and seasonality. His report includes the first detailed section and ground plan of an excavated feature in the region (see Figure 10 and Vignette 3 for details).

Figure 9: Natural History Society of New Brunswick campsite at Bocabec, 1883, based on a watercolour sketch by Bessie Whitney. *Bulletin of the Natural History Society of New Brunswick* (10).

Vignette 3: A Stone Age Village at Bocabec

Phil's Beach was an excellent location for a large encampment. The site was relatively flat, with a sea-beach on the south side for landing canoes and a freshwater spring to the east of the site. Nearly 30 depressions were recorded at the site, which were interpreted as the floors of precontact dwellings (or "huts"). The excavation consisted of a trench dug through the largest of these depressions, which was later found to incorporate three adjacent dwellings. These were labelled A to C. An earlier hearth feature, labelled "1" on Matthew's map, was discovered at the site. Matthew (1884, 9) placed these features in two separate occupations (components). The earlier occupation was on the original beach, and the later occupation was further back from the shore and on top of an existing midden. The earlier component contained larger tools made from coarser materials, more harpoon heads, and more fish bones. The dwellings of the second occupation were "conical" pit-houses, with a layer of clean beach gravel at the base and a raised earthen bench around the inner wall. Large stones around the walls and at the entrance were identified as supports for poles. Floors were littered with ash, charcoal, pottery sherds, and food debris, and occasionally new gravel and hearth stones were added. Matthew (1884, 24) opines a winter occupation of the site, based on the orientation of the dwellings out of the prevailing wind, and other evidence that stone tools and pottery were being made indoors. Assuming that the dwellings were contemporaneous, Matthew estimates a population of up to 120 for the existing portion of the village (1884, 13).

The faunal remains recovered from the site indicate a rich resource base, including beaver, moose, deer, hare, fox, bear, and marine mammals (Matthew 1884, 22). Bones of various birds were present, including wading, aquatic, and arboreal species. Fish bones indicated that cod, herring, sculpin, and shark were taken. Shellfish species were dominated by clam, but included horse-mussel; long-whelk; round-whelk; small, purple-shell rock-periwinkle; bonnet limpet; a single large scallop; and sea urchin. Several species of land snail were present. As from other sites in the area, very few botanical remains were recovered. However, the excavators did recover some charred seeds from a

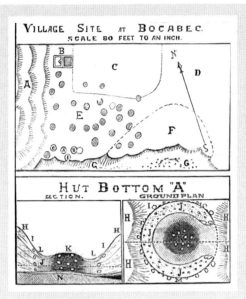

Figure 10: Top: George Matthew's profile and ground plan of an excavated feature at the Bocabec site, New Brunswick. *Bulletin of the Natural History Society of New Brunswick* (10). Bottom: Bocabec beach today. Photograph by Jason Jeandron.

hearth feature, including beach peas, a round seed the size of a radish seed, and a few grass seeds. The beach pea was gathered by the historic Mi'kmaq of New Brunswick (Speck and Dexter 1951, 257).

Most of Matthew's report focuses on the description of artifacts recovered by the expedition, which included pottery, lithics, and bone and ivory specimens. He identified a "pottery-yard" on the west side of dwelling A, based on the presence of clay deposits (1884, 13). He noted that a good source of clay for pottery-making was available at the site, but that the potters instead used the material from the seashore near the low tide mark. Pottery from the site indicates that both grit and shell were used to temper the clay. Matthew even notes the presence of residues on the outside of many potsherds. He identifies at least 10 different design elements on the pottery, including what we, today, would refer to as fabric-impressed, dentate, pseudo-scallop shell, and cord-wrapped stick impressions (1884, 13–14). These designs were comparable to known collections from Oak Bay and Maquapit Lake.

Matthew (1884, 17) suggests that stone tool manufacturing was conducted near the central fireplaces, based on clusters of debitage at these locations. The finished tools included projectile points, scrapers, bifaces, and ground stone axes. Most of these tools were made from local lithics, while the Saint John River is indicated as another possible source area. Matthew also speculates on tool functions and interprets the large quantity of scrapers from dwelling C as evidence of woodworking activities (1884, 19). Bone and ivory tools included a variety of modified beaver incisors, awls (bodkins), needles, harpoon points, and scored pieces. One of the latter pieces, with parallel notching on the back, is identified as a "tally stick" or gaming piece. Snow (1980, 197, Figure 5.6) refers to similar pieces from Maine as gaming or magical bones. Matthew notes that bone needles often were found at the backs of dwellings, opposite the entrance. Miscellaneous artifacts included a stone pendant decorated with crossed lines in the form of a lattice, and two kinds of powder stored in clam shell valves (i.e., galena, which occurs near the Digdeguash Inlet, and pulverized horse-mussel shells). The galena (lead sulphite) was probably prepared to be used as a pigment, while the crushed shell was likely used as a temper in pottery paste.

2: PRACTISING ARCHAEOLOGY IN THE MARITIMES

Early Fieldwork in Prince Edward Island

The short-lived Natural History Society of Prince Edward Island (1889–92) included archaeology as one of its subjects of inquiry (O'Grady 1993, 11). While the group did not undertake excavations, they were aware of the presence of shell middens on the island. The first reported excavation was conducted by the prominent American archaeologist, Jessie W. Fewkes, best known for his work in the American Southwest (Buchanan 1999, 15; O'Grady 1993). Like Baird, Fewkes was affiliated with the Smithsonian Institution. While on vacation on the island in 1896, he was told of a shell midden near Rustico, which he later described as consisting of a deposit of oyster and clam shells measuring 250 m^2 in size and 25 cm deep (Wallace 1989). His less-than-meticulous trenching of the midden was reported the same year in the *American Antiquarian* (Fewkes 1896). The more intriguing finds included two stone celts (axe heads), a copper bead, and a toggling harpoon point fashioned from walrus tusk. John Newson, the proprietor of the Seaside Hotel where Fewkes stayed, was probably his main informant and collaborator. When the Society was re-organized in 1899, Newson was the new president, and the name was changed to the Natural History and Antiquarian Society (Watson 1899a). The first annual outing of this group included visits to the Mi'kmaw encampment at Rocky Point and the ruins of Fort La Joie (Watson 1899b). Newson exhibited some projectile points and the tooth and claw of a bear from the Rustico site at a meeting in November 1901 (Wake 1995, 32).

Early Professional Period (1913–1960)

The term "professional archaeologist" first appears in literature around 1900, although the formal introduction of archaeology as a specialty began in the 1890s (Christenson 2011, 4, 14). The period from 1913 to 1960 saw the first fieldwork in the Maritimes organized by professional archaeologists, yet it was a period of slow growth for the discipline, both here and overseas (Bintliff 1986). The years of political and social upheaval associated with two world wars and the economic depression of the 1930s were partly responsible for this situation. Furthermore, until the 1960s, only a handful of professional archaeologists practised in the entire country, and they were assisted by a dedicated group of amateurs (Wright 1985, 425). The hiring of Harlan I. Smith by the Archaeology Division of the Geological Survey of Canada in 1911, followed a year later by William J. Wintemberg, was of significance to the archaeological study of the Maritimes (Figure 11). Wintemberg concentrated his research efforts on eastern Canada. In 1913–14, they worked together on two important shell midden sites in Nova Scotia (Smith and Wintemberg 1929; Smith 1917; Figure 12). They also surveyed much of the north coast of New Brunswick; the Northumberland Strait shore of Nova Scotia, from Pugwash to Merigomish; parts of the north coast of Prince Edward Island; and parts of the south shore of Nova Scotia (Wintemberg 1914).

Excavation techniques were not yet of a high standard and featured the digging of deep trenches through shell middens. Concerning his work at the Eisenhauer shell midden, Wintemberg (1914, 385) writes, "I spent some nine days, some days with as many as four assistants, excavating one of the largest, the Eisenhauer shell-heap, and secured five large boxes of

Figure 11: Early professional archaeologists: William J. Wintemberg and Harlan I. Smith. Canadian Museum of History negatives 55792 and 76087.

Figure 12: Harlan I. Smith excavation at Merigomish shell midden, Nova Scotia, 1914. Smith and Wintemberg 1929, Plate IIA.

specimens, all of which were Indigenous, and showed no signs of European influence." They also collected artifacts, and acquired some as gifts, and studied collections at Dalhousie University, the Nova Scotia Provincial Museum, and the Natural History Society of New Brunswick. Wintemberg even visited the Rustico shell midden on two occasions. During the 1913 survey, he surface-collected an unfinished pipe and adze blade. On his return in 1937, he dug test pits and collected several hundred artifacts, including a copper bead (O'Grady 1993, 15). When Wintemberg died in 1941, Diamond Jenness wrote that without question "he was the leading authority on Canadian archaeology" (1941, 66).

Other notable research from the first two decades of the twentieth century includes the survey work of Warren K. Moorehead in northern Maine and southwestern New Brunswick in search of "Red Paint" burials. During the last two weeks of July 1914, Moorehead conducted a canoe survey of the upper Saint John River area, from Edmundston to Meductic (Figure 13; Moorehead 1922, 233–38). His crew tested near a Wolastoqwey

2: PRACTISING ARCHAEOLOGY IN THE MARITIMES

Figure 13: Warren K. Moorehead and "The Force" at their camp on the flat below Grand Falls, NB, 1914. From lantern slide 409 (Me.WKM,559), Robert S. Peabody Museum of Archaeology, Phillips Academy, Andover, Maine.

village at the mouth of the Madawaska River, and Indigenous guides led him 50 km up the river in search of the source of a black "flint" used for stone tool manufacturing. Later in the week, they sunk several hundred test pits within a 4 km radius of the mouth of the Tobique River and recovered some flakes and biface fragments from pits dug in the modern Maliseet village at Tobique. One of their guides, John Devoe, gave them a list of nine precontact sites between Tobique and Saint John. They tested at least two of these, at Woodstock and Meductic. Moorehead considered Meductic to be the largest and most extensive site they found in New Brunswick and noted the private collection of a local farmer. His crew recovered hundreds of chipped stone artifacts and pottery fragments from test pits and surface-collecting at this site.

When plans were being made to establish a provincial museum in New Brunswick, the Natural History Society offered its collections and library, which were transferred to the new museum in 1932 (Squires 1945, 17–19). These collections included the original archaeological specimens from the Gesner collection and those collected by members of the Society. The New Brunswick Museum opened on August 16, 1934. T.C. Currelly, director of the Royal Ontario Museum of Archaeology, gave one of the opening speeches, and Chief William Polchies, of the Saint John Wolastoqiyik, attended in full regalia, including a silver medal given to his people by Queen Victoria (Squires 1945, 22).

In 1935, Mrs. J.C. Webster had 12 cases installed in the grand gallery for oriental and archaeological materials. This exhibit included materials transferred from the Natural History Society, which were augmented by a bequest in 1943 of more than 2,500 artifacts found in New Brunswick by the late William Hale. A collection of models of wigwams, canoes, toboggans, and deadfalls by E.T. Adney was added to the ethnological exhibits. Some materials were also set aside as visual learning aids in the museum's education program.

Archaeological research in the region came to a virtual standstill between 1914 and the 1950s. In New Brunswick, archaeology was continued in the upper Saint John River area by avocational archaeologists (e.g., Adney 1933; Clarke 1974). George Clarke built an extensive collection of pre-contact materials during his explorations on the Saint John, Tobique, and Miramichi rivers, much of which was put on public display in Woodstock and is now entrusted to the University of New Brunswick (Woolsey 2013). In the northeast, Gorham (1928) reported a Contact period burial at Red Bank, on the Miramichi River, and Wintemberg (1937) tested an Early Woodland burial site in the same area. Wintemberg (1942, 130–34; 1943) also made the first attempt to integrate the precontact ceramics of the Maritimes into a broader North American scheme.

In Nova Scotia, anthropologist Frank Speck (1924) describes a possibly Contact Period slate human figurine found at an old campsite on the west bank of the Clyde River, Shelburne County, which now resides in the National Museum of the American Indian, Washington, DC (Figure 14). The

Figure 14: Carved slate anthropomorphic figurine collected by folklorist MacEdward Leach at an old campsite on the Clyde River, Nova Scotia. National Museum of the American Indian, Smithsonian Institution (#121754). Photograph by Ernest Amoroso. Courtesy Patricia Nietfeld.

artwork on the figurine is reminiscent of the Woodland period incised stones from Holt's Point, Passamaquoddy Bay (Fowler 1966a; Hammon 1984). According to Roger Ray (1977, 18) the face of the figure was rubbed with grease, and he notes that bear grease was used to nourish an individual's "soul spirit" and is believed to have been used to invoke dreams that revealed where to hunt. Ray (1977, 19) also depicts a historic Penobscot (Penawapskewi) wooden figure with movable joints, which shares many similarities with the Clyde River figurine, and especially the features of the head and face and body form.

Fieldwork in northern Maine sponsored by the Peabody Museum during the 1930s was extended into New Brunswick by Douglas Byers after World War II (Sanger 1979c, 12–13). Survey work was resumed in Passamaquoddy Bay and along the upper Saint John River during the 1950s (Stoddard 1950). Stoddard also briefly visited southeastern New Brunswick during his 1950 survey and later conducted an excavation at the Graham site, an early historic Mi'kmaw dwelling in the Richibucto area (Stoddard and Dyson 1956).

J. Russell Harper (1956, 1957) excavated a Contact period burial site at Portland Point, Saint John Harbour, under the auspices of the New Brunswick Museum. According to David Sanger (1987, 89), he also may have tested the McAleenan shell midden site at Digdeguash Harbour in the mid-1950s. The Portland Point report includes the description of a 1955 amateur excavation of another Contact period burial in Pictou, Nova Scotia. Harper conducted additional work at this site in 1956 (Harper 1957). The avocational archaeologist, Kenneth Hopps, opened a small museum on his property, where he exhibited materials from the excavation and even sold copies of Harper's 1957 published report.

In 1957, John Erskine was doing botanical fieldwork for the Nova Scotia Provincial Museum in the Port Joli area. The author Thomas Raddall had explored several shell middens in the area and convinced Erskine (1998, 4–5) that someone should record the location of these sites before they disappeared. Erskine tested nine sites in 1957 and went on to sample dozens more over the next 10 years. As he began to work in earnest, he received encouragement and guidance from Douglas Byers (1960, 5–7) and produced several reports for the Provincial Museum (Erskine 1958, 1959, 1961).

The first conference on archaeological research in the Maritimes was held at Citadel Hill in Halifax, on October 31, 1959 (Anonymous 1959). The meeting was chaired by Donald Crowdis, curator of the Provincial Museum (1940–65). Eighteen delegates were in attendance and reports were given by John S. Erskine, Jane McNeill, J. Russell Harper, H.L. Cameron, and Douglas Byers. Erskine reviews previous research conducted in Nova Scotia and his three field seasons on shell midden sites in southwestern Nova Scotia. He points out that virtually nothing was known about the "pre-shell-heap" cultures. McNeill reports on the condition of the Provincial Museum's collections of archaeological and ethnological materials and notes that one precontact collection of 250 specimens seems to be missing (i.e., the Patterson Collection). Harper describes his fieldwork in New Brunswick and Pictou, Nova Scotia (1956, 1957). Cameron describes his use of aerial photography at historic sites in Nova Scotia (1954, 1956, 1958). Byers shows slides of his research in Maine and points out the similarity between materials recovered at sites in that area with those found in Nova Scotia. In an afternoon panel discussion, many issues debated included the need to formulate legislation for the protection of archaeological sites, as well as the need for detailed site surveys, salvage operations, the training of local archaeologists, and a suitable publication outlet. This meeting was a promising beginning, and plans were made to make it an annual event. Unfortunately, there was a lapse of 26 years before the next meeting would convene, with a new generation of archaeologists.

Modern Professional Period (1960–Present)

The 1959 Conference on Archaeology in Nova Scotia was a watershed in the history of archaeological research in the Maritimes. For the first time, local participants met and identified the problems they faced. The impact of the meeting was immediate. Erskine branched out to survey other parts of Nova Scotia, and even visited New Brunswick and Prince Edward Island. In 1962, he learned of the Palaeo site at Debert, Nova Scotia, and relayed the information to Byers (Erskine 1998, 5; Figure 15). As a result, the first large-scale professional excavation of a precontact site was conducted at Debert, which also involved a geological survey for the sources of the lithic materials found at the site (Borns 1966; Byers 1966; MacDonald

Figure 15: John Erskine photograph of the Debert Palaeo site, July 1962. John S. Erskine Photograph Collection (E1).

1966; Stuckenrath 1966). The project was conducted by Byers and received funding from the United States National Science Foundation and the Canadian and Nova Scotian governments. George MacDonald's (1968) report on the site has become a classic publication in Palaeo research. We now know that the Debert area was just beginning to inform us on the earliest inhabitants of this region (Bernard et al. 2011; Julien et al. 2008).

Interest in the Merigomish area was renewed at the beginning of the 1960s. John Erskine (1961) explored the Merigomish Islands in 1960 and tested three sites, two precontact and one historic. In particular, he isolated two undisturbed areas at Smith's Shell-Heap D, now designated BjCo-02, where he found Middle and Late Woodland projectile points and moose and deer bone. In 1978, David Keenlyside (1980b), with the Canadian Museum of Civilization, reported that all but one of the shell middens reported by Smith and Wintemberg had been destroyed by coastal erosion. In 1993, Ronald Nash took a St. Francis Xavier University field school to the Millar site at Kerr's Point, which was first recorded by Patterson (Snow 1994). Finally, Michelle Lelièvre (2012) conducted doctoral research with the University of Chicago on Maligomish Island in 2007–08. Her fine-grained analysis of the shell midden on Maligomish changed the focus of local shell midden research to the study of midden composition. In particular, she addressed the presence of the eastern oyster in Late Woodland middens, which distinguishes it from deposits on the Atlantic and Bay of Fundy coasts (Lelièvre 2017c).

Until recently, it was believed that Matthew's original field notes on the Bocabec site were passed on to other members of the Society and eventually destroyed. Instead, they were rediscovered by Jason Jeandron (personal communication) at the New Brunswick Museum. At least part of the Phil's Beach collection also ended up in the New Brunswick Museum, where it was mixed with other collections. In 1979, these materials were restudied by Jennifer Bishop (1983). The surviving collection consists of 38 lithic specimens, 23 bone/ivory artifacts, and 96 ceramic sherds. Bishop's study involved an updated description and quantitative analysis of these artifacts, and an attempt to date the two occupation levels at Phil's Beach. In the 1880s, Matthew had no way of accurately dating the two components. He noted that the absence of European artifacts suggested a precontact date for both occupations, yet the dwellings had many similarities with historic Indigenous wigwams (p. 28). Based on the ceramic analysis, Bishop (1983, 56) dated the earlier occupation to c. 1,700 ^{14}C yrs BP and the later occupation to c. 900–400 ^{14}C yrs BP. Using the ceramic chronology of Petersen and Sanger (1991), the two occupations can be associated with the early-middle Middle Woodland (c. 2,150–1,350 ^{14}C yrs BP) and late Middle to Late Woodland (c. 1,350–400 ^{14}C yrs BP). The fabric-impressed pottery was missing from the museum collection. This material could date either to the Early Woodland (c. 3,050–2,150 ^{14}C yrs BP) or to the reoccurrence of fabric-impressed pottery in the late Late Woodland (c. 650–400 ^{14}C yrs BP). It appears that the site was used over a long span of time, during the Middle to Late Woodland periods.

Since 1960, archaeology has expanded in four sectors across Canada: government, museum, university, and the private sector (Turnbull 1977). Early research in the 1960s was dominated by two large federal agencies, the Archaeological Survey of Canada (National Museums of Canada) and the National Historic Sites Service of Parks Canada. The Archaeological Survey is responsible for all precontact research conducted by the federal government and is conducted primarily through the Atlantic Provinces Archaeologist, a position first held by Richard Pearson. Parks Canada is responsible for research conducted at National Historic Sites and Parks. The latter includes mostly historic sites, but a few precontact sites have been excavated by Parks Canada archaeologists (e.g., Ferguson 1986; Wallace 1987) and precontact material culture is often encountered at early historic sites in the region. For example, during a field survey at the early seventeenth-century Habitation site, Nova Scotia (Cameron 1956), besides a large quantity of historic artifacts, sherds from two precontact pottery vessels and three projectile points were collected (Deal and Butt 1991, 1).

Today, regional research is conducted mainly through the auspices of provincial agencies (e.g., Ferguson 2004). In Nova Scotia, archaeology falls under the jurisdiction of the Department of Communities, Culture, and Heritage, and the mandate of the Nova Scotia Museum; in New Brunswick, it falls under the mandate of the Archaeological Services Unit of the Department of Tourism, Heritage, and Culture. While John Erskine was considered the unofficial Provincial Archaeologist in Nova Scotia (Fitting, 1973, 57), Brian Preston became the first official Curator of Archaeology in 1968, and Christopher J. Turnbull became the first Provincial Archaeologist of New Brunswick in 1973. In Prince Edward Island, the responsibility for archaeology initially fell to the Director of Archives for the Department of Education. In 2010, a new Aboriginal Affairs Secretariat and Provincial Archaeologist's office were created, and Helen Kristmanson became the first Provincial Archaeologist (Kristmanson 2010).

The Nova Scotia Museum (NSM) is the only museum in the region that has its own archaeology program, with a collection of over half-a-million artifacts. The Department of Communities, Culture, and Heritage (CCH) is responsible for issuing permits, and the recording and storage of precontact materials. The Museum, which operates within CCH, also offers an annual research grant aimed at projects that focus on threatened sites, the restudy of collections, or community outreach programs. Information on Nova Scotia archaeology is disseminated via the Internet, exhibits, articles, and curatorial reports. Work began on a new archaeological gallery in 1991, which opened in 1997 and continues to be refreshed. The New Brunswick Museum eventually passed over its precontact collection to the Archaeology Branch in the Old Soldiers Barracks in Fredericton, where it remains today as a research collection. The Archaeology Branch, now called Archaeological Services, issues permits for New Brunswick and has an active research program. It produces a manuscript series that includes reports on major archaeological projects.

A single system of site designation has been adopted across the country (Bordon 1952), yet policies and responsibilities relating to archaeology still vary considerably (Foulkes et al. 1984). Over time, legal provisions for the protection of archaeological sites have improved. In New Brunswick, the Historic Sites Protection Act (1976) became the guideline for the protection of sites. The Act is invoked when a site is slated for protection, and a permit is then required before the site can be altered or excavated (Turnbull 1977, 3). In 1980, the Nova Scotia Museum became responsible for precontact and historic sites, including those under water, and for material culture through the Special Places Protection Act (1989), and Robert Ogilvie became the first Curator of Special Places. The Act includes guidelines for archaeological survey and excavation and research involving collections. Prince Edward Island has revised its heritage policies under the Archaeology Act (2006). The 1970s also saw the formation of the Council of Maritime Premiers, an interprovincial committee that sponsors and co-ordinates research across the region, including archaeology (Davis 1998, 158). The Council was expanded to include Newfoundland and Labrador and is now the Council of the Atlantic Premiers.

Funding for archaeological research was dramatically increased during the 1960s (Wright 1985, 429), with increased budgets for universities and for federal and provincial government agencies. Some research was funded by National Research Council grants (1966–69) and by the Canada Council (1967). In 1978, the Social Sciences and Humanities Research Council of Canada was formed out of the Canada Council and became a major sponsor of archaeological projects. The Council of Canadian Archaeologists was organized in 1966 as a lobbying group for issues concerning Canadian archaeology. Two years later, the Canadian Archaeological Association (CAA) was established. The journal produced by the CAA, the *Canadian Journal of Archaeology* (*CJA*), is one of the major publication venues for Canadian archaeology. Another important national publication medium is the Mercury Series of the Archaeological Survey of Canada. In New Brunswick, Archaeological Services publishes a Manuscripts in Archaeology series and a more polished memoir series. The Nova Scotia Museum produced its first overview of precontact archaeology in the 1970s (Hayward 1973) and began publishing summaries of permit reports in its Curatorial Report series and produces the occasional special publication. The NSM launched an e-publication program that facilitates the publication of recent research and newsletters. There is no comparable publication source in Prince Edward Island, but several important popular archaeology articles have appeared in the *Island Magazine*. Publication is part of the mandate of the Council of Maritime (now Atlantic) Premiers (e.g., Deal and Blair 1991). Several small independent publishers (i.e., Nimbus Publishing) have produced popular volumes on archaeology, and access to reports on research has been greatly enhanced by the Internet. In 2010, the Nova Scotia Museum began posting a current research report series online.

During the 1970s, full-time archaeologists were hired at two Nova Scotia universities, namely Stephen Davis at Saint Mary's University and Ronald Nash at St. Francis Xavier, and Francis Stewart taught part-time at the University of New Brunswick. The two Nova Scotia institutions soon were providing locally trained archaeologists. A report of the Council of Maritime Premiers (MCAC 1978) recommended the development of a basic curriculum in regional archaeology in the local universities, but this was never fully implemented. Eventually, two full-time archaeologists, David Black and Susan Blair, were added to the anthropology faculty of the University of New Brunswick. Anna Sawicki also taught archaeology on a part-time basis at the University of Prince Edward Island. James Tuck, of Memorial University of Newfoundland, began training archaeology graduate students in the 1970s, including some who were working in the Maritimes and, more recently, archaeology MA students have come out of the University of New Brunswick program. The author was added to the Memorial University faculty in 1986 as a Maritimes specialist. Summer archaeological field schools have been offered periodically through these institutions since the mid-1970s, as well as through the Department of Earth and Environmental Science of Acadia University. Newly trained students generally sought work in provincial and federal departments and museums. Today, more jobs are created in the private sector, including employment as staff members or seasonal workers with contracting companies (see Davis 1998, 160). New Brunswick and Nova Scotia both have active amateur archaeology societies, which include a variety of avocational archaeologists, students, and professionals. These groups have formal meetings, field trips, and guest lecture series.

With a more formal infrastructure, archaeological fieldwork in the region increased dramatically over the second half of the twentieth century, yet the work was unevenly distributed. Coastal areas were targeted because of the threat of site destruction due to rising sea levels (Davis 1980, 1983; Simonson 1978). In New Brunswick, fieldwork has focused on Passamaquoddy Bay and the Chiputneticook-St. Croix drainage, the Tobique River area and Lakes Region of the Saint John River drainage, and the Miramichi and Tracadie areas of the northeast. Relatively little work has been done along the Bay of Fundy shore from Passamaquoddy Bay to the Minas Basin, the lower Saint John River area, and along the numerous river drainages of eastern and southeastern New Brunswick. In Nova Scotia, research has focused on the area around Halifax and Dartmouth, the South Shore, Lake Kejimkujik and Lake Rossignol, the western Minas Basin, the Shubenacadie drainage, and portions of the Northumberland Strait shoreline (also see Davis 1998, 158–59). Preston (1989, 1991) identified 10 areas of Nova Scotia that were poorly studied, including large portions of Guysborough County and Cape Breton Island. In Prince Edward Island, archaeological research has been concentrated on the large bays along the gulf coast and the coast opposite Cape Breton Island (Buchanan 1999). Most of the southern and western shores have not been surveyed. Furthermore, the occasional recovery of artifacts offshore by scallop draggers in the Bay of Fundy and off Prince Edward Island indicates that many early sites are now deep under water (Keenlyside 1984a; Stright 1990; Taylor 2020).

Close ties developed between archaeologists in Maine and the Maritimes during the 1970s and a series of informal meetings were held. The main objectives of these meetings were to discuss current developments in each area and to seek consensus on classification systems and terminology (Sanger 1973b, 8–9). The meetings were discontinued by the 1980s, yet the research links have survived. A regional Archaic workshop held in

October 2001, at the University of Maine, Orono, resulted in an important collaborative publication (Sanger and Renouf 2006). The Nova Scotia Museum initiated an annual workshop for professional archaeologists in 1985. These meetings have continued to this day and generally involve most of the archaeologists working in Nova Scotia and a few from elsewhere in the region. A wide range of provincial and national issues are addressed at these meetings (see Davis 1998, 160).

As mentioned above, since the 1970s there has been a growing concern among Indigenous peoples in North America over the recovery and treatment of precontact human remains and artifacts (Mackie 1995). This was an important issue in 1993 when the Canadian Archaeological Association began consultations with Indigenous communities across the country for the purpose of drafting an agreement on ethical conduct concerning Indigenous heritage and archaeological research. In the Maritimes, a series of meetings, workshops, and/or talking circles were conducted. A number of universal concerns were recognized (after Allen 1996, 19), including the need (1) to respect sacred sites, including burial places; (2) for more consultation and communication between the two groups on heritage issues; (3) for more Indigenous training and educational opportunities in the field of heritage studies; (4) for fuller participation in heritage projects; (5) to respect oral traditions and Indigenous interpretations, especially during archaeological impact assessments; and (6) to report finds in a timely and understandable format. The resulting document is a tentative statement of mutual concerns, which can be used to develop more specific local protocols (Allen 1996).

Bringing It All Together

The beginnings of archaeology as a discipline in the Maritimes can be traced to the naturalists of the nineteenth century, who usually were wealthy avocational scientists who formed societies and gave lectures on various topics, including archaeology. The most important figures to archaeology were Abraham Gesner, Loring W. Bailey, and George Matthew in New Brunswick and George Patterson in Nova Scotia, while Americans Spencer F. Baird and Jessie W. Fewkes made key contributions. The early naturalists were aware of the exciting research being done on shell midden sites in Denmark and the new methodologies being developed for archaeology (see Chapter 3). The societies even established their own small museums, which would become the nucleus of provincial collections.

Archaeology in the early twentieth century was impeded by the two world wars and the depression of the 1930s. However, the inter-war period saw the first significant publication by professionally trained archaeologists in the region (i.e., Smith and Wintemberg 1929). Fieldwork continued to be sporadic until the 1960s and was mostly in the hands of a few dedicated avocational archaeologists, such as George Clarke in New Brunswick and John Erskine in Nova Scotia. The Citadel Hill conference in 1959 was a watershed in Maritimes archaeology. Representatives from the Nova Scotia and New Brunswick museums, along with Douglas Byers of the Peabody Museum at Harvard and aerial photographer H.A. Cameron, discussed key issues that included the training of local archaeologists, the need for more detailed surveys, and suitable publication outlets. These same issues were still on the agenda of the next conference in Halifax in 1985.

The 1960s signalled the beginning of a new era for archaeology throughout Canada. The Canadian Archaeological Association was formed in 1968 to promote archaeological research across the country. New funding and publication options were becoming available. The first large-scale professional excavation in the Maritimes was conducted at Debert (MacDonald 1968). Nova Scotia appointed its first Curator of Archaeology in 1968 and New Brunswick its first Provincial Archaeologist in 1973. New guidelines were established for the protection of archaeological sites and collections, and eventually Prince Edward Island followed suit. Archaeologists were hired at the major universities in the Atlantic region, which led to the training of a new generation of archaeologists.

Despite a marked increase in archaeological activity in the Maritimes since the 1960s, it remains a vastly under-studied region in eastern North

America. Today, much of the fieldwork is driven by cultural resource management concerns and academics are slow to incorporate new findings from this work. What we need is a more inclusive and coordinated approach, involving academics, government archaeologists, contract archaeology groups, and Indigenous organizations. Indigenous organizations like the Archaeology Research Division of the Kwilmu'kw Maw-klusuaqn Office and the Maliseet Advisory Committee on Archaeology do essential work of mediating between government agencies and Indigenous communities. Critical to this process is an ongoing collaboration with local Indigenous communities.

THE WHY AND HOW QUESTIONS

ACCORDING TO MATTHEW JOHNSON (2019, 2), theory covers the why questions in archaeology, while methodology covers the how questions. Theory determines why we excavate a certain site, or why we save the animal bones and pieces of charcoal. Methodology determines how we go about doing this and what we do with the materials we collect. Another popular use of the term "theory" is as a hypothetical construct, such as Darwin's theory of evolution. In either sense, theory deals with ideas, concepts, and thought. "Method" implies action and is usually the result of theoretical reflection. Problems can be solved by the development of new methodology. In archaeology, these problems generally relate to the recovery of material remains, mapping the landscape, and the dating of deposits. The following chapter charts the growth of theoretical thought in archaeology in the Maritimes and the methods (techniques) developed to address regional archaeological problems (see Vignette 4). This discussion will illustrate how our understanding of the precontact period has changed over time.

The Archaeological Record

Before reviewing the development of theory and method in the region, we should consider what archaeologists study. Since the late twentieth century, the term "archaeological record" has been a popular reply. In a now classic 1985 paper, Linda Patrik discusses the confusion over the use of this term in the archaeological literature. It was used varyingly to refer to the things or populations that existed prior to deposits as a receptacle for them (i.e., the ground), material deposits, material remains, archaeological samples, and archaeological reports (Patrik 1985, 29). Precisely, the archaeological record refers to the physical remains of the past, which archaeologists use to interpret past lifeways. In a practical sense, when archaeologists refer to the archaeological record, they usually mean all the information amassed from decades of archaeological survey, excavation, and laboratory analysis for their specific region. It is the archival record of the archaeologist from which he/she interprets the past. There are many holes in this record for the Maritimes, due to varying standards of recovery and record-keeping, and the vagaries of site and material culture preservation. However, recovery standards have improved dramatically over the years as more professional archaeologists have worked in the region.

In the early years of archaeology in the Maritimes, no official record of sites existed. To find a site you had to go to an area and ask the local people if anyone had a collection of Indigenous artifacts or knew of any ancient campsites. We still do this today, but it is usually part of a well-planned regional survey. Indigenous place names and oral histories can also give clues to important places (see below). Some sites are obvious, like the enormous shell middens in Passamaquoddy Bay and along the south shore of Nova Scotia. Sometimes vegetation changes are a clue to a site location. For example, plum trees, berry bushes, and pigweed (any of several varieties of *Amaranthus retroflexus*, a mild-flavoured edible plant with small but nutritious seeds) often grow around former Indigenous campsites. Sites also occur quite often at the mouths of rivers and streams, which were used as transportation routes and as fresh water sources. Others are found near lithic stone tool quarrying sites. Likely sites can be ground-tested for evidence of precontact occupation. For older sites, the landscape may have changed considerably since the time of occupation. Deeply stratified sites, like the Boswell site along the Annapolis River near Kingston, Nova Scotia, would likely have been missed using standard ground-testing methods (Deal et al. 2022). A chance discovery of Terminal Archaic artifacts along the shore pointed to the possible presence of an early site. Many Archaic and Palaeo sites are believed to be offshore due to sea level rise and can only be located and studied by using expensive underwater techniques (Stright 1990).

In terms of interpreting the archaeological record of the Maritimes, archaeologists focus on information relating to past material culture and sites of past human activity. Past material culture exists in the form of man-made objects (artifacts), plant and animal specimens (ecofacts), and human remains. It also includes non-portable evidence of human activity or features, such as the structural remains of dwellings, hearths, and pits. Indigenous activity sites include village sites, campsites, cemeteries, and locations of resource extraction and processing.

Precontact cultures are identified by a shared technology, settlement and subsistence patterns, and social system that existed during a specific period. Technology refers to tools and shelter and to the acquisition of the raw materials used for their manufacture. Archaeologists have developed a specialized terminology for the analysis of different finished tool forms (see Figures 16 and 17). The archaeological evidence for technology includes the tools themselves, archaeological traces of former shelters, and the identification and distribution of the utilized raw materials.

Certain rock (lithic) and mineral resources were important to Indigenous populations in the region. In the precontact period, flakeable (knappable) lithics were the raw materials for the manufacture of hunting and processing tools. Indigenous populations in the Northeast sought out the best-quality lithic materials in each region and certain higher-quality lithics were distributed over long distances (see Chapter 6). Cherts from coastal Labrador and the Quebec interior made their way to the Maritimes and Maine, especially towards the end of the precontact period (Cox 2021). Cherts, chalcedonies, and rhyolites from certain Nova Scotian quarries were highly prized. Harder stone, ground and polished to make woodworking tools (e.g., axes and adzes), and clay for pottery-making

3: THE WHY AND HOW QUESTIONS

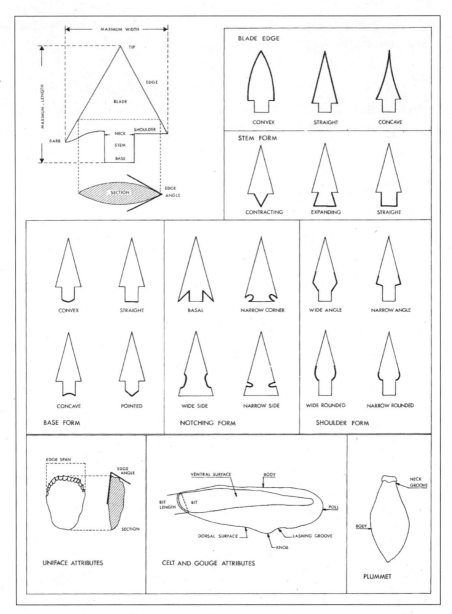

Figure 16: Illustration of lithic and ground stone tool terminology (from Deal 1985, Figure 15). Figure by Michael Deal and Angel Gómez-Miguelanez (adapted from Sanger 1973, Figure 4, and Allen 1981, Figures 13, 16).

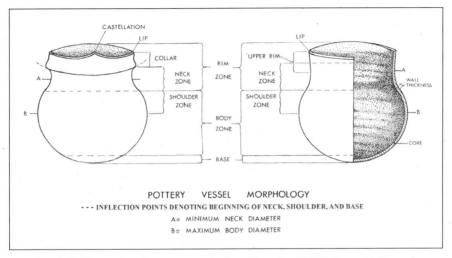

Figure 17: Illustration of pottery terminology (from Deal 1985, Figure 8). Figure by Michael Deal and Angel Gómez-Miguelanez (adapted from Allen 1981, Figure 32, and Marois 1979).

were widely available within the region. Copper was an important material for making both spiritual and domestic items throughout the late precontact period (Hanley et al. 2022; Monahan 1990). Only small amounts of copper were available locally, so raw copper was most likely acquired through trade, at first from distant sources, then regional sources, and eventually through trade with European fishermen (Whitehead 1991; Whitehead et al. 1998).

"Subsistence patterns" refers to the economic practices related to the acquisition and use of food resources by precontact peoples. Archaeologists interpret subsistence practices from plant and animal remains and from the tools used to acquire and process food. "Resource use" in archaeological terms relates to the natural resources that formed the basis of precontact technologies and subsistence practices. "Settlement patterns" refers to the distribution of human populations throughout their habitat and across the landscape. Archaeologists interpret settlement patterns from different types of sites and their distribution, and this can be equated with precontact land-use practices (see below). "Social system" refers to the social, political, and spiritual beliefs of an archaeological culture. Much of the archaeological evidence for social systems is derived from artifact forms and decorations and from burial practices that often imply the social roles and statuses of individuals.

While individual archaeologists may focus their research activities on specific problems and specific time periods, they all share certain goals (Fagan 2006, 63–66). When archaeologists search out and excavate pre-contact sites, they are contributing to our understanding of the local and regional cultural sequences. Therefore, an important goal of archaeological research is the reconstruction of culture history, or the sequence of archaeological cultures within the region. Individual sites may have been occupied many times by many different groups of people. The artifacts and features left at a site help us to understand how it was used. Thus, another important goal of archaeological research is the reconstruction of past lifeways, or how people lived on a day-to-day basis and how they organized themselves. The interpretation of archaeological remains is affected by various local conditions that are referred to as "site formation processes" (Schiffer 1987). These processes include cultural and natural factors affecting the preservation of material culture and sites, such as coastal erosion, soil acidity, and farming practices. On a larger scale, archaeologists have tried to identify cultural processes that account for change in material culture and human behaviour over time, such as migration, diffusion, acculturation, and technological innovation. In addition, Fagan (2006, 66) holds that a fundamental objective of modern archaeology is to conserve, manage, and preserve the archaeological record for future generations. Archaeological sites are under constant threat of destruction due to human activities and climate change.

Vignette 4: Methods in Maritimes Archaeology

Archaeologists use a variety of analytical methods to study materials from pre-contact sites. Here are the principal methods used in the Maritimes:

Geographic Information Systems (GIS). This computing method is commonly used for capturing and displaying different forms of spatial data in the form of maps. For example, data from different sources representing the locations of archaeological sites, resources, place names, and trails can be placed on a single base map or aerial photograph to show relationships at different times. GIS technology can also overlay, or combine, data sets from geophysical surveying techniques, such as magnetometry, resistivity, and ground-penetrating radar (GPR) for the study of buried cultural features. Drones now can be used to acquire aerial photographs, including Lidar, which uses laser light to penetrate vegetation to produce high-definition site maps. Consulting groups like Boreas Heritage Consulting Inc. are bringing GIS and advanced technology to cultural resource management projects in the Maritimes, while magnetometry and GPR techniques and drone-based photogrammetry have been used successfully on Indigenous sites in Newfoundland and Labrador (Erwin et al. 2018; Williamson 2019; Wolff and Urban 2014).

Paleoethnobotany. The term "ethnobotany" was coined in 1895 to describe the study of plants used by Indigenous peoples (Ford 1978, 33). The field was later broadened to include plant remains from archaeological sites. This subfield, which is referred to as "paleoethnobotany," or "archaeobotany," concerns the recovery and analysis of archaeological plant (floral) remains as a basis for understanding past human and plant interactions. The paleoethnobotanist in the Northeast studies preserved plant remains recovered from archaeological deposits (Deal 2008a).

Palynology. The study of ancient (fossil) pollen from sites or, more often, from nearby lake or bog deposits can provide clues concerning the ancient climate (or the paleoenvironment) at the time the site was occupied (e.g., Mudie and Lelièvre 2013; Spooner et al. 2014). This work is often done by archaeologically trained palynologists.

Stable Isotope Analysis. This popular tool for studying changes in the diets of past human and animal populations entails the analysis of stable carbon ($\delta^{13}C$) and nitrogen ($\delta^{15}N$) isotope ratios (Burchell and Harris 2018, 115) through the study of bone collagen (i.e., the protein fraction of bone) in archaeological specimens. In Nova Scotia, isotope sclerochronology (i.e., the study of shell growth over time) has been used to study the season of occupation of Port Joli shell midden sites (Betts et al. 2017). This technique has also been used to study organic residues adhering to, or absorbed into, the walls of pottery vessels to determine food preparation techniques and vessel function (Deal et al. 2019; Taché and Craig 2015).

Stratigraphic Analysis. A common method for determining the sequence of the occupation of a site is to examine the layers of soil (sediment) and cultural deposits (strata) accumulated on a site over time. The stratigraphic layering of deposits can be used as a tool for dating the cultural layers (components) relative to one another. This method is used in conjunction with radiocarbon dating and perceived changes in artifact design and decoration to develop a cultural timeline for the site (see Vignette 5 and Figure 42).

Zooarchaeology. This is the study of animal (faunal) remains from archaeological sites (Murphy and Black 1996). In the Maritimes, coastal shell midden sites have produced the most complete record of precontact animal use due to the tendency of the decomposing shell to reduce the natural acidity of the soil that erodes calcium (bone). At interior sites, animal remains sometimes survive as calcine (charred) bone from hearth (fireplace) deposits.

Development of Archaeological Theory and Method

Archaeological theory and methodology in this region have always closely followed contemporary research in Europe and the United States. Naturalist groups working on shell midden sites in the nineteenth century were exposed to current writings on evolutionary archaeology. These archaeologists, often referred to as the unilinear evolutionists, adopted an evolutionary model for culture change over time. Most prominent anthropologists of the day, like Lewis Morgan (1877), believed that human cultures progressed in a single line of development from savagery to civilization. While a racialized hierarchy is prominent in his book *Ancient Society*, Morgan's feelings about race are ambiguous, as he was a vocal supporter of Indigenous rights in America (Hume 2011). What later archaeologists took away from this work was the notion that the stimulus for cultural change was environmental stress, and change was expressed in terms of technology, that is, through the invention or adoption of new tools.

While the cultural evolution model follows a Darwinian perspective, Bruce Trigger (1989, 139) traces the intellectual framework for scientific archaeology to the Enlightenment philosophers of the eighteenth century and their notions of progress, reason, and conjectural history. These concepts were already influencing Danish researchers early in the nineteenth century as they were laying the foundations of a scientific approach in archaeology. Christian Thomsen revived an evolutionary model of the Roman philosopher Lucretius in his reorganization of the Danish National Museum collections. This model, known today as the Three Age System, uses the historic development of stone, bronze, and iron tools as a device for chronologically ordering archaeological materials. As Trigger notes (1989, 140), Thomsen had "demonstrated for the first time how archaeological data could be ordered chronologically and explained without reference to written records or oral traditions." This scheme was used successfully by J.J.A. Worsaae (1849) to interpret the stratigraphic levels in his excavations in Danish bogs and, later, by Daniel Wilson (1851) in his influential treatise on Scottish archaeology, *The Archaeology and Prehistoric Annals of Scotland*. Wilson's book introduced the new system to the English-speaking world, along with the new term "prehistoric," referring to history before written records (Ash 1985, 15), although it appears that he adapted the term from earlier Scandinavian terminology (Rowley-Conway 2006). Early local naturalists, like L.W. Bailey, would have been aware of Wilson's research when he attempted the first classification of precontact artifacts in New Brunswick (Black 2009). Another Dane, Sven Nilsson

(1868), showed that comparative ethnography could be used to determine the function of precontact stone and bone tools.

The naturalists of the Maritimes in the mid-nineteenth century were quite aware of current developments in archaeology. Although the Three Age System was not fully applicable to this region, the "Stone Age" designation was in use by the 1870s (Gilpin 1874) and widely used thereafter (e.g., Bailey 1887; Matthew 1884; Patterson 1890; Piers 1895). Wilson's term "prehistoric" was also being used by the 1870s to refer to precontact Indigenous history (Dawson 1878, 41; Patterson 1877, 24). Even before Morlot's (1861, 1863) reports on Danish shell midden studies, Daniel Wilson, now immigrated to Canada, had published instructions on the careful excavation, recording, and transport of human remains and associated artifacts in the widely circulated periodical *The Canadian Journal* (1855, 346–47). He travelled throughout North America and published several archaeological papers, much of which was included in his major work *Prehistoric Man* (Wilson 1862; see Kehoe 2002).

Towards the end of the nineteenth century, a general dissatisfaction with the effects of the Industrial Revolution led British archaeologists to question the value of technological progress. Further, as nationalism was growing throughout Europe, people became interested in tracing their ancestry into the distant past. Gradually, historical sequence began to replace technological progress as the most important characteristic of cultural change (Trigger 1989, 145). Seriation, based on changing trends in artifact design and decoration, was developed as a technique for identifying cultural change over time (Petrie 1899). Grahame Clark (1954) developed an ecological approach to the study of how archaeological cultures adapted to their environments. Archaeologists like Gordon Childe (1925) began talking about archaeological cultures and their movements over the European landscape. American archaeologists also began to identify archaeological cultures and culture areas (Holmes 1914). Initially, they assumed that there had been little cultural change over time; therefore, surviving cultures could be used to interpret precontact sites using a direct historical approach (Deal 2017; Lyman and O'Brien 2001). Gradually, culture-historical sequences were developed for the different culture areas based on stratigraphic excavation and seriation, beginning with the American Southwest (Kidder 1924).

Post-World War II America saw a renewed interest in evolutionary theory and an increase in multidisciplinary research. The radiocarbon dating technique, developed by chemist Willard Libby (1952), allowed the refinement of culture historical sequences to include pre-ceramic cultures. Technological progress again was associated with cultural development over time (e.g., White 1949). Julian Steward (1955) stressed the importance of ecological adaptation to cultural change. Cultural materialists like Marvin Harris (1968, 1979) claimed that environmental, technological, and economic factors were the major determinants of human behaviour. Artifacts were perceived as the material manifestation of human behaviour. Archaeologists also became more interested in delineating theory and method in their discipline. Willey and Phillips (1958) outlined a culture-historical model for explanation in archaeology that progressed from observation (fieldwork) to description (culture historical integration) to explanation (processual integration). They also clarified the interrelationships of certain significant archaeological concepts, namely, component, phase, horizon, and tradition (see below).

The professionals working in the Maritimes were influenced by the culture-historical approach. By the early twentieth century, they understood that the Maritimes were part of a larger Northeast culture area. Attempts were made to identify specific precontact cultures, such as Moorehead's "Red Paint People," and their geographical distribution within the region (Sanger 1979a).

Gradually, a general historical framework was established for the Northeast that identified the earliest cultural manifestation as Palaeo (or "Palaeoindian"), followed by a few interrelated Archaic cultures and a succession of Woodland cultures (e.g., Byers et al. 1943). The use of radiocarbon dates allowed these archaeological cultures to be placed into distinct temporal periods: Palaeo (c. 11,000–8,000 ^{14}C yrs BP), Archaic (c. 8,000–3,000 ^{14}C yrs BP), and Woodland (c. 3,000–1,500 ^{14}C yrs BP) (see Vignette 5). Today, we also recognize a Contact (or sometimes Protohistoric) period, to identify the time between first European contact and first permanent settlement (c. AD 1500–1600) (Gullason et al. 2008). Researchers in the Maritimes have attempted to integrate the local sequences into the better-known sequences of New England and Ontario, with varying success (e.g., Byers 1959; Wintemberg 1942, 1943).

The 1960s saw a greater divergence of archaeological theory and method in Great Britain and the United States. In the US, Lewis Binford (1962) spearheaded a movement (the "New Archaeology") to make archaeology more scientific, with greater emphasis on quantification of archaeological data, more general explanations of archaeological phenomena, and more borrowing from other disciplines. Archaeologists became concerned with how sites were formed and the differential preservation of archaeological materials (Schiffer 1987). This movement developed into the modern processual archaeology. While British archaeologists were not immune to the lure of the New Archaeology (e.g., Clarke 1968), it was influenced more by a need for broader social theory in archaeology. Processualists often referred to the archaeological record as "transformed" material culture, while post-processualists conceived it as a "text" to be read by archaeologists (Patrick 1985). Today, most North American archaeologists can be linked to some form of processualism, although various alternative post-processual approaches have become popular. Critical or revisionist approaches, such as gender studies and Indigenous archaeology, have made archaeologists more aware of alternative interpretations of the past. Even older approaches, such as cultural ecology (Steward 1955), have been updated to be more compatible with social theory (Johnson and Hunn 2010).

The professional archaeologists working in the Maritimes after 1960 were still struggling with the development of a regional culture-historical sequence. Dating of the initial Palaeo occupation was established from the excavations at Debert (Stuckenrath 1966). The Late Archaic period was coming into focus (Sanger 1973a; Tuck 1975, 1978a, 1978b). But the Late Palaeo and Early Archaic periods were referred to as the "Great Hiatus" (Tuck 1984, 14–17). Archaeologists are beginning to understand these periods (MacCarthy 2003; Murphy 1998; Suttie 2007; Sanger and Renouf 2008). Much more information has been accumulated concerning the Woodland period and a detailed seriation of ceramics has been devised by James Petersen and David Sanger (1991). Culture change still is discussed largely in terms of independent (*in situ*) development, diffusion, population pressures, or migration. Archaeologists have become more concerned with site formation, both at the site and at regional levels. Coastal erosion continues to be a pressing issue for this region (Betts and Hrynick 2021, 12; Davis 1980, 1983; Simonson 1978), so that there is an emphasis on the testing and excavation of coastal sites in danger of erosion. The collection of plant and animal remains did not become routine practice until the 1980s (with some exceptions: Deal 2008a; Murphy and Black 1996).

The basic and integrative archaeological units presented by Willey and Phillips (1958, 40–43) have been added to the regional terminology. A short-lived local or regional manifestation of an archaeological culture is called a "phase." Researchers divide their sites into distinct components representing archaeological phases (or culturally homogeneous stratigraphic units), so that sites are often referred to as single-component or multi-component. Many sites in the Maritimes have Early, Middle, and Late Woodland components, as well as a historic component. Classes of artifacts, or groups of related materials, recovered from a site (or feature) are often referred to as "assemblages" (e.g., a ceramic assemblage, or a burial assemblage). The basic units of component and phase are integrated within the regional sequence through the notions of horizon and tradition. A "horizon" refers to the spatial continuity of an archaeological culture. An early Palaeo Clovis horizon is believed to stretch across North America, with many local variants. A "tradition" is a temporal continuity of a technology or social form, such as a specific style of stone tool or a distinctive form of burial (e.g., the Moorehead Burial Tradition). Another term used occasionally is "complex," which Fladmark (1978, 150) defines as a "consistently recurring assemblage of artifacts or traits which may be indicative of a specific set of activities, or a common cultural tradition," such as fish weir complex (Petersen et al. 1994) or site complex (Woolsey 2018).

Archaeologists use several different techniques to place sites and artifacts within a regional timeline. The stratigraphy, or depositional layers, within a site is not always easy to read. Sometimes, at multi-component sites, distinct cultural layers overlap in some areas and not in others. Multi-component post-Archaic sites are often very shallow in this region, with two or more components occurring in a deposit 10–15 cm deep. In areas with such slow accumulation of sediments, each cultural group using the site is likely to disturb earlier deposits in heavy-use areas. Even short-term, post-abandonment disturbances, such as plowing, can create havoc with the stratigraphy of such shallow archaeological sites. By contrast, sites along some major river systems are deeply stratified due to periodic flooding (Allen 2005; Deal et al. 2022; Petersen 1991; Petersen and Putnam 1992).

Vignette 5: Building a Timeline for the Maritimes

Today, most sites, features, and artifacts are dated through association with wood charcoal or other organic materials such as shell that can be dated using the radiocarbon dating method. This is an absolute dating method that is based on the radioactive decay of Carbon-14 (^{14}C). Libby's technique relied on the assumption that the ratio of radioactive Carbon-14 and normal Carbon-12 remained constant over time. Dendrochronological (tree-ring) studies proved that there have been variations in the atmospheric concentration of Carbon-14 over time. Today, radiocarbon dating laboratories provide both uncorrected and corrected (or calibrated) dates. Most older publications report the uncorrected dates, and that practice is also used in this volume. A more recent method of radiocarbon dating, known as the accelerator mass spectrometric (AMS) technique, can be used to determine dates on very small samples. Most of the reported radiocarbon dates for the Maritimes are included in the Canadian

Archaeological Radiocarbon Database (CARD) maintained by the Canadian Museum of History (CMH) and the Laboratory of Archaeology (LOA) at the University of British Columbia. MacInnes (2021) recently used this database in a promising new "dates as data" approach to explore the precontact population dynamics of the Maritime Peninsula, which indicated a boom-and-bust dynamic that appears to correspond to the major technological periods.

The seriation of precontact ceramic styles has provided the framework against which archaeologists in northeastern North America can interpret local and regional culture histories for the Woodland period (Petersen 1985, 6–8; Ritchie 1985). In 1991, an elaborate ceramic chronology was proposed for Maine and the Maritimes by James Petersen and David Sanger (1991) based on comparisons of ceramic stylistic, morphological, and physical attributes with associated radiocarbon dates from dozens of Woodland sites. The model distinguishes between direct and general associations between Carbon-14-dated samples and ceramics. Direct associations indicate a clear connection between the Carbon-14 date and ceramic vessel(s), such as recovery from the same feature or physical contact between the dated charred organic sample and the ceramic sherd. All other associations are less reliable and are given a general ascription. This chronology replaced a long-standing tripartite system with a seven-part chronology that was designated Ceramic Periods One through Seven (see Table 2). Adrian Burke (2022) has developed a promising model for changes in Woodland projectile point styles in the region to correspond to the Peterson and Sanger model (see Chapter 6).

Table 2. Petersen and Sanger (1991) Ceramic Period Subdivisions and Temporal Equivalents.

Ceramic Period Subdivisions	Temporal Equivalents
Ceramic Period 1 (Early Woodland)	ca. 3050–2150 ^{14}C yrs BP
Ceramic Period 2 (early Middle Woodland)	ca. 2150–1650 ^{14}C yrs BP
Ceramic Period 3 (middle Middle Woodland)	ca. 1650–1350 ^{14}C yrs BP
Ceramic Period 4 (late Middle Woodland)	ca. 1350–950 ^{14}C yrs BP
Ceramic Period 5 (early Late Woodland)	ca. 950–650 ^{14}C yrs BP
Ceramic Period 6 (late Late Woodland)	ca. 650–400 ^{14}C yrs BP
Ceramic Period 7 (Contact)	ca. 400–200 ^{14}C yrs BP

Helen Kristmanson (1992) proposed a refinement of the Petersen and Sanger model for southwestern Nova Scotia, based on 20 radiocarbon and two thermoluminescence (TL) dates from five sites. Kristmanson's study concluded that their Ceramic period divisions are widely applicable, yet there is considerable variation in the date ranges for each period in different portions of the Maritime Peninsula. This finding is supported by Bourgeois's (1999) research along the Saint John River in central New Brunswick. Further, based on her work at Gaspereau Lake, Woolsey (2020) recommends five new subperiods between 1,650 and 950 ^{14}C yrs BP.

In 1993, the thermoluminescence (TL) dating technique was used for dating ceramics at the St. Croix site, Nova Scotia. These samples were processed at the Luminescence Laboratory at the Department of Earth Sciences, Dalhousie University, by Dorothy Godfrey-Smith. The TL dating technique is preferred over radiocarbon dating since it provides a date for the ceramic sherd itself rather than from associated charcoal. However, field collection procedures are more rigorous for TL analysis and there are more opportunities for both natural and cultural contamination. An earlier attempt to apply TL analysis to four specimens from the Brown site (BeCs-3) was abandoned due to contamination problems (Sheldon 1988, 40). Basically, TL dating works on the principle that small amounts of energy accumulate in the minerals in the clay matrix of a ceramic vessel (as trapped electrons). When a ceramic piece is fired, some of the accumulated energy is released as light and energy begins to build up again in the vessel. After excavation, a ceramic sherd can be reheated to release the energy accumulated since its original firing. The light from the reheating, known as the thermoluminescent signal, can be used to calculate the time elapsed since the vessel was last heated. The six TL dates determined for St. Croix ceramics do not completely agree with the Petersen and Sanger chronology and therefore support Kristmanson's conclusion that some local and intraregional variation exists in the ceramic chronology (Godfrey-Smith et al. 1997).

Indigenous Forms of History

Unlike the linear structure of history followed by Western society, Indigenous history is embodied in oral traditions and art. There are two kinds of stories: historical anecdotes and traditional, both of which are expressed in the form of symbolic narratives (*sensu* Sable and Francis 2012, 54–57; Smith and Walker 1997, 365). Wabanaki stories undoubtedly have their roots in precontact oral traditions, yet many elements of Western storytelling traditions have been incorporated over the last 500 years as storytellers would interweave different tales into story cycles as the situation dictated. These stories are an essential way of passing on important information from generation to generation, and they link Indigenous peoples to the landscape. Nash (1997, 67; also Burke 2003) posits that a cognitive archaeology approach may "reconstruct something of what people perceived of various ancient landscapes through myth and the contemporary vernacular arts." Wabanaki storytelling may also be an undervalued mechanism for investigating climate change, in that it charts cultural connections to disappearing resources (Daigle et al. 2019, 782; Brooks and Brooks 2010).

Stories are crucially important for revealing the interconnections of the spiritual and material worlds (Dickason 1998, 23). The traditional Indigenous world is brimming with animating spirits believed to reside in animals, plants, inorganic objects, and geographic formations. For the Wabanaki, the key to the relationship between human and other-than-human beings is respect (Robinson 2014, 673). Animals are "persons," in that they share a common essence with humans (Hornborg 2008, 22). Animals, including the extinct giant beaver (Beck 1972), play important roles in many stories, in which they interact with humans or transform into humans, or humans transform into animals. Many of these stories serve as lessons in moral behaviour relating to the respectful treatment of animals. One manifestation of this respect that is important to archaeology is the spiritual connotation in the treatment of animal bones (Wallis and Wallis 1955, 107ff.). For example, the bones of moose should never be burned or given to dogs but should either be used to make something or be buried (Robinson 2014, 675). According to LeClercq (1910, 226), the Mi'kmaq:

> never burned, further, the bones of the fawn of the moose, nor the carcass of martens; and they also take much precaution against giving the same to the dogs; for they would not be able any longer to capture any of these animals in hunting if the spirits of the martens and of the fawns of the moose were to inform their own kind of the bad treatment they had received.

In relation to their hunting dogs, Denys (1908, 430) reports that "as to the bones, they are not given any, for fear of damaging their teeth, not even those of the Beaver." As with the moose and marten, he goes on to say that if the dogs could eat beaver bones, the beaver would no longer give themselves as food. Such taboos have direct implications for the interpretation of archaeological faunal assemblages found in domestic contexts.

Many of the traditional Wabanaki stories feature a culture hero (*kinap*) called Kluskap ("Gluskabe," or "Glooscap"), who had supernatural powers and was generally noble-minded and generous to humans. Kluskap was the great teacher of the Indigenous peoples (Nicolar 1893, 5), who taught them the use of fire and tobacco, and the making of pottery, fishing nets, and birchbark canoes, as well as the difference between good and evil and the spiritual power in all things. Silas Rand (1894, xliv) gives the following summary of Kluscap's situation:

> Glooscap was unmarried. A venerable old lady whom he called grandmother kept house for him, and a little fellow named Abistănāooch' (Marten) was his servant. He could do anything and everything. The moose and the caribou came around his dwelling as tame as cattle; and the other beasts were equally obsequious. The elements were entirely under his control. He could bring on an intensity of cold when he chose, which would

extinguish all the fires of his enemies, and lay them stiffened corpses on the ground.

Gerald Gloade (2008), program development officer, Confederacy of Mainland Mi'kmaq, studied the stories collected by Silas T. Rand from Mi'kmaw storytellers in Nova Scotia to identify all the locations mentioned and link them to material culture collected at these places. His final map included more than 50 places from across Nova Scotia. Many of the stories are tied to local natural history, including the tidal expansion of the Minas Basin, climatic change, the formation of certain geological features (e.g., Kluscap's grandmother's pot on Partridge Island), and the former presence of giant beavers in Nova Scotia (also see Sable and Francis 2012; Newsom 2017, 95–96, 120). Certain places are closely tied to the great horned serpent (Jipijka'm) and its link to geological events (Gloade 2008, 246). The stories of Kluscap's battle with a wizard in the form of a giant beaver ranges from Cape Breton to the Minas Basin area, to Kluscap's camp at Blomidon and his grandmother's campsite on Partridge Island (and in another version to Brier Island, Digby Neck).

The Kluskap stories often have interesting implications for archaeology. For example, the Mi'kmaw story "A Wizard Carries Off Glooscap's Housekeeper" includes the following episode:

> His next halt was on the north side of the bay, at Spenser's Island. There Glooscap engaged in a hunting expedition on a somewhat large scale. A large drove of animals was surrounded and driven down to the shore, slaughtered, and their flesh sliced up and dried. All the bones were afterwards chopped up fine, placed in a large stone kettle, and boiled so as to extract the marrow, which was carefully stored away for future use. Having finished the boiling process, and having no further use for the kettle, he turned it bottom upwards and left it there, where it remains in the form of a small round island, called still by the Indians

[Mi'kmaq] after its ancient name, *Ooteomtil* (his kettle; that is, Glooscap's kettle). (Related by Mi'kmaw storyteller Thomas Boonis, of Cumberland, June 10, 1870; cf. Rand 1894, 291-92)

The practice of extracting bone grease and marrow from the bones of deer, moose, or caribou (i.e., cervids) is often present at archaeological sites in the form of bone fragments discarded at campsites (e.g., Betts et al. 2017, 31; Morin 2020). These are sometimes found in association with broken pottery vessels, which may have been used for boiling the bones. The stone kettle in the story may have originally been an earthenware cooking pot or birchbark vessel (Taché et al. 2008, 69). These were replaced by copper kettles during the Contact period, and in the stories told by the storytellers of Rand's time.

Bonnie Newsom (2017, 91) recounts a Panawahpskewi (Penobscot) story called the "Ghost Hunter," in which a woman is watched over through the winter by her husband's ghost. This one short story incorporates several useful elements that complement archaeological settlement studies on the Penobscot River, such as the notion of "interior" places that are accessible by canoe that can be reached by travelling "upstream" for three days from the woman's parent's home prior to winter (Newsom 2017, 90-91). The story contains elements of "agency, choice, and unpredictability in the human experience" and embedded notions of "seasonal movement, activity areas, mode of transportation, and social organization" (Newsom 2017, 91). All of these concepts are relatable to archaeological interpretations of precontact lifeways.

The stories are filled with instances of landscape transformation, like the story of Kluskap's kettle. Humans and other-than-humans can be transformed into islands, trees, and rock formations. Sable and Francis (2012, 74) note that beavers are often used in the stories to talk about changes in the landscape and waterways (e.g., the story in Chapter 4 of the formation of the Minas Basin). They also describe several "Grandfather" and "Grandmother" rocks from Nova Scotia and New Brunswick, which act as guideposts on the landscape (Sable and Francis 2012, 43-46). These formations have their own spiritual essence, and it is customary to leave an offering when you pass. Allen and others (2004, 9; Sable and Francis 2012, 75–76) recorded a story relating to the rocks known as the "flowerpots" in the Rocks Provincial Park, New Brunswick. According to Mi'kmaw Elder Michael Francis of Big Cove First Nation, for hundreds of years before the arrival of the Europeans, powerful beings (*Kinaps*) prepared great feasts at large annual gatherings of people at this location. When European missionaries came, they convinced the people that their enemies might see the carved sign poles used to guide people to the location. Once the sign poles came down, the large cooking pots turned to rock and became the flowerpots. It is significant that when large cooking pots are found in archaeological contexts, they are often interpreted as feasting vessels. Caves can also be sacred places associated with traditional stories, where people go to fast or hold ceremonies (Sable and Francis 2014, 47–49).

One enduring aspect of traditional Indigenous culture is that place names have survived European contact and settlement. There is a long tradition of research into the place names of the Indigenous peoples of the Maritime Peninsula (e.g., Anderson 1919; Ganong 1964; Sanger et al. 2006). Early European maps of the region incorporate both Indigenous and European place names, going back to the early sixteenth century (Ganong 1964, 75–81). Keith Basso's influential 1996 publication on Western Apache place names emphasized that place names structure geography and at the same time preserve cultural information. Implicit in many Indigenous systems is the notion that meaning is not inherent in landscape but is provided by people — places are a result of the relationships that people cultivate and maintain in the landscape (Creese 2018). For people living by hunting and gathering, like the precontact and early historic peoples of the Maritimes, it was important to name landmarks on travel routes. Place names can be highly descriptive of the local landscape, as seen from certain vantage points, and as mnemonic devices they allow later generations to recreate the same view and be spiritually connected to their ancestors. Some place names can represent economic activities or real events that took place at a location (e.g., hunting and fishing locations or eel weirs) and thus are directly relatable to archaeological research. Others may relate to traditional events, such as those tied to the story of "Kluscap and the Giant Beaver," and at the same time serve as maps for navigating a wide landscape (Sable 2011; Sable and Francis 2012, 50–53, 65–68). In these and other ways, place names are important elements of oral tradition and important links to Indigenous ideology.

According to Dickason (1998, 23), art was a form of "control-power" that was "aimed at communication with and evoking the co-operation of plant and animal spirits." Shamans used performance (e.g., costume, masks, and instruments) and art when seeking help from the spirits to control weather, interpret dreams, cure the sick, or aid in the hunt (Erickson 1978b, 6–7). Shamans are well documented by the seventeenth-century chroniclers (Lescarbot 1928, 104–05; Biard 1959, 77, 119, 121; LeClercq 1910, 216–23, 229; Denys 1908, 417; Maillard 1758, 37–39). They also are featured in many of the more traditional stories (Smith and Walker 1997). Ray (1977, 6–7) illustrates a birchbark box lid dating to at least the early nineteenth century, which depicts a Peskotomuhkati shaman dancing in a special gown and playing an old-style birchbark rattle. Ray suggests that the shaman is chanting an invocation to communicate with the spirit world. Dance is also closely tied to song (chants), music, and dreams. According to Sable and Francis (2012, 78) these art media encode information about the environment, including the stars, seasons, directions, the nature of reptiles and birds, and especially regarding the safe collection of medicinal plants.

Visual arts also were produced to please the spirits and often represented personal totems. Early Europeans reported images on wigwams, a moose painted on the sail of a shallop, and body tattoos of snakes, crosses, and sun images. For example, LeClercq (1910, 217–20) identifies the image of a shaman's animal helper that adorned the outer cover of his medicine bag. Some objects, like those made from shiny metals, crystals, and shell, were imbued with spiritual significance. Such objects frequently are found in archaeological contexts (e.g., Leonard 1996, 48–49). When Kluscap dresses his aged companion with gemstones from Blomidon, she at once

3: THE WHY AND HOW QUESTIONS

becomes young and beautiful (Rand 1894, 291). This area is still important to modern gem hunters, and places like Amethyst Cove (BhD3:03) once had a precontact campsite, which was destroyed by coastal erosion.

The Wabanaki were proficient mapmakers. In 1602, the ship of explorer Bartholomew Gosnold encountered a Mi'kmaw trading shallop with a crew of eight men off the coast of southern Maine. The Mi'kmaw "captain" drew Gosnold an accurate map of the nearby coast using a piece of chalk (Kupperman 2000, 5–6; Lewis 2008, 68). On November 9, 1761, Aikon Aushabuc, a Mi'kmaw chief, made a gestural map using the thumb and forefinger of his left hand to explain the current geopolitical situation to a captive Englishman named Gamaliel Smethurst (Lewis 2008, 68–69). A kind of expedient map on birchbark, called *wikhikon*, was used as a form of communication. Mallery (1894, 330–49; also Speck 1940, 80–81; Prins 1994, 112–14) illustrates a number of these maps from throughout the Wabanaki region, dating to the early nineteenth century, which he categorized as notices of departure, direction, or condition. Some of the maps relayed considerable geographic information and details on hunting activities. Mallery also illustrates an earlier *wikhikon* of direction made by Mi'kmaw scouts in the early seventeenth century, to warn the rest of their party that enemy warriors had been observed in canoes on the lake going toward the outlet of the lake and probably down the river (Mallery 1894, 341; Figure 18).

Figure 18: Mi'kmaw *wikhikon*: notice of direction map, warning of a Peskotomuhkatiyik war party. Note the 10 dots representing individual warriors, the canoe and porpoise symbol for the Peskotomuhkati, and the direction arrow (Mallery 1894, 341, Figure 2.1).

Settlement and Subsistence

The late precontact inhabitants of the Maritimes were foraging peoples (or hunter-gatherers). They left no evidence of a developed time-reckoning (or calendric) system, like the Classic Maya of Mesoamerica, but would still have had a perception of time based on time indication, in which seasonal and biological cycles were followed (Lucas 2005, 68). Seasonal changes in weather and the availability of desired plants and animals would have influenced settlement stability. Furthermore, the periodic movements of people across the landscape (or forager mobility) are influenced by several factors, including the nature of resources, level of food storage, trade, territoriality, social and gender inequalities, work patterns, and demography (Kelley 1992, 43–44).

Information on land and resource use forms the basis for our understanding of the ecological context of precontact societies and their related mobility strategies. Land-use patterns can be equated with archaeological settlement distribution and seasonality, while resource use relates to the natural resources that formed the basis of precontact technologies and subsistence practices (Deal 2002). Following Lewis Binford (1980), we can also make a distinction between residential mobility and logistical mobility. The former relates to the movement of all members of a campsite or village from one location to another, while the latter involves the movement of small groups or individuals to and from residential sites (Kelley 1983, 278). In logistical terms, mobility can involve short trips for general foraging, specific tasks, or resource monitoring. For example, Scots Bay, on the Bay of Fundy, is believed to be a marginal area for habitation but where small groups visited in the summer and early fall months to quarry stone for tool production and trade.

When Ganong (1899) compiled the first comprehensive list of possible precontact sites in New Brunswick, he had to rely primarily on the early historic literature, modern Indigenous informants, and place-name nomenclature. In fact, he was able to consult only four archaeological sources (i.e., Bailey 1887; Baird 1882; Goodwin 1892; Matthew 1884). Since that time hundreds of precontact sites have been identified and many have been excavated. Ganong's study, which locates sites and resources within seven Indigenous districts, essentially is a model of precontact settlement and subsistence. Like other such models of the nineteenth century, it followed a direct historical approach (Davis 1998; Deal 2017). Indigenous settlement and subsistence patterns reported by early explorers and settlers were merely projected back into the precontact period.

Ganong (1904) also recognized that resource availability and diversity were closely integrated with Indigenous settlement location and size. He recognized that sites were located along navigable waterways, such as main branches of large rivers and at the mouths of these rivers at the coast (also see Lewis and Sable 2014). Travel was by canoe and the main river and lake systems were connected by short portages (Ganong 1901, 1913a, 1913b, 1914). Ganong (1899, 1904) suggested that precontact peoples established habitation and campsites according to the most important resources along these waterways, then looked for certain requisite conditions for habitation. These criteria included a well-drained and dry site location, with an adequate canoe landing area, preferably in an exposed location for viewing approaching parties and to allow a breeze to remove insects (Ganong 1904, 24–26). Also important were access to fresh spring water for drinking, firewood, and a grove of white birch for construction purposes. Ganong's (1904, 23–24) principal resources were listed as "environmental factors affecting settlement." His general categories are relevant today, although faunal resources are given priority over floral and other natural resources.

The first comprehensive settlement and subsistence model of the modern era was developed by Bernard Hoffman (1955). His model relied on ethnohistoric sources yet was sensitive to the changes to Indigenous culture that resulted from European contact (Figure 19). Hoffman presented a simple cyclical model of the late precontact period, which featured summer coastal habitation and a winter inland hunting season. This information was presented on a circular chart, which included seasonally available fauna, the size of social groupings, and area of resource exploitation. It was originally presented as a model for the Mi'kmaw area, but a basic cyclical model was generally accepted for the entire region.

As archaeological data began to accumulate, Hoffman's model was called into question. David Sanger (1971a) was the first to point out that the model was inconsistent with archaeological information from northern Maine. Faunal evidence from Maine shell midden sites suggested a winter coastal occupation for the late precontact period. Subsequent fieldwork in Passamaquoddy Bay indicated a similar pattern for southwestern New Brunswick (Sanger 1982, 1987; Stewart 1989). Sanger (1987) comments

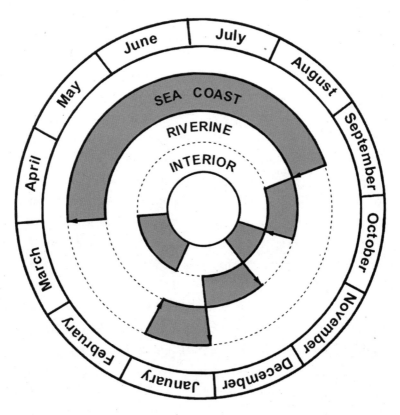

Figure 19: Hoffman's seasonal round subsistence model for the Mi'kmaq (adapted from Hoffman 1955, 152).

that this apparent reversal in settlement use was a result of the intensification of the fur trade during the late sixteenth century, in which Indigenous peoples hunted fur-bearers in the winter and moved to the coast in the summer to trade with visiting Europeans. Subsequently, various other models have been developed to account for late precontact land and resource use within the region (e.g., Black 1992; Burke 2000; Burley 1983; Davis 1986; Nash and Miller 1987; Nash et al. 1991; Sanger 1987; Snow 1980). For the most part, these models were devised to make sense of settlement and subsistence data for relatively small study areas. Important elements of the models are characteristics of the local landscape, site size and distribution, and the faunal record. Most of the models were developed before there was any substantial archaeobotanical record, and lithics generally were ignored (Deal 2002).

Many typologies have been developed for classifying archaeological sites. For example, K.C. Chang (1972, 18) classified sites according to characteristics of site permanency. He identified seven basic settlement types based on season of site use (seasonality), and/or length of occupation, and the number of cultural components (or depositional units) represented. The least permanent type is the single event, which he equates with an overnight camp. The people leaving this type of site had little time to alter the landscape, develop facilities, and create disposal areas. The next level of permanency is the seasonal site, which represents a single season of occupation. These are specialized activity camps/structures, such as resource extraction camps (e.g., hunting, fishing, and mining). These sites may have specialized facilities and cached implements. It is unlikely that such sites would have much material culture of high social or economic value, since it is likely that all useful materials would be removed upon abandonment (Deal 2008).

Chang's third settlement type represents sites like the previous one, but these were used seasonally for several years, which would allow for more extensive development of structures and facilities. Because the site would be occupied and abandoned each year, it would have many similarities to a permanent occupation, except for the seasonal nature of the toolkit and facilities. There might be some caching of site-specific tools. Settlement type four is the many-season site, visited each year for many years (and presumably for at least one generation). Such sites are more likely to have semi-permanent structures devoted to spiritual practices, as well as local cemeteries. At settlements with cemeteries, there is always a steady flow of domestic items, heirlooms, and/or spiritual artifacts from the site to burial assemblages. The last three settlement types are full-season occupations. Type five is a one-year occupation. A full range of annual activities would be expected, but like the single seasonal site, there would be a low level of development of facilities, and activity and disposal areas. Settlement type six represents the continuous occupation of a site for several years before abandonment. This would be like type seven, the permanent settlement, except that the latter would be more deeply stratified. Precontact settlements in the Maritimes would correspond to the first four of Chang's types, yet no structures related to spiritual activities have been discovered, except possible sweat lodge features during the late Woodland Period (Hrynick and Betts 2014, 2017, 7–10; Nash and Stewart 1990, 69; see Chapter 6). A few sites have associated burials, but cemeteries usually are separated from settlements.

Economic Analysis

Gary Crawford and David Smith (2003) use the term "Northeastern Coastal Pattern" to describe the economy of precontact peoples of the Maritime Peninsula, which was mainly hunting and gathering, with some groups to the south doing limited gardening by Late Woodland times. We know this because a major development of the modern professional era in the far Northeast has been the systematic recovery and analysis of precontact plant (floral) and animal (faunal) remains. These studies have given us a glimpse at the diet of precontact peoples in the region, as well as the use of plants for medicines and the use of plants and animals in tool manufacture and construction activities. Furthermore, species ubiquity (presence or absence) relates to the seasonality of site use and the site environment at the time of occupation. Unfortunately, the acidic soils of the region are not kind to bone and plant remains. The best source of specimens is coastal shell midden deposits where the lime from deteriorating shell counteracts the natural acidity of the soils (e.g., Betts et al. 2017; Black 1993, 2017; Murphy and Black 1996), or from charred plant and animal remains recovered from hearth features. Specimens from interior (non-shell midden) sites are relatively rare (e.g., Deal 1986).

Although the archaeological evidence is far from complete, it is obvious that precontact populations of the Maritime Peninsula used a broad and diverse range of natural resources. Faunal (animal) remains recovered from archaeological sites represent a wide range of the available modern species, as well as extinct species such as sea mink (*Neovison macrodon*) and great auk (*Pinguinus impennis*). Fur-bearing mammals were widely distributed throughout the region. Riverine fish species, and especially the anadromous Atlantic salmon (*Salmo salar*) and catadromous American eel (*Anguilla rostrata*), were particularly valuable resources. Shellfish were important in certain areas, especially during the late precontact period. Archaeological evidence of plant use is beginning to accumulate, but at a slow pace due to considerable preservation problems (Deal 2008a). The present archaeological evidence is obviously only a small fraction of the species collected in precontact times. Nutshells and seeds from various wild fruits are represented in charred form, but the green parts of plants and flowers used for herbal medicines, food, and beverages do not survive in the acidic soils. Wood, bark, and plant fibres only survive under exceptional preservation conditions. In this case, detailed studies of traditional knowledge are particularly valuable to archaeological interpretations.

An interest in animal bones and shell, known today as zooarchaeology, has its beginnings in the late nineteenth century (Murphy and Black 1996). Several naturalists of the period made identifications of vertebrate and invertebrate species and even looked at cut marks on bone. George

Matthew (1884, 23) was the first researcher to send faunal material outside of the region for expert advice (i.e., to Daniel Wilson in Toronto and to J.W. Dawson in Montreal). After this promising beginning there was a hiatus until the publication of the Smith and Wintemberg (1929) volume on shell midden excavations at Mahone Bay and Merigomish Harbour in Nova Scotia. Both authors gave careful treatment to the faunal remains and tools made from bone and teeth. John Erskine carried on the shell midden studies in Nova Scotia during the 1950s and 1960s (Erskine 1960). He was aware of the importance of the faunal materials collected, but initially had difficulty finding experts to help him with species identifications. Eventually, he received assistance from Evan Hazard (University of Michigan) with the mammal bones, while Pierce Brodkorb and Lowell Bernstein (University of Florida) identified the bird species represented; A.H. Leim (St. Andrews Biological Station) made initial identifications of shellfish specimens, and J.C. Medcof (Department of Fisheries) helped him with the fish specimens (Erskine 1998, 90–92). With the modern professional era, after 1960, faunal analysis became a routine part of most archaeological excavations. Several studies have focused on site seasonality and paleodiet (e.g., Black 1992; Rojo 1987; Stewart 1989).

Botanist R.P. Gorham was the first researcher to recognize the significance of archaeological plant remains in the region. In a now classic paper, Gorham (1943) reports charred plum pits (*Prunus nigra*), recovered by avocational archaeologist Frederick Clarke, in "ash pits" (hearths) at the late precontact Meductic site. The common occurrence of plum trees at Indigenous sites and the recovery of charred specimens at Meductic led Gorham to propose that the precontact Indigenous peoples of New Brunswick were intentionally planting this species around their campsites. In other words, they were practising a form of arboriculture. Gorham (1928) was also responsible for salvaging two sections of matting from a Contact period copper kettle burial discovered at Red Bank, on the Miramichi River, in 1927. These were later studied by Wendell S. Hadlock and botanist W.E. Steckbeck of the University of Pennsylvania (Hadlock 1947). J.R.

Harper (1956, 40–51) also recovered a fibre-woven specimen from a Contact period burial at Portland Point. He compared this fibre-woven artifact with those recovered at Red Bank and with others from the Contact period Hopps burial site (BkCp-1), Pictou, Nova Scotia (Harper 1957). During the 1970s, textiles were recovered from an Early Woodland burial mound at Red Bank, New Brunswick (Turnbull 1976). The Hopps materials were re-studied (Whitehead 1987) and another Contact period specimen was identified from a burial at Northport, Nova Scotia (Whitehead 1993, 43). Gordon (1995, 1997) studied the construction techniques of the Hopps site textiles. Most of the archaeological specimens were twined with rush (*Scirpus* sp.), reed (*Juncus* sp.), or basswood fibre (*Titia americana*) and represent bags and baskets for carrying food (e.g., eggs or fish) or possibly clothing (Gordon 1997, 97).

During the 1980s, Hal Hinds, a botanist from the University of New Brunswick, identified charred seeds recovered from the Fulton Island (BlDn-12), Diggity (BfDa-01), and Mud Lake Stream (BkDw-05) sites in western New Brunswick (Deal et al. 1991, 175; Foulkes 1981). Hinds's work inspired the author and David Christianson (Nova Scotia Museum) to begin paleoethnobotanical research in Nova Scotia. With the help of the Curator of Botany at the Nova Scotia Museum, Alex Wilson, a comparative collection of modern seeds was put together from the museum's herbarium collection of dried plants. Speck and Dexter's (1951, 1952) reports on modern Mi'kmaw and Wolastoqwey plant use served as a guide for the selection of specimens for the reference collection. This collection was first used in 1985 for the identification of archaeobotanical materials from the Bliss Islands, Passamaquoddy Bay (Warman 1986), and the Melanson and Indian Gardens (BaDg-2) sites in Nova Scotia (Wells 1987; Deal 1990). During the 1990s, additional paleoethnobotanical laboratory work has been undertaken by archaeology students at Memorial University. Unpublished student reports concerning nine New Brunswick sites and six Nova Scotia sites were summarized by Lackowicz (1991). Additional macrobotanical remains have been identified at five sites on the Bliss Islands (Black

Figure 20: Clam Cove 2004, illustrating on-site hand screening of shell midden sediments (Roger Lewis and Sara Halwas). Photograph by Michael Deal.

1993, 52–55; Blair and Black 1991), the Skull Island burial, Shediac Bay (Leonard 1996), the Jemseg and Meadows sites on the Saint John River drainage (Monckton 2000), and in southwestern Nova Scotia (Deal and Halwas 2008; Deal et al. 2011; Halwas 2006; Figure 20).

Reflections on the Past

Archaeological theory and method in the Maritimes have followed similar trends in the United States and Europe since the time of the naturalists. Archaeology has evolved from a largely humanistic to a more scientific discipline, with the adoption of a wide array of scientific methods. Considerable effort has been put into improving our understanding of the historical timeline of archaeological cultures and technological change, along with associated environmental change. Techniques for finding, excavating, and mapping archaeological sites and regions, and identifying plant and animal remains, tool functions, and site seasonality have been steadily improving. The overall effect is the building of a more robust archaeological record.

As Dickason (1997, 23) points out, history to Indigenous peoples is about "defining perceptions of themselves." Oral narratives often concern events relating to transformations in Indigenous lifeways; such narratives do not adhere to a Western sense of linear time but are designed to teach important knowledge practices in terms and analogies relatable to the experiences of the modern audience. While relatively few historic events are recorded, important information on the Indigenous realities and codes of behaviour are transmitted, along with practical information on dealing with other-than-human beings, collecting medicinal plants, reading the landscape, and making maps.

4

PEOPLING A NEW LAND

THE EARLIEST HUMAN INHABITANTS of the Maritimes are known to the modern Mi'kmaq simply as the "Ancient People" (*Sa'qewe'k L'nuk*; Lewis 2006a), but in archaeological terminology they are often referred to as the Palaeo peoples (or "Palaeoindians"). The Palaeo period for the Northeast dates approximately from 12,000 to 8,000 ^{14}C yrs BP, and can be divided into Early, Middle, and Late subperiods based on the seriation of diagnostic stone projectile point styles (Newby et al. 2005, 148–50). Bradley (2001) further identifies several regional phases, at least four of which are relevant to the Maritimes (see below). The diagnostic artifact of the Palaeo material culture is the fluted projectile point, that is, a stone weapon tip with one or two long flakes removed from the base to facilitate hafting to a wooden spear with the aid of bone foreshafts. The ancient people had a variety of other tool forms made from stone, bone, and wood. While preservation conditions in the Northeast are not kind to organic artifacts, bone and ivory artifacts (even some on mammoth bone) have been found at Palaeo sites in western North America and Florida. Bradley (1995) reports that six basic forms have been identified, including double-bevelled bone tools, bone and ivory projectile points, a cylindrical ivory knapping billet/burnisher, a spear shaft straightener, an awl, and a bone bead. The double-bevelled bone tools, which are the most common form, have been variously interpreted as foreshafts for spears, sled runner segments, or

4: PEOPLING A NEW LAND

Figure 21: Palaeo period sites on a map by Dominic Lacroix representing the North Atlantic coast shorelines at 9,000 ^{14}C yrs BP. Dots represent Early and squares represent Late sites: 1. La Martre, 2. Cap du Renard, 3. Sainte-Anne-des-Monts, 4. Magdalen Islands sites, 5. Geganish (Ingonish Island), 6. Mitis, 7. Tracadie River, 8. Odaswanokh (Little Narrows), 9. Basin Head, 10. Rimouski, 11. Jones, 12. Savage Harbour, ▶

sections of ceremonial staffs (e.g., Bradley 1995; Dunbar and Webb 1996). The foreshaft interpretation is now well-entrenched in the literature (e.g., Wright 1995, 33, Figure 3).

Palaeo artifacts have been found throughout the Maritime Peninsula and the adjacent Magdalen Islands (Figure 21). However, only a handful of sites have been excavated, including the Debert and Belmont sites in Nova Scotia (Vignette 7; Davis 1991b, 2011; MacDonald 1968, 2011), the Jones site on Prince Edward Island (Keenlyside 1985a, 1985b; MacCarthy 2003), and the Vail, Michaud, and Varney Farm sites in Maine (Gramly 1982; Petersen et al. 2000; Spiess and Wilson 1987). In the Maritimes, Bonnischen and others (1991) reported only 16 sites and isolated surface finds for the entire period: four in New Brunswick, six in Nova Scotia, and six in Prince Edward Island. This sparsity has been filled out somewhat by more recent finds and studies of private collections. For example, Early Palaeo lithic assemblages recovered from Forest City, Maine (Hudgell et al. 2013) and Pennfield, Charlotte County, New Brunswick (Suttie et al. 2013) are helping to fill in the former geographical gap between the Vail and Debert sites. A reworked fluted point was surface-collected in 2012 from the Sable River estuary in southwestern Nova Scotia (Betts et al. 2018). Many more sites are known from Maine and New England, which give us a general model for interpreting the Palaeo materials from the Maritimes. In fact, Wright (1995, 29) uses the term "Debert/Vail complex" to refer to a shared cultural tradition centred in the Maritimes and northern New England during the Early Palaeo period.

◀ 13. Point Deroche, 14. New London Bay, 15. North Tryon, 16. Hogan-Mullin, 17. Cape Spear, 18. Amherst Shore, 19. Debert and Belmont sites, 20. New Horton Creek, 21. Medford, 22. Melanson area sites, 23. Windsor, 24. Kingsclear, 25. Gaspereau Lake sites, 26. Quaco Head, 27. Munsungun Lake, 28. Forest City and Pirate Cove, 29. Pennfield, 30. Pierce-Embree, 31. Blackman Stream, 32. Esker, 33. Vail, 34. Varney Farm, 35. Michaud, 36. Nicholas, 37. Hedden, 38. Bull Brook.

The Setting

Prior to the arrival of humans, northeastern North America was almost completely covered by ice. At the time of glacial maximum, ca. 18,000 ^{14}C yrs BP, the only unglaciated portions of the Maritime Peninsula were offshore islands and peninsulas that now are part of the broad Continental Shelf, including Georges Bank and Sable Island (Pielou 1991, 138–46; see

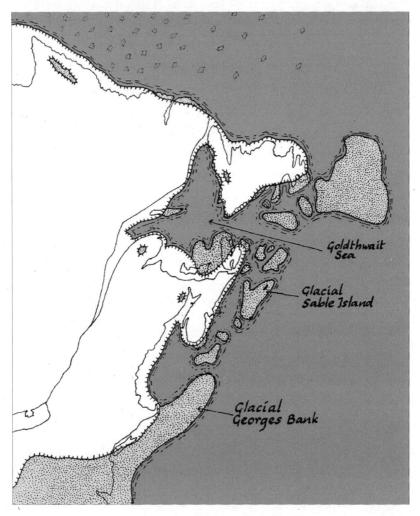

Figure 22: Glacial maximum on east coast ca. 18,000 ^{14}C yrs BP, indicating the Goldthwait Sea (adapted from Pielou 1991, Figure 6.4, 139).

Figure 22). The Cape Breton Highlands, the Magdalen Islands, and northeastern Prince Edward Island probably were part of a larger land mass that bordered the Goldthwait Sea — the ancestral Gulf of St. Lawrence. Such areas served as refugia for many hardy species of flora and fauna. For years, fishermen trawling the Georges Bank have pulled up specimens of ancient mammoth and mastodon teeth (Edwards and Emery 1997). According to Pielou (1991, 141), the vegetation of glacial Georges Bank probably consisted of a mixture of tundra, which attracted mammoths, and coniferous parkland and black spruce, which attracted mastodon. Refugia to the north would have been more thinly vegetated, with low shrubs and herbs covering glacial Sable Island. Large active animals, including wolves and caribou, could have moved freely among the refugia. The flora and fauna from these unglaciated areas would have migrated to the mainland as the glacial ice retreated and contributed to the modern flora and fauna of the region (see Vignette 6).

Vignette 6: Retreat of the Great Glacier

Donald Soctomah (2005, 3–4) relates the following account of the Peskotomuhkati (Passamaquoddy) story of the melting of the Great Glacier that covered the Maritime Peninsula. In this account, Nipon, the embodiment of summer, along with her grandmother Komiwon (the rain) and the warm winds, does battle with Pun (the winter) and the cold winds, freeing the land of ice and allowing humans to inhabit the north. Although defeated, Pun still returns to the region each year.

In the far old time there lived near the sun a beautiful woman, Nipon, her name meant summer. Green was her garment all of fresh leaves, and beautiful flowers covered her wigwam. She had a Grandmother, Komiwon, the rain, who dwelt far away. But when Komiwon came to visit her grandchild, one thing she always said whenever she left Nipon: "One thing I bid you with hardest warning, to one thing I bid you with a strong will, you should never seek in your wanderings the Lahtoqehsonuk, the land of the north, for there dwells Pun the winter, a deadly foe. You will surely find him should your feet fall in the Lahtoqehsonuk. Your Lahtoqehsonuk beauty will leave you, your green dress fade, your hair turn gray, your strength become weakness." Nipon gave little attention to Komiwon, the rain. One fair morning, she sat by her wigwam in the bright sunshine, looking at the Lahtoqehsonuk, the northlands. All that Nipon saw seemed strangely lovely as if enchanted. No human being was in the northland but over it all was beautiful sunshine. There she saw at a long distance a wonderful land, broad shining lakes, high blue mountains, bright rolling rivers, all strange and sweet. Something came over her, she didn't know if it was a dream or a voice. There was no help, she must rise and go to the land of Lahtoqehsonuk, in the northland. Up rose Nipon, on to the north she walked. Then she heard a voice, the voice of the rain. "Listen, my daughter! If you go to the northland, Pun, the winter, will surely kill you!" Nipon would not listen to the warning. She could not stay still, for a spell was on her. She kept walking to the north for many days, for many moons. Still the sun shone, still she saw a beautiful country of mountains and rivers, until one day Nipon noticed that she was followed. The land went onward; as she traveled, all around her was nothing but sunshine. Stopping a little to think of the wonders, she heard a whisper, the voice of the rain, "Stay, my daughter!" It made her willful, she still kept on. Still the Pun country went on before her, and something she had never known before came over her. She felt cold! An unseen power now drove her onward. Still the mountains went on before her; the green leaves of her garment grew yellow and faded and were blown away by the grim wind. Her long hair turned gray and white; the sun grew dim and then shone no more. She was very weak. The beautiful mountains were heaps of snow; the beautiful rivers and lakes were all of ice in the northland. Komiwon, the rain, was sad. She looked around; no smoke was rising in Nipon's wigwam. "She has not returned," said Komiwon, so in her fear she went to the wigwam.

All was silent, the boughs and flowers, which covered the wigwam, were all yellow and faded. "My child, my child, you are caught by the cruel Pun, by the wicked winter, there in the north." Immediately she called for her bravest warriors, the ever-Invisible Spirits. These were their names: Sawonehson, the south wind; Cipenuk, the east wind; and Sonutsekoton, the warming southwest wind. "Quickly," she cried, "travel away to the Lahtoqehsonuk, fight like heroes, and use all your power to rescue Nipon from Pun, the winter, fly to the north!" The wind warriors, unseen by man, flew like lightning on their long journey. As they entered the Lahtoqehsonuk, Pun felt ill. He called all his chieftains, Great Lahtoqehsonuk, the terrible North wind, and the wild northwestern wind, the chill northeast wind, with all the frosts, sleet spirits, snow spirits, and every chill of the killing cold that dwell in the north. "Fly," he cried, "for our enemies are coming up from the south land, the homeland of Nipon, the summer!" Even as he spoke, the sweat dropped from him, his face grew thin, his feet seemed smaller. "I feel them coming, fly to battle!" The mighty winged giants flew to the fight, great snowflakes and heavy hailstones met and melted with the great raindrops. Winds were loud and roaring thunder, storm against storm. The drops of sweat grew bigger on Pun's cheeks; on Nipon's head the hair grew whiter and whiter. Louder and louder the winds were blowing, snow was falling thicker and thicker, but the driving rain and the mild south winds were even warmer, and bigger. The drops on Pun's face grew, his strength had left him, down he fell and, in his falling, his leg was broken. "I must perish if this lasts longer," he cried. "Set Nipon free, she it is who caused this." As the words were spoken, the winds were silenced. Snow and rain ceased. Turning her back to the Lahtoqehsonuk and Pun, the winter, weary Nipon set out on her long journey. As old as she was, she fled from the north, her white hair the color of the snows, worn out in her weakness in its chilling frosts. Many moons passed. Still she traveled, the sun grew warmer, days and shadows were ever longer, the air was softer and greener grew the mountains. Freed from ice, rivers were rushing, lakes were shining in the sunlight, flowers were unfolding to the warm breezes. Weary Nipon was weary no longer. Her heart grew lighter, her hair grew darker, and her face was fairer, brighter and younger, becoming all she had been in her early beauty. The butterflies knew her again and fluttered around her, and all the flowers greeted her with perfume in sweet voices as she went past. She was near when the clouds grew thicker, rain drops falling, showers pelting, white water falling and thunder roaring. Still she went on, her path lit by wild lightning until in the midst where

> the clouds were darkest, she found the wigwam and entered the door. There, as if dying, lay Komiwon, the ancient rain-mother, weaker and older, worn and weary. "You, my daughter," she said to Nipon, "you well might have killed me by disobedience. You have brought suffering on me and all things. But for my battle with Pun, the winter, all life would have perished. Never again while life is in me, can I venture on such a struggle. Be this your warning, or else the Pun, the cruel winter, will conquer all things and ice and snow will cover the world forever and ever."
>
> Source: Reprinted from Soctomah (2005). Courtesy of Donald Soctomah.
>
> In a similar Mi'kmaw story Gluskap (the first human) moves his people from Nova Scotia to the south to recruit the Goddess of Summer to come to Nova Scotia and create the four seasons (at the expense of the God of Winter), while leaving only one giant chunk of ice on the Cobequid Mountains (Gloade 2007, 248).

Around 13,000 years ago, the retreat of ice from the coast of Maine led to a "marine transgression" (Struiver and Borns 1975) and the formation of an extensive coastal bay. Subsequent crustal rebound reversed the transgression and by 12,000 ^{14}C yrs BP the modern coast of Maine was formed. At about the same time, in the northern part of the Maritime Peninsula, salt water inundated the western end of the Goldthwait Sea to form the vast, inland Champlain Sea. It covered over 20,000 square kilometres and spread westward nearly to Lake Ontario. This was a cold-water sea inhabited by whales (bowheads, humpbacks, finbacks, belugas, and harbour porpoises) and seals (ringed, harp, and bearded), and fish species such as tomcod and three-spined stickleback (Pielou 1991, 217). It would last for 2,000 years, until crustal upwarping (isostatic rebound) drained the salt water and formed the freshwater channel we know as the St. Lawrence River. Sea levels were as much as 60 m. lower in some areas, and a broad plain, known as "Northumbria," linked Prince Edward Island with the mainland. To the northeast of Prince Edward Island, the Magdalen Plateau extended out to the Magdalen Islands and northeastern New Brunswick to form the southern bank of the Gulf of St. Lawrence.

The Early Palaeo period occupation of the Maritimes, and south to New England, roughly coincides with a cooling period known as the Younger Dryas stadial, which dates from 11,000 to 10,000 ^{14}C yrs BP (or 12,900 to 11,600 cal yrs BP). The radiocarbon dates from the Debert site range from about 11,106 to 10,043 ^{14}C yrs BP (or 13,148 to 11,736 cal yrs BP). It is generally difficult to correlate paleoecological work with perceived trends in the precontact period, yet Newby and others (2005) argue convincingly that climatic changes involved in the Younger Dryas resulted in changes in floral and faunal populations that directly impacted human resource procurement strategies. They use comprehensive fossil pollen records for species that give the best indication of overall vegetation change to reconstruct vegetation patterns in the region at 1,000-year intervals. Climatic conditions during the Younger Dryas coincided with large areas of tundra-like vegetation north of spruce woodlands. The spruce population in the Maritimes shifted southward, while sedges (open tundra vegetation) and remnant glaciers expanded (Newby et al. 2005, 145–47). At the end of the Younger Dryas period, the tundra-like vegetation was replaced by widespread closed forests, including temperate conifer and deciduous populations. Their reconstruction also indicates that regional vegetation patterns during the Younger Dryas would have been suitable for caribou herds migrating long distances, like the modern George River Herd of northern Quebec and Labrador. The mixed deciduous forests following the Younger Dryas were probably more suitable to solitary cervids like moose and deer (Newby et al. 2005, 151). Lothrop and others (2011) suggest that this abrupt warming period at the end of the Younger Dryas (ca. 10,100 ^{14}C yrs BP, or 11,600 cal BP) also coincided with a decline in Palaeo fluting technology and new regional site distributions.

First Settlers

There has been considerable speculation as to the timing and nature of Palaeo people's arrival and occupation of the Maritime Peninsula. The movement of these early hunter-gatherers is generally linked to changing environmental conditions, the movement of caribou herds, and the availability of suitable lithics for stone tools. Gramly (1999, 4) suggests that the Lamb site may have belonged to a pioneering group that established a migration route north and east of the Ohio River, and eventually on to northern Maine and the Maritimes (also see Lothrop et al. 2016, 206). The existence of the Champlain Sea during the Younger Dryas period may have greatly influenced human migration. Dincauze and Jacobson (2001, 122) speculate that people travelling east along early Lake Ontario and the shores of the Champlain Sea may have been lured there by the biotic richness of adjacent woodlands, wetlands, and tundra. Besides caribou and beaver, summer-nesting waterfowl could have provided meat, eggs, and feathers (Dincauze and Jacobson 2001, 123). Bird-hunting would have required some sort of netting technology. Loring (1980, 21, 35; also see Robinson 2012) notes that several concentrations of Palaeo sites are associated with the Champlain Sea shore, which may represent frequent visits by small hunting parties, possibly attracted to the rich marine biota of the Champlain Sea (i.e., seals, whales, and possibly walrus).

Curran (1999, 21) points out that peoples using fluted points probably were drawn northward in search of resources, rather than by population pressures at home. Dena Dincauze argues that some of the largest Palaeo sites in the Northeast, including Debert, may have been marshalling areas, occupied by groups who had just entered a new territory, and that such sites became "focal places used for the gathering, arranging, and allocating of resources and information" (Dincauze 1996, 10). She notes that previous interpretations included the use of these sites as camps and lookouts for intercepting migrating caribou herds (i.e., episodic reuse), or seasonal hunting aggregation camps, family camps, or social aggregation camps where information was shared and marriages arranged (Dincauze 1996,

6–7). For example, George MacDonald (1982, x) suggests that variations in fluted projectile point styles indicate that the first inhabitants of the region formed several distinct groups, rather than a homogeneous population. Dincauze (1996, 8) lists criteria that would apply to pioneer marshalling sites, including distance to other large sites, archaeological visibility (rarity), use of earliest fluted point style, evidence of only one or two lithic sources, distinct artifact clusters (features), richness of the artifact assemblage in each cluster, and stylistic conformity. Debert certainly is a strong candidate for a marshalling area under these criteria. If it were an aggregation site for smaller local groups of people, you would expect to see much more variability in lithic resources. However, the mathematical odds of discovering the first pioneer encampment in the region must be phenomenal. The scarcity of large sites in the Maritimes may be merely a result of the submergence of other large sites and the small number of researchers working in the area. Marshalling may also have involved shorter expansions, in which case, Debert may be one of several such sites in the region.

The Early Palaeo Peoples

Bradley and others (2010) have proposed a chronology for the New England–Maritimes region that includes a Middle Palaeo period (ca. 10,300 to 10,100 ^{14}C yrs BP; or 12,200 to 11,600 cal BP). We have very little evidence at present for the Middle Palaeo in the Maritimes and, since it includes a continuation of fluted-point technology, it is included with the Early Palaeo in this discussion. The earliest human inhabitants of the Maritime Peninsula were part of a wider North American Palaeo cultural manifestation, identified in the west with the Clovis cultural tradition. The great separation in time and unique environments makes it difficult to compare these people with modern Indigenous cultures. However, based on numerous modern studies of hunter-gatherer (foraging) societies, the Palaeo peoples were likely egalitarian (i.e., they shared resources), maintained a low population density, lacked territoriality, practised a minimum level of food storage, and had a flexible, closely related, family-based composition

(Kelly 2007, 15). As Wright (1995, 24) points out, a social system that could maintain a consistent technological tradition while colonizing such a vast area is difficult to imagine. However, even small-scale societies share a common social order that pervades the complex interrelationships of the people in the group, how they are led (i.e., by elders, spiritual mediators, great warriors, or great hunters), as well as how they relate to their deceased ancestors, the forces of nature, and the landscape.

People of the Northeastern Palaeo tradition probably used at least two residential "base camps" (i.e., warm- and cold-season camps), and logistical camps for a variety of subsistence tasks, such as hunting, and quarrying sites (Gramly and Funk 1990). Gramly (1982) considers that some archaeological sites, like Bull Brook, Massachusetts, and Whipple, New Hampshire, may have been the warm- and cold-season camps for the same group. Palaeo quarrying sites are rare, but they have been identified in areas around Munsungun Lake, in northeastern Maine (Bonnichsen 1981).

Palaeo peoples of the region usually are portrayed as caribou hunters, although this concept is supported more by vegetation reconstructions than by actual faunal material. Caribou bones are known only from the few sites in New England and Ontario and, possibly, Michaud, Maine (Lothrop et al. 2011, 562; Spiess et al. 1985; Spiess and Wilson 1987; Storck and Spiess 1994). Caribou may have been only a seasonal resource (Spiess et al. 1985). Bonnichsen and others (1991) note that a wide variety of habitats was available in Palaeo times, and that Palaeo subsistence patterns may have been quite diverse. So far, the only other fauna associated with these early sites are beaver, arctic fox, hare, and various unidentified species of mammal, fish, and bird. However, it is assumed that Palaeo peoples also hunted seals and possibly walrus (e.g., Keenlyside and Anderson 2009, 375). Anadromous fish species, such as salmon and gaspereau, were plentiful. Jackson (1987) imagines that the earliest Palaeo people of southern Ontario may have hunted mastodons. Mastodons and mammoths may have overlapped with Palaeo people on the Maritime Peninsula, but an association has yet to be demonstrated (Bourque 2001, 17–19; Hoyle et al. 2004; Odale et al. 1987). Plant remains are even less common at Palaeo sites. The only specimens found in this region come from the Hedden site, southern Maine (Asch Sidell 1999, 197), which produced seeds of four species of edible fruit, including raspberry/blackberry (*Rubus* sp.), bunchberry (*Cornus canadensis*), bristly sarsaparilla (*Aralia hispdia* Vent.), and grape (*Vitis* sp.).

Recent ice-patch archaeology in the Yukon (Farnell et al. 2004; Hare et al. 2004) has prompted speculation that the remnant ice sheets on the Maritime Peninsula during the Younger Dryas may have attracted both caribou and their human predators (Stea and Mott 1998). For example, Pelletier and Robinson (2005) suggest that Early Palaeo people from Bull Brook, Massachusetts, may have travelled the 400 km to Munsungun Lake to obtain chert from local quarries, but also to take advantage of caribou at nearby ice patches in summer. According to Stea (2011, 69), small ice caps of unknown size and thickness probably existed in the Cobequid Highlands and Prince Edward Island at the time Debert was occupied. Keenlyside and Kristmanson (2016, 65) mention that even though much of Prince Edward Island was glaciated during the Early Palaeo period, hunters may have come there to hunt caribou on the ice sheets. Furthermore, ice may have facilitated the storage of meat for early hunters (Hare et al. 2004, 261).

The Vail Palaeo site is believed to be contemporary with Debert. It is located along the ancient Magalloway River system in northeastern Maine, which was excavated in 1980 by Richard Gramly (Buffalo Museum of Science). It is depicted as a single-occupation, warm-season, caribou-hunting camp (Gramly 1982). Located at a constricted part of the river valley, it was ideal for intercepting migrating caribou. The range of artifacts recovered from Vail was like that from Debert, including Debert-style eared, fluted projectile points. The raw materials used were probably acquired from deposits in northwestern and north central Maine or northern New Hampshire (Gramly 1982). Further to the south, at the Michaud site, on the Androscoggin River, a shallow-based style of fluted projectile point was recorded (Spiess and Wilson 1987). Lithic use and manufacturing patterns at this site imply a long-distance quarrying practice, rather than collection on annual visits to quarries or acquiring raw materials through trade (Spiess and Wilson 1989).

> ## Vignette 7: Debert/Belmont Complex
>
> The best-known Palaeo archaeological site in the Maritimes is at Debert, Nova Scotia. The first published reference to the site is attributed to private collector W.A. Dennis of Kentville, who was known for looting sites and purchasing collections from other collectors with little concern for provenience. Dennis had bought a small collection of artifacts from the site from E.S. Eaton and reported the site to the editors of *American Antiquity* (Cotter 1962, 456). This note caught the attention of John Erskine (1964), who, along with geologist W.A. Take, was granted permission to investigate the site, which was located on Department of National Defence property (Fitting 1973, 57). Erskine notified his long-time advisor Douglas Byers, who in turn enlisted the support of the National Museum in the subsequent excavation of the site. In fact, Debert became the first modern professional archaeological excavation in Nova Scotia, under the direction of George MacDonald (National Museum) and Douglas Byers (Peabody Foundation). MacDonald's 1968 report on the excavation became an immediate classic in Northeast archaeology. In 1989–90, Stephen Davis (1991b) identified two additional sites at Belmont, which is within a kilometre of Debert (Figure 23), and the total site count now exceeds six (Brewster et al. 1996, 82; Rosenmeier et al. 2010, 130).
>
> The Debert site is located on a low-relief surface, sloping south from the Cobequid Hills, at about 30 m above mean sea level. Below is a flat plain and the Debert River. The site has been described as a high-altitude, caribou-hunting base camp (MacDonald 1968). Tuck (1984) suggests that several family groups may have congregated at this site for a co-operative hunting enterprise. MacDonald (1968) identified 11 living areas at the site, each with two or more hearth features, some pits, and artifact clusters. Firewood from the hearths has been identified as almost exclusively spruce. Structures erected at the site may have had wooden frames, with hide coverings, and moss for insulation (Tuck 1984).

4: PEOPLING A NEW LAND

Figure 23: A visit to the Belmont site, 1990. Background, left to right: Stephen Davis, Laird Niven, Mike Sanders, David Keenlyside; front: Helen Kristmanson, Valery Monahan, Aaron Butt, and Stephen Powell. Photograph by Michael Deal.

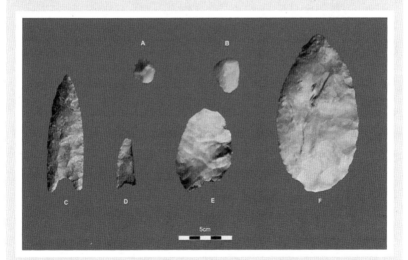

Figure 24: Selected Palaeo tools from the Debert site: (A) graver (engraving tool), (B) uniface (scraper), (C–D) fully fluted, eared projectile points, (E–F) bifacial knives. Courtesy Nova Scotia Museum.

The Palaeo toolkit is known to us almost entirely from lithic artifacts (Figure 24). At Debert, MacDonald reported spear points, drills, and perforators with large flakes (channel flakes) removed from their bases to facilitate hafting. The projectile point style is generally described as being eared and fluted (see below). Other tool forms included gravers (for engraving wood and bone), bifacial knives, and side scrapers. Local raw materials were used to make hammerstones and anvils, while better-quality raw materials were acquired elsewhere. The most common raw material was chalcedony, which is believed to have been quarried along the north shore of the Minas Basin between Five Islands and Parrsboro (Davis 2011, 18; MacDonald 1968, 61). It appears that the local toolmakers attempted to conserve the better raw materials through heating to improve flaking qualities and by using a bipolar core technique to produce small, sharp flakes from cobbles using stone hammers and anvils.

In 1972, the Historic Sites and Monument Board designated Debert as a National Historic Site of Canada. Nova Scotia was granted protection of the site in 1976, under the Historic Sites Protection Act. Following the discovery of the Belmont sites, the Confederacy of Mainland Mi'kmaq initiated a project called "Mi'kmawey Debert" to foster the protection and public interpretation of the sites (Julien et al. 2008). In October 2005, they hosted a special workshop at Debert to address the future of the Debert/Belmont sites. Canadian and American scholars and community elders took part in a roundtable discussion of common research issues, interdisciplinary cooperation, and cultural resource management concerns relating to the sites. It was the first time that members of the original Debert excavation team were able to share their perspectives on the sites with current researchers in a public forum. The short-term benefits from this workshop were a new publication updating the research on the sites (Bernard et al. 2011) and an archaeological survey to assess previously untouched portions of the protected area. This collaboration was followed by a paper that tackled the problems of the discrepancy between the site's dates and those derived from regional palaeoclimatic data and the relative chronology of the sites within the Debert/Belmont complex (Rosenmeier et al. 2012).

Lithic Styles of the Maritime Peninsula

Dramatic changes to the regional flora and fauna at the end of the Younger Dryas would have forced the Palaeo peoples to develop new procurement strategies, including changes to their lithic toolkit. The most significant difference is the replacement of fluted projectile points with non-fluted forms (Newby et al. 2005; Wright 1995, 35). This technological change is generally used to signify the beginning of a new era in Palaeo occupation, known simply as "the Late Palaeo Period." Researchers in Maine and the Maritimes have tried to avoid naming lithic and ceramic types. Instead, emphasis has been placed on attribute analysis. This method is more inclusive of rarer styles and avoids the proliferation of named types that causes confusion when comparing projectile point and ceramic styles between regions in the Northeast. However, named types from other areas are not ignored when drawing comparisons. Three broad stylistic variants characterize the projectile points of the Maritime Peninsula, namely, fully fluted projectile point styles, single-fluted (and non-fluted) point styles, and non-fluted point styles (see Figure 25 and Table 3). Dates for these stylistic changes are based on radiocarbon dates from only a few sites, and, therefore, are tentative (see Dumais 2000; Keenlyside 1985a; Spiess et al. 1998).

The earliest Palaeo projectile points used in the region, ca. 10,800–10,500 ^{14}C yrs BP, are large spear points with basal fluting on both sides. The two major styles are illustrated by point forms from the Bull Brook site, Massachusetts, and the Debert site, Nova Scotia. Fluted points from Bull Brook generally range from 7 cm to 10 cm in length and have straight to slightly excurvate (i.e., curved outward) sides and moderate basal concavities. The flutes vary from one-third to one-half the length of the point. The point is held in place between two bone foreshafts, which fit into the flutes. These points also exhibit grinding on the edge of the blades on the lower half of the point, so as not to cut the lashing that holds the point and foreshafts in place. This style of projectile point is widely distributed in New England. In Maine, they have been identified from at least five sites and numerous isolated finds (Spiess et al. 1998, 214–17; Spiess and Wilson 1987, 193–200).

Table 3. Selected Palaeo Projectile Points from Small Collections and Isolated Finds.

Location	Context	Raw Material	Source
Fully Fluted, Shallow Indented Base:			
Kingsclear, NB	Isolated Find	Munsungun Chert	Turnbull 1974b
New Horton Creek, NB	Isolated Find	Banded Green Chert	Turnbull & Allen 1978, 447
Medford, NS	Isolated Find	North Mtn Chert	MacDonald 1965
Fully Fluted, Deeply Indented Base (Eared):			
Quaco Head, NB	Isolated Find	Chert	MacDonald 1968, 124, fig. 24b
North Tyron, PEI	Isolated Find	Chalcedony	Bonnichsen et al. 1991, 6
Amherst Shore, NS	Isolated Find	Chalcedony	Davis & Christianson 1988
Gaspereau Lake Site, NS	BfDb-5	Chert	Murphy 1998, 46
Dartmouth, NS	Isolated Find	Chalcedony	Davis & Christianson 1988
Sable River estuary, NS	Isolated Find	Chalcedony	Betts et al. 2018
Single Fluted (or Non-Fluted):			
Red Bank, NB	Hogan-Mullen	White Quartz	Turnbull & Allen 1978, 150
Melanson, NS	Isolated Find	Red Quartzite	Erskine 1998, 12, plate 2
Gaspereau Lake, NS	BdDf-1	Tan Quartzite	Laybolt 1999, 50, 218
Gaspereau Lake, NS	BdDf-1	Chert	Laybolt 1999, 50, 218
Ingonish, NS	Geganisg site	Rhyolite	Nash 1978, 136

4: PEOPLING A NEW LAND

Non-Fluted, Parallel Flaked:

French Lake, NB	Isolated Find	Chert	Keenlyside 1984b, 6
Cape Spear, NB	Isolated Find	Chert	Suttie 2014
Point Deroche, PEI	Isolated Find	Grey Veined Chert	S. Buchanan, pers. comm.
Windsor, NS	Isolated Find	Chert	S. Davis, pers. comm. 2016
Gaspereau Lake, NS	BfDb-5	Quartzite	Murphy 1998, 46
Yarmouth, NS	Isolated Find	Chert	Davis & Christianson 1988

Figure 25: Palaeo projectile point styles discussed in the text: (A) fully fluted style, Kingsclear, New Brunswick, (B) fully fluted, eared style, Quaco Head, New Brunswick, (C) single-fluted style, Melanson, Nova Scotia, (D) non-fluted, parallel flaked style, Windsor, Nova Scotia, (E) triangular style, Savage Harbour, Prince Edward Island. A and B courtesy of the Government of New Brunswick; C photograph by Michael Deal; D courtesy of Stephen Davis; E courtesy of James Tuck.

Three specimens of this fully fluted, shallow-based style are known from the Maritimes. The first was found by a collector at Kingsclear, New Brunswick (Turnbull 1974b; see Figure 25). It appears to be manufactured from Munsungun chert (Bonnichsen et al. 1991, Figure 1.2g; MacDonald 1968, 124, Figure 24d). The second artifact was collected by a field hand on a farm in Medford (near Blomidon), Nova Scotia. In a letter to John Erskine, George MacDonald (1965) noted that this point is made from nearby North Mountain material. The specimen is now believed to be in a private collection in the United States. The third specimen was picked up from the creek bed at New Horton Creek, New Brunswick, about one km north of the Bay of Fundy (Turnbull and Allen 1978, 447). It is described as lanceolate, with excurvate edges, a concave base, lateral grinding, and retouch on both sides after fluting. It is made from a banded green chert that may have been heat-treated before knapping.

The second major style is characterized by spear points from the Debert and Belmont sites in Nova Scotia (Davis 1991b, 2011; Ellis 2004, 2011; MacDonald 1968). The Debert excavation produced 140 whole and fragmentary points in virtually all stages of manufacture, which range from 3 cm to 10 cm in length (MacDonald 1971, 32–33). They feature recurved (i.e., curved backward) edges, parallel to converging margins, and deeply indented bases (< 0.6 cm). Projectile points of this style are found primarily in Maine and the Maritimes but are known from as far west as the Lamb site below Lake Ontario (Gramly 1999). They are well represented at a cluster of sites in northwestern Maine, including the three sites at Vail, four other sites, and two isolated finds (Gramly 1982; Spiess et al. 1998, 236–37; Spiess and Wilson 1987, 199).

Six isolated finds of this fully fluted, eared point style are known from the Maritimess (Table 2). MacDonald (1968, 124, Figure 24b; Bonnichsen et al. 1991, Figure 1.2f) reports a large specimen from Quaco Head, New Brunswick. Another was collected about 4 km inland from North Tyron, Prince Edward Island (Bonnichsen et al. 1991, 6, Figure 1.2h). In Nova Scotia, a specimen was collected from a sandy beach along the Amherst shore in an area that was probably grassland in Early Palaeo times (Bonnichsen et al. 1991, 6, Figure 1.2e; Davis and Christianson 1988, 190). Murphy (1998, 46) discovered a similar specimen when he re-analyzed the material recovered by John Erskine in 1967 from the Gaspereau Lake site (BfDd-5), in central Nova Scotia. This specimen is missing a tip and one ear but exhibits the deeply concave base and double fluting of this style. A specimen collected at a private residence in Dartmouth, Nova Scotia, is described as a fluted point preform, made from the brecciated chalcedony specific to the Debert site, and similar in appearance to a specimen depicted by MacDonald (1968, Figure 20a; Christianson 1991; Davis and Christianson 1988). It is described by Christianson (1991, 8) as representing the manufacturing stage immediately before the first channel flake is removed to form the first flute. The final example is a point collected in 2012 on the Sable River estuary (i.e., the Pierce-Embree site), which is believed to be a re-worked fluted point made from a variegated, multicoloured, translucent chalcedony (Betts et al. 2018).

Three lanceolate bifaces (or preforms) made from a high-grade, light grey chert were recovered from the Pirate Cove site, Spednic Lake, New Brunswick (Figure 26; Deal 1984a, 24–25). This site is located approximately five km northeast of the Early Palaeo site at Forest City (Hudgell et al. 2013). It was first recorded by local avocational archaeologist J. Bliss Goodwin. The artifacts were surface-collected at an eroding beach face. The original site would have afforded an excellent view of the main body of Spednic Lake to the south. These points exhibit a high degree of workmanship, with parallel thinning flake scars but no basal grinding or fluting. One specimen exhibits a fracture pattern similiar to artifacts from the Vail site (Arthur Spiess, personal communication 1984). One additional specimen from the site is a large biface of reddish-brown jasper, which also exhibits fine bifacial retouch. The one complete lanceolate specimen has slightly excurvate sides. These specimens are tentatively attributed to the Palaeo period, based on the quality of raw materials and level of workmanship compared to Archaic and Woodland chipped stone tools from southwestern New Brunswick.

The second major style variant, dating to ca. 10,100–10,050 ^{14}C yrs BP, is characterized by small (>6 cm long) projectile points with excurvate sides, narrow bases, and shallow basal concavities (>2 cm). Some specimens have short flute scars on one side, and some exhibit lateral grinding. This style may represent a transitional technological form between the early fluted and late unfluted spear points (i.e., the Middle Palaeo fluted

Figure 26: Pirate Cove visit, October 1983, with complete biface *in situ*. Photographs by Michael Deal.

point form described by Bradley et al. 2010). Most specimens come from the Nicholas site, Maine. Newby and others (2005, 148) point out the close similarity between these points and the named Holcombe point style from the Great Lakes area. Boudreau (2008, 6) describes the Holcombe point as having convex blade edges, concave or nearly straight base, ground stem edges, a maximum width at or above mid-base, and about half of them are fluted on only one side. Other specimens have been found in Maine at two sites, along with two isolated finds (Spiess et al. 1998). A single radiocarbon date of 10,090 ± 70 ^{14}C yrs BP is associated with this point style at the Esker site (Spiess et al. 1998).

In the 1960s, John Erskine (1998, 12, plate 2) reported a lanceolate spear point in the collection of Ellis Gertridge of Gaspereau, Nova Scotia, which he believed to be very similar to the Holcombe named type. The Gertridge specimen was collected from the huge, multicomponent site at Melanson, along the lower reaches of the Gaspereau River. It has a distinctive fluting scar (~1.5 cm long) on one side (MacCarthy 2003, Figure 3.7). Unfortunately, the Gertridge collection was dispersed after Ellis died and the whereabouts of this specimen are presently unknown. Laybolt (1999, 49–50) also reports convex-sided, straight-based, single-fluted specimens from two sites on Gaspereau Lake. A specimen very similar to the Melanson find was recovered by Ronald Nash (1978, 136) from uncertain context at the Geganisg site, which is the well-known rhyolite quarry site on Ingonish Island, Cape Breton. This island was attached to the mainland prior to 4,000 years ago and the quarry appears to have been in use from Palaeo to Woodland times. The specimen is made from Ingonish rhyolite (Nash 1978, Figure 1). One additional, unfluted point, tentatively attributed to this period, comes from a private collection from the Indian Gardens site, southwestern Nova Scotia. It measures 6.3 cm long, and 3 cm wide. A projectile point from the Hogan-Mullin site (CfDk-1), Red Bank/Sunny Corners, New Brunswick, may also represent this style. The specimen was originally recovered from an excavation by William Wintemberg in 1930, from a disturbed context. It is described as a lanceolate point with a slightly concave base, convex lateral edges, basal thinning on both faces, and a single fluting scar (Turnbull and Allen 1978, 150). It also features grinding on both base and lateral edge junctions and portions of the basal concavity. It is made from white quartz. The Palaeo affiliation of this and a second similar point from the same site has recently been questioned, based on raw material, flaking characteristics, and the fact that all other artifacts from the site seem to date to the Woodland period (Leonard 2005, 13–14).

From ca. 10,000–8,000 ^{14}C yrs BP Palaeo peoples in the region used non-fluted projectile point styles. Two distinct, widely distributed styles are known from the Maritime Peninsula. The first style is characterized by long (6 cm to 10 cm), thin bodies with finely executed parallel flaking, and generally have a flat base and sometimes feature small side notches. They are best known from seven sites on the Gaspé Peninsula, Quebec, and four sites and nine isolated finds from northern Maine (Benmouyal 1987; Chapdelaine and Bourget 1992; Chalifoux 1999; Chalifoux and Burke 1995; Doyle et al. 1985; Dumais 2000; Dumais et al. 1993; Laliberté 1992; Petersen et al. 2000; Sanger et al. 1992). Varney Farm, Maine, has produced six dates, with one at 9,410 ± 190 ^{14}C yrs BP and five clustering between 8,700 ± 60 and 8,380 ± 100 ^{14}C yrs BP. Radiocarbon dates from three Quebec sites range from 8,400 to 7,800 ^{14}C yrs BP, indicating that Late Palaeo occupation in the Gaspé probably began later, around 8,000 ^{14}C yrs BP (MacCarthy 2003).

Specimens representing this style are relatively rare in the Maritimes, but have been recovered from the Gaspereau Lake area, Nova Scotia, along with isolated finds from Windsor and the Little Narrows site, Cape Breton (Keenlyside 1984b, slide 7b; Keenlyside 1984c; Laybolt 1999; Murphy 1998). A complete specimen, with small side notches, was recently reported from Windsor (Stephen Davis, personal communication, 2016; Figure 25). Although the point was brought to the site in landscaping fill, the presence of other points of this style at Gaspereau Lake suggest that it originated in the general area of Windsor. Murphy (1998, 47) reports a finely parallel-flaked point from the Gaspereau Lake site (BfDb-5:193), recovered from a disturbed context (see Keenlyside 1984b, slide 7b). Davis and Christianson

(1988, Figure 2a) report another complete parallel-flaked point collected from a small terrace above the harbour at Yarmouth, Nova Scotia. It is described as lanceolate, with slightly concave base, slight basal ears, and co-lateral flaking. Keenlyside (1984b, slide 7a) reports a lanceolate point of this style as an isolated find from French Lake, New Brunswick, and Turnbull and Allen (1988, 252) note that at least two "Plano-like" points have been collected from the Saint John River Valley. Brent Suttie (2014b) recently reported an additional lanceolate point from an isolated find off Cape Spear, on the Northumberland Strait shoreline opposite Prince Edward Island. This specimen has an interesting combination of features, including a long lenticular shape, parallel flaking on both faces, as well as basal thinning by the removal of a small channel flake and two small notches in the sides, presumably for securing the point to a shaft (Suttie 2014b, 9). Scott Buchanan photographed a parallel-flaked point with a small stem, possibly a reworked point, which was found in a house garden at Point Deroche, Prince Edward Island. It is made from a fine grey chert with black veins (Deal 2016, 48).

The second Late Palaeo style variant was originally identified by David Keenlyside (1985, 82) as having a broad triangular outline, with excurvate lateral edges and a pronounced rounded, indented base. Basal thinning occurs as step fractured flake scars on one or both faces, but basal-edge grinding is generally absent. Basal tangs (or ears) seem to be intentionally asymmetric. Twenty-two specimens from Prince Edward Island averaged 5.1 cm long, 3.2 cm wide, 0.65 cm thick, and 0.61 cm in basal depth (Keenlyside 1985, 82). This point style is associated with the Gulf of St. Lawrence area, and particularly Prince Edward Island. Bradley (2001) refers to these points as "Maritime Triangle," while Leonard (2005) calls them "Southern Gulf" points. Most specimens were recovered at sites in Prince Edward Island, including the Jones site, Basin Head, and Greenwich, and isolated specimens come from New London Bay, Savage Harbour, St. Peter's Bay, and Little Harbour (Keenlyside 1985; Bonnichsen et al. 1991; MacCarthy 2003). Keenlyside (1985, 81) also identifies two isolated finds on the Tracadie River, New Brunswick, at Tracadie Lagoon (CiDf: 3) and along the estuary. Survey work on the Magdalen Islands has produced isolated finds at three sites (McCaffrey 1986). Further study of private and museum collections in New Brunswick and Nova Scotia would likely turn up additional examples.

Late Palaeo Peoples

The Late Palaeo period roughly coincides with the beginning of the Holocene Epoch (ca. 10,000 to 8,000 ^{14}C yrs BP), which brought warmer weather and the gradual development of a woodland flora and fauna to the region. Surprisingly, we know even less about this period than we do about earlier Palaeo times (Keenlyside 2011). This scarcity of data usually is attributed to either a near depopulation of the area or the more likely scenario that most sites were located along the now inundated shoreline.

In her review of the Late Palaeo manifestation on the Maritime Peninsula, Michelle MacCarthy (2003) characterizes the population as highly mobile groups of generalized hunter-gatherers. She envisions groups of interrelated families sharing specific lithic resources; Munsungun chert in the Varney Farm area of Maine, De Landes Formation cherts on the Gaspé Peninsula sites, and Ingonish rhyolites on Prince Edward Island. Furthermore, she suggests (2003, 173) that the raw materials may have had symbolic value, linked to cultural identity. It is likely that smaller groups met at specific sites to exchange raw materials, arrange marriage partners, and cooperate at peak times in hunting and fishing of specific species.

At present, two distinct groups can be identified in the Maritimes: one using parallel-flaked, unfluted projectile points and the other using small, trianguloid projectile points. The unfluted points of the former group have obvious similarities to the Plano-like styles of the Great Lakes region, suggesting that they originated there and travelled along the St. Lawrence drainage to the Gulf. The second group may have developed *in situ* from the Early Palaeo fluted point culture. Both groups had sites in coastal locations, implying the seasonal use of coastal resources.

Steven Loring (1980, 35) suggests that ancestors of the unfluted point users may have developed marine mammal hunting skills along the Champlain Sea.

Interior triangular point-using populations appear to have been more restricted in their movements, possibly due to the degeneration of the spruce forest environment through the spread of pine. Remnant stands of spruce along water margins may have drawn some groups to coastal areas. David Keenlyside (1985) offers the explanation that both Palaeo peoples living along the eastern coast of the Maritime Peninsula and the lower St. Lawrence River may have had a marine adaptation focused on peak seasonal occurrences of seal and walrus. He refers to this as a "Palaeomarine Adaptation" (c. 9,500 to 9,000 ^{14}C yrs BP). This development may account for the scaled-down version of the fluted projectile point used during this period. The Jones site assemblage also included a barbed fluted point (see Vignette 8). Keenlyside (1985) links the late Palaeo marine adaptation to the Maritime Archaic cultural pattern that developed later in the same area. Furthermore, MacCarthy (2003, 169) agrees that the superficial similarity of the small, fluted points and later Dorset Palaeoeskimo endblades may indicate a similar form of technological adaptation to marine mammal hunting.

Vignette 8: The Late Palaeo Sites

Three sites from the Maritime Peninsula will serve as examples of the Late Palaeo contexts encountered by archaeologists in the region: namely, Varney Farm in western Maine, the Rimouski site on the Gaspé Peninsula, and the Jones site on Prince Edward Island. Varney Farm is a single component site overlooking the Nezinscot River floodplain. The site produced 47 parallel-flaked projectile points, representing at least 19 complete points, along with drills, scrapers, and biface fragments (Petersen et al. 2000). Much of the site was disturbed, but one feature found in an undisturbed context was dated to 9,410 ± 190 ^{14}C yrs BP. Five additional dates ranged from 8,700 ± 60 to 8,380 ±

100 ^{14}C yrs BP. The excavators preferred the earlier date, but the more recent dates are in line with samples from the Rimouski site. As MacCarthy notes (2003, 32), this overlapping is coincident with later Archaic populations living in the area.

The Rimouski site is located on the north shore of the Gaspé Peninsula, about 1.6 km from the St. Lawrence River. Like most of the Gaspé sites, it is situated on a raised marine terrace (ca. 135–140 m above sea level) at the limits of the marine invasion of the Goldthwaite Sea (Dionne 1990). The excavation of the site in the early 1990s (Chapdelaine and Bourget 1992) produced parallel-flaked projectile points, like those from Varney Farm, along with small retouched flakes and scrapers. Several activity areas were identified, including one believed to be associated with working hides. The radiocarbon dates for the site indicate a relatively late occupation.

The Jones site is a multi-component site located on an elevated headland on the north shore of St. Peter's Bay, Prince Edward Island. It is the only site among the three in the Maritimes claimed to produce *in situ* Late Palaeo artifacts. First excavated by David Keenlyside and Anna Sawicki in 1983 (Keenlyside 1985) and revisited by Michelle MacCarthy in 2001, Mr. and Mrs. Roland Jones amassed a collection of stone tools from the site in the 1960s, including nearly 50 parallel-flaked projectile point fragments. The points are triangular in outline, with bifacial trimming, basal indenting, and thinning, and pronounced barbs (i.e., Bradley's "Maritime Triangular" point). They range from 30 to 70 mm in length. The earliest stratum of the site (c. 80 cm below surface) produced the base of a triangular point, while a complete point was surface-collected at the eroding edge of this layer. Keenlyside and Kristmanson (2016, 67) indicate that nearly 100 of these points have been found on the Island, and that most are made from Ingonish rhyolite from Cape Breton Island. Accordingly, the easiest route to the quarry source was by boat from the South Lake area across the Northumberland Strait to Margaree, Cheticamp, or Mabou Harbour areas, and from there across the island.

When Michelle MacCarthy revisited the site, she discovered evidence of disturbance in the suspected Palaeo layer, and she noted that the four radiocarbon dates all fall within the last 2,000 years (2003, 57; Figure 27). One re-evaluation of the impacts of coastal submergence off the north shore of

Figure 27: Michelle MacCarthy at the Jones site, Prince Edward Island, 2001. Photograph by Michael Deal.

Prince Edward Island has led to the thought that the Jones site likely dates to the Late Archaic, and the distinctive projectile points from here, and similar ones from the Magdalen Islands, are a "re-invention" of the Early Palaeo point style as harpoon endblades used for hunting sea mammals (Lacroix et al. 2011).

The Ancient Ones

Despite some issues with radiocarbon dates and potential disturbance at the two major Early and Late Palaeo sites (MacCarthy 2003; Lacroix et al. 2014; Davis 2011; Rosenmeier et al. 2012; Stea 2011), we still have a fair picture of the first inhabitants of the Maritimes. The ancient peoples were descended from a widespread Palaeo culture, known as the Clovis. Over many generations, descendant groups moved along the southern Great Lakes and Champlain Sea, presumably following migrating herds of caribou, which were attracted to the ice-margins. By 11,000 years ago, people using a modified version of the Clovis fluted spear point arrived in the Maritime Peninsula and occupied sites at Vail and Debert. The people at Debert may have been the first to enter the Maritimes, via eastern Maine and New Brunswick. However, coastal sites from this period are inundated, so there may have been earlier populations along the northern Maine and southern New Brunswick coasts. Lithic sources along the northern coast of the Minas Basin likely were discovered as the Debert people entered the area. The climate at the time was relatively cool and the area was covered with tundra-like vegetation and remnant spruce forest. Ice patches to the northwest of the site in the Cobequid Hills would have attracted migrating caribou. Only stone tools have been found at the known sites, but these reflect a hunting-related technology. Tools made from bone and ivory are known from sites further west. Animal and plant remains are rare from sites in the Northeast, but recovered specimens indicate that their diet included caribou, beaver, hare, arctic hare, and unidentified species of bird and fish, along with various edible berries.

It would be presumptuous to compare the lifeways of the ancient peoples with those of modern Indigenous peoples. However, we believe that they lived and travelled in small extended family groupings. All known human groups follow some sort of traditional social order. Leadership may have been entrusted to successful hunters or knowledgeable elders. Elders are respected members of all Indigenous societies for their accumulated wisdom and memories of the past. They are the conduit of oral history. Shamans may have played important roles, as the keepers of spiritual knowledge. These groups likely migrated between camping sites during at least two seasons of the year to take advantage of the resources in their area, with logistical trips for peripheral resources like lithic quarries. Family-based groups may have joined with other groups at times to exploit certain resources, such as migrating caribou or anadromous fish runs. Larger groupings would also provide opportunities to trade and to arrange marriages.

The Late Palaeo to Archaic transition is still poorly understood. Long, slender parallel-flaked spear points replace fluted points to the west, but evidence in the Maine–Maritimes region is sporadic. Small triangular points with basal indentations and barbs may be a Late Palaeo (or Archaic) re-invention of early fluted points but designed for sea mammal hunting. It seems likely that both forms are part of a marine-oriented technology that was developing in the Gulf of St. Lawrence area.

5

THE LONG AGO PEOPLE

KAREN PERLEY OFFERED the Wolastoqwey term *Pihce* (Long Ago) for the Archaic period of the Maritimes (Blair 2004a, 137). These "Long Ago" people are known to us from a few key archaeological sites (see Figure 28). We are gradually learning more about Indigenous lifeways during the Early and Middle Archaic periods (ca. 9,500 to 6,000 years ago), but there is a notable absence of archaeological sites on the coasts until the Late Archaic (Sanger 2006, 245). The Early and Middle Archaic periods were once referred to as the "Great Hiatus" (Tuck 1984; Sanger 2006, 230) and various hypotheses were presented to explain the relative lack of evidence. One prominent hypothesis featured an unproductive boreal forest environment with a low carrying capacity for human population, which predicted that there were few archaeological sites to be found (Fitting 1968). This theory was brought into question as more palynological data were gathered (Petersen and Putnam 1992) and deeply buried Early and Middle Archaic components were found in the Maine interior.

Sanger (1975, 1979a) and Tuck (1975) offered hypotheses related to sea level change on the Maritime Peninsula. According to Jim Tuck (1975), there may have been substantial coastal populations during the early Holocene, but that their sites have since been inundated by rising sea levels throughout the region. He felt that there was continual occupation of the coastal areas of the North Atlantic from Late Palaeo times to European contact, which he referred to as the "Northeastern Maritime Continuum" (Tuck 1975). Sanger (1975) suggested that the Gulf of Maine and Bay of Fundy were too shallow to permit the circulation of sea water, which resulted in a relatively low level of marine resources during the early Holocene.

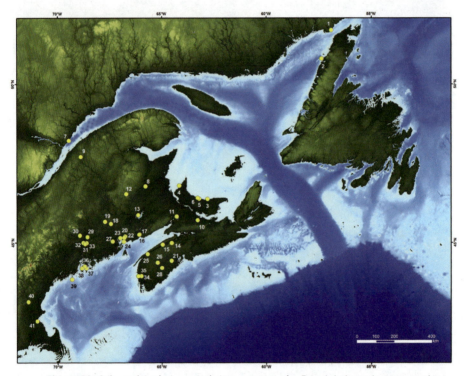

Figure 28: Selected Archaic period sites on a map by Dominic Lacroix representing the North Atlantic coast shoreline around 6,000 ^{14}C yrs BP: 1. L'Anse Amour, 2. Port au Choix, 3. Canavoy, 4. Rix and Wedge sites, 5. Robinson's Island, 6. Rustico Island, 7. Cap-de-Bon-Désir, 8. Gerrish, 9. Ruisseau-des-Caps, 10. Steele's Island, 11. Beausejour Beach, 12. Big Clearwater, 13. Cow Point, 14. Gaspereau Lake, 15. Boswell, 16. Portland Point, 17. Bentley Street, 18. Diggity, 19. Mud Lake Stream, 20. Mill Lake Bluff, 21. Governor's Island, 22. Canal Beach, 23. Teacher's Cove, 24. Rum Beach, Bliss Islands, 25. Bear River, 26. Eel Weir sites, 27. N'tolonapemk, 28. Indian Gardens, 29. Passadumkeag River sites, 30. Sharrow & Brigham sites, 31. Sunkhaze Ridge, 32. Hirundo & Young sites, 33. Gilman Falls, 34. Tusket Falls sites, 35. Bain, 36. Nevin, 37. Deer Island sites, 38. Turner Farm, 39. Stanley, 40. Neville, 41. Boyleston Fish Weir.

In a later article, he added that lower sea levels at this time affected river gradients, making them too steep to be used by important anadromous fish species (Sanger 1979c). Further, he remarked on the scarcity of identified interior sites as being due to a lack of research and systematic archaeological surveys of interior areas. He also suggested that the material culture of the Early and Middle Archaic in the Maritime Peninsula might not resemble that of contemporary sites in northern New England. Research since the 1970s has begun to fill in some of the missing information and archaeologists no longer speak of a great hiatus.

The Setting

Studies of plant pollen (palynology) now are available for more than 30 sites across the Maritimes (Dredge et al. 1992; Mayle and Cwynar 1995, Figure 2; MacQuarrie 2001). They provide a general model of climate and vegetation change for the region, which indicates a gradual northeastern movement of forest regimes. After 8,000 years ago, there was a rapid climatic warming to as much as 2.5° C above the present annual average temperature (i.e., the Hypsithermal interval). A pine (*Pinus*), birch (*Betula*), and oak (*Quercus*) forest dominated the region during the Early Archaic. By Late Archaic times, a hemlock (*Tsuga canadensis* (L.) Carr.) and oak forest had developed in Nova Scotia and New Brunswick, and a hemlock and white pine (*Pinus strobus* L.) forest had developed in Prince Edward Island (Anderson 1980; Anderson et al. 1989). Temperatures began to fall to modern levels after 4,000 years ago, and a spruce (*Picea*), birch, and beech (*Fagus grandifolia* Ehrh.) forest developed in Nova Scotia and New Brunswick, while a hemlock-birch-beech association predominated on Prince Edward Island.

Research by scientists from the Geological Survey of Canada is also providing a clearer picture of coastal submergence in the region. Seismostratigraphic mapping of the Magdalen Plateau is providing new insights into the postglacial history of the shoreline of the northern end of the Maritime Peninsula (Josenhans and Lehman 1999). For example, 9,500 years ago a vast freshwater lake existed between Prince Edward Island and the Magdalen

Islands. Sea levels for the region at 7,000 years ago were 30 m below the present level. By 5,000 years ago they were 15 m below present and the land link from Prince Edward Island to Nova Scotia and New Brunswick was broken (Keenlyside 1984a, 26; Keenlyside and Kristmanson 2016).

Georges Bank became submerged around 4,000 years ago, resulting in increased tidal activity in the Gulf of Maine and Bay of Fundy. This resulted in cooler water that attracted new species of fish, sea mammals, and sea birds, as well as the development of deeper estuaries that attracted anadromous fish (Atlantic salmon, Atlantic shad, and gaspereau), and bogs that attracted waterfowl. According to Shaw and others (2010), the rapid breakdown of a barrier of sediment at the entrance to the Minas Basin, ca. 3400 ^{14}C yrs BP, caused a tidal expansion, drop in water temperature, and increased tidal currents and turbidity that changed the inner estuary from a lagoonal-mesotidal to macrotidal environment. This led to the disappearance of Archaic period oyster beds (Bleakney and Davis 1983) and expansion of soft-shell clam beds in the area. The authors compare this catastrophic event with an old Wabanaki story involving the culture hero Gluskap and Giant Beaver (Leland 1884, 63–64; Rand 1894, 236), which appears to indicate that the destruction of the barrier was witnessed by Indigenous people and passed on through oral tradition (Shaw et al. 2010, 1089–1090).

The modern shoreline was established by 3,000 years ago. Archaic period artifacts have been recovered by scallop draggers from submerged sites in the Gulf of Maine, Bay of Fundy, and Northumberland Strait (e.g., Black 1997; Crock et al. 1993; Keenlyside 1983, 1984a, 2006; Price and Spiess 2007; Stright 1990; Turnbull and Black 1988). These specimens include large ridged ulus, large bifaces, grooved (or knobbed) plummets, adzes, and full-channelled gouges. Ulus are crescent-shaped tools, often hafted, that are used commonly in the Arctic regions for butchering large sea mammals and splitting fish. A biface and plummet recovered by draggers off the shore of Eastern Blue Hill Bay, Maine, are believed to date to the Late Palaeo and Early or Middle Archaic periods (Crock et al. 1993). Draggers have also brought up artifacts off the shore of Mount Desert Island, including three large bifaces, one made from Kineo rhyolite, three plummets, a ground slate point, and ground stone gouge and adze (Crock et al. 1993; Price and Spiess 2007; also see Kelley et al. 2010). The Penobscot Bay site is located under about eight metres of water off the eastern end of Deer Island, Maine. Artifacts recovered by divers and draggers at this site include an ulu, ground stone adzes, and biface fragments, and these are believed to date to the Middle and early Late Archaic (Stright 1990, 439).

In the Maritimes, two large, ridged ulus have been recovered in Passamaquoddy Bay (Turnbull and Black 1988), one from off the northeastern coast of Prince Edward Island (Keenlyside 1984a) and two others from off Digby Neck, Nova Scotia (Fader 2005; Taylor 2020, 131). A multibeam bathymetric survey off Digby Neck in 1999 indicated a submerged ridge jutting three nautical miles offshore from Sandy Cove, at the location of one of the ulu finds, along with associated walrus bones (Fader 2005). According to Fader (2005, 6–10; also Taylor 2020, 131), the ridge would have protruded into the Bay of Fundy during a period of lower sea level (c. 9,000–5,000 years ago), providing a broad beach where early hunters could have processed large sea mammals like walrus. A stemmed slate knife has also

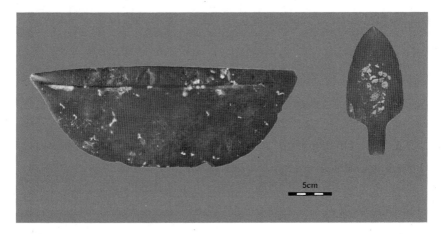

Figure 29: Archaic period artifacts recovered off Digby Neck, Nova Scotia: (left) slate ulu from three nautical miles (5 km) offshore from Sandy Cove; (right) stemmed slate knife from 15 nautical miles (28 km) offshore. Courtesy Nova Scotia Museum.

been recovered 15 nautical miles off Digby Neck (Anonymous 1989; Figure 29). A full-channelled Archaic gouge was recovered off Indian Island, between Deer Island and Campobello Island, Passamaquoddy Bay, by marine biologists dragging for scallop samples (Black 1997). Virtually all these materials are believed to pre-date the Late Archaic period on the Maritime Peninsula and seem to lend support to Tuck's hypothesis of continual coastal occupation. With the loss of these coastal sites, we are forced to reconstruct the Early and Middle Archaic sequence largely from surface-collected materials from sites in under-surveyed interior areas.

Early and Middle Archaic in Maine and New England

Sanger (2006, 31) points out that archaeologists working in the Maritime Peninsula have not yet identified a transition from the Late Palaeo to Early Archaic period. There is currently only one site in Maine, Blackman Stream, on the Penobscot River, that has both Late Palaeo and Early Archaic components, which are separated by one metre of sediment (Sanger et al. 1992). Sanger (2006, 231) suggests that the Late Palaeo record in the Gaspé, which Dumais (2000) has dated to 9,000–8,000 ^{14}C yrs BP, may have co-existed with Early Archaic peoples in central Maine. Archaeologists working in New England and further south have developed an Early and Middle Archaic cultural sequence based on diagnostic projectile point styles, known as the Neville-Stark Complex (c. 8,000–6,000 ^{14}C yrs BP). Early Archaic styles consisted of a series of stemmed and bifurcate-base points, primarily associated with the Southeast and Mid-Atlantic areas. The Neville site, located on the Merrimack River, New Hampshire, served as the model for the Early and Middle Archaic sequence in New England (Dincauze 1975). The site is identified as an interior fishing camp, based on ground stone woodworking tools; net sinkers; and large concentrations of mercury in sediments. Projectile points and spearthrower weights (or bannerstones) provide evidence of hunting. A series of distinctive projectile point styles were identified. Neville points had triangular blades and tapering stems, and dated to between 8,000 and 6,500 ^{14}C yrs BP. Stark points had less distinct shoulders and pointed stems, and dated between 6,500 and 6,000 ^{14}C yrs BP.

The spear thrower (atlatl) is a device used by Archaic hunters across eastern North America. Archaeological evidence indicates that they consisted of a short shaft (probably made of wood or cane) with a handle (of wood or antler) at the proximal end and an antler hook at the distal end. The hook received the hollow base of the spear (or dart), which was probably also made of wood or cane. While a few handles and hooks have survived in archaeological contexts, the shafts have never been recovered. What survives more often is the spear thrower weight, which appears in a variety of forms. These were secured along the shaft of the atlatl below the hook. One study of these weights shows that they served as a counterbalance that allowed the hunter to remain poised to make an overhand throw (Kinsella 2013). The counterweight took stress off the crucial arm muscles for several additional minutes while waiting for the right moment to strike. Kinsella (2013) links the use of this tool to the hunting of white-tailed deer, which became available across the Northeast during Archaic times with the development of deciduous forests.

We must assume that a wide range of perishable tools also were being used during this period. For example, the large Archaic cemetery (c. 8,000–7,000 ^{14}C yrs BP) at Windover, Florida, produced only five lithic artifacts (including three stemmed projectile points) compared to 119 tools made of bone, antler, marine shell, and wood (Doran 2002). The latter includes atlatl handles, barbed projectile points, fishhooks, pins, awls, punches, carved bird bone tubes, and tortoise shell containers. Paleodietary analysis at this site indicates a subsistence strategy based on riverine fauna and terrestrial flora, but with fruits being more important than nuts (Tuross et al. 1994).

Archaeologists in Maine and the Maritimes looked through existing collections for examples of the diagnostic projectile point styles known from New England. Spiess and others (1983a) identified only 13 Early Archaic points in Maine, and these were found primarily west of the Penobscot

River drainage. They discovered 357 Middle Archaic points but, again, the numbers were much greater in southern Maine and trailed off to the north. A series of stratified sites near Rumford, on the Androscoggin River, provide the best evidence of this lithic complex in Maine, with dates associated with Neville points c. 8,000–6,500 ^{14}C yrs BP and Stark points c. 6,400 to 5,700 ^{14}C yrs BP (Spiess and Mosher 2006). Sanger (2006, 237) notes that this complex appears to be better suited to the uplands of western Maine and a dependency on large game than on the marshy environments farther to the east.

Gulf of Maine Archaic (ca. 9,500–6,000 ^{14}C yrs BP)

Sanger's "incomplete data" hypothesis may have considerable merit for understanding the Early and Middle Archaic on the Maritime Peninsula. The excavation of deeply stratified interior sites in central and northern Maine has led to the reinterpretation of the Archaic material culture from the region. Robinson and others (1992) have coined the term "Gulf of Maine Archaic Tradition" to describe the Early and Middle Archaic manifestations for the Gulf of Maine watershed. This tradition amounts to a "technological pattern" consisting of a diverse ground stone toolkit and a chipped stone industry featuring quartz scrapers (unifaces) and non-diagnostic projectile points. The absence of diagnostic projectile points partly explains why so few sites had been identified for the period. Stone spear points still may have been used, but at sites away from riverine areas (Will 2012, 1). Will (2012, 28; Will 2017, 18) believes that the pattern originated as a cultural response to localized environmental changes in the region during the early Holocene. A specialized toolkit was developed to accommodate new subsistence opportunities, especially related to wetland, riverine, and maritime habitats. Will (2017, 17) also points out that there was no effort to acquire exotic lithic materials, as we see in earlier and later cultural traditions.

Robinson's model suggests that projectile points were less important to subsistence practices in the region, or they were being made from more perishable materials, such as bone. There is a danger that people not using stone projectile points, or making them from other materials, will be excluded from the archaeological record (Robinson 1996a, 2–3), and similar situations may account for other gaps in the regional sequence. An important artifact of the Gulf of Maine pattern is the full-channelled gouge that was previously considered to date to the Late Archaic period. Associated with this elegant gouge are ground stone rods, which may have been used to sharpen the cutting edges of the gouges.

The Brigham and Sharrow sites located near the confluence of the Piscataquis and Sebec rivers, central Maine, are important to our understanding of the Gulf of Maine Archaic Tradition (Petersen 1991; Petersen and Putnam 1992). These sites contained materials from the period of lightest occupation at the Neville site (i.e., pre-5,000 ^{14}C yrs BP), including diverse ground stone tools and unstandardized core, cobble, and uniface tools (Dincauze 1993, 13). Ground stone tools included full-channelled gouges, rods, small chisels, celts, projectile points, and plummets. Bifaces are rare, while core tools and unifaces are more common. Chipped stone tools are made predominantly from local raw materials. A large charred and calcined faunal collection indicates that a wide variety of fauna was exploited, including large and small mammals (i.e., deer, beaver, muskrat, and black bear), anadromous and catadromous fish species, and unidentified species of bird, turtle, and snake (Spiess 1992). Other New England sites with important early Holocene components include the Blackman Stream, Gilman Falls, North Wind, Little Ossipee North, and Ellsworth Falls sites in Maine (Byers 1959; Sanger 1996a; Sanger et al. 1992; Will 2012, 2017), and the Eddy and Wadleigh Falls sites in New Hampshire (Bunker 1992; Maymon and Bolian 1992).

It is generally believed that most ground stone tools were mounted in some form of organic haft. Moreover, the morphology of each tool suggests the type of hafting used and the use wear and damage on the tool points to its function (Brzezicki 2015, 97). Brzezicki (2015, 97–100) identifies four types of hafts, namely, elbow, socketed elbow, bound, and socketed. Elbow hafts are made from sections of a tree or sapling trunk that have a trunk or root connection point, such that the completed tool looks like a human arm bent at the elbow joint. For socketed elbow hafts, the poll (non-impact) end of the artifact fits into a special hole or "socket" carved into the handle. Brzezicki describes the bound half as "constructed using sapling trees, fastened by wrapping the artifact at the hafting element (i.e., a groove) with the sapling tree, and the saplings are lashed together to form a handle" (2015, 97). The socketed haft is made from a branch or section of tree trunk with an opening carved where the poll end of an artifact will be fitted, and the haft is then lashed to the artifact. According to Brzezicki (2015, 115), elbow hafts were common throughout the Archaic, while socketed elbow hafts were used only during the Early Archaic; bound hafts were used during the Early Archaic and again during the Transitional Archaic; and socketed hafts occur only in the Woodland period.

A significant site in the traditional Peskotomuhkati area of northeast Maine/southwest New Brunswick area is N'tolonapemk ("Our Ancestors Place"), at the outlet of Meddybemps Lake at Dennys River. This site was a traditional stopping place on an important canoe route that linked interior regions with the coast by way of the St. Croix and Dennys rivers (Brigham et al. 2001, 27; Brigham et al. 2006; Soctomah et al. 2012). It was periodically occupied from the Early Archaic period to the Contact period as a base camp for procuring resources from the surrounding forests, wetlands, lakes, and rivers. Bones of alewife or gaspereau (*Alosa pseudoharengus*) found throughout the sequence suggest that this was an important anadromous fish harvesting location for the last 8,000 years. The earliest occupants of N'tolonapemk also fished for perch, sucker, and eels, hunted large mammals, and hunted or trapped beaver, muskrat, woodchuck, various birds, and turtles, and collected wild plants and nuts (UMF-ARC 2002, 16). Early Archaic structures (surviving as housepits) at the site were circular, probably covered with bark or hides, and occupied spring through fall. All artifacts from the site are made from stone, and include quartz cores used as raw material for tools, quartz scrapers (unifacial tools), sandstone abrading tools, chopping tools, and hammerstones, as well as gouges for woodworking and stone rods for sharpening them. The near absence of stone projectile points suggests that bone spear points were more common. Occupation was sparse during the Middle Archaic, but the people probably continued the subsistence strategies of the earlier inhabitants. One important tool found in the Middle Archaic component at the site was an ulu (thin, semicircular knife), like contemporary forms found on interior lakes in the Maritimes (see below).

Robinson (1992, 2006) also identified a Middle Archaic burial complex believed to be associated with the latter part of Gulf of Maine Archaic Tradition. The Morrill Point burial complex (ca. 8,000 to 6,000 ^{14}C yrs BP) features full-channelled gouges, rods, adzes, celts, whetstones, unifacial tools, red ochre, and burial locations on gravel knolls and ridges, away from occupation sites. So far, four sites have been identified as belonging to this complex, including Sunkhaze Ridge and Passadumkeag in Maine, Table Lands, New Hampshire, and Morrill Point, Massachusetts (Robinson 1992, 79–86). This form of burial does not appear in the Maritimes until the Late Archaic (Sanger 2006, 240–41). Gilman Falls contains a metamorphic rock suitable for making stone rods and, indeed, rods were found in all stages of manufacture (i.e., crude blanks, and nearly complete and complete specimens) — and the site is located only a 10-km canoe ride from Sunkhaze Ridge (Sanger 2000, 154).

Early and Middle Archaic in the Maritimes

As in Maine, researchers in the Maritimes have tried looking for diagnostic Early and Middle Archaic projectile points like those found on contemporary sites further to the south. Suttie (2007) reports two bifurcate-base projectile points from New Brunswick, which may indicate Early Archaic links with New England. Only eight Middle Archaic "Stark-like" projectile points have been reported for the Maritimes (Deal et al. 2006). Furthermore, less than a dozen spear thrower weights are known from the region. Suttie (2005, 46–47, Figure 2.9) illustrates seven specimens from New Brunswick, while Deal and Rutherford (2001, 146, plate 8) report four specimens from Nova Scotia. Most of these are fragments of the winged style of spear thrower weight. Bourque (2001, 43–45) attributes this style to the Middle Archaic in Maine, but winged style weights have also been recovered from later Archaic contexts elsewhere in New England (e.g., Haviland and Power 1994, 52–54; Mournier 2003, 169–70).

The archaeological evidence for the Early and Middle Archaic in the Maritimes was re-examined by Brent Murphy (1998), who found it to have a close affinity to the Gulf of Maine Tradition. He identified 122 artifacts from more than 30 site collections in the region. His model suggests a similar toolkit, including ground stone, full-channelled gouges and rods; and a scarcity of bifaces, quartz core and uniface flake technology, bone and antler technology, and specialized mortuary artifacts (Murphy 1998, 95). Site locations suggest an interior lacustrine and riverine settlement pattern, while coastal occupation cannot be ruled out. Murphy also suggests a variable subsistence pattern based on terrestrial mammals, anadromous and catadromous fish species, and sea mammals. The Cap-de-Bon-Désir site, Quebec, has produced seal bone fragments dating to ca. 7,310 ^{14}C yrs BP, which lend some support to Murphy's model (Ploude 2000, 6). The Mill Lake Bluff site (BhDq-08) has produced the first example of a Middle Archaic quartz core and uniface technology for the Maritimes, dating to around 6,120 ± 90 ^{14}C yrs ago (Suttie 2007, 2013).

Artifacts from public and private collections in the Maritimes are recovered primarily from large interior lake systems in Nova Scotia and New Brunswick (Deal et al. 2006, Table 1; see Figure 30). In Nova Scotia, sites on Lake Rossignol, Grand Lake, and especially Gaspereau Lake (see Vignette 9) have produced 36 full-channelled gouges, six rods, and 16 ulus, of which five have ridges to facilitate hafting. In New Brunswick, sites on the Chiputneticook Lakes (i.e., Spednic and Palfrey lakes) in western New Brunswick, and the Lakes region (i.e., French, Maquapit, and Grand lakes) in central New Brunswick, have produced 36 full-channelled gouges, 16 rods, and 11 ulus, nine of which are ridged. In 1967, David Sanger (1967, 23) excavated at a location on the banks of the Saint John River, opposite the modern town of Meductic, just ahead of rising water from the Meductic Reservoir. He uncovered two large choppers, resembling ulu preforms,

5: THE LONG AGO PEOPLE

Figure 30: Selected Archaic artifacts from the Maritimes. Early/Middle Archaic: (E) full-channelled gouge, (G) ridged ulu; Late Archaic: (A) knobbed plummet, (B–C) large, side-notched projectile points, (D) shallow-grooved gouge, and (F) adze/gouge. Images A, D–E, and G from Spednic Lake, and F from Cow Point, courtesy the Government of New Brunswick. Image B from the Roger's site, Scots Bay, and C from Indian Gardens, courtesy the Nova Scotia Museum.

and other poorly formed tools below the plow zone and fluvial deposits that he suggests are like artifacts from deeply buried Middle Archaic sites in the Penobscot Valley in Maine. He believes that other Early and Middle Archaic sites are likely to be buried under fluvial deposits along the Saint John River.

Only four specimens can be tentatively identified to this period in Prince Edward Island, including three full-channelled gouges and a large, ridged ulu. One gouge with a long, shallow channel and wide bit was reported from the Rix site (CfDb-1), near Miminegash (Sawacki 1984). The other two gouges are from the Montaque River area, on the opposite side of the island. One specimen, donated to the Garden of the Gulf Museum in 1957, is of uncertain provenance. The second specimen was excavated by a bottle collector from a flat, raised terrace at the edge of a former farmstead property along a small tributary of the Montaque River. It was recovered from a dark, organic deposit underlying a layer of oyster shells, itself beneath a nineteenth-century midden deposit. This site has yet to be tested by professional archaeologists. An ulu was recovered by a scallop dragger off East Point, at approximately the 20-m bathymetry contour, in the general proximity of what appears to be a drowned river.

Vignette 9: Gaspereau Lake

As part of his examination of archaeological collections from the Maritimes, Murphy (1998, 39–60) re-interpreted the materials recovered by John Erskine (1998, 16–40) at the Gaspereau Lake (BfDb-5) site, in Nova Scotia. This site is located at the lake outlet to Gaspereau River, about 27 km from the mouth of the river at Minas Basin. The lake was dammed in 1921, so that the current water level is unnaturally high, and the site is submerged most of the year. Erskine excavated the site in the late fall of 1965. He discovered that the site consisted of a series of occupation floors with numerous, sometimes overlapping, hearth features. Murphy discovered that Erskine's earliest component for the Gaspereau Lake site was very similar to the Middle Archaic component of the Sharrow site in Maine (Petersen 1991) and by extension to the "Gulf of Maine Tradition" (see Robinson and Petersen 1992).

The Gaspereau Lake materials include the bit end of a full-channelled gouge, two rods, three crude plummets (or pre-plummets), and two damaged spearthrower weights (Figure 31). The latter includes a "triangle of slate" that was surface-collected at the site (BfDd-5: 78) and the central portion of a "winged" spearthrower weight collected nearby (Deal and Rutherford 2001, 146, plate 8). The chipped stone assemblage includes two contracting stem projectile points, flakes, choppers, and scrapers. Erskine interpreted the site as a small hunting/fishing camp. The Gaspereau Lake/Gaspereau River drainage system was one of the most heavily used waterways in precontact Nova Scotia,

5: THE LONG AGO PEOPLE

Figure 31: Archaic assemblages from the Gaspereau Lake site. Early/Middle Archaic: (A) rod, (B) pre-plummet, (C–D) contracting-stem style projectile points, and (E) bit end of a full-channelled gouge. Late Archaic: (F) narrow-bladed slate bayonet/knife, (G–H) eared, side-notched projectile points, (I) broad, side-notched projectile point, (J) broad-bladed slate bayonet tip, (K) celt, and (L) plummet. Photograph by Roy Ficken, Photographic Services, Department of Biology, Memorial University, 2001.

from Palaeo times to the present (Laybolt 1999). This broad interior lake provides easy access to many other lakes, while the river is a major source of anadromous gaspereau, or alewife (*Alosa pseudoharengus*). The river also runs close to the major source of White Rock quartzite, which is a dominant chipped stone raw material used on the system, along with cherts from nearby North Mountain.

The Gaspereau River estuary is also close to the fowling marshes and shellfish beds of the Minas Basin (Nash et al. 1991, 214). Today, soft-shell clam (*Mya arenaria* L.) and mussel (*Mytilus edulis* L.) are the dominant shellfish species in this area. However, Marine biologists from Acadia University have documented a 4,400-year-old forest and an extensive oyster (*Crassostrea virginica*) bed off Long Island, in the Minas Basin (Bleakney and Davis 1983). These areas were exposed by an outflow channel of the Gaspereau River through the intertidal mud flats over two km offshore. Oyster shells, measuring up to 20 cm in length, have been recovered, and three specimens produced an average radiocarbon date around 3,800 ^{14}C yrs BP. We know that oysters were available as early as 6,000 ^{14}C yrs BP along the coast of Maine (Bourque 2001, 45–46; Sanger and Belknap 1987; Sanger and Sanger 1986), and it seems likely that the Minas Basin beds also were available throughout the Archaic period.

Late Archaic (ca. 6,000–4,500 ^{14}C yrs BP)

Archaeologists working in the Maritime Peninsula recognize two distinctive Late Archaic cultural traditions. One tradition is primarily a coastal marine adaptation that was originally referred to as the "Red Paint" people, because of their extensive use of red ochre in burials (Sanger 1979a; Willoughby 1935). Warren K. Moorehead (1922) and his excavation crew, which he called "The Force," travelled extensively in northern Maine and western New Brunswick in search of Red Paint cemeteries. Both Moorehead and Willoughby considered them to be an extinct culture (Sanger 2000, 146). Sanger (2000, 154) suggests that the "Red Paint" burials were probably just part of a cultural tradition shared by more than one ethnic group on the Maritime Peninsula that related to a set of spiritual beliefs unknown today. When these beliefs changed irrevocably around 3,800 ^{14}C yrs BP, red ochre all but disappeared from the graves, many of the distinctive artifacts dropped out of the archaeological record, and cremation burial replaced inhumation (Sanger 2000, 154). Today, researchers in Maine refer to them as the Moorehead Burial Tradition of the Moorehead Phase of the Late Archaic (Bourque 1995). However, some authors link this burial tradition with a broader coastal adaptation called the Maritime Archaic Tradition, which stretches from the mid-coast of Maine to northern Labrador (Renouf 1999, 20; Tuck 1975, 1991). Betts and Hrynick (2021, 141–43) consider the Moorehead Tradition as a branch of the broader Maritime Archaic, consisting of various local complexes. The second cultural tradition is an interior adapted Archaic tradition, which shared a projectile point style with the Late Archaic culture of the Lower Great Lakes and Upper St. Lawrence River Valley region. The geographical boundary between the interior and coastal populations is difficult to define, because the two cultural traditions had a few common tool forms. In particular, the interior assemblages in the area include ground slate points and ulus (Robinson 1996b; Cox 1991), as well as bone points. These tools are believed to appear first in coastal Archaic areas. The assemblages of coastal sites often include projectile points and spearthrower weights that are more diagnostic of interior or more southern archaeological cultures.

The earliest Late Archaic site in the Maritimes is a small cemetery, known as the Gerrish site, which is located on a high terrace overlooking the Southwest Miramichi River at Quarryville, in northeastern New Brunswick. This site consists of a deep pit feature filled with ochre-flecked silt, lined at the base with a layer of cobbles and stone slabs, with a connecting feature containing four large ochre-coated bifaces and a chipped and ground stone celt (Allen 1989; see Figure 32). According to Allen (1989, 33) this site resembles the early Maritime Archaic cemetery at Forteau Point, southern Labrador, which has been dated to around 5,000 ^{14}C yrs BP (Tuck 1976, 48–49; Tuck 1978a, 58–59).

5: THE LONG AGO PEOPLE

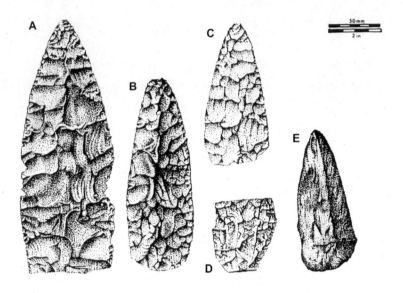

Figure 32: Late Archaic Gerrish site artifacts: (A–D) bifaces, (E) pecked and ground stone celt (note that biface (B) is depicted in Black 2011, Figure 7). Courtesy the Government of New Brunswick.

Interior Late Archaic (6,000–4,500 ^{14}C yrs BP)

There are two hypotheses concerning the origin of the interior Late Archaic people of the Maritime Peninsula. Some authors link them to the Laurentian Tradition, which is the eastern component of the broad Lake Forest Archaic (Snow 1980). The Lake Forest cultural manifestation extends from the Great Lakes to the St. Lawrence River estuary. Bruce Bourque (1995) believes that the Laurentian Archaic manifestation in the Maritime Peninsula may represent an actual migration of people into the interior portions of Maine and New Brunswick, during an early phase of the northern New England Laurentian sequence, known as the Vergennes Phase (Cox 1991). Some authors link the Laurentian Tradition with the Hathaway burial tradition (c. 5,100 ^{14}C yrs BP), which appears at six sites in central Maine, while others associate it with the Small Stemmed Point

Tradition from the coast of Maine (Robinson 1996b, 4–10). The Hathaway assemblages include forms of greenstone tuff gouges and adzes, pendants, bannerstones, a serrated biface or knife, plummets, full-channelled pebble weights, and polished pebble strike-a-lights (Robinson 1996b, 4). The appearance of the Laurentian Tradition in the area seems to coincide with the development of a mixed hardwood forest in the Northeast. Sites are found in interior riverine and lacustrine contexts and are generally disturbed. Laurentian technology and site locations suggest a hunting and fishing subsistence pattern based on white-tailed deer, beaver, rabbit, and freshwater and anadromous fish species.

David Sanger and Bonnie Newsom (2000), based on their work in the Howland Reservoir area, believe that the interior "Laurentian" Archaic was an *in situ* development from the Gulf of Maine Archaic people, involving the addition of certain artifact classes and the reduced use of others. They identify a biface tradition that appears in Middle Archaic sites around 6,000 ^{14}C yrs BP, which precedes the addition of side-notched Laurentian projectile points around 5,000 ^{14}C yrs BP. In other words, the Vergennes Phase described by Cox (1991) represents the adoption of side-notched points, ulus, and plummets by the Indigenous Middle Archaic population (Sanger and Newsom 2000, 17). They also note that each of these tool forms has its own unique history and may have been added to the inventory at different times. Mosher and Spiess (2004, 29–30) identify another proto-Laurentian component (c. 6,000–5,000 ^{14}C yrs BP) at Site 108.58, at the confluence of Mattamiscontis Stream and the Penobscot River. Zone III at this site produced a huge adze, a steep-bitted quartz endscraper, ridged hammerstones, slate point fragments, and quartz and Kineo rhyolite cobble cores. There were no side-notched, chipped stone projectile points, but they are found at nearby contemporary sites.

At N'tolonapemk, around this time (ca. 5,900–4,800 ^{14}C yrs BP) the inhabitants were using many of the tools of earlier periods, with the addition of short-channelled gouges, net sinkers, and thick projectile points with serrated margins (UMF-ARC 2002, 20–21). The Late Archaic component at the site suggests a larger occupation and produced a greater variety of animal remains, including deer, bear, loon, hare, and swordfish, and a greater variety of seeds and berries, including a possible sunflower seed fragment. One intriguing artifact dating to ca. 4,300 ^{14}C yrs BP is a stone animal figurine, resembling a sea mammal, that may have been a fishing lure, a gauge for making fishing nets, or a personal ornament (Soctomah et al. 2012; UMF-ARC 2002, 21).

Two styles of projectile points found on the Maritime Peninsula are reminiscent of Laurentian Tradition points. These are side-notched and triangular, "eared" points. Side-notched points are frequently large, with parallel to concave blade edges and basal grinding. Cognates are known from Ontario and New England, where they are identified with the "Otter Creek" style (e.g., Sanger 1975; Sanger et al. 1977). Radiocarbon dates associated with this side-notched style from other regions range from ca. 6,500–4,500 ^{14}C yrs BP (Ritchie 1980, 89). Sanger (2006, 238) suggests that it may not be a coincidence that these styles appear in the Maritime Peninsula during the development of hardwood forests, which is an attractive habitat for deer and moose.

The best-known Laurentian Archaic site in the Maritime Peninsula is the Hirundo site, in northern Maine (Sanger and MacKay 1973). Hirundo is located on the right bank of Pushaw Stream, which drains water from Pushaw Lake and, eventually, into the Penobscot River. Near the site is a long stretch of rapids that would have teamed with salmon, shad, and alewife during the spring spawning season (Sanger and MacKay 1973, 37). The exploitation of these anadromous fish species was probably the main reason for selecting this location as a campsite. Charcoal from a hearth feature dates the Laurentian component at this site to about 4,295 ± 95 ^{14}C yrs BP.

Assemblage 2 from this site contained numerous large, side-notched projectile points, as well as a perforated abrasive stone, slate points, rods, a shallow-grooved gouge, plummets, and a winged spearthrower weight. Sanger and MacKay (1973, 37) indicate that the stratigraphy for this site is ambiguous. Bourque (1995, 228) suggests that there is probably some mixing of components and that the Laurentian component probably predates the hearth feature. Excavation of a single component site with Vergennes-like elements, at site 95.20, on the Grand Falls drainage, produced three radiocarbon dates averaging 5,073 ± 112 ^{14}C yrs BP (Cox 1991). Bourque (1995, 228) notes that these are very close to Vergennes Phase dates from elsewhere in the Northeast.

The Laurentian projectile point styles represent another problem for determining the boundaries between coastal and interior populations, since they appear to be distributed throughout the Maritimes. Unfortunately, the only example found *in situ* is a large side-notched point recovered at the Big Clearwater Brook site (CdDq-1), at the mouth of the main Southwest Miramichi River. The point was recovered in the basal stratum of the site, which was separated by a thick sand layer from an overlaying ceramic-bearing deposit (Pearson 1962, 15), similar to the situation at the Transitional Archaic Boswell site in Nova Scotia (Deal et al. 2022). This site is one of several small sites along the upper Big Clearwater, which were popular with local collectors. Clarke (1974, 142ff.) describes this body of water as a cold, clear, rapid stream with two falls, which is well known for its salmon and trout populations. It is also an important transportation route connecting the central plateau (below the Southwest Miramichi) and the Tobique River areas.

Twelve large, side-notched specimens are also known from six site collections on the Chiputneticook Lakes and two specimens from Magaguadavic Lake, in southwestern New Brunswick (Deal 1984a). However, this style is rarely found east of the Saint John drainage. Deal and Rutherford (2001) report only 16 specimens, from 14 different sites in Nova Scotia (see Figure 30). Most of the Nova Scotian sites are distributed along the present northern coastline of both mainland Nova Scotia and Cape Breton Island, with some examples known from southern Cape Breton and the Gaspereau Lake and Lake Rossignol areas (Deal and Rutherford 2001). Erskine (1998, 29) reports the discovery of an agate specimen of this style that was unearthed from a diatomaceous earth deposit in Tiddville Marsh

(Factory Bog), Digby Neck, from a depth of about 1.2 m and measuring 12 cm in length and 3.5 cm in maximum width. An additional specimen was identified in a collection from Steele's Island, in Tatamagouche Bay (Deal 1996, 30), and specimens are also known from Savage Harbour and St. Peter's Bay, Prince Edward Island.

The triangular points are smaller in size and possess characteristic flaked "ears" at the base. Similar forms are known from southern New England, dating between ca. 5,000–4,000 ^{14}C yrs BP, and are identified with the "Lamoka" style (Ritchie 1980, 91). Seven specimens have been identified in five site collections from the Chiputneticook Lakes and one specimen from Magaguadavic Lake (Deal 1984). Deal and Rutherford (2001) report eight specimens from Nova Scotia: six from Gaspereau Lake, one from Rafter Lake, and one from Indian Gardens. Their distribution is primarily in the western half of Nova Scotia, and all three are located on large interior lakes beside stream or river outlets. A single specimen has been reported from the Wedge site, near Miminegash, Prince Edward Island (Sawicki 1984).

Coastal Late Archaic (5,000–3,800 ^{14}C yrs BP)

The coastal Late Archaic is characterized by coastal habitation sites and elaborate cemeteries. Subsistence patterns varied throughout the region. Swordfish, cod, and sturgeon are believed to have been important in the Gulf of Maine (Spiess 1992), while sea mammal hunting was more likely along the coasts of the Maritimes. Barbed and toggling harpoons, and bone and slate points, probably were used for harvesting seals and swordfish. Short-stemmed projectile points were used for hunting deer, moose, and possibly caribou in Nova Scotia. Beavers were important for their teeth and hides. Tools also included chipped stone butchering knives, bone scrapers, needles and awls, and ground stone woodworking tools. Woodworking tools likely were used in the construction of house frames, weir stakes, bowls, and artwork, and possibly dugout canoes. The diagnostic tool form of this period is the slate bayonet, which often is associated

5: THE LONG AGO PEOPLE

with burials. One burial collection of bayonets from Union, Maine, even had the impressions of a twine woven reed bag or mat etched across the artifacts (Bourque 1995; Whitehead 1987; Figure 33).

There has been considerable debate concerning the nature and origins of the coastal population of the Maritime Peninsula during the Late Archaic. The history of this debate is reviewed by Bourque (1995, 225–31). Byers (1959, 242) was the first researcher to suggest that coastal Archaic peoples of the Northeast, including Maine and the Maritimes, might have followed a marine adaptation, based partly on the recovery of swordfish remains at the Nevin site. Tuck (1984, 1991) opines that the coastal Late Archaic of the Maritimes and adjacent areas of Maine is a regional variant of a broader maritime cultural manifestation that extended from southern Maine to northern Labrador, and from the island of Newfoundland west to the St. Lawrence estuary. This "Maritime Archaic Tradition" focused on the hunting and fishing of marine species, although the major species exploited varied from region to region. Wright (1995, 180) suggests that cultural

Figure 33: Late Archaic slate bayonets from Union, Maine, with textile etching. Courtesy Bruce Bourque, Maine State Museum, Augusta.

similarities over this vast area during the Late Archaic probably can be attributed to a few interrelated factors, including "a shared technology, a similar way of life, interlocking trade networks, a common cosmological view, and the mobility of marriageable females" all within a framework of exogamous, partrilineal hunting societies. Because of the difficulty of establishing a long temporal continuity for the important Maritime Archaic traits south of the Gulf of St. Lawrence, Bourque prefers to view this period as a "horizon" that resulted from shared technologies and ceremonial behaviour (1995, 229–30) or distinct, but socially connected, cultures (2013, 150).

Bruce Bourque (1995) treats the Late Archaic of coastal Maine and southwestern New Brunswick and Nova Scotia as a separate development out of a local Middle Archaic culture. He has coined the term "Moorehead Phase" for this cultural manifestation (Bourque 1992, 26–39). Bourque has also identified a widespread coastal Archaic culture known as the Small Stemmed Point Tradition (dating to around 5,000 ^{14}C yrs BP) as the immediate ancestors of the Moorehead people (2013, 53–54). He suggests that their stemmed points, which often were made from white quartz, were fitted into sockets at the end of spear shafts. The Early Moorehead elongated oval whetstones with a hole for suspension first appear in a Small Stemmed Point context (Bourque 2012, 70). Furthermore, he points to evidence that these people were the first in the region to hunt swordfish, which was continued by their Moorehead descendants. Bourque (2012, 8) also notes that the Small Stemmed Point Tradition may have extended their range across the Bay of Fundy into Nova Scotia. Although the evidence for this surmise is presently equivocal (Tuck 1984, 27), it does fit with the later presence of Moorehead-like and Transitional Archaic material culture in southwestern Nova Scotia (e.g., Sanger 1991a). The clearest evidence of small, stemmed points was found at the Bain site, in southwestern Nova Scotia (Sanger and Davis 1991).

Bourque suggests that a trading partnership existed between Maine and Newfoundland and Labrador, and he feels that large, white pine dugout canoes may have been traded north (2013, 147). Although no Archaic period canoes have been found in the region, a white pine dugout canoe found at Val-Comeau, northeastern New Brunswick, was dated by dendrochronology to AD 1557 (Laroque 2013; Pickard et al. 2011). This find indicates that a precontact dugout canoe tradition existed in the region, but they may have been used alongside moosehide boats and birchbark canoes (Sanger 2009c). The fact that Moorehead burials have not been found east of Cow Point, on the Saint John River, may indicate the eastern portions of the Maritimes were largely bypassed. Long slate bayonets that characterize the coastal Archaic, possibly local stone imitations of swordfish bills, may also have been distributed to the north through trade, and possibly in exchange for Ramah chert points (Bourque 1994, 27). Bourque also identifies the north as a possible source for powdered red ochre, pyrite fire kits, and polished slate gouges with scoop-shaped cavities, while pie-shaped and wide hexagonal forms of bayonets may have western origins and were imported or copied locally (2013, 61, 80, 87, 96). According to Bourque (2013, 87–88), certain artifacts have ceremonial value and suggest that some of the Moorehead phase burials were those of shamans. The artifacts include Ramah chert points, mica, pyrites, exotic projectile point styles, polished northern woodworking tools, banded slate bayonets, woodpecker beaks, and shark teeth. On the other hand, local projectile point styles, adzes, gouges, plummets, fire kits, and water-worn pebbles are more representative of community membership.

The clearest evidence of coastal Late Archaic habitation sites comes from the Turner Farm and Stanley sites in Maine (Bourque 1975, 1995, 2012). No structures were uncovered in Occupation 2 at Turner Farm, but large working areas were identified, along with several hearth and pit features. Five human burials, with red ochre, were excavated, as well as five dog burials. This component also provided the first faunal assemblage from a Late Archaic site in the Maritime Peninsula. It included swordfish, seal, white-tailed deer, sea mink, a herring-sized fish, and soft-shell clam. Based on the faunal data, Bourque (1975) suggests a settlement pattern consisting of summer maritime hunting and fishing, fall and spring riverine fishing, and winter interior hunting. The Stanley site, on Monhegan Island, near Pemaquid, Maine, has not been systematically excavated, but the Stanley collection contains a similar range of material culture to Turner Farm (Figure 34), including a large sample of swordfish remains (Eldridge 2007; Sanger 1975, 62). No Late Archaic habitation sites have been excavated in the Maritimes, but ground slate points and bayonets are quite common from collections in this area (Deal and Rutherford 2001).

Subsistence patterns undoubtedly varied throughout the region. Swordfish (*Xiphias gladius*) and Atlantic cod (*Gadus morhua*) are believed to have been important marine resources in the Gulf of Maine (Spiess 1992; Spiess and Lewis 2001, 154), while sea mammal hunting was probably more important along the coasts of the Maritimes. Keenlyside (1999, 56;

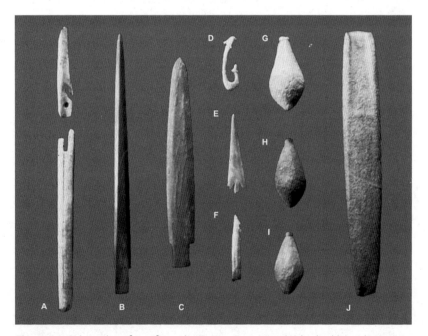

Figure 34: Selected artifacts from the Turner Farm site: (A) barbed bone harpoon and harpoon foreshaft of swordfish bill (*rostrum*), (B) narrow, hexagonal slate bayonet, (C) broad, hexagonal slate bayonet, (D) bone fishhook, (E) small, ground, slate point, (F) barbed bone point, (G–I) plummets, and (J) short-grooved gouge. Courtesy Bruce Bourque, Maine State Museum, Augusta.

Keenlyside 2001) has argued that walrus (*Odobenus rosmarus A.*) was an important resource in the Gulf of St. Lawrence region dating back to Late Palaeo times. Historically, this species was valued for its oil, hides, meat, and ivory. Walruses prefer islands, loose-ice, and shallow seas, and they were still widely distributed in the Gulf of St. Lawrence and North Atlantic coastal areas during the early historic period, and especially at Miscou Island, New Brunswick, the Magdalen Islands, and Sable Island (Kingsley 1998; McCaffrey 2016).

Keenlyside (1999, 59-61) notes the recovery of walrus remains from archaeological contexts in the Atlantic region, including a walrus tusk from the Middle Archaic L'Anse Amour burial, Labrador, and a walrus

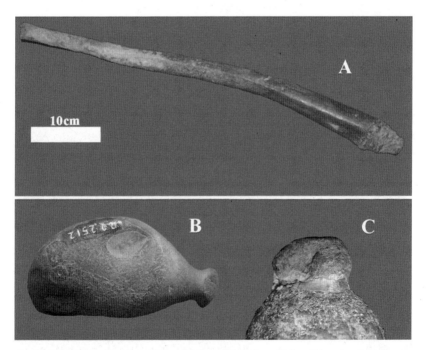

Figure 35: Selected artifacts from the Beausejour Beach site: (A) walrus baculum (*Os penis*), (B) plummet that appears to be a marine effigy, and (C) plummet exhibiting remnants of what has been tentatively identified as marine eelgrass (*Zostera* sp.) wound around the suspension groove. Photographs courtesy Colin MacKinnon, Emeritus, Canadian Wildlife Service, Sackville, New Brunswick.

ivory tool from the Late Archaic Port au Choix cemetery, Newfoundland (also see Keenlyside and Andreasen 2009, 375–77). He suggests that the large, ridged ulus recovered offshore in the Maritimes may have been lost while hunting and butchering walrus or seals along the fringes of ice flows. Large ovate bifaces, like one found near the mouth of the Aboushagan River, Robichaud, New Brunswick, may also have been used in sea mammal butchery (Leonard 2002, 6, Figure 15).

A cache of grooved plummets and a walrus baculum (*Os penis*) was found at site BlDb-10, Beausejour Beach, Cumberland Basin, Bay of Fundy (Figure 35; MacKinnon 2003a). Originally there were 48 specimens, but the total has gradually risen to 123, including one specimen with remnants of what has been tentatively identified as marine eelgrass (*Zostera* sp.) wound around the suspension groove (Colin MacKinnon, personal communication, 2012). A sample from the baculum has been AMS dated to 3,710 ± 50 ^{14}C yrs BP (Beta-139755, CMC-1537; D. Keenlyside personal communication, 2001). At 57 cm in length, this specimen is undoubtedly from a full-grown adult, and probably an individual over 15 years old (see Fay 1982, 35). Grooved (knobbed) plummets are generally thought to be net weights used in a coastal fishing technology. Arthur Spiess (personal communication, 2001) has suggested that the association of the baculum with plummets may indicate that it was used as a fishing club. Walrus baculum clubs are known from the central and western Arctic and the Northwest Coast of British Columbia (e.g., Mathiassen 1927, 83, 160).

An additional 45 grooved plummets have been reported in New Brunswick, and 52 in Nova Scotia. Only three specimens are known from Prince Edward Island, of which two pieces of uncertain provenance are in the McCord Museum collections (Moira McCaffrey, personal communication, 2001). Like the bayonets, they have not been found north of the Lakes region in New Brunswick. Bourque (2012, 71–72) identifies two distinct weight classes of plummet at Turner Farm, with smaller specimens weighing between 20 to 420 grams and larger specimens from 610 to 1260 grams. He suggests that the larger plummets were used as sinkers for cod fishing.

None of the Beausejour plummets fall in the larger size range (MacKinnon, personal communication, 2021). Some small plummets have zoomorphic shapes, including both aquatic and terrestrial mammals. One specimen was recovered by a scallop dragger in 2001 off Seacow Head, in the Northumberland Strait, which, according to David Keenlyside (2006), closely resembles a Stimpson's whelk (*Colus stimpsoni*). An even more spectacular specimen recovered from a Late Archaic cemetery at Portland

Figure 36: Late Archaic artifacts from Portland Point, Saint John: (A) ground slate knife or projectile point, (B–C) knobbed plummets, (D) plummet in the form of a sea mammal, and (E) ground stone object. Courtesy of the Government of New Brunswick.

Point, New Brunswick, which was used on the cover of Jim Tuck's 1984 volume (Figure 36), appears to represent a sea mammal (Harper 1956; Jeandron 1996, 11). One of the Beausejour plummets appears to be a crude fish effigy (MacKinnon, personal communication, 2012).

The recovery of large oyster shells along with Archaic period artifacts by scallop draggers off the coast of Maine sometimes indicates the presence of precontact oyster shell middens (Spiess et al. 1983b, 93). Evidence for Archaic shellfish exploitation has been found elsewhere in Maine and New England (Sanger and Belknap 1987; Brennan 1974). According to Spiess (2017, 111), clams and other shellfish may have been a primary source of protein for coastal people in Maine during both the Archaic and Woodland periods, and the location of clam beds during the Woodland may have been a major factor in settlement size, duration, and intensity. Marine biologists from Acadia University have documented a 4,400-year-old forest and an extensive oyster bed off Long Island in the Minas Basin (Bleakney and Davis 1983). This is consistent with a radiocarbon date of 4,200 ± 200 ^{14}C yrs BP acquired in 1955 from tree stumps in a drowned forest at nearly Avonport (Cameron 1956, 7). The Long Island oyster beds were exposed by an outflow channel of the Gaspereau River through the intertidal mud flats over two kilometres offshore. Oyster shells measuring up to 20 cm in length have been recovered, and three specimens produced an average radiocarbon date around 3,800 ^{14}C yrs BP. Today, oyster beds are found only in the warmer waters of northeastern Nova Scotia and Cape Breton Island (Stewart 1984), but oyster shells are relatively common in late precontact middens and oysters commonly appear in Mi'kmaw oral tradition (Black and Whitehead 1988, 17, 24). It is likely that the submerged oyster bed off Long Island and others along the Nova Scotian coast were utilized during Archaic times.

Moorehead and his crew excavated numerous boneless cemeteries and burials in Maine but came up empty in their survey of the Upper Saint John and St. Croix River drainages in New Brunswick (Moorehead 1922, 233–38; also see Belcher et al. 1994; Smith 1948). A large boneless cemetery was excavated at Cow Point, located on a channel between Grand and Maquapit lakes, New Brunswick, by David Sanger (see Vignette 10). Another small, disturbed cemetery was excavated by Russell Harper (1956) at Portland Point, in the Saint John harbour. It produced gouges, plummets, abraders, hammerstones, a ground slate point, and a plummet in the form of a marine effigy (Figure 36).

The Nevin site, near Blue Hills, Maine, has the best organic preservation of any of the Moorehead burials. Skeletal analyses of the 19 individuals buried at Nevin indicated that the Late Archaic population had a high protein diet and were in good health, with minimal indications of chronic disease (Bourque and Krueger 1994; Shaw 1988, 73). This site was excavated in the 1930s by Douglas Byers and Frederick Johnson of the Peabody Museum (Byers 1979). Organic artifacts included harpoon foreshafts made from swordfish bills, barbed harpoons, points and small bird darts, moose-bone daggers, needles, skate teeth beads, and even modified human bones. The incised designs on the moose-bone daggers from Nevin, along with the incised bayonets from Cow Point and elsewhere, may represent the earliest precontact decorative tradition in the Maritime Peninsula. A wide variety of design motifs was produced but, unfortunately, the symbolic significance for these motifs has been lost (Wright 1995, 210).

Sanger (1991a) considers that Moorehead phase peoples were also boating across the Bay of Fundy to southwestern Nova Scotia. In fact, the diagnostic slate bayonets seem to be more common in Nova Scotia than in New Brunswick. Deal and others (2006) report 55 slate bayonets that represent two basic subclasses. Twenty-nine specimens have long, narrow blades, with hexagonal or biconvex cross-sections, and straight or contracting stems. Decorative elements occur on three specimens. These are variants of the bayonets found at the Cow Point site (Sanger 1973a; Figures 37–38). Although relatively rare, these specimens are widely distributed.

The remaining 26 specimens are characterized by broad blades, hexagonal cross-sections, and contracting stems. Most of the stems are notched. Two of these specimens are relatively large and are believed to have come from naturally eroded burials. The workmanship on the slate bayonets is quite variable, and some examples of the smaller version of this class exhibit evidence of use-wear. Based on the stratigraphic record of graves at Cow Point, these functional slate bayonets may be the more recent of the two styles. Except for one specimen found on the Tantramar Marshes (Turnbull 1988), this form is found exclusively in western New Brunswick.

Ten slate projectile points were collected at Barren Lake, near the southwestern coast of Nova Scotia (Davis 1991c, plate 2). This area is closest to the northeastern coast of Maine, where this artifact class seems to occur most often (e.g., Smith 1948, 44–46; Willoughby 1935, 55ff.). The Nova Scotian examples can be characterized as barbed, biconvex in cross-section, and having a straight stem. A section of a ground slate

Figure 37: Portable stone artwork. Late Archaic: (A–C) engraved images on narrow slate bayonets from Cow Point; Woodland: (D–H) engraved pebbles from Holts Point. Courtesy of the Government of New Brunswick.

harpoon head found along the Mersey River, in southwestern Nova Scotia, is also believed to date to the Late Archaic (Deal et al. 2006, 262).

The "narrow-stemmed" points of this period have straight stems and straight blade-edges. Examples frequently exhibit the striking platform at the base of the stem. Shoulder form, predominantly rounded, differs from the frequently angular forms seen on examples from other parts of the Maritime Peninsula. Similar forms are dated at ca. 3,700 ^{14}C yrs BP in New Brunswick (Sanger 1973a) and ca. 5,000–4,000 ^{14}C yrs BP in Maine (Bourque

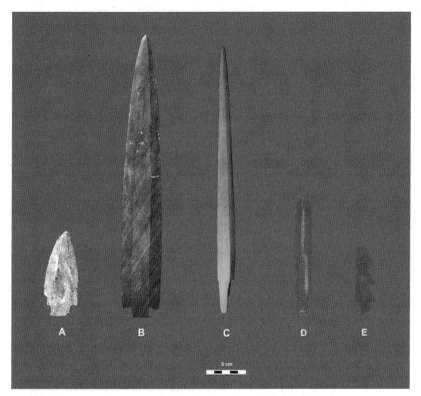

Figure 38: Late Archaic ground slate implements. (A) knife (Elmsdale, NS), (B) broad-bladed barbed bayonet (Milton, NS), (C) narrow-bladed, slate bayonet (Cow Point, NB, (D) knife with incised decoration (Indian Gardens, NS), and (E) barbed point (Mersey River, NS). (A–B) John S. Erskine Photograph Collection (E69). (C) courtesy of the Government of New Brunswick. (D–E) courtesy the Nova Scotia Museum.

1975, 40). At least 52 specimens are known from 25 site collections in Nova Scotia (Deal and Rutherford 2001). Their distribution in Nova Scotia is at principally interior riverine/lacustrine locations in the west. To date, no specimens have been recovered east of the Shubenacadie River.

Vignette 10: Cow Point

In 1914, Moorehead (1922, 233–38) and his excavation crew travelled extensively in northern Maine in search of "Red Paint" cemeteries. They also spent three weeks in western New Brunswick paddling and shovelling their way down the Saint John River. Fortunately, for later archaeologists, Moorehead was unaware of the Late Archaic burials excavated by amateurs in the Lakes region in the late nineteenth century. In fact, the collections at the New Brunswick Natural History Society museum included considerable Archaic materials from this region (Banville 1970). Wintemberg (1913) noted that the 13 ground stone bayonets in the collection were all from Grand and Maquapit lakes, and included a wide variety of styles, with diamond shaped, oval, elliptical, and oblong hexagonal cross-sections.

David Sanger was the first professional archaeologist to investigate the Grand Lake area. His excavation of the Cow Point cemetery (BlDn-2) is our model for Late Archaic burial practices in the region (Tuck 1978a, 1991, 39ff.). The 1970 fieldwork, along with earlier excavations by local collectors, uncovered at least 60 burial features (Sanger 1973a, 16; 1991b, 75). Radiocarbon dates from the site indicate that the cemetery was in use around 3,800 years ago. The artifact collection from this site is dominated by ground stone tools, including two classes of ground slate bayonets, two classes of celts, short-grooved gouges, grooved (knobbed) plummets, and three classes of abrasive stones. Thirteen of the slate bayonets exhibit delicate, incised decorations, with nine distinctive motifs, some of which were revived in later artistic traditions in the Atlantic region (Lee 1999; Figure 37). Sanger (2000, 152) notes that the ground slate points were "unsuited to offensive tasks," and may have been placed decoration-side-up to make a final spiritual connection between the deceased and the living during burial. The Cow Point collection included 76 narrow, ground slate bayonets, while 23 additional specimens are known from other sites, including at least 13 from the Lakes region, two from the Oromocto River drainage, three from Lake Utopia, and three from the Reversing Falls Portage Route in the city of Saint John. Five of the specimens from the Lakes region exhibit incised designs like those from Cow Point (e.g., Kain 1901). Only 11 of the broad-bladed slate points are known to be from New Brunswick, including eight from Cow Point, one from an unspecified site in the Lakes region, one from Spednic Lake, and two fragments of a single specimen found below water in front of the Canal Beach site, Lake Utopia (Suttie 2007, 43).

Transitional (or Terminal) Archaic

Towards the end of the Late Archaic there is a new cultural presence in the Maritime Peninsula. It is generally agreed that there was a movement of people, identified with the Susquehanna Tradition, into the region as early as 4,000 ^{14}C yrs BP (Bourque 1992, 39–43, Bourque 1995; Deal 1986; Sanger 1975, 2005, 23–24; Spiess et al. 1983b, 97–98; Tuck 1991). The Susquehanna (Transitional Archaic) people can be characterized by a distinctive tool-making tradition and the practice of cremation burial. They made broad-bladed, stemmed projectile points and drills. These points are also known as "broadpoints" or "broadspears" and are related to similar styles of the "Savannah River Complex." The named styles that have cognates in the Maritime Peninsula are "Atlantic/Snook Kill," "Susquehanna Broad," and "Orient Fishtail." These three styles represent distinct phases in Transitional Archaic technological development. Each of these styles has been identified at the Boswell site, Nova Scotia (Campbell 2016; Deal et al. 2022). In the south, these point styles are also associated with spearthrowers and grooved axes. The distribution of broadpoints in New England also corresponds with the distribution of steatite (soapstone) bowls. The Susquehanna were originally considered to be the technological innovators responsible for the transition, via soapstone vessels, towards the use of pottery in the Northeast (Tuck 1978b, 37–39). However, Kenneth Sassaman

(1999, 93) points out that soapstone technology was not part of the original migration but was adopted in some areas at least 200 years later and was contemporary with early pottery traditions. The relationship between the Susquehanna Tradition and other interior and coastal groups is a matter of debate, as is their relationship in time to historic Indigenous cultures in the Maritime Peninsula (Wright 1995, 181). Turnbull and Allen (1988, 255) indicate that the Susquehanna appear to mark the beginning of closer cultural contacts with continental areas, as opposed to the North Atlantic.

The argument for a Transitional Archaic migration into the Maritime Peninsula is based on criteria derived from Rouse's (1958) research on migration theories (see Sanger 1975; Bourque 1995, 252–53). First, a homeland for the tradition can be identified in southern New England, with ties to archaeological cultures in the southeast. Second, elements of the Susquehanna tool assemblages appear over a broad area of eastern North America in a short period of time, around 3,800 BP (Bourque 1995, 253). Third, environmental conditions were favourable. Swordfish and deer are believed to be important species to the resident Late Archaic population, but not critical resources for Susquehanna Archaic peoples. Sanger (1975, 61; 2006, 242) points out that after 5,000 ^{14}C yrs BP the increase in tidal amplitude caused a decrease in the numbers of swordfish in the Gulf of Maine and a concomitant increase in the soft-shell clam. Bourque (2012, 49; Bourque et al. 2008) remarks that overfishing is an important factor in the disappearance of swordfish and decline of large cod by 3,600 ^{14}C yrs BP, which were replaced by meso-predators like flounder, sculpin, and dogfish. The cooling climate was unfavourable to deer. Fourth, Sanger (1975) points out that all systems of this archaeological culture are present in Maine and adjacent New Brunswick. Both habitation and mortuary sites have been identified, as well as a toolkit comparable to those of southern New England. By contrast, the later Adena manifestation in the Maritime Peninsula appears to be represented only by a mortuary subsystem. Fifth, Sanger points out that no suitable alternate model has been put forward.

Dincauze (1975, 27) agrees with the migration hypothesis but suggests that it was a movement of small groups of people, with a distinctive technology, rather than a mass migration. Certainly, the Transitional Archaic presence is stronger in Maine than in the Maritimes, with only transient population east of the St. Croix River drainage and southwestern Nova Scotia. However, Bourque (1995, 247) sees the migration as a movement of large groups of people into Maine following the demise of the Moorehead phase. Bourque also feels that this migration was a short-term (c. 3,800–3,500 BP) infiltration of an exploratory nature. He bases this interpretation on significant north–south differences in technology (i.e., the scarcity of steatite bowls and spearthrower weights) and what he sees as a one-way, north–south distribution of exotic lithics (Bourque 1995, 247).

It was originally thought that they did not move beyond the Saint John drainage in New Brunswick and the Shubenacadie River in southwestern Nova Scotia (Deal and Rutherford 2001). However, the presence of a Late Transitional Archaic component at the Beausejour Beach site (BlDb-10), on the extreme eastern end of the Bay of Fundy (MacKinnon 2003b), and possible fishtail-like projectile points in collections in Prince Edward Island, point to a late push to parts of the far eastern Maritime Peninsula (Deal et al. 2006). Many of the grooved axes in collections from the Maritimes probably also date to this period. It is rare to find more than one specimen associated with any given site, although a small cache of Transitional Archaic grooved axes and celts is reported by Davis (1982) from a site (BfDr-8) on a small islet off the southeast coast of Deer Island, Passamaquoddy Bay.

The "Northeastern Susquehanna Tradition" is characterized by a more diversified subsistence pattern than that of the resident Archaic populations. Sites are located both on coastal and interior riverine and lacustrine locations. Tuck (1978b) suggests a deer-bear-moose hunting focus. Evidence from Turner Farm indicates that coastal groups also exploited deer, seals, waterfowl, cod, and shellfish (Spiess and Lewis 2001, 155). Wright (1995, 192) points out that early coastal fishing technology in

New England is demonstrated by the Boyleston Fish Weir site in Boston (Décima and Dincauze 1998), as well as on Sabasticook Lake in central Maine (Peterson et al. 1994). Tuck (1991, 53) suggests that the richness of resources evident at Turner Farm might not be applicable to other Transitional Archaic sites along the Gulf of Maine/Bay of Fundy coast. At interior sites, anadromous fish exploitation is indicated by calcined fish bones and characteristics of site location (Borstel 1982; Deal 1985; UMF-ARC 2002). Sanger (2006, 243) points out that the Susquehanna originated in the mid-Atlantic region, where they were adapted to hardwood forests and nut-bearing trees. Evidence from Maine indicates the use of beechnuts at Turner Farm and acorns at sites along the Kennebec River and Merrymeeting Bay (Bourque et al. 2006; Spiess and Hedden 2000). A decrease in dependence on the dugout canoe in favor of birchbark canoes may have begun during Transitional Archaic, or even earlier (Sanger 2009c). According to Betts and Hrynick (2021, 149) this would fit with an economic model in which birchbark canoes were used to access the headwaters of major rivers and hardwood forests of the interior, and especially for nut-gathering. In other words, the birchbark canoe was the ideal vehicle for exploiting interior resources.

Early Transitional Archaic (ca. 4,000–3,400 ^{14}C yrs BP)

The Turner Farm site provides our best evidence of the Early Transitional Archaic in Maine (Bourque 1975, 1995). The Susquehanna Archaic occupation, which dates to about 3,600 ^{14}C yrs BP, includes three basin-shaped "living floors" covered with beach gravel and littered with bone and artifact refuse. The living floors range from three to five metres in diameter. One of these living floors is encircled with fire-cracked rock, suggesting a tent ring, and another feature is partially encircled by post moulds, suggesting a wood-framed structure (Bourque 1975, 39; Tuck 1991, 53). The lithic component includes broad-bladed projectile points, drills, chipped stone knives, scrapers, and pestles. Several other Susquehanna components have been identified at sites in northern Maine (Bourque 1992, 39–43; Cox 2021, 30–32).

Transitional Archaic cremation burials have been found intruding on earlier Archaic red ochre burials, as at the Walter B. Smith site on Alamoosook Lake (Moorehead 1922, 140; also see Borstel 1982). An extensive cemetery was discovered at Turner Farm, which was only explored to determine its limit (Bourque 1995 145–65). Two burial clusters were uncovered: earlier unburned inhumations in the south and secondary cremation burials in the north. Cremation burials include some elaborate bone and antler artifacts, which are sometimes ceremonially "killed." The burials include well-designed marine hunting equipment and artifacts with symbolic importance, including maxillae of wolf, fox, and bobcat, and turtle-shell rattle fragments with associated small quartz pebbles. Also included were decorated bone objects, incised bone "gaming pieces," and 12 small cylindrical copper beads (Bourque 1995). A single Transitional Archaic cremation burial has also been identified at Ruisseau-des-Caps, in the Gaspé area (Dumais 1978). The burial is situated on a terrace, about 20 m above the St. Lawrence River. It consists of an elliptical-shaped pit, about 25 cm deep, and 1.2 m long, with its long axis oriented to the north. The burial contained small, calcined bone fragments without red ochre, and has been dated to $3,720 \pm 90$ ^{14}C yrs BP. The grave inclusions were utilitarian items, including two broad-bladed projectile points, a drill and drill tip, biface fragments, a possible pestle, and an abrading stone.

In New Brunswick, the densest occupation of Early Transitional period peoples is along the Chiputneticook–St. Croix drainage and Passamaquoddy Bay, where their material culture has been identified at several sites, including the Bliss Islands, Deer Island, Teacher's Cove, Canal Beach, and Site BgDq-39 near Pennfield (Black 2000, 94; Black 2018; Davis 1978, plate Vd, h; Suttie 2007; Suttie and Nicholas 2012; Suttie et al. 2013). However, the only excavation of an undisturbed Early Transitional component is at Mud Lake Stream (Deal 1986; Vignette 11). Transitional Archaic artifacts are relatively rare east of the St. Croix River drainage, but a few diagnostic broad-bladed projectiles have been identified along the Saint John River drainage, in surface-collected materials from Woodstock, Grand

Lake, and Portland Point. The Portland Point component consists of seven artifacts recovered from disturbed contexts (Harper 1956), including three Transitional Archaic projectile points, a drill, and three soapstone bowl fragments (Jeandron 1996, 12–13). The projectile points include a complete "Snook Kill" specimen and basal fragments representing two Late Archaic styles. Brent Suttie (2007, 44) reported three additional Transitional Archaic specimens (a drill and two projectile points) from a disturbed context at the Canal Beach site, Lake Utopia.

A site at Beausejour Beach (DlDb-10) extends the reach of Transitional Archaic to the eastern end of the Bay of Fundy (MacKinnon 2003b). A Transitional Archaic component was identified stratigraphically about 3 m above the Late Archaic component, which was associated with a submerged forest. The component consists of a fire-related feature and a nearby scatter of stone tools. The feature contained fire-cracked rock, charcoal, bone, lithic detritus, and red ochre. Faunal specimens from the feature were identified as knuckle bones of black bear (*Ursus americana*). The artifacts included a bifacial knife, a chipped adze with ground bit, and three broad-bladed projectile points. Originally, the site was in a forested area above the bay. Two charcoal samples from the hearth were dated to 3,270 ± 60 ^{14}C yrs BP (Beta-176431) and 3,330 ± 70 ^{14}C yrs BP (Beta-176432). These dates seem to be late for the tool forms recovered at the site, which may indicate that the feature is from a separate Late Transitional component.

More than 20 Nova Scotia sites have produced Transitional Archaic material culture (Deal et al. 2006), mostly in southwestern Nova Scotia. Several sites cluster along the Lake Rossignol–Mersey River and the Gaspereau Lake–Gaspereau River drainage systems. In 1967, John Erskine identified an Early Transitional Archaic component at the Gaspereau Lake site (BfDb-05), which consisted of six broad-bladed projectile points and a fully grooved axe (Erskine 1998; Murphy 1998; see Figure 31). A large ground stone adze was recovered at Pennfield, which has been dated to ca. 4,000 cal. BP (Brezicki 2015, 29, 34), while two grooved celts were recovered at the Boswell site, which show evidence of being used in a grubbing or pulling motion (Campbell 2015, 161). A ¾ grooved axe in the George Frederick Clarke collection from Moosehead Lake, Maine (Brzezicki 2015, 212), as well as a finely crafted specimen recovered at Melanson by Ellis Gertridge (Figure 39), probably date to this period.

Laybolt (1999) identified six additional sites on Gaspereau Lake with Transitional Archaic material culture. Since 2007, CRM Group has been testing sites on Gaspereau Lake and has identified five sites with Transitional Archaic components and the familiar range of tools, including broad-bladed projectile points, drills, and large end scrapers like those identified by David Sanger in Passamaquoddy Bay (Sanders 2014). Sanders and others (2014) recently reported Transitional Archaic artifacts from a cluster of four sites along the Mersey River. Broad-bladed projectile points have also been recovered at Indian Gardens (BbDg-10), Bear River (BdDk-4), Eel Weir VI (BbDh-6) (Christianson 1985, 9; Connolly 1977; Ferguson 1986), and Governors Island, on the Lahave River (Pentz 2013, 76). Site locations in Nova Scotia suggest a preference for river outlets on large lakes, although rising sea levels may have inundated coastal sites.

Importantly, a collection from Tusket Falls (AiDi-17), near Yarmouth, includes eight projectile points, a drill,

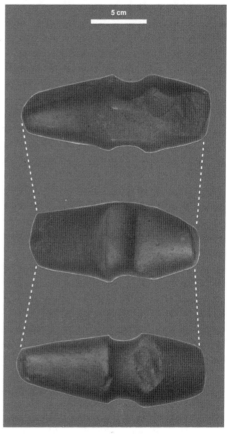

Figure 39: Three views of a Transitional Archaic ¾-grooved maul (or axe) from Melanson, Nova Scotia (Ellis Gertridge Collection). Compiled from photographs by Michael Deal.

5: THE LONG AGO PEOPLE

and a shallow-grooved gouge (Davis 1991b; Glen 2016, 19, Figure 9; Sanger and Davis 1991, 70). Sanger (2006, 243) noted that some of the Tusket Falls artifacts appeared to be made from rhyolites with coastal Maine affinities. He thinks that Transitional Archaic peoples from Maine were making 160-km canoe trips to southern Nova Scotia (Sanger 1991a; Sanger 2006, 243). Burke (2006, 415) also notes that small amounts of North Mountain lithics have been reported in Archaic sites in the Penobscot River Valley of Maine, suggesting a persistent connection between the two areas over time.

The base of a broad-bladed point was collected, along with a biface, along the Annapolis River at the Boswell Site, in South Farmington, in 2009 (Deal 2013). A chipped stone celt with a ground bit was found on the same

Figure 40: Selection of Transitional Archaic artifacts from the Boswell and Wilkins sites, 2011–2016: (A) bipointed biface (Wilkins), (B) ovate-base biface, (C–D) contracting stem points, (E) broad contracting stem projectile point, (F) contracting stem projectile point, (G) expanding stem strike-a-light, (H–I) complete and partial drills, and (J–K) celts. Photograph by John Campbell.

property, which is like specimens from southwestern New Brunswick and northern Maine in Transitional Archaic or Early Woodland contexts (e.g., Sanger 2008, 21–33). Since 2015 work at the deeply stratified Boswell site uncovered a large assemblage of Transitional Archaic artifacts from two distinct components (Figures 40–41; Campbell 2016; Deal et al. 2022).

Figure 42 represents the north wall profile of Unit 55 at Boswell and illustrates the stratigraphic column for the main excavation area. Level 1,

Figure 41: Stepped excavation at the Boswell Site, 2014, showing John Campbell and Erin McKee collecting and recording samples for paleoethnobotanical and paleoenvironmental study. Excavating in the background are Josh McLearn and Jodi Howe. Photograph by Michael Deal.

which has the most organic content, has two subdivisions: Level 1a is the sod layer, with actively growing vegetation. Level 1b corresponds to the Late Woodland deposit in Area 1 but appears to be culturally sterile in Area 2. Level 2 is a layer of burnt sediments and charcoal, which overlays two Middle Woodland deposits (Levels 3–4) and is believed to represent the remnants of a forest fire. Level 5 is a sterile fluvial deposit about 40–50 cm deep. Level 6 is the Late Transitional Archaic deposit. It overlays another fluvial deposit, about 20 cm deep (Level 7). Level 8 is the Early Transitional Archaic deposit. Level 9 is another sterile fluvial deposit, which extends to the 2.5-m depth limit of the excavation. Four radiocarbon dates from the early component range from 3,710–3,606 ^{14}C yrs BP (4,144–3,849 cal BP),

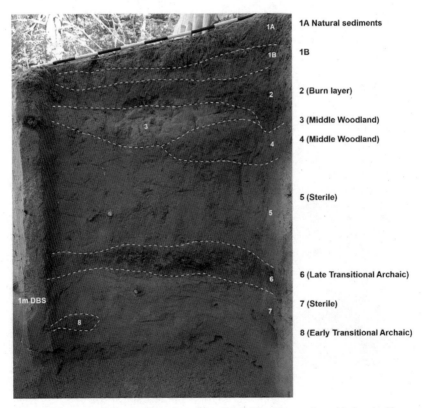

Figure 42: Boswell site north wall profile of Unit 55 with stratigraphic levels. Photograph by Michael Deal, 2018.

while two late component dates range from 3,288–3,211 ^{14}C yrs BP (3,570–3,362 cal BP). One of the early features at the site is interpreted as a lithic knapping station, based on a distinctive cluster of thousands of rhyolite flakes and a perforated abrading stone (Deal et al. 2022).

The lithic artifacts exhibit a wide range of raw materials, including some imported (e.g., Vinalhaven and Kineo rhyolite) and some local (e.g., North Mountain rhyolites and White Rock quartzite) materials. The Annapolis River has long been a highway for the movement of people and trade between central and southwest Nova Scotia. Similar deeply stratified sites excavated in central Maine have aided in the revision of the cultural sequence in that area (Mack and Clark 2016; Putnam 1994; Sanger et al. 2003), and it is likely that the Boswell site will allow for a revised interpretation of the Archaic–Woodland transition in central Nova Scotia (see below).

Late Transitional Archaic (ca. 3,400–3,000 14C yrs BP)

In Maine, broad-bladed projectile points and knives seem to disappear by 3400 ^{14}C yrs BP (Spiess and Petersen 2000). However, there is growing evidence for a Late Transitional Archaic presence in the region, in the form of broad, side-notched (fishtail-like) projectile point styles (as at the Boswell site). The fishtail style appears to be a variant (or re-invention) of the "Orient" fishtail style of New England. Steatite bowls are also believed to be associated with these later styles but are rare on the Maritime Peninsula. Ground stone tools in general appear to get smaller during this period (Brzezicki 2015, 29).

Passamaquoddy Bay and Cobscook Bay are referred to as the Quoddy region. Due to coastal erosion, the Transitional Archaic represents the earliest coastal archaeological record for this region, but that record is relatively limited (Sanger 2012, 252). Earlier artifacts have been found offshore. David Black (2000; 2022, 84) identifies a Late Transitional Archaic assemblage in the intertidal zone at the Rum Beach site (BgDq-24) in Passamaquoddy Bay, which he dates to between 3,600 and 3,000 ^{14}C yrs BP. This site has produced distinctive Late Traditional Archaic tool forms and exotic lithics like those found at Maine sites. In 2018, he updated the Rum Beach inventory and reviewed other collections from Pasamaquoddy Bay. He believes the Quoddy region was fully integrated into a broadpoint (Transitional) Archaic "interaction sphere" (Black 2018, 65). Sanger (2008) believes that it is more like a stylistically similar cultural pattern, but that the Quoddy Transitional Archaic was a distinct manifestation. He points out that the few known Transitional sites in the Cobscook Bay area, such as Eastport (or Moose Island) and N'tolonapemk, have Transitional Archaic assemblages that are quite different from those recorded further south. He describes a Quoddy Transitional Archaic with slightly different projectile points, large scrapers, and an incipient blade tool tradition (Sanger 2012, 262). In fact, he identified the large unifacial scraper, like those found at Teacher's Cove, Carson, St. Croix Island, Eastport, and N'tolonapemk, as the defining artifact of the Quoddy Transitional Archaic. Black (2022, 102) notes that Transitional Archaic peoples of the Quoddy region preferred dull-coloured, porphyritic, and flow-banded rhyolites, obtained either locally or through exchange.

Sanger (2008, 31) believes that easterly expansion along the Maine coast would have been inhibited by the combined effects of a dense spruce-fir forest, with few nut-bearing trees, and a less productive and more hostile littoral (seashore) zone. He favours the portage route that connects the Penobscot River with both the St. Croix and Saint John rivers via the Eel River (known historically as the "Maliseet Trail"). This scenario could explain the early component at Mud Lake Stream, and the later appearance of Transitional Archaic material culture to the south in Pasamaquoddy Bay and the Lower Saint John River Valley. Blair (2004b) identifies a Late Transitional Archaic presence ca. 3,000–2,870 ^{14}C yrs BP (3,390–2,930 cal BP) on the lower Saint John River, based on radiocarbon dates from the Fulton Island and Jemseg Crossing sites.

Additional evidence for a Late Transitional Archaic presence in New Brunswick exists in the form of steatite bowls recovered from two sites in the Lakes region, and vessel fragments from the Portland Point and Bentley

Street sites in Saint John (Jeandron 1996, 12; Suttie 2005, 44–45). The two nearly complete bowls from Maquapit (or French) and Oromocto lakes (Figure 43) are like the two-lugged varieties reported for New England (Fowler 1966b), where they most likely originated. Suttie (2005, 44) suggests that the Oromocto bowl may have been ceremonially "killed" (intentionally broken) to accompany a deceased individual, a practice that has been reported elsewhere in the Northeast (Ritchie 1980, 170).

The tidal expansion of the Minas Basin coincides with the Late Transitional Archaic in Nova Scotia (ca. 3,400 ^{14}C yrs BP). On the eastern edge of the Chignecto Peninsula, evidence of Transitional Archaic occupation has been found at a site at Qospemk (Neville Lake), which dates to around 3,300 ^{14}C yrs BP (Lelièvre et al. 2022). To the west of the Minas Basin, at the Boswell site, two radiocarbon dates are associated with hearth features from a distinct Late Transitional Archaic component, which generally

Figure 43: Steatite bowl recovered by Moses H. Perley at Oromocto Lake in 1896. Courtesy the Government of New Brunswick.

lacks rhyolite, and includes fishtail-style (wide, side-notched projectile points) dated to ca. 3,288 ± 24 ^{14}C yrs BP; UOC-8802, and native copper nodules (ca. 3,311 ± 38 ^{14}C yrs BP; UOC-1207). These nodules comprise the earliest known use of copper in the Maritimes, while Early Transitional copper beads at Turner Farm are the earliest in the larger Maritime Peninsula. Fishtail-like points have been identified from three areas of Prince Edward Island, including two specimens from the Canavoy site (CcCq-1) in Savage Harbour and three from sites in St. Peter's Bay (Deal et al. 2006). Early Woodland, Meadowood-style points are also well represented in the Canavoy collection. Another fishtail-like specimen is recorded for Robinson's Island (CcCt-1), Rustico Bay, which is made from Ramah chert.

Vignette 11: Mud Lake Stream

BkDw-5 produced the first *in situ* Transitional Archaic component identified in the Maritimes. The site is situated below a series of rapids on Mud Lake Stream, which drains Mud Lake into Spednic Lake (Figure 44). The Transitional (Susquehanna) component is represented by two features in the basal stratum of the site. Charcoal samples from the two features date the component to

Figure 44: Mud Lake Stream site in foreground, southwestern New Brunswick. Courtesy the Government of New Brunswick.

5: THE LONG AGO PEOPLE

Figure 45: Stemmed projectile points from Mud Lake Stream. Courtesy the Government of New Brusnwick.

about 4,000 years ago. These features produced 14 broad-bladed points and fragments like the Snook Kill style of New England (Figure 45), as well as three drill fragments, two small bifaces, and a chipped stone celt. A fully grooved axe and an ovate plummet, which were collected on the beach in front of the site, are believed to be part of the Transitional Archaic component. A stemmed graver recovered at the Diggity site (DjDu-17), Spednic Lake (Deal 1984b), is stylistically like the Mud Lake Stream specimens and may be a reworked stemmed point (also see Ritchie 1980, 151). The chipped stone tool assemblage from this site is very similar to that of the Hirundo/Young sites (Borstel 1982). Eight of the chert specimens are made from a poor grade of chert and are heavily bleached. The only faunal remains recovered from the component were 31 calcined fish bones, 14 of which have been identified as alewife, or gaspereau (*Alosa pseudoharengus*; Deal 1986, 89).

Certain factors indicate a possible ceremonial or mortuary function for feature 1, which contained seven large bifaces and the calcined fish bones (Figure 46). These include the presence of charcoal, a relatively high phosphorous content, predominantly heat-damaged artifacts, and the presence of what appear to be "killed" (intentionally damaged) artifacts, while the lack of both red ochre and human remains is not uncommon in Early Transitional Archaic features (Borstel 1982, 61; Dincauze 1975, 29, 31). Dincauze (1975, 31) proposes a possible relationship between ceremonial features and spring fishing sites like Mud Lake Stream.

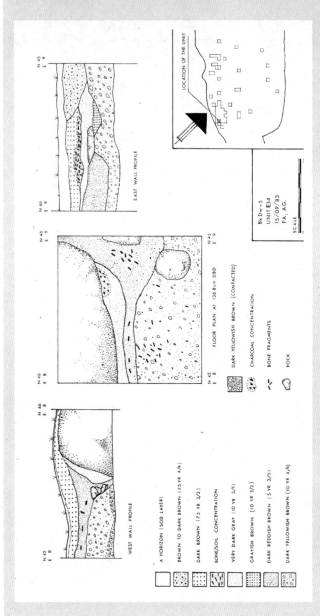

Figure 46: Feature 1, Mud Lake Stream. Drawing by Angel Gómez-Miguelanez, Archaeological Services, Fredericton. Courtesy the Government of New Brunswick.

Archaic–Early Woodland Transition

The transition from Archaic to Woodland in the Maritimes is often a contentious issue. In 1975, Sanger suggested that the Transitional Archaic (Susquehanna) Tradition may be the basis for later Algonquian-speaking cultures in Maine and New Brunswick. In 1984, Tuck argued that the Maritime (Coastal) Archaic are more likely ancestors for later Indigenous peoples in the Maritimes, based on the lack of Transitional Archaic sites in eastern portions of New Brunswick and Nova Scotia. Rutherford (1990a), in his study of Late Archaic and Early Woodland projectile points, found a greater similarity between Moorehead Phase (Coastal) Late Archaic points and Early Woodland points. He completely rules out a connection between the Transitional Archaic and Early Woodland biface technology and favours an *in situ* development from the resident Late Archaic population. Rutherford's conclusions are generally in agreement with those of Tuck (1991), yet he differentiates between Moorehead and Maritime Archaic populations.

Wright (1999, 575–76) presents four possible scenarios for the transition from Archaic to Woodland manifestations in the Maritimes. First, the Early Woodland people descended from the local Transitional Archaic (Susquehanna-derived) culture. Second, they descended from an Indigenous culture that arose from a Late Archaic base, which readily interacted with peoples to the south and north and shared several material and mortuary traits. Third, they were an amalgam of intrusive Transitional Archaic people and local Indigenous peoples. Finally, there was a territorial divide during the Transitional Archaic period between the western and eastern portions of New Brunswick and Nova Scotia, which presumably dissolved by 2,500 ^{14}C yrs BP. Wright suggests that options two or four are the most likely, based on available information. In any event, Wright (1999, 582) suggests that the Transitional Archaic contracting stem projectile point forms gave rise to the parallel, expanding, and pointed stem forms of the later Woodland.

The impact of the Transitional Archaic expansion in New Brunswick and Nova Scotia is quite different. Some Transitional Archaic influence reached the Quoddy region, but it is not a well-defined tradition (Sanger 2008, 20). Black (2000, 101) sees a continuity from fishtail forms to wide, side-notched Early Woodland forms in the Quoddy region. Blair (2004b, 293–395) suggests that the Saint John River Valley was the cultural boundary for the spread of the Transitional Archaic, and that there is not a sharp delineation between Late Transitional Archaic and Early Woodland in that area. When Sanger returns to the evidence from western New Brunswick in 2012, he argues that the Transitional Archaic manifestation in the Quoddy region (c. 3,400–3,000 ^{14}C yrs BP) represents a distinctive littoral zone adaptation with links via interior waterways to the Saint John River and, furthermore, that this can be linked to the historic cultural developments of the Wolastoqiyik and Peskotomuhkatiyik.

There appears to be a more robust presence of the Transitional Archaic in Nova Scotia. At the Boswell site, we see a strong Early Transitional Archaic component, with several examples of imported lithics, which may be slightly later than the Transitional Archaic component at Mud Lake Stream. This situation is followed by a depositional gap at the site, then a Late Transitional Archaic component, with projectile point styles and lithic materials that closely resemble Early Woodland material culture. There is no Early Woodland (Meadowood-like) component at Boswell such as that found at Mud Lake Stream (Deal 1986), which may indicate that the Boswell Late Transitional Archaic component is a true transitional Archaic/Woodland component, especially if Wright's scenario four is correct. If option four is correct, we may be seeing at least three separate regions at this time, namely, southwestern New Brunswick (the St. Croix and Saint John river drainages and the Quoddy region), southwestern Nova Scotia, and eastern New Brunswick, Prince Edward Island, and central-eastern Nova Scotia (see Sanger 2008, 2). Other Early Woodland peoples to the west may also have a bearing on the origins of the modern Indigenous populations (McEachen 1996).

Increasing Cultural Complexity

The Archaic (Long Ago) people left a complicated archaeological record on the Maritime Peninsula. The record for the Early and Middle Archaic (ca. 9,500–6,000 ^{14}C yrs BP) has been seriously compromised by rising sea levels and by the fact that existing sites are often deeply buried along the major river systems. Over the Archaic period, the population gradually increased and settlements expanded to fill the landscape. For over four millennia of Archaic development, populations had to adapt to climatic changes and fluctuating resource richness. Populations on the Maritime Peninsula adopted different technology and economic practices from those of peoples to the south, due to a cooler and wetter environment.

The first distinctive cultural tradition to be recognized is the Gulf of Maine Archaic, an Early and Middle Archaic technological tradition that developed in the Gulf of Maine watershed. This area includes coastal northern Maine, southwestern New Brunswick, and the Bay of Fundy coast of Nova Scotia. Eastern New Brunswick, Prince Edward Island, and eastern Nova Scotia may have been more focused on the Gulf of St. Lawrence and Atlantic seacoast, but with a similar technology. Early and Middle Archaic toolkits are characterized by a variety of ground stone tool forms, chipped quartz unifaces, full-channelled gouges, rods, and non-diagnostic projectile point styles. By the Middle Archaic, the ulu was added to the kit. Local raw materials were preferred over exotic lithics. In the Gulf of Maine watershed, this new toolkit was devised to exploit wetland, riverine, and lacustrine habitats, with large and small mammals, anadromous and catadromous fish species (e.g., alewife and eel), waterfowl, reptiles, and shellfish. The Gulf of Maine burial complex featured red ochre and burials on ridges, away from settlements.

The Late Archaic (ca. 6,000–3,800 ^{14}C yrs BP) features distinct interior and coastal cultural traditions. The interior manifestation may be an extension of the Laurentian Tradition, which extends westward to the Great Lakes and northward to the Gulf of St. Lawrence drainage. Some authors believe that Laurentian peoples migrated eastward into central Maine and

New Brunswick. Others believe that the interior tradition developed out of the existing Middle Archaic population, with the addition of Laurentian side-notched projectile points, ulus, and plummets. The change in technology is associated with the development of mixed hardwood forests and a hunting/fishing subsistence pattern focused on white-tail deer, beaver, rabbit, and anadromous fish. The coastal Archaic is identified as the Moorehead Tradition, which shares many similarities with the Maritime Archaic of Newfoundland and Labrador, and the north shore of Quebec. This adaptation was maritime and based on fishing and sea mammal hunting that varied by area (e.g., swordfish in the Gulf of Maine and seals and walrus along the Gulf of St. Lawrence and Atlantic coasts). The Moorehead Tradition developed out of an earlier Indigenous tradition, with the addition of swordfish swords and slate bayonets (some spiritual and some utilitarian). They appear to have carried on an active trading relationship with the Maritime Archaic, which brought Ramah chert south from Labrador and bayonets towards the north. The Moorehead burial tradition probably developed out of the earlier red ochre burial tradition.

The Transitional (Terminal) Archaic (ca. 4,000–3,000 ^{14}C yrs BP) appears to usher in closer ties to Archaic populations to the south and west, rather than the North Atlantic. It is generally agreed that, at this time, there was a migration of people from what is today New England into the Maritime Peninsula. The migrating group is usually identified as the Susquehanna Tradition, which brought a distinctive tool tradition and the practice of cremation burial. Their toolkit included broad-bladed projectile points and drills, along with new tool forms, like grooved axes, pestles, and the weighted spearthrower. They followed a more diversified subsistence pattern, which included both coastal and interior resources. Coastal sites utilized deer, seals, waterfowl, cod, and shellfish, while interior sites exploited nut trees (e.g., beech and oak), bear, deer, moose, and anadromous fish (e.g., alewife). The nature and extent of the migration are debated. Those migrating from New England appear to have had a strong presence in northern Maine and southwestern Nova

Scotia, weaker in southwestern New Brunswick, and only transient in the rest of the Maritime Peninsula.

The Early Transitional Archaic (ca. 4,000–3,400 ^{14}C yrs BP) is best known from the Turner Farm site in Maine. This site produced habitations that likely had circular, wood-framed structures and tents, and a cemetery with both inhumation and cremation burials. The cremation burials often had ceremonially "killed" artifacts and items of spiritual or symbolic importance (e.g., turtle-shell rattles and animal jaws). Early Transitional Archaic material culture is widespread in southwestern Nova Scotia, which is not surprising since it is likely that there were close contacts with the Maine coast since the Late Archaic. So far, the only excavated site is a fishing station (i.e., the Boswell site) along the Annapolis River, which connects the western and central parts of Nova Scotia. An earlier fishing site at Mud Lake Stream, in the New Brunswick interior, may be an important link in the spread of Transitional Archaic culture to Passamaquoddy Bay, and possibly the Saint John River. The Late Transitional Archaic (ca. 3,400–3,000 ^{14}C yrs BP) is more problematic, as there appear to have been distinctive regional cultural traditions developing in the Maritimes, such as the Quoddy region, Lower Saint John River, and southwestern Nova Scotia. Significant traits include wide, side-notched (fishtail-like) projectile points and large scrapers, use of copper, and a preference for local raw materials. Considerable debate continues over the importance of the Transitional Archaic culture to the development of Early Woodland, which is likely to vary according to region.

6

THE CLAY POT PEOPLE

THE PEOPLE OF THE WOODLAND PERIOD (ca. 3,000 to 500 ^{14}C yrs BP) were the first people in the Maritimes to embrace pottery-making (Davis 1991d; Leonard 1995; Figure 47). In fact, in the Peskotomuhkati timeline developed by Soctomah and others (2012), this period is referred to as the *Qahqolunsqey*, or "Clay Pot" period. Pottery (or ceramic) vessels are durable, can be made from local materials, and serve a wide variety of functions, including cooking, serving, and vermin-proofing storage. The Early Woodland in the Maritimes is marked by the arrival of pointed-base vessels covered with fabric impressions, which are generally identified as a variant of the widespread Vinette 1 style of pottery (Taché 2005; see below). These vessels are rare in the region and in the Maritime Peninsula in general. Fragmented fabric-impressed vessels have been identified at the Mud Lake Stream, Jemseg, and Portland Point sites in New Brunswick (Bourgeois 1999, 43–44; Deal 1986), and at the Rafter Lake, St. Croix, and End of Dyke sites in Nova Scotia (Davis 1991d, 96; Godfrey-Smith et al. 1997, 253; Woolsey 2018, 273; Figure 48). They are equally rare in Maine, although they have been recovered at the Knox, Great Diamond Island, Bob, and Turner Farm sites, and a large collection of 38 fragmented vessels was recovered at N'tolonapemk, near the Maine/New Brunswick border (Belcher 1989; Bourque 2001, 76; Mack et al. 2002, 72; Newsom 2020;

Petersen and Sanger 1991, 118–23; UMF-ARC 2002). By Middle Woodland times, pottery was ubiquitous in the region. However, actual evidence of pottery production is quite rare beyond the recovery of various implements believed to have been used for decorating pottery vessels, as well as

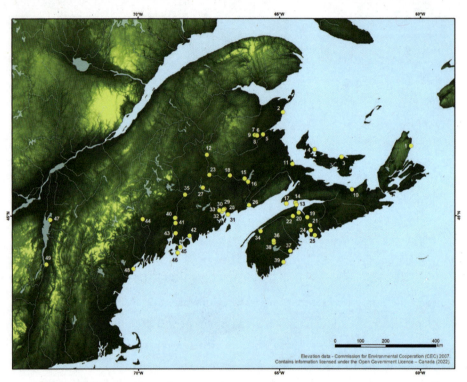

Figure 47: Selected Woodland period sites on the Maritime Peninsula: 1. Geganish (Ingonish Island), 2. Tracadie River, 3. Canavoy, 4. Pitawelkek, 5. Forks, 6. Wilson and Howe sites, 7. Augustine and Mejipke sites, 8. Tozer, 9. Oxbow, 10. Merigomish Harbour sites, 11. Skull Island, 12. Shiktehawk (Bristol), 13. Clam Cove, 14. Davidson Cove, 15. Fulton Island, 16. Jemseg, 17. Cape d'Or, 18. Eqpahak Island, 19. St. Croix, 20. Melanson, 21. Rafter Lake, 22. End-of-Dyke (Gaspereau Lake), 23. Meductic, 24. Frostfish Cove, 25. Skora (White's Lake), 26. Saint John Harbour sites, 27. Mud Lake Stream, 28. Carson, 29. Bocabec, 30. Holt's Point, 31. Weir site, Bliss Islands, 32. Ministers Island, 33. St. Croix Island, 34. Bear River, 35. Mattawamkeag, 36. Merrymakedge, 37. Port Medway, 38. Eel Weir sites, 39. Port Joli sites, 40. Bob, 41. Eddington Bend, 42. Watson, 43. Mason, 44. Embden, 45. Goddard, 46. Knox, 47. Boucher and Swanton sites, 48. Great Diamond Island, 49. Orwell.

a few features that have been interpreted as pottery firing pits (Kristmanson and Deal 1993, 75; Newsom 2017, 169; Sanger 1996b, 523).

Karen Taché and Owen Craig (2015) propose that the adoption of ceramic vessels during the Early Woodland may be associated with large seasonal gatherings, like spring anadromous fish runs, and the preparation of aquatic resources. They further suggest that the low quantity and small size of ceramic vessels may reflect the primary use of these vessels for cooking and consuming fish at feasting events or the preparation of fish oils for exchange. Their findings are based on a combination of carbon and nitrogen isotope and lipid analyses on Early Woodland (Vinette I) ceramics and residues from the greater Northeast, although not including the Maritime Peninsula. Their results are clearest for coastal sites, while vessels from inland sites may be associated with more complex mixtures of food sources (Taché and Craig 2015, 183–86). Bonnie Newsom studied the choices (agency) involved in Early Woodland pottery production at 10 sites in Maine. She states that the combination of excurvate rims and feldspar temper in vessels from Turner Farm implies that the vessels were used for cooking or processing seal blubber or fish oil (Newsom 2022, 333).

As discussed in the previous chapter, the actual transition from Archaic to Woodland is not clear in the archaeological

Figure 48: Vinette-like vessel from the Boucher site, Vermont. Note triangular designs. The photograph originally appeared in *Archaeology of Eastern North America* 18, 23. Courtesy *Archaeology of Eastern North America* and the Eastern States Archaeological Federation.

record. Holyoke and Hrynick (2022, 4) hold that the Woodland period should be viewed more as a temporal designator than as a useful model for facilitating interpretive process. The Woodland is a continuation from the Late or Transitional Archaic culture. Local projectile point styles developed out of earlier Archaic forms: narrow, straight, and contracting stemmed points in southwest New Brunswick and Nova Scotia, and straight-stemmed, followed by small, expanding-stemmed points further east (Burke 2022, 199). The lithic toolkit included large scrapers, which become smaller in the Middle Woodland, and polished stone celts, abraders, and a variety of rough stone tools (Wright 1999, 572). At some point, they adopted pottery-making, perhaps through matrilocal marriage arrangements (Woolsey 2022). Woolsey (2022, 394–96) estimates that the earliest vessels represent a minor addition to the Woodland toolkit (also see Wright 1999, 571–72), and they may have been used more in feasting and trade than in everyday cooking (Taché and Craig 2015). At some point, they received an infusion of new ideas from the west through the "Meadowood Interaction Sphere" (Taché 2011, 86–89). They added Meadowood-style side-notched projectile points to their toolkit, and perhaps Vinette-like pottery was introduced at the same time. Although evidence of Meadowood influence is widespread in the region, it is not continuous (see below).

We have a substantial amount of archaeological information on faunal, floral, and inorganic resource use for the Woodland period in the Maritimes (Deal 2002, 2008a). Smoked fish, eels, shellfish, fowl, grease and oils from various animals, and animal pelts were prized. Archaeological evidence indicates a marked increase in the utilization of beaver during the Woodland and prior to European contact, which Crader (1997, 235) explains may be due to an increased importance of beaver for clothing. Eel weirs are common in some areas (Lewis 2006b). A wide variety of edible wild berries, fruits, and grapes, along with nuts (acorns, butternuts, beechnuts, walnuts), and groundnut tubers were available in the Maritimes. Plant-fibre mats, bags, and baskets, as well as birchbark artifacts, have been recovered in archaeological contexts (Deal 2008a). Several important lithic sources are known in the region (e.g., Burke 2000) and native copper is available in Nova Scotia. Indigenous resource exploitation shows considerable local variation and potential for intra- and interregional trade (Deal 2008a; Deal et al. 2011; Nash and Miller 1987).

Meadowood Early Woodland (c. 2,800–2,200 ^{14}C yrs BP)

The impact of Meadowood culture in the Maritimes has long been acknowledged (Turnbull and Allen 1988, 256); yet, the pervasiveness of this impact was not established until the 1990s (McEachen 1996). At least seven habitation and three burial sites have been identified in the region, along with numerous artifacts in private collections. In fact, there is more evidence for Meadowood in the Maritimes than further south, suggesting closer ties between the lower Great Lakes area and the Maritime Peninsula than with New England. Wright (1999, 572–73) states that the arguments for a Meadowood presence in the Maritimes were not convincing, but it seems that he was unaware of the fieldwork at Jemseg (Blair 2004a) or of McEachen's regional review. McEachen (1996) considers that the Meadowood presence in the Maritimes was an actual population movement, linked to an east-to-west interaction sphere that involved exchange of goods, and later, of spiritual ideas and paraphernalia. He likens the Meadowood manifestation to the early hypothesized Susquehanna migration from northern New England. Habitation and mortuary sites are found in the area and virtually the entire range of Meadowood material culture has been recovered. The latter includes side-notched projectile points and drills, cache blades, slate gorgets, birdstones, copper awls, pecked and polished celts, and Vinette-like pottery. Finely crafted cache blades, or bifaces, are a common feature of the Meadowood lithic assemblages, which Taché (2011a, 147–48) believes were produced mainly as prestige items for long distance trade. McEachen suggests a tentative settlement and subsistence model for the Maritimes. Habitation sites are located on terraces beside major river systems, while cemeteries are located near habitation

6: THE CLAY POT PEOPLE

sites or on the coast. Subsistence is believed to be primarily a riverine/lacustrine, hunting and fishing pattern. Site locations indicate that freshwater and anadromous fish were important resources.

Meadowood-like sites have been identified in southwest, central, and northeast New Brunswick. At least three suspected Early Woodland sites are known from the Red Bank area, along the northwest Miramichi

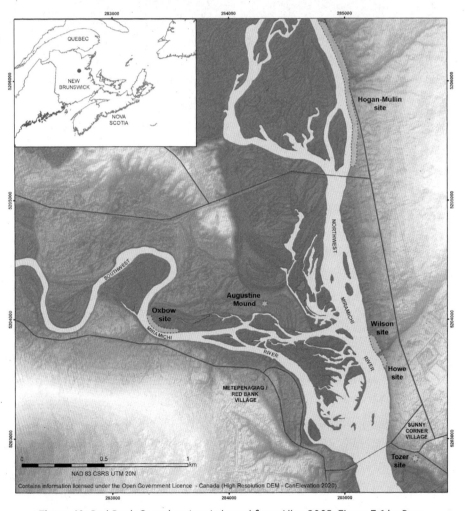

Figure 49: Red Bank Complex sites (adapted from Allen 2005, Figure 7.6 by Bryn Tapper).

River (Figure 49). The Tozer site consists of two circular features containing a few calcined bones and typical Meadowood grave inclusions (McEachen et al. 1999; Wintemberg 1937). The latter included 17 red ochre-stained cache blades, one lanceolate and one stemmed biface, a copper awl, and a nearly complete slate gorget (Figure 50). The cache blades were originally believed to be made from chert originating in the Great Lakes area, but geochemical and petrographic analyses suggest a local source (McEachen et al. 1999). Three nearby sites have also produced Early Woodland materials, but all have been damaged by plowing. The Wilson site is a campsite, about one kilometre above Tozer, which has produced cache blades, side-notched projectile points and drills, and double-ended and triangular scrapers. The Howe site, located on an elevated terrace above Wilson, and Hogan-Mullin, located further upriver, have produced Meadowood-style projectile points.

Figure 50: Tozer site artifact assemblage: copper awl, gorget fragment, and cache blades. Photograph courtesy the Government of New Brunswick.

6: THE CLAY POT PEOPLE

Excavations at the Jemseg site, in the Lakes region, New Brunswick, uncovered a large Meadowood habitation area (McEachen 2004). Artifacts recovered from this area included ground stone celts, abrading stones, hammerstones, scrapers, two Meadowood-style projectile points, and Vinette-like pottery. The pottery sherds were found in a hearth feature with radiocarbon dates of 2,140+/-60 and 2,520+/-70 ^{14}C yrs BP. One feature, containing red ochre but no artifacts, is believed to be a burial. Birdstones were also collected by George Clarke from along the Tobique and Saint John rivers. The Gaugenn site, on the Tobique, which has been dated to about 2,890 ^{14}C yrs BP, has produced artifacts thought to be made from Mistassini quartzite from Quebec (McEachen et al. 1999, 161).

Three Meadowood features were excavated at Mud Lake Stream, on the Chiputneticook–St. Croix River drainage, southwestern New Brunswick (Deal 1985, 1986). A small burial feature that had been partially eroded at the beach face contained faunal elements that have been identified as dog, beaver, and a salmonoid fish species. No human remains were included, which means that it may have been a dog burial. Several artifacts, some of which were intentionally broken, were placed in the grave, including a slate gorget, a side-notched projectile point, and a serrated biface (Figure 51). Five sherds of fabric-impressed pottery were recovered within a one metre radius. A small cache of nine Meadowood projectile points was also discovered. A third feature believed to be associated with the Meadowood component contained only a calcined fragment of a barbed bone point, which has been dated to about 2,750 ± 80 ^{14}C yrs BP (Beta 23443).

Meadowood sites and materials are known almost exclusively from the southwestern part of Nova Scotia. Meadowood-style projectile points have been identified on Lake Kejimkujik and on the short section of the Mersey River connecting this lake and Lake Rossignol (Ferguson 1986). The Eel Weir complex is a group of sites associated with a series of triangular-shaped, stone fish weir bases along the Mersey River. These weirs are believed to have been used to capture eels in the fall and gaspereau in the spring. At Eel Weir Site 6, five Meadowood-style points were recovered.

6: THE CLAY POT PEOPLE

Similar points have been recovered at the Merrymakedge site, which is a multicomponent site at the north end of Lake Kejimkujik.

A Meadowood campsite has been reported at Rafter Lake, which drains into St. Margaret's Bay (Davis 1977, 1991d, 96). A possible semisubterranean dwelling has been identified, with a hearth feature containing a Vinette-like potsherd and a Meadowood-style projectile point. The dwelling is oval

Figure 51: Lithic artifacts recovered from Feature 20, Mud Lake Stream: (A–B) end scrapers, (C) side-notched projectile point, (D) gorget, (E) side scraper, (F) biface fragment, (G) side-notched projectile point, (H) biface, (I) two conjoined biface fragments, (J) serrated biface. Courtesy of the Government of New Brunswick.

in floor plan and measures approximately 3.5 x 2.5 meters. This site is probably an interior extractive site, located on an anadromous fish run.

In 1992, an avocational archaeologist excavated two Meadowood features on his property in Port Medway (McEachen 1996). The first was a small circular pit (Feature 1) with an artifact cluster, including Meadowood points, cache blades, copper awls, gorgets, and red ochre. It is believed to be a burial pit, although no bones were recovered. Feature 2 was a row of artifacts, about one metre long, which consisted of side-notched projectile points, cache blades, abraders, birdstone fragments, celts, and hammerstones. The function of this feature is unknown, but it seems to be associated with the burial pit. The site may represent a burial or ceremonial site situated near the rich fishing grounds of the Medway River. An alternate explanation is that the two ceremonial features represent caches associated with traditional feasting activities.

The St. Croix site, a large village on the St. Croix River, Hants County, Nova Scotia, has also produced a Meadowood component, underlying a Middle Woodland component (Deal et al. 1994). This site is at the head of tide for the St. Croix River, which drains into the Avon River and Minas Basin. Furthermore, it is at the northern end of an important historic portage route, via the Ponhook Lakes to the Atlantic. The main reason for choosing this site most likely was the spring runs of salmon and gaspereau. The Meadowood materials included sherds of Vinette-like pottery and a side-notched projectile point made from an exotic material, which has been identified by Moira McCaffrey (personal communication, 1996) as Mistassini quartzite (Figure 67e). This piece may have been an heirloom, since virtually all the other chipped stone artifacts were made from Scots Bay cherts, White Rock quartzite, or local quartz.

Three alternative models have been put forth to explain the Meadowood phenomenon in the Northeast. Ritchie (1955) argues that it was based on the spread of a burial cult. A second and economic model champions an exchange network that allows more stability in local subsistence systems (Granger 1978). Third, Taché (2011a) argues that the Meadowood phenomenon is best explained by a sociopolitical model, involving the increasing control over time of Onondaga chert cache blade production and the exchange of this commodity for other exotic raw materials and finished prestige goods (e.g., native copper, marine shells, gorgets, birdstones, ceramic tubular pipes, quartz crystals), as well as perishable items like animal hides. In the Meadowood core area, this economic base involved the emergence of elite corporate kinship groups who controlled resources, used cemeteries to signify resource ownership (such as prime fishing locations), and enlisted skilled specialists in the production of exotic items. Taché (2011a) stresses the importance of storage of the food surpluses to the Meadowood core area since such surpluses become a capital for exchange.

Our best evidence on large-scale storage in the Maritimes comes from Red Bank, New Brunswick. Allan (1991, 16; 2005, 65, 71) recorded more than 60 large storage pits, or underground food storage vaults, along the higher terraces surrounding Red Bank (Metepenagiag), New Brunswick. Details on these sites were not published, but she briefly describes the vaults as being as deep as 2 m and 4–5 m in diameter, dug into heavy gravel to allow drainage. No artifacts or ecofacts were recovered, but one site left evidence of bark or sod roofs. Of interest is the Mejipke (formerly Two Hole) site, which is located on the terrace between the Early-Late Woodland Oxbow site and the Early Woodland Augustine burial mound. Allan suggests that the pits were used for storing pots and baskets of dried and smoked fish, smoked fowl, fruits, nuts, and wild grains. She further suggests that the vaults are at least 1,200 years old, and that these features could have been used during the Early Woodland period. Blair and Ward (2013, 13–14; also Blair and Rooney 2022, 133–34) report that more than 120 such pit features are now known along the terraces of Metepenagiag, and that they may have been used, based on faunal remains and stable isotope analysis, as smoking pits for the bulk processing of anadromous fish. In particular, Blair and Rooney (2022, 158–59, 162–63) stress that sturgeon has been an important species for Metepenagiag for the last 3,000 years, both as a food source and for its spiritual connection to the people of the community. Suttie (2006) suggests that these pits were probably used cyclically for smoking fish and preserving foods. Similar features are known from other Woodland period sites, such as Eel Weir 6 on the Mersey River (Ferguson 1986). These pits may be earlier versions of the Wolastoqwey "barns" described by John Gyles on the Saint John River in the late seventeenth century (see Hall 2015, 20–21).

Easy access to interior and coastal resources and the presence of large storage features suggest the possible accumulation of food surpluses. Metepenagiag may represent the kind of wealthy community associated with the sociopolitical model favoured by Taché. It was a densely populated area throughout the Woodland period. Furthermore, prestige items are known from both Meadowood (copper items and slate gorgets) and late Early Woodland Middlesex burials (e.g., copper beads, Ohio pipestone, and exotic cherts; see Turnbull 1976). Together with the evidence of intentional breakage of prestige items and the possibility that Meadowood cache bifaces were being made from local materials by local craft specialists, we have a community with the potential to encourage successful traders and the development of social inequalities.

Small amounts of native copper were collected in the region, but probably not in large enough quantities for trade. Early Woodland archaeological evidence of copper consists of finished items at the Tozer (Meadowood burial) and Augustine (Adena burial) sites at Red Bank. They were originally believed to be made from Great Lakes copper, but an electron probe microanalysis on one specimen indicates a Cape d'Or origin (Jarratt 2013, 151). Levine (2007, 181) suggests that up to 65 per cent of the Early Woodland specimens may have been made from Nova Scotian sources. Levine (1999, 189; also see Taché 2011b, 63) notes that nineteenth-century reports on the Bay of Fundy deposits talk of copper nuggets weighing several pounds. Leonard (1996, 80–102; also Monahan 1990) suggests that the Lake Superior source seems to dry up by the Middle Woodland period, when local copper was substituted for making tools, such as awls and blades. However, a recent comprehensive study of precontact copper artifacts indicates that Lake Superior copper is absent from the Maritimes, which means that Bay of Fundy copper may have been more prevalent in the past (Hanley et al. 2022, 252–53). The local copper-working industry featured the cold-hammering (and possibly annealing) of small copper nuggets into sheets and bars that were made into a variety of artifacts. Leonard (1996) listed 26 archaeological sites in the Maritimes where native copper artifacts have been found. Precontact copper sources in New Brunswick probably include Clark Point, Passamaquoddy Bay, and Southwest Head, Grand Manan Island. Both appear to be primary copper sources, existing as copper nuggets (nodules) and as narrow veins or patches in trap rocks (Sabina 1965, 24, 29). At least six source areas also have been identified in Nova Scotia, including the well-known source at Cape d'Or.

The three Meadowood features excavated at Mud Lake Stream (Deal 1986) are the most difficult to reconcile with Taché's model. She suggests that cemeteries were used to signify resource ownership, such as prime fishing locations. It is possible that the burial (Feature 20) at Mud Lake Stream was a human interment (long since disintegrated) that included charred animal remains from a burial feast (including a possible dog sacrifice; see Chapter 7), thus marking a claim to this important fish exploitation location. The nearby N'tolonapemk site supports the presence of Meadowood in the St. Croix River area between about 2,800 to 2,150 years ago (UMF-ARC 2002, 24–25). It is located at the Denys River outlet of Meddybemps Lake, with access to nearby productive wetlands. Like Mud Lake Stream, it marked an important interior resource location, where alewife was abundant. The presence of exotic lithics from New Brunswick, Nova Scotia, and New York indicates that the people of this area were involved in a widespread exchange system, at least involving lithics. Gaps persist in the Meadowood record for the Maritimes. The evidence is strongest in northeastern New Brunswick but remains sporadic everywhere else. If the Meadowood manifestation represents an actual migration of people, then it may be confined to northeastern New Brunswick, while elsewhere the local Indigenous people were adopting some Meadowood practices.

Middlesex Early Woodland

Towards the end of the Early Woodland (c. 2,800–2,200 ^{14}C yrs BP), many of the inhabitants of the Maritime Peninsula adopted a new mortuary pattern. Researchers in the Maritimes tend to view this cultural manifestation as a diffusion of Ohio Valley Adena spiritual elements into the region, rather than a migration of people (Clermont 1978; Rutherford 1990b; Turnbull 1976; Wright 1999). It is basically seen as an Adena mortuary system with distinctive burial inclusions, grafted into a Meadowood-like cultural system, which is referred to in the literature as Middlesex. Wright (1999, 555) suggests that this mortuary complex may represent travelling priests/shamans who were overseeing a formal spiritual system with a prescribed set of burial items. In the Maritime Peninsula, Middlesex sites are found primarily along the St. Lawrence River drainage, the eastern coast of New Brunswick, and south-central Nova Scotia. The northeastern sites tend to be found in clusters, including the Boucher, Swanton, and Orwell sites in northern Vermont, the Augustine and McKinlay sites in New Brunswick, and the Esson and Whites Lake (or Skora) sites in Nova Scotia.

The Northeastern Middlesex burial assemblage has certain characteristics that distinguish it from Ohio Valley burials. For example, the pecked and polished adze blades of the Adena are replaced by chipped and ground adze blades, like those also found in some Transitional Archaic contexts. This difference may be significant, since chipped and ground adzes appear to be the most widespread Middlesex artifact found in private collections in the Maritimes. The large, stemmed projectile points of the Adena have lobate-shaped bases, while most eastern versions, notably excluding the Boucher specimens, tend to be square-based. Furthermore, pottery appears among the burial goods on the Maritime Peninsula but is rarely found in Adena burials. The reel-shaped gorgets that are common in the Ohio Valley are replaced by angular-shaped slate gorgets in the Northeast. Wright (1999, 595) finds that the incorporation of local elements may reflect the adaptability of the Adena spiritual system. Other artifacts, including the blocked-end tubular pipes and large bifaces, appear to come directly from the Ohio area, while copper beads are made from regional copper (Hanley et al. 2022). A similar range of burial inclusions have been recovered from contemporary sites in New England (Ritchie and Dragoo 1959).

The Champlain drainage in Vermont probably was an important segment of the Adena trade network, which extended along the southeastern Great Lakes, and the Hudson, Ohio, and St. Lawrence rivers (Heckenberger et al. 1990). Middlesex burials were discovered in 1861 at Swanton and Orwell (Willoughby 1935, 85–86, 92–100). Forty-four graves were identified at Swanton, including both primary and cremation burials, and two burials were found at Orwell. Twelve tubular pipes were recovered at Swanton, including one with a thunderbird (fishhawk) motif, which is a powerful spirit being in the Northeast (Lenik 2012). Other offerings include gorgets, amulets, boatstones, pendants, and copper and shell beads. The Boucher site features 69 graves, of which 44 are primary and 23 are cremations, and two burials include both primary and cremation burials (Heckenberger et al. 1990a, 1990b). Red ochre and black graphite were commonly used in burials. The diagnostic grave inclusions include at least 12 complete and fragmented tubular pipes and more than 3,000 beads of rolled copper and shell. A nearly complete, conical pottery vessel, identified as Vinette 1 style, was decorated with triangular designs (Haviland and Power 1994, 99; see also Figure 48). Organic remains included an extensive collection of cloth made from vegetable fibre, leather bags, and cordage. Faunal materials included beaver incisors, bear teeth and jaw fragments, dog bones, and whole snakes and fish. An animal "medicine" hide bag from Feature 94 contained a bone fishhook and bones from several animals, including coiled snakes (Heckenberger et al. 1990, 200).

Middlesex sites seem to be relatively rare in Maine. Best known is the Mason site, near Orland (Moorehead 1922, 46ff.). Mason is a Late Archaic cemetery, but at least three graves are intrusive Early Woodland features. Tubular pipes link these burials with the Middlesex Tradition. Other offerings include copper beads and a chert blade. Across the Maine–New Brunswick border, at Ministers Island, Saint Andrews, a Middlesex burial was discovered beneath a Middle/Late Woodland shell midden (Sanger 1986). This feature has been radiocarbon-dated to 1,930 +/- 110 ^{14}C yrs BP. The grave inclusions consist of red ochre, a fragment of matting, 31 complete and 126 fragmented copper beads, two bifaces, one bipoint, a cigar shaped rod, strike-a-light, five celts, and two giant shark teeth. Shark teeth are known from burial contexts from Late Archaic to Woodland times, and according to Betts and others (2012) were both a symbol of a maritime lifeway and a creature of transformational and spiritual power through which a person (such as a shaman) could access supernatural powers.

Avocational archaeologist George Frederick Clarke (1974, 79) collected a chipped and ground adze blade from the Forks site, at the confluence of the south and north branches of the Miramichi River, which is now recognized as a diagnostic Middlesex artifact. Clarke also excavated in 1932, at Bristol, near the confluence of the Shiktehawk and Saint John rivers, where he unearthed a large cache of bifaces (1974, 112–24). The evidence from this site was revisited by Brent Suttie (2010), who attributes the bifaces to the Middlesex (Adena). The site is situated on the important Shiktehawk–Miramichi portage route described by Ganong (1899, 252). The most significant Middlesex sites in New Brunswick are the Augustine burial mound and the McKinlay site in Red Bank (see Vignette 12). However, additional Adena-related artifacts have been recovered at the Fulton Island, Ministers Island, and Navy Island sites (Foulkes 1984; Sanger 1987).

Two Middlesex burial sites are also known from the Halifax-Dartmouth area in Nova Scotia. In the late nineteenth century, the Esson site was destroyed by construction work in Dartmouth and the exact location was not recorded. The only artifact known to survive from the site is a large, blocked-end tubular pipe, now in the Nova Scotia Museum collection, although Brian Preston (1974, 4) identified an additional adze and two grooved axes that may also be from the site. A second mound was opened by a bulldozer during land-clearing for a subdivision at Whites Lake, outside of Halifax. This mound, known as the Skora site, featured a cremation burial with a large collection of burial inclusions (Davis 1991b).

6: THE CLAY POT PEOPLE

The latter included three chipped and ground stone adze blades and seven square-stemmed projectile points. A second burial contained calcined human bone fragments and seven chalcedony flakes. Two radiocarbon samples date the site to around 2,200 ^{14}C yrs BP. Chipped and ground stone adze blades recorded in three collections around the Minas Basin also suggest Middlesex burial practices in that area (Deal 1988). An Adena-style projectile point was also found in 1965 by George MacDonald at the mouth of the North River, on Gaspereau Lake. Further to the south, a blocked-end tubular pipe and two large projectile points were reported in Yarmouth County collections (Davis 1991b).

Vignette 12: Augustine and McKinlay

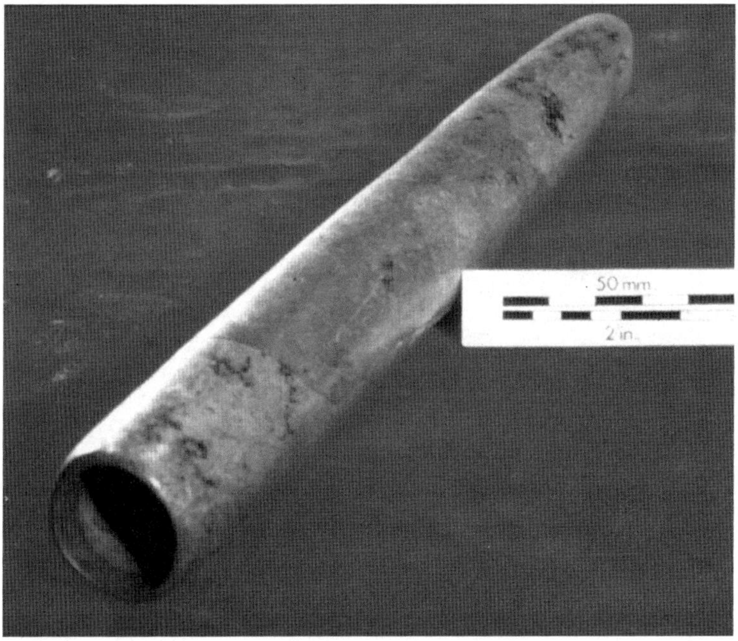

Figure 52: Blocked-end tubular pipe from the Augustine mound. Courtesy Archaeological Services, Fredericton, Government of New Brunswick.

The Augustine mound site is located on a high terrace above the southwest Miramichi River (Turnbull 1976, 1978; Blair and Rooney 2022, 135ff.). Chris Turnbull received the first-ever permit issued in Canada to do archaeological research on Indigenous land, with the condition that the human remains were to be reinterred in the burial mound after study. The mound contained 11 burials, some with lavish grave offerings. The diagnostic Middlesex artifacts included blocked-end tubular pipes (Figure 52), gorgets, bifaces, large square-stemmed projectile points, and chipped and ground stone adze blades. Copper salts from the thousands of copper beads aided the preservation of organic materials, including braided thongs for beads, textile fragments, cedar bark matting,

Figure 53: Excavation at the deeply stratified Oxbow site, Red Bank, New Brunswick. Photograph from Allen 1991, 30. Courtesy the Government of New Brunswick.

twilled and pleated basketry, hafted beaver teeth, and a wooden spear shaft fragment. Some of the burials were blocklifted and sent to the Canadian Conservation Institute for laboratory excavation.

Materials from a second Red Bank area Middlesex grave are housed in the British Museum. The artifacts were purchased from a local man in 1909 and were not known to Canadian archaeologists until after the Augustine excavation. Wright (1999, 600) notes the high similarity between the Augustine and McKinlay assemblages. The exact location of the McKinlay site is uncertain except that it was in the Red Bank/Sunny Corner area. The collection consisted of two individuals encased in birchbark, in a pit about 60 cm deep (Turnbull 1988b). The museum collection includes four tubular pipes, copper beads, gorgets, a boatstone, stemmed projectile points, scrapers, bifaces, and five celts. The collection includes pottery sherds of a local ware, like others recovered at Augustine and the bottom level at Oxbow (Figure 53). One sherd was decorated with a trailed, sectioned-triangle motif like the decoration on the Boucher vessel.

Middle and Late Woodland Periods (ca. 2,200–500 ^{14}C yrs BP)

In the archaeological literature, the Middle and Late Woodland peoples usually are treated as a cultural continuum, distinguished by minor changes in technology. Historic ethnic divisions are often projected back to the Middle Woodland period (e.g., the ancestral Mi'kmaq, Wolastoqiyik, and Peskotomuhkatiyik). Archaeologists working in the Maritimes generally agree that an unbroken cultural sequence spanned the 1,500 years before European contact (Tuck 1984, 71). As mentioned above, our understanding of earlier Woodland occupation is clouded by archaeological evidence of contact with neighbouring Indigenous peoples (McEachen 1996). Allen (1993, 32) posits that the Peskotomuhkatiyik and Wolastoqiyik are descended from one of the earlier Archaic cultures known to have inhabited southwestern New Brunswick (also see Rutherford 1989). The ancestral Mi'kmaq also may have developed out of a local

Archaic culture, although some researchers believe that they are descended from groups that migrated into the area along the St. Lawrence drainage at the beginning of the Woodland period (Fiedel 1991). It is also possible that many linguistic elements were adopted from the west along with Meadowood material culture.

Several cultural traits during the Middle Woodland period differentiate it from the Early Woodland. A series of new decorative styles appear on pottery, and there is greater variation in vessel forms, which implies more specialized uses (Staplefeldt 2009). Three common styles occur, namely, pseudo-scallop shell, dentate, and cord-wrapped stick (Figures 54–56). Other evidence of an artistic tradition appears in the form of incised pebbles at the Holt's Point site in Passamaquoddy Bay and petroglyphs in Maine, New Brunswick, and Nova Scotia (Lee 1999). At Holt's Point, 40 siltstone or slate pebbles were discovered with distinctive geometric designs, including an arch and triangle, herringbone, crossed central arch,

Figure 54: Pottery vessel rim from the Diggity site, featuring pseudo-scallop shell design elements, associated with the Middle Woodland period (from Deal 1984b). Courtesy the Government of New Brunswick.

6: THE CLAY POT PEOPLE

Figure 55: Dentate stamped vessel found by divers on the Kennebecasis River in southern New Brunswick. Photograph by Kora Stapelfeldt.

Figure 56: Pottery rim sherd collected by D. London at Ring Island, Maquapit Lake, New Brunswick, 1900. Note cord-wrapped stick design elements. Photograph by Kora Stapelfeldt.

and crosshatching motifs (Hammon 1984; Fowler 1966a; see also Figure 37). The famous petroglyphs of Lake Kejimkujik are generally believed to date to the contact and historic periods but some petroglyphs in eastern Maine and New Brunswick may date to the precontact period (Hedden 1985; Snow 1977; Tapper and Moro Abadia 2021; see Vignette 13 below).

Residue studies in the Maritimes have focused on Middle and Late Woodland pottery. Early results indicate a more terrestrial mammal vessel use for interior Proto-Wolastoqwey and Peskotomuhkati sites (i.e., Fulton Island and Mud Lake Stream), while the residues from Nova Scotia Proto-Mi'kmaw sites suggest a more marine vessel use (Deal et al. 2019). One residue sample, from End-of-Dyke, Gaspereau Lake, produced a marine signature. Marine residues from an interior lake site signal the cooking of anadromous fish (such as gaspereau) and/or the catadromous American eel (*Anguilla rostrata*), both of which were important in the Mi'kmaw diet. Several of the Nova Scotia residues may have had a terrestrial plant or nut component. Unfortunately, aquatic biomarkers had not been identified until after the original study. However, the findings are reinforced by a study in New Brunswick, in which researchers ran bulk stable isotope samples for residues from 29 vessels from the Miramichi region, in traditional Mi'kmaw territory; 22 from sites along the Saint John River, in traditional Wolastoqwey territory; and 12 samples from sites in Passamaquoddy Bay, in traditional Peskotomuhkati territory (Suttie 2014a). Stable isotope values suggest a predominantly marine diet for the Mi'kmaw area and a more terrestrial mammal/freshwater fish/bird diet for the Wolastoqwey and Peskotomuhkati areas. When we compare the stable isotope values from the original study, two Fulton Island samples conform to the latter area, while Mud Lake Stream samples are indeterminate. In addition, Kelly-Anne Pike (2013, 161) reported stable isotope values for 14 Proto-Mi'kmaq from a Woodland period cemetery at Old Mission Point, in northern New Brunswick, which suggests that they relied primarily on marine resources for their dietary protein. Certainly, pottery vessels became more numerous and larger during the Middle and Late Woodland periods, which may indicate a gradual switch to the more generalized use pattern (e.g., the cooking of food mixtures) reported in the historic period.

New pottery styles are accompanied by new projectile point styles, which show considerable variability across the region. Several variants on a contracting stem style, called "Tusket" by John Erskine (1998, 88), seem to originate in Nova Scotia and Prince Edward Island (Buchanan 2011; Figure 57). In Burke's model (2022, 199), Middle Woodland projectile point styles

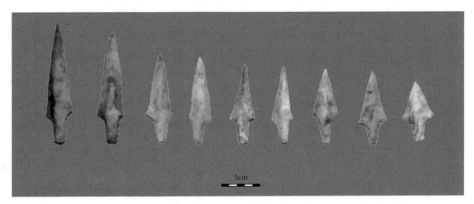

Figure 57: Early Middle Woodland contracting stem project point cache, surface collected by Jim Legge at Gaspereau Lake, Nova Scotia. Photograph by Michael Deal.

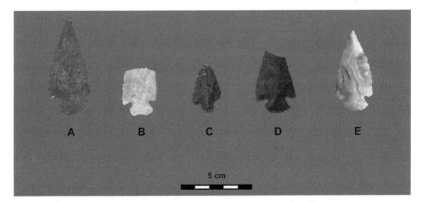

Figure 58: Middle Woodland corner-notched projectile points from Clam Cove, Scots Bay, Nova Scotia. Note (A–D) are from site excavations conducted in 1988–1989 and 2004–2005, and (E) was collected at the site by a Scots Bay resident. From photographs by Michael Deal.

in the southwestern part of the Maritime Peninsula include stemmed and side-notched points, with contracting stem points in Nova Scotia, followed by side- and corner-notched points after c. 1,560 ^{14}C yrs BP. In the northeast, bipointed/contracting stem points are followed by wide, straight or contracting stem points; and, after c. 1,350 ^{14}C yrs BP, by side- and corner-notched points. Burke notes that there is a clear technological change in the late Middle or early Late Woodland to primarily side-notched and corner-notched varieties, which are not found outside the Maritime Peninsula (2022, 209; see Figure 58). Anderson and Hrynick (2019) suggest that the large bifaces that are associated with Woodland deposits in the Passamaquoddy Bay area may have been hafted for use as knives, rather than preforms for producing projectile points.

There is a more widespread use of good, local lithic sources during the Middle and Late Woodland. Lithics from Scots Bay, White Rock, Washademoak Lake, Munsungun Lake, and Ingonish Island are all heavily used. An increase in small scraping tools also has been found, which may be associated with the development of birchbark technology. Wooden parts of canoes and baskets require finer workmanship.

Our first solid evidence of precontact dwellings for the region is dated to the Middle Woodland in coastal Maine and Passamaquoddy Bay, and first was identified by Matthews (1984). Several sites have semisubterranean house pits, which are 10 cm to 60 cm deep. Floor plans indicate that these structures were oval in outline, with elevated benches around the perimeter and hearths near the door (Sanger 1976, 1996b, 522–23; 2010). These are believed to be winter dwellings, with sunken floors serving to conserve heat. The exteriors were probably conical pole and birchbark constructions, insulated with hides and mosses. Hrynick and Black (2016) provide an impressive review of the topic, which updates work in the Quoddy region since Sanger's study. They suggest that the wigwam form of structure persisted throughout the Woodland and into the historic period, along with associated social patterns (Hrynick and Black 2016, 58).

Fieldwork in the Port Joli area of southwestern Nova Scotia, expanding on Erskine's early work (1959), identifies dwelling features at multiple sites (Hrynick and Betts 2017, 2019), and explores the evidence for Woodland period gender relationships at different scales in the archaeological spectrum (Hrynick and Betts 2022). Hrynick and others (2012; Hrynick 2011) offer a detailed excavation of a domestic structure at a Late Woodland, Port Joli, shell midden site (AlDf-24). Despite multiple reoccupations, artifact distributions within this feature are believed to conform to the partition of dwelling space by sex and age, as described in the ethnohistoric literature (especially LeClercq 1910). Interior summer dwellings appear to have been less substantial, with house poles merely sitting on the surface, with no subsurface excavation. Two additional dwelling features were identified at the Jack's Brook site (AlDf-30), at Port Joli, and a third feature is interpreted as a sweat lodge, based on ethnographic, ethnohistoric, and archaeological evidence (Hrynick and Betts 2014; 2017, 7-10). Nash and Stewart (1990, 69) report another possible "sweatbath" feature at the Melanson site, on Gaspereau River. These are rare examples of the ceremonial use of space at precontact sites in this region.

The elaborate burial practices associated with the Middlesex manifestation in the region do not survive into the Middle Woodland period. Simple, primary burials replace cremation and secondary burials. Grave inclusions are more rudimentary or non-existent.

A palynological study of a shell midden at Maligomish (Indian Island), Nova Scotia, found that the pollen assemblages of cores taken from in the midden were comparable to those from marine and lake cores within a 50 km radius for the later Middle and Late Woodland periods (Mudie and Lelièvre 2013). Despite some mixing, the midden sediments appear to reflect local environmental changes during the Woodland period. Changes in seawater temperature and rising sea levels affected shellfish bed location and the relative abundance of different shellfish species (e.g., Lelièvré 2017c). In general, shellfish exploitation became more important to the economy of some areas within the region, such as

Passamaquoddy Bay, the Northumberland Strait, and the South Shore of Nova Scotia. For example, Betts (2019, 351) indicates that clam flats appear around 1,500 years ago in the inner harbour at Port Joli and ushered in about a thousand years of intensive shellfish exploitation. Erskine had identified "clam drying sites" in the Port Joli area in the 1950s, which Betts (2019, 91) confirmed as specialized clam-processing areas associated with the Middle Woodland period.

In southern Maine, the population adopted corn, bean, and squash horticulture and became more sedentary during the Late Woodland. Fieldwork around the historic French fort at Colonial Pemaquid indicates that corn, and possibly bean, horticulture was being practised in that area around AD 1445 (Spiess and Cranmer 2001). Conditions for Indigenous horticulture were favourable in certain parts of the Maritimes, yet there is no paleoethnobotanical evidence to support its activity in the precontact period. Hall (2015) argues from the ethnohistoric evidence that the Wolastoqiyik were growing corn, and possibly beans and squash, on the upper reaches of the Saint John River before the Europeans arrived. Archaeological evidence shows groundnut vegiculture and plum arboriculture were being practised in the region before European contact (Leonard 1996).

It is often difficult to distinguish between Middle and Late occupations at archaeological sites in the Maritimes, although Betts (2019) makes a clear distinction between Middle and Late occupations in the Port Joli area (see below). The Middle and Late designations for this period are based primarily on stylistic shifts in ceramic designs (e.g., Petersen and Sanger 1991). Woolsey (2017) notes that the hard-bodied, thin-walled, and elaborately decorated vessels of the Middle Woodland are replaced by coarser-tempered, expediently decorated vessels during the Late Woodland. She attributes this change to a move towards standardization and mass production. Exotic lithic materials are less common in Middle Woodland site collections, although they begin to appear again in some areas during the Late Woodland. However, lithic workmanship appears generally to decrease by the Late Woodland.

6: THE CLAY POT PEOPLE

Vignette 13: Beginnings of a Rock Art Tradition

Bryn Tapper (2020) brings rock art research of the Maritime Peninsula into the broader traditions of the Algonquian-speaking peoples of central and eastern Canada and northern New England. In central Algonquian areas, this tradition reaches back to the Archaic period, while in the east, it has been dated back to the Woodland (Lenik 2002, 66) and reached Newfoundland during the historic period (Gaulton et al. 2019). Rock art sites often comprise extensive panels supporting overlapping motifs. Like the Wabanaki stories, these panels contain a mixture of traditional and Western elements inscribed over decades, if not centuries. Rock art motifs vary widely, ranging from figurative to abstract imagery, created for both esoteric and more mundane purposes. Motifs include figurative forms depicting humans, animals, and spirit beings important to Indigenous cosmology (Bryn Tapper, personal communication, 2020). Imagery also depicts Mi'kmaw subsistence practices such as hunting and fishing scenes, as well as the canoes and sailing vessels used for transport. Rock art sites often combine precontact and postcontact elements, which record glimpses of the Indigenous reaction to the encroachment of European culture (e.g., Molyneaux 1989; Tapper and Moro Abadia 2021). Precontact sites often exhibit abstract images associated with traditional shamanistic rites, while postcontact imagery is more often biographical, with scenes that chart the rapidly changing world that Indigenous peoples experienced following European contact. Images of domestic structures, churches, clothing, and everyday objects are common (Tapper and Moro Abadia 2021, 306; also see Robertson 1973). One petroglyph at Kejimkujik Lake, Nova Scotia, appears to depict an earthenware pottery vessel: a relic of precontact times. Early studies of rock art in the Maritime Peninsula focused on stylistic and formal variation, but since the mid-1970s research has made more frequent reference to Indigenous world views and oral traditions, and paid attention to the importance of the rock art site and surrounding landscape, all of which help to reveal the underlying ideologies and meaning of the images (Tapper 2020, 6; Tapper and Moro Abadia 2021).

A common belief shared by Algonquian-speaking groups is that rock art was made by "Little People" (known as *mihkomwéhsisok* to the Peskotomuhkati, and *wiklatmu'j* to the Mi'kmaq) who live in rocks and cliffs along the shorelines of lakes and rivers and who warn travellers of impending dangers; or who were sought by Medicine Men for spiritual knowledge and medicine (Zawadzka 2019, 83; also see Molyneaux 1980; Tapper 2020; Walker 1996). In eastern Maine, Hedden (2004) notes the shamanistic nature of rock art and links the extensive petroglyph tradition at Machias Bay with the changing roles of shamans over a period of three millennia. Elsewhere in eastern Maine, Panawahpskewi (Penobscot) rock art from Embden on the Kennebec River and from Grand Lake Stream (Hedden 1985, 2022; Lenik 2002, figure 45) focuses on sexual imagery. Snow (1977, 47) notices a strong connection between shamans, sexuality, and petroglyphs. The sexual content seen at many petroglyph locations likely was made by shamans to demonstrate and enforce their power through an expression of sexual prowess. Further, Snow (1977, 48) suggests that canoe transportation motifs represent a shamanistic metaphor for magical transformation or cosmic journeying. Hedden (1985, 6) views the unbridled sexuality of the Panawahpskek images as intended to enhance fertility in the animals they hunted and reflects the transition to incipient horticulture and trade that gave shamans more free time to indulge their fantasies. While sexual imagery is less common in the Wabanaki region as compared to central Canada, some historic rock art sites include similar imagery, such as "copulation" motifs at Kejimkujik Lake (Molyneaux 1984a, Figure 5d) and at Kwipek in Nova Scotia (Whitehead 1992; Tapper 2021, 6), and at Conception Bay in Newfoundland (Gaulton et al. 2019, Figure 5e). Hedden (1985, 7) regards the relative absence of overt male sexuality at Wabanaki sites as a possible congruence of rock art and oral traditions, in that Wabanaki stories emphasize the rather "proper" Gluskabe (Kluskap) as compared to the more irreverent tricksters in the stories of the central Algonquian-speaking peoples.

Subsistence Patterning

Ongoing research reveals evidence that the transition from Middle to Late Woodland is characterized by the exploitation of a wider range of local resources, interregional trade, and possibly the adoption of limited horticultural practices. The region has a diverse landscape of highland ranges, lowland plains, large interior lakes, expansive and smaller river systems, and numerous coastal bays and inlets. Palynological studies indicate a change in the forests of the region around 2,000 ^{14}C yrs BP, which led to today's Acadian Forest region, in which red spruce, balsam fir, yellow birch, and sugar maple are dominant species, with lesser amounts of red and white pine. The Atlantic region can be further divided into a few distinctive subregions, based on local variations in tree species.

Floral Resources

Archaeologists in the Maritimes have been actively collecting plant remains only since the 1980s (Deal 2008a). Archaeological specimens consist primarily of macrobotanical materials, such as charred seeds, nut shells, and plant fibres. Considering the extensive use of plant materials for food, medicine, and tools by the historic Indigenous populations, it is obvious that we have much more to learn about plant use in the precontact period. Fewer than 50 plant species have been identified from archaeological sites in the region. The most commonly occurring macroplant remains from late precontact sites in the Maritimes consist of cherry and plum pits, and raspberry (or blackberry) seeds. These species produce edible fruits and certain plant parts have valued medicinal properties. Other species with edible fruits, recovered from archaeological sites, include partridgeberry, strawberry, blueberry, bunchberry, gooseberry, and elderberry.

Nut kernels have provided an important food source in eastern North America since Archaic times. Late precontact sites have yielded specimens of butternut, hazelnut, beechnut, and acorns. Butternuts are known to grow naturally only in New Brunswick and have been recovered from the Fulton Island and Meadows sites, on the Saint John River, as well as at a Middle Woodland site in the Gaspé (Foulkes 1981; Trembley 1997; Varley 1999, 43). Charred butternuts were recovered from a shell midden site at Port Joli, Nova Scotia, suggesting that they were being exchanged with other parts of the region (Betts 2019, 335–38; Deal et al. 2011). Kevin Leonard

(1996) has identified hazelnut and beechnut at the Skull Island site, Shediac Bay.

Hardwoods were used as firewood, construction materials, and tool hafts. Softwoods could also be used as tool hafts, as the only archaeological example from the Maritime Peninsula is a white cedar (*Thuja Occidentalis*) haft for a bifacial knife (Anderson and Hrynick 2019). Birch was a particularly important species since its bark was used for making wigwams, canoes, containers, and burial shrouds. Birchbark has been recovered from burial sites dating from the Early Woodland to the historic period. Stephen Monckton's (2000, 2004) analyses of charred wood from the Jemseg and Meadows sites indicates that a wide variety of fuel woods were used in the Lakes region of central New Brunswick, including maple, beech, ash, oak, birch, ironwood, pine, and spruce, which he believes were collected randomly from the forest floor. At coastal and island sites, occupants would have been forced to rely more heavily on conifers, such as pine, balsam fir, hemlock, and spruce, for their firewood.

The earliest specimens of plant fibres recovered from archaeological sites in the Maritimes include twine and rush woven textiles from the Early Woodland Augustine burial mound (Turnbull 1976) and the possible marine eelgrass binding around the suspension groove on a Late Archaic plummet mentioned above. Two small fragments of woven matting manufactured from strips of arborvitae bark were recovered from a Contact period burial site at Red Bank (Hadlock 1947). Another charred fragment from Portland Point is made from hemp dogbane (*Apocynum cannabinum*). The woven artifacts from the Contact period Hopps site include numerous fragments of mats, bags, and cordage (Harper 1956, 40–51). Ruth Whitehead (1987) and Joleen Gordon (1993, 1995, 1997) have identified a variety of construction materials, including rush, reed, cattail leaf, the bark of white cedar and basswood, and beach grass. Some fragments are made from the inner bark of an unidentified conifer species. Indirect evidence of plant fibre industries is available in the form of fabric impressions on ceramics. Positive casts of these impressions sometimes permit the identification of original structures, such as cordage twists, but the raw materials are rarely identifiable (Petersen 1996).

Abrams and Nowacki (2008) believe that the management of both fruit and mast (nut and acorn) trees was widely practised in precontact times in eastern North America. For example, among the food plants listed above, Canada plum may be of importance. It grows wild throughout New Brunswick but is most densely clustered along the upper Saint John and Restigouche rivers, the mouth of the St. Croix River, and the lower portion of the Miramichi River. It is also found in the Annapolis Valley and Tatamagouche areas of Nova Scotia. The common occurrence of plum trees at Indigenous sites and the recovery of charred plum pits at Meductic led R.P. Gorham (1943) to propose that the precontact peoples of New Brunswick were intentionally planting this species around their campsites. Kevin Leonard (1996) recovered plum pits from a late precontact burial at the Skull Island site, Shediac Bay, and has revived Gorham's theory concerning Indigenous arboriculture. Additional evidence for possible plum arboriculture comes from the discovery of nine plum pits in a leather pouch that accompanied a Contact period female burial from Northport, Nova Scotia.

The Skull Island site also produced 75 grams of charred groundnut (*Apios Americana*) tubers. This species was an important food resource in the early historic period and likely was introduced much earlier in precontact times (Leonard 1996). Today, groundnut is most common in southwestern and parts of central Nova Scotia. Leonard (1996) also reviews the evidence for possible Mi'kmaw horticulture during the Contact period. He cites Lescarbot's assertion that the Mi'kmaq once cultivated corn, beans, and squashes, only to abandon the practice when they began to acquire foodstuffs through trade with the French. Further evidence is provided by Pierre Arsenault's 1714 account of Mi'kmaw gardens of corn at Shediac and Richibucto, and John Giles's late seventeenth-century account of Wolastoqwey gardens of corn and storage practices at Meductic (also see Hall 2015). As Leonard points out, both areas, along with portions of southwestern New Brunswick, possessed suitable climatic conditions for corn horticulture. Historical accounts indicate that the Mi'kmaq were growing tobacco during the early seventeenth century. Monckton (2004) identified corn kernels and cupule (*Zea mays*) fragments, and a single possible tobacco seed from the Jemseg site. Unfortunately, the cultural context for these specimens is presently unclear, and other specimens of uncharred squash seeds and a single charred barley seed are believed to date from the period of European settlement.

Faunal Resources

A wide variety of animal species were hunted or harvested by the Woodland peoples of the region, including land and marine mammals, birds, freshwater and marine fish, and shellfish. Today, the diversity and richness of faunal resources varies considerably by ecological zone within the region. Although the archaeological record for faunal resources in the region is far from complete and is plagued by the differential preservation of coastal and interior samples, it demonstrates that this situation also existed in the late precontact period when it affected local patterns of resource exploitation (e.g., Burley 1981, 206).

Fur-bearing animals were important to precontact peoples as a source of food and clothing and most species are widely distributed over the region. The species most often recovered from archaeological sites are the beaver, river otter, muskrat, hare, marten, fisher, black bear, whitetailed deer, caribou, and moose. The now-extinct sea mink has been reported from at least one site in Passamaquoddy Bay and another on Spednic Lake, and in larger numbers in northern Maine (Black et al. 1998; Deal 1986, 89; Robinson and Heller 2017, 94–97). The non-fur-bearing land mammal species include the porcupine and dog. Dog (*Canis familiaris*) remains are often found at sites on the Maritime Peninsula, dating back to the Archaic period (Mann 2021, 18–20). Mann (2021, 20–25) suggests that they probably served similar roles in precontact and historic times as valued hunting companions and, occasionally, for food (e.g., for feasting or during times of meat shortage).

6: THE CLAY POT PEOPLE

Bone and antler tools are common at coastal shell midden sites, including projectile points, awls, needles, combs, and leister prongs (e.g., Sanger 1987, 51–55; Figure 59). The teeth of beaver and various carnivores, such as the fisher, sea mink, and river otter, were also made into tools and pendants (Tyzzer 1943). Marine mammals are represented by harbour seal, hooded seal, grey seal, sperm whale, and harbour porpoise. Seals were hunted for their oil and skins by the Mi'kmaq of the northeast coast of New Brunswick and Prince Edward Island, and in early historic times these commodities became important in their trade with the Europeans

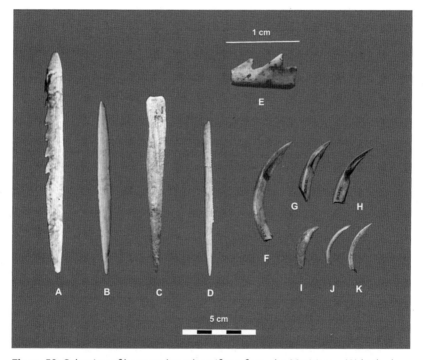

Figure 59: Selection of bone and tooth artifacts from the Maritimes: (A) barbed leister point and (B) bone needle, Merigomish, NS, (C) bone awl, Upper Path Lake Brook, Port Joli, NS, (D) bone pottery-decorating tool, Ministers Island, NB (see Kristmanson and Deal 1993, 75), (E) barbed bone point (calcined), Mud Lake Stream, NB, (F–K) animal tooth tools, Gooseberry Point, Campobello Island, NB. (A–B) courtesy Nova Scotia Museum, (C) John S. Erskine Photograph Collection (E150), (E–K) courtesy of the Government of New Brunswick.

(Prins 1996, 99–100). Atlantic walrus also was available to Indigenous peoples in these areas (Keenlyside 1984b, 11).

More than 30 avian species have been identified at sites in the Maritimes (e.g., Black 1992, 235–36; Erskine 1966). Migratory bird species are particularly useful for interpreting the season of occupation of precontact sites and, therefore, mobility patterns (Stewart 1989, 62–64, 67). Waterfowl could be hunted on the marshes and bogs of eastern New Brunswick, the Minas Basin of Nova Scotia, and on numerous marshy lakes in central New Brunswick (Ganong 1904b, 23).

The Bay of Fundy, the Gulf of St. Lawrence, and the Atlantic coast of Nova Scotia have varying currents, tidal amplitudes, and water temperatures (Scott and Scott 1988). These factors affect the diversity and productivity of fish and shellfish species in these areas. Marine fish species recovered from late precontact sites include herring, Atlantic cod, longhorn sculpin, Atlantic sturgeon, monkfish, harbour pollock, haddock, flounder, and hake. Of importance were anadromous species, such as Atlantic salmon, gaspereau (alewife), and American shad, which were available in great numbers during spawning season. The fish returned yearly to certain rivers where they could be captured easily at waterfalls, tideheads, and along narrow thoroughfares between lakes. Freshwater or "landlocked" Atlantic salmon are found in many of the interior lakes. Ganong (1904b, 24) even suggests that the catadromous species, the American eel, may have been the most important fixed resource for determining campsite and village locations. Several harvesting locations are known in the Maritimes. Weirs were used in some areas to catch eels and other fish, such as salmon and sea trout, on their downstream movement. Ronald Nash (1978) has also stressed the importance of eel fishing through ice in eastern Nova Scotia.

Another important fixed resource is the great variety of shellfish along the shorelines of the Maritimes. The most important species utilized along the Bay of Fundy coast was the soft-shell clam. Shells of this species form the bulk of most coastal midden deposits in Passamaquoddy Bay. Sea urchin is common in some insular shell middens. Clams often are considered a starvation food source, but Sanger (1987, 72) thinks that they may have had a pivotal role in adaptation to a marine environment. They can be gathered easily by all family members and they are edible throughout the winter. Black and Whitehead (1988) suggest that shellfish preservation and storage practices may have been developed in the precontact period, and Betts (2019, 91; Erskine 1962) reports large Middle Woodland clam-drying middens at Port Joli. Along the Gulf of St. Lawrence coastlines of New Brunswick, Nova Scotia, and Prince Edward Island, the Atlantic oyster is the most important species, along with the hard-shell clam or quahog, surf clam, soft-shell clam, and the common mussel.

Inorganic Resources

Lithic materials constitute the most significant class of inorganic resources collected by the precontact peoples of the Maritimes. These include a variety of knappable rocks for making chipped stone artifacts, less brittle varieties of rock utilized for hammerstones, anvils, and pecked and ground stone tools, as well as certain clays and minerals. The inorganic raw materials that we have the most information about are native copper and knappable lithics. Throughout the late precontact period, Indigenous peoples in the Maritimes were acquiring small amounts of native copper. During the Middle Woodland period, copper was collected and made into tool forms such as awls and blades (Leonard 1996, 80–102; Monahan 1990). This practice persisted until the Contact period, when copper and brass kettles became available through trade with Europeans and pieces of worn-out kettles were reworked for other functions, such as the tinkling cones worn by Mi'kmaw women (Whitehead 1991) and domestic tools such as knives (MacKinnon and Colpitts 2006).

All known source areas for native copper in the region occur along the Bay of Fundy and Minas Channel, with the best-known source being at Cape d'Or (Gloade 2020). These appear to be primary copper sources, existing as copper nuggets (nodules) and narrow veins or patches in trap rocks (Sabina 1965, 24, 29). Certain lithic source areas became well known in precontact times and lithics from those areas were widely distributed within the region. Primary sources in New Brunswick are found along the Tobique River (Burke 2000), at Washademoak Lake, central New Brunswick (Black and Wilson 1999; Jeandron 1997; Matthew 1900), and along the Bay of Fundy coast, while a few minor source areas have been identified along the coast of Passamaquoddy Bay (Crotts 1984; MacDonald 1994). Two other major lithic sources areas, formerly in Wolastoqwey territory in Maine, are the Munsungun Lake and Kineo-Traveller formations (Bonnischen 1981; Doyle 1995; Pollock et al. 1999). Small quantities of lithics from the Mistassini region of central Quebec and Ramah Bay in Labrador have been identified in archaeological sites in the region. These two lithics are very difficult to distinguish visually, but each has been differentiated using geochemical techniques (Rutherford and Stevens 1991). These lithics are believed to have arrived in the region over an exchange network that followed the east coast south from Labrador to New England (Loring 1988).

Chalifoux and Burke (1995) identify two quarries and several workshop sites at Grand Touladi Lake, in the Témiscouta region of Quebec. This region consists of a series of lakes and rivers that connect the upper Saint John and St. Lawrence rivers. It formed part of the early historic Wolastoqwey territory. Touladi lithics, which form part of the Cabano Formation, are described as fine-grained homogeneous cherts, varying in colour from black to grey to bluish green (Burke 2000, 178–79). This material is rarely found in secondary deposits. Touladi cherts represent the dominant material for archaeological sites in the Témiscouta area. Access to the Saint John River drainage means that this material is likely to be present, but unidentified, in lithic assemblages of sites along the central and southern portions of the river.

Munsungun lithic materials have been described as deep red wine, dark green, dark grey, or black cherts, moderately fine-grained, massively textured, weakly translucent at the edges, and having excellent conchoidal fracture (Doyle 1995, 306). Burke (2000, 189–92) writes that most of the Munsungun chert used during Palaeo times was collected at the source, but that late precontact peoples may have collected loose fragments from secondary deposits in streams and around the lakes in the area. A second lithic source area in Maine is the Kineo-Traveller Mountain region. Fragments of Kineo rhyolite (or felsite) were spread widely over central and eastern Maine as glacial till. Unsurprisingly, it occurs commonly in archaeological assemblages of the region (Burke 2000, 223; Doyle 1995). This lithic material has been described as a green-grey, glassy, porphyritic rhyolite, containing phenocrysts of feldspar, tiny glass beads of quartz, and several accessory minerals (Doyle 1995, 304). This material occurs occasionally in archaeological assemblages in Passamaquoddy Bay (MacDonald 1994, 36).

In Nova Scotia, the primary source of cryptocrystalline lithics is North Mountain, along the Bay of Fundy, while White Rock quartzite and Geganisg cherts also were in demand. North Mountain is a huge block of basalt along the Bay of Fundy coast that yields a variety of chalcedonies, agates, and jaspers (Dostal and Dupuy 1984, 247; Sabina 1965, 41–46). Knappable lithics can be quarried or collected at several locations extending from Cape Blomidon around Cape Split and southwest to Digby Neck. The most accessible deposits are at either end of this range, with 12 locations along Digby Neck and 22 locations at the northeastern end. The most extensive deposits are associated with the Scots Bay Formation, and a workshop site has been identified at Davidson Cove (see Vignette 14). Another important Nova Scotian source is the Geganisg quarry site on Ingonish Island, off northern Cape Breton Island (Nash 1978). This material has been classified as a medium-grained, grey-to-black rhyolite, with pronounced foliation, and Ingonish Island rhyolite is petrologically quite different from mainland Cape Breton rhyolites (Barr and Raeside 1998, 30). Specimens have been visually identified at sites along the eastern coast of New Brunswick and Nova Scotia, on Prince Edward Island, and on the Magdalen Islands (Keenlyside 1990, 14; Martijn 1989, 212; McCaffrey 1986, 153). Unfortunately, part of the site has eroded away since Nash's excavation (Donovan 2009, 333).

Scots Bay Lithics

The principal source of lithic resources along North Mountain, Nova Scotia, is in the Scots Bay and Blomidon peninsula. Scots Bay lithics fall within the general class of sedimentary microcrystalline silicates commonly called chert. In both the geological and archaeological literature, the term "chalcedony" is more often applied to these deposits. Chalcedony is one of several subvarieties of chert distinguished by colour, texture, internal structure, and water content. According to geologist John Thompson (1974, 151–52), the Scots Bay chalcedony is characterized by a structure of well-defined polyhedral blocks, few, or no, water-filled cavities, and as colourless or light brown in transmitted light.

The relationships between common siliceous materials based on their crystal size and arrangement are illustrated in Figure 60. In archaeological terminology, chalcedony includes the fibrous subvarieties of cryptocrystalline quartz, while chert, as a subvariety of cryptocrystalline quartz, is granular in nature (e.g., Crabtree 1967, 12; Crotts 1985, 48; Hammer 1976,

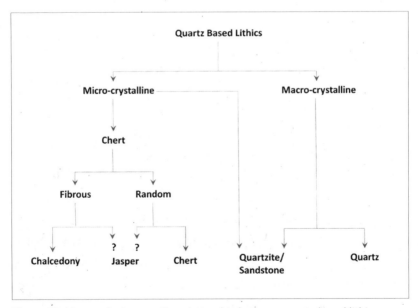

Figure 60: Hammer's chart on the relationship between quartz-based lithics (adapted from Hammer 1976, 42).

40–41). In practice, the light colour and waxy luster of chalcedony are important for archaeological identification. The Scots Bay lithics include the variegated subvariety of chalcedony known as "agate" and the more difficult to categorize subvariety "jasper." Crabtree (1967, 12) considers jasper an impure form of chalcedony that derives its distinctive red or yellow colour from inclusions of iron-based clay (1967, 12). Ross Creek is the source of a distinctive dark-brown jasper.

Decades of geological research have established that the depositional environment for the Scots Bay limestones, which were subsequently replaced by chalcedonies, was a shallow, freshwater lake associated with the chalcedony-rich deposits of Cape d'Or and the jasper-producing deposits on Isle Haute (Crosby 1962; Klein 1962; Thompson 1974). Throughout this area, the chalcedonies occur either as replacement nodules in limestone or siltstone, or as extensive bedded deposits in limestone (Thompson 1974, 144). According to Thompson, the nodules are typically red, reddish brown, and brown due to disseminated hematite, and they are generally cylindrical in shape, with their axes lying parallel to the paleocurrent direction (1974, 144). The nodules in limestone can be up to 30 cm in diameter and two metres in length. Chalcedony beds in limestone are generally less than five centimetres thick and predominantly blue-grey in colour (Thompson 1974, 152). Geochemical analysis by Thompson (1974, 154) indicated chemical differences between the nodules and beds, with the nodules being higher in silica and lower in all other targeted elements.

Several locations of chalcedony beds were recorded in 1964 by geologists from the Nova Scotia Museum, in conjunction with archaeological work at the Debert Palaeo site. Except for two areas with abundant chalcedony veins, these beds are thin and isolated. Nodules of chalcedony also are scattered on the beaches of most of the large coves. The coves nearer to the point are difficult to reach on foot due to high cliff faces, sometimes over 60 m above the shoreline. Of the four archaeological sites identified, only the shell midden site at Clam Cove (BhDc-5) has evidence of seasonal use over an extended period.

The source area along Scots Bay forms part of what Thompson calls the Scots Bay Formation. It has several major outcrops of chalcedony. Two of these are reached easily on foot, while access to the other outcrops is limited by tidal activity. Water-worn nodules of chalcedony can be gathered along the entire shoreline of this area and exposed chalcedony beds are common. However, the only precontact workshop site known in the area is associated with the outcrops at Davidson Cove.

Vignette 14: Davidson Cove Quarry and Workshop

Quarrying and workshop areas haved tended to be neglected by archaeologists due to the vast quantities and lack of variety in the materials collected (Ericson 1984). However, they can be viewed as the initial stages of a tightly integrated system that involves the selection, modification, distribution, and consumption of lithic materials (Ericson 1984). They can provide valuable information on quarrying procedures, tools, and strategies for initial lithic reduction, and a wealth of analyzable debitage (Bryan 1950; Purdy 1984; Ritchie and Gould 1985). One pioneer in lithic quarry studies estimated that nine-tenths of the initial reduction materials were wasted (Holmes 1919, 178), and experimental studies tend to support this assertion (e.g., Newcomer 1971). Other studies have focused on tracing lithics from various sites to their source locations for economic analysis (e.g., Gramly 1980).

The extensive workshop area at Davidson Cove lies on the eastern bank of Thorpe Brook, where it flows into Scots Bay, Nova Scotia (Figure 61). Davidson Cove has been known to geologists for decades for its chalcedony outcrops, but the workshop area was not officially recorded as an archaeological site until July of 1988 (Deal 1988). At that time, the site was mapped and tested, and column samples were collected from a profile along the shore face.

The workshop site extends up Thorpe Brook for at least 25 m and along the shore face parallel to the Bay for about 40 m. It is situated on a ridge about 6 m above the basalt shore and well above the highest high tide level. Erosion witnessed along the shore face is primarily due to winter storms and freeze-

6: THE CLAY POT PEOPLE

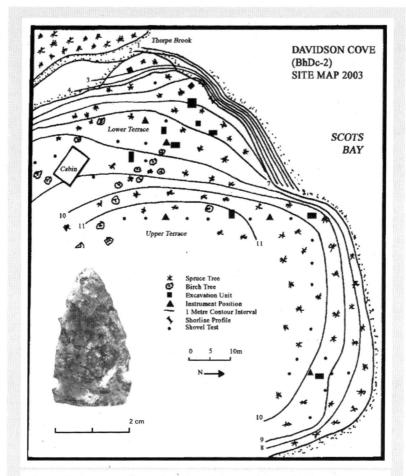

Figure 61: Site map of Davidson Cove lithic workshop, 2003, with insert of a Late Woodland side-notched projectile point recovered at the site in 1988. Drawing and photograph by Michael Deal.

thaw activity rather than to tidal action. A 20-square-centimetre column sample was taken from a profile along this shore face to provide an estimate of production intensity at the site. A thick layer of debitage was recorded at the base of the initial humus layer and the upper portion of the underlying layer of silt. The ratio of sediment to lithics by weight for each of these layers was 0.81, while the ratio of sediment to lithics by volume for each layer was identical at

2.4. In addition, 15.9 kilograms of flakes, core fragments, and quarry blanks were collected from a single one-metre-square test unit. The debitage was primarily chalcedony, with a wide range of colour variation.

While it is likely that both bedded chalcedony and nodules were used for making quarry blanks, decades of visits by geologists and rockhounds have resulted in the defacement of the bedded deposits by metal picks. The presence at the site of three small quartzite hammerstones and one hammerstone/anvil indicates that initial reduction was done using a hard hammer technique. The 20 quarry blanks collected were bifaces with very generalized morphologies, and most of them seem to have been discarded because they could not be reduced to the desired thinness. This assumption is based on the relatively large nodes of material left in the midsections of most discarded specimens.

A subsequent excavation in 2003 confirmed our original understanding of the site as a large lithic workshop area. Crude bifaces and biface fragments were found along with hammerstones in most units. Large end scrapers were also common and may have been used for working wooden billets used in lithic reduction. The distribution of debitage hints at the organization of production at the site. The presence of a lithic dump, along with the predominance of larger cores and fragments in units near the shore face, suggests that that area was used for the initial reduction of cores. Pressure flakes from biface manufacture were found in greater quantities at the back of the lower terrace and suggest that finer work was done in this area. The lithic debitage was sorted into three categories, namely, cores and core fragments, reduction flakes, and pressure flakes. The latter was arbitrarily set at less than 1 square cm. The artifact assemblage included 44 bifaces, 50 biface fragments, 9 bipolar cores, 3 gravers, 30 hammerstones/anvils, 3 projectile point fragments, 13 scrapers, 5 uniface fragments, and 11 utilized flakes and cores. Catherine Jalbert's study of the debitage from Davidson Cove and other sites in the Minas Basin area confirms its primary use as a quarry/workshop site, as the site itself produced 100 per cent Scots Bay materials, compared to 77 per cent at the nearby Clam Cove site and 48.2 per cent at the St. Croix site, on the St. Croix River (2011, 102). She believes that the workforce at the site was likely composed of both experts and novices, based on the quality of discarded bifaces and characteristics of the fracturing they exhibit (Jalbert 2011, 61–100).

Lithic Distribution

North Mountain lithics shed some light on the nature of regional lithic distribution. Two lines of evidence from Davidson Cove suggest a Middle to Late Woodland period utilization of the Scots Bay chalcedonies. The first is a radiocarbon date of 1,540 ± 110 ^{14}C yrs (Beta 29379), derived from a charcoal lens that was completely encased in debitage, and therefore is believed to date to a time when the workshop was in operation. The second piece of evidence is a small, side-notched, Late Woodland projectile point from test unit one, which is the only finished tool recovered from the site. Furthermore, all other diagnostic artifacts thus far recovered from the Scots Bay area can be dated confidently to the Middle or Late Woodland period. The chalcedony sources, including outcrops and glacial till, are reported in rock and mineral guides for the region (Morrill and Hinchley 1959, 1981; Sabina 1965), but do not necessarily represent sources exploited in precontact times. In fact, the only other identified Indigenous chalcedony workshop in the Maritimes is on Washademoak Lake on the Saint John River drainage (Black and Wilson 1999; Crotts 1985, 51; Gesner 1839, 60; Matthew 1900, 62–63).

In Nova Scotia, chalcedonies are found only along the Bay of Fundy shore from Digby Neck to Blomidon, and at Cape d'Or (Figures 62 and 63). It is significant that Fundy shore chalcedony is rarely encountered east of the Shubenacadie River (e.g., Nash 1986, 29, 39), while chalcedonies from the Cape d'Or/Parrsboro area have been identified at the Palaeo site at Debert (MacDonald 1968) and eastwards into Pictou County. The Scots Bay sources may have been accessed by water from the Minas Basin area (e.g., Blair 2010), although the water route around Cape Split to the quarry sites can be hazardous. Overland trails also were possible but would greatly limit the amount of lithic material collected. The most abundant use of these chalcedonies is along the Minas Basin and up the Gaspereau River to Gaspereau Lake. The southward distribution of Fundy shore chalcedony seems to follow well-known historic portage routes to the Atlantic, namely, via the Shubenacadie and Musquodoboit rivers in central

6: THE CLAY POT PEOPLE

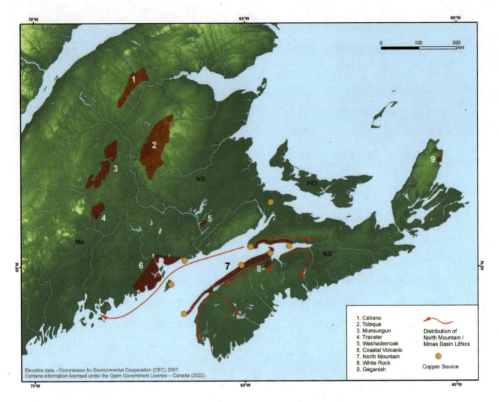

Figure 62: Map indicating the approximate locations of major lithic and copper source areas mentioned in text, with arrows showing possible distribution routes of North Mountain and Minas Basin lithics. Map by Michael Deal and Bryn Tapper.

Nova Scotia and via the Mersey River in southwestern Nova Scotia (see Deal et al. 1987; Sable 2011, 161–62). The source areas on Digby Neck have not yet been surveyed by archaeologists. They may have provided the chalcedonies for inhabitants of the southwestern coast and may also have moved along the Mersey route via Bear River. The distribution of this high-quality lithic material within western Nova Scotia may reflect late precontact sociopolitical organization in the region. It corresponds closely to one of the seven Mi'kmaw political districts of *Kespoogwit*, which stretches from Cape Sable to the Shubenacadie and Musquodoboit rivers (Biard 1959, 89; Lewis and Sable 2014; Speck 1922, 93–105).

6: THE CLAY POT PEOPLE

Figure 63: Lithic cores (i.e., blocks of raw material) from Scots Bay (NS) and Washademoak Lake (NB) as displayed in the Great Hall, Queen's College, Memorial University, 2009. Photographs by Catherine Jalbert.

Since stone tools were largely replaced by iron ones during the Contact period (Bailey 1969), we have no clear record of the possible sociopolitical role of lithics within the region. Ethnographic data from other areas suggest that quarry sources are generally held in common among groups of hunter-gatherers. However, the production of generalized quarry blanks at Davidson Cove seems to indicate that the workshop knapper did not know the consumer, therefore raising the possibility that lithics were used in some form of intraregional exchange (see Ericson 1984, 6). If consumption was local, workshops might be expected to produce a wider variety of finished tools to reduce transport loads (see Ericson 1984; Gramly 1980). However, it is possible that fewer finished tools were produced to reduce the amount of time spent at workshop sites.

If Scots Bay chalcedonies were being used in a lithic exchange system, it is likely that access was restricted to local families or communities. While the ethnohistoric literature hints at a complex political hierarchy of chiefs and councils (Nietfeld 1981), this structure is probably a product of contact with non-Mi'kmaq, as well as the Eurocentric views of the early chroniclers. The lowest level of this hierarchy is probably our most useful model for the precontact era. It consists of a local leader responsible for a group of related families who shared a specific summer camp. In historic times, each of these families controlled specific hunting territories around lakes and river courses (Speck 1922). Summer meetings were important for arranging marriages, settling disputes, and cooperating on economic projects.

In the precontact era, summer would be the ideal time for excursions to the quarry sites on the Fundy shore. Quarry blanks and some finished tools produced at Scots Bay were probably taken to summer camping areas, like Melanson, on the Gaspereau River. If the quarry blanks were made intentionally for exchange with other local groups within the district, this exchange was most likely on a small scale, such as infrequent exchanges between family groups along the borders of hunting territories or at contact points along major portage routes. While this discussion of the distribution of Scots Bay chalcedonies is largely speculative, it does seem to correspond to available archaeological and ethnohistorical information. At the very least, we can say that Scots Bay chalcedony was a valuable and widely distributed commodity during the Middle and Late Woodland period in western Nova Scotia.

Significant quantities of Scots Bay lithics, along with Cape d'Or copper, made their way to northern Maine. Cox (2022, 81) considers the Goddard site, in eastern Penobscot Bay, to have been perhaps the largest Late Woodland occupation in Maine between AD 650 and 950. He describes it as a large summer village and important gathering place in an Indigenous trading network (i.e., a gateway site). It received exotic lithics from quarries throughout New England, as well as from Ramah Bay in Labrador and the western Minas Basin. More than 700 artifacts were made from Nova Scotia lithics, including 98 completed tools (i.e., projectile points, bifaces, and end scrapers). Other contemporary sites with significant amounts of Nova Scotia lithics include the Watson site, on Frenchman's Bay, and Mattawamkeag, on the upper Penobscot River (Cox 2021, 75; Cox and Kopec 1988). Cox believes that trading was indirect, or down-the-line trading, involving several communities between the source and distribution site. Black (2022, 102–03) also notes that brightly coloured cryptocrystalline cherts from Nova Scotia, Maine, and the New Brunswick interior were favoured in the Quoddy region during the Late Woodland.

Settlement and Subsistence Models

Several settlement and subsistence models have been developed for the precontact populations of the Maritimes. The earliest models, dating to the nineteenth century, followed a direct historical approach, in which accounts of the early explorers and settlers were projected back in time. The first comprehensive model of the modern era was developed by Bernard Hoffman (1955, 152). Hoffman's model also relied on ethnohistoric sources, yet he was sensitive to the changes to Indigenous culture that resulted from European contact. Hoffman presents a simple cyclical model of the late precontact period, which featured summer coastal habitation and a winter inland hunting season. This information was presented on a circular chart that included seasonally available fauna, the size of social groupings, and the area of resource exploitation. It was originally presented as a model for the Mi'kmaw area. However, combined with the work of Speck among the Penobscot (1940), a basic cyclical model was generally accepted for the entire Maritime Peninsula (Sanger 1996b, 514; 2000, 155). As archaeological data began to accumulate, Hoffman's model was called into question. David Sanger (1971) pointed out that the model was inconsistent with archaeological information from northern Maine, where faunal evidence suggested a winter coastal occupation for the Late Woodland period. Subsequent fieldwork in the coastal Quoddy region suggests a similar pattern for southwestern New Brunswick. Sanger (1987) contends that the apparent reversal in settlement use was a result of the intensification of the fur trade during the late sixteenth century, in which Indigenous peoples hunted fur-bearing animals in the winter and moved to the coast in the summer to trade with visiting Europeans.

Based on two decades of coastal surveys of Boothbay Harbor and East Penobscot Bay, Maine, David Sanger introduced a two-population model for the Woodland period in Maine (1982, 1996b, 1996c). Research at coastal shell middens indicated that precontact people moved around regularly to exploit different resources, but only within the littoral (shore) zone (Sanger 1996b, 515–18; 2000, 158). Sanger subsequently proposes that different populations may have inhabited the coast and interior regions during this period, each adapted to a different environment. This model was supported by studies of coastal and interior cordage twist patterns of fibre perishables used in pottery manufacture (Petersen 1996). Bonnie Newsom (2017) tested the two-population model by examining potters' choices in production over time in three ecological regions along the Penobscot River (i.e., coastal, head-of-tide, and interior). Her extensive analysis of fabric composition, and of shape and decorative characteristics, revealed a shared common heritage (or macrotradition) that indicated a level of social interaction throughout the area. The fabric twist dichotomy remains, but she also discovered distinctions in the production of pottery in each region. At the head-of-tide, at the Eddington Bend site, compact fabrics and high lip diversity indicated larger, hotter firing processes, where several families converged at the site to produce pottery vessels of a variety of functions (Newsom 2017, 204–05). At interior sites, vessels with thicker walls and higher inclusion densities indicated a domestic scale of production and vessels more suitable for transport. At coastal sites, the mechanical strength of pottery decreased over time and lip diversity was scant, suggesting a move to more standard, stable production and a somewhat sedentary lifestyle (Newsom 2017, 205–06). Newsom's study conceives a more complex situation than the two-population model and highlights several common features of Indigenous lifestyles, including "flexibility, fluidity, and mutability" (Newsom 2017, 211).

Dean Snow (1980, 42ff.) depicts a general dualistic settlement pattern for the Early and Middle Woodland cultures along the northeast coast up to the Saint John River, featuring interior summer camps and winter coastal occupation. His model for the Late Woodland has been referred to by Sanger as a "centralistic" resource exploitation pattern, involving larger settlements on the major rivers, from which collecting trips were made to inland and coastal resource sites. According to Sanger (1987, 140), Snow's Early-Middle Woodland model appears to be refuted by evidence of possible year-round occupation at some coastal sites, while a lack of evidence for large inland village sites brings his Late Woodland model into question. As an alternative to Snow's model, Sanger proposes that nucleation into larger villages in river valleys like the Saint John began after European settlement, when Indigenous populations were devastated by diseases and felt a need to assert their control over riverine trade routes.

Sanger (1987, 113) characterizes coastal Passamaquoddy Bay sites as cold-weather residential camps, from which small groups sortied to exploit local resources at logistical camps. He adopts a generalized hunting-gathering subsistence pattern for this region that he terms an "effective working territory." Shellfish obviously were an important factor in site location, while various nearby marine and terrestrial habitats were extensively exploited. Boating technology allowed for a larger marine (versus terrestrial) catchment area. However, tidal ranges in the region would have greatly affected the scheduling of activities, in that canoeists would try to avoid the wider intertidal zone in favour of sheltered coves.

David Black (1992, 2003, 2013) has presented a detailed ecologically based analysis of late precontact occupation of the Bliss Islands, Passamaquoddy Bay. During the Middle Woodland period, the Bliss Islands may have been utilized periodically during both the warm and cold seasons and, possibly, year-round. He suggests a maximum population density during the Middle and early Late Woodland period, which coincided with a period of high productivity in shellfish species due to a stabilization of the local shorelines. Both summer and winter sites and dwelling remnants are identified. Black presents a pattern of fauna exploitation involving shellfish collecting in the winter and spring, deer hunting in spring and summer, birding in the summer, vertebrate fish harvesting from traps and weirs in summer and fall, and grey seal hunting in winter. By contrast, Late Woodland camps are warm-season occupations, and faunal assemblages indicate a greater emphasis on hunting and less emphasis on littoral resources, with the hunting of harbour seals in spring and early summer, harvesting of herring and cod, and birding in summer, and deer and moose hunting in fall. Patton and others (2022, 272) present an updated model for the Late Woodland Quoddy region featuring fragmented shoreline settlements of closely related households that exploited microlocal resources, based on the diversity of vertebrate and invertebrate faunal remains and site structure.

Betts (2019) presents a model for the Port Joli area that also recognizes major shifts in site location and site structure between Middle and Late Woodland occupations. Middle Woodland peoples relied more heavily on shellfish exploitation and left behind deep processing middens (Betts 2019, 355–59). Some sites represent year-round occupation. With a decline in shellfish productivity, Late Woodland peoples relied more heavily on cod and hare in winter and hunted more cervids and less waterfowl. The area was abandoned by the late seventeenth century.

The Chiputneticook–St. Croix drainage area is believed to be the principal interior resource area for the ancestral Peskotomuhkatiyik. The St. Croix River is not easily navigable. Little evidence exists of campsites along the river, especially between the West Grand and Chiputneticook Lake systems. Sanger (1986, 154; 1987, 132) envisages that the St. Croix may not have served as a major interior waterway at all, and that the interior and coastal inhabitants were two different populations. Archaeological evidence from Spednic Lake affirms that two settlement areas at opposite ends of the lake were used as bases for fishing, hunting, and birding expeditions from later spring to fall (Deal et al. 1991, 172). A winter occupation cannot be demonstrated or ruled out. The remaining sites are widely dispersed along the lake, including sites on islands and the tips of long, narrow peninsulas.

Dean Snow (1980) was the first author to give detailed consideration of precontact settlement and subsistence patterning on the Saint John River. He believes that ancestral Wolastoqiyik lived in semi-permanent villages located on salt water. These villages could range as far north as the Lakes region, which sits at the head of tide for the Saint John River. Snow's model involves logistical movements of small, family-based groups from these villages into upstream forests in the winter and to coastal encampments in the late spring and summer as important resources became available. According to Snow (1980, 47), winter campsites were scattered along the shores of the river and its ponds, lakes, and most tributaries, and summer campsites were found on the coast. Snow feels that the European fur trade had little effect on the Wolastoqiyik, since they followed a relatively mobile and diffuse settlement/subsistence pattern. He also suggests that whatever incentive there was to adopt horticulture disappeared with the intensification of the fur trade. Thus, semi-permanent villages, regular seasonal scheduling, and a dense population led to development of a more complex sociopolitical system. According to David Sanger (personal communication, 1998), Snow's model appears to be based primarily on Speck's (1940) characterization of the Penobscot (Panawahpskewi) in Maine, which he applies wholesale to the Saint John River region without adequate confirmation from archaeological evidence.

In a study of the major lithic source areas at Témiscouta, Tobique, and Munsungun, Adrian Burke (2000) reviews the archaeological evidence for settlement and subsistence patterning for the interior of the Saint John River waterway. He considers three possible scenarios, but eventually settles on a model with two distinct populations. The interior population is characterized by small, mobile, family-based groups that used the major lithic resources as part of their annual round. The coastal group is considered more sedentary, with a specialized coastal economy. Lithics are an important element in the social and economic interactions between the two groups.

David Burley (1981, 207) characterizes the protohistoric Mi'kmaq of the Northeast as generalized hunter-gatherers, using a centralized residential site from which to exploit resources in two or more areas. His model for the late precontact period emphasizes the importance of fishing and food preservation, the gathering of shellfish, and sea mammal hunting in spring and midwinter, and the year-round hunting of ungulates. Pat Allen (1991, 2005) suggests that during the fall, residents of the Oxbow site on the southwest Miramichi began to move to winter camps on upper terraces, where large storage pits were filled with pots and baskets of dried and smoked fish, smoked fowl, fruits, nuts, and edible grains. With some local resource variation, this model might be extended to the coastal lagoon-estuary localities at Tracadie and Kouchibouquac. Keenlyside (1990, 32) notes that prime fishing locations on the Tracadie River drainage, such as prominent points of land or shoreline locations where the channel changes direction, were clearly an important consideration in the choice of habitation sites. The occurrence at Tracadie sites of exotic lithics from Cape Breton Island, the Bay of Fundy, and Ramah Bay seems to lend more support to the notion of a regional exchange for the late precontact period (Keenlyside 1990).

6: THE CLAY POT PEOPLE

Ronald Nash and Virginia Miller (1987) reconsider Hoffman's model citing new faunal evidence for eastern Nova Scotia and Cape Breton Island and opt for a more generalized subsistence pattern for the late precontact period in that area. Faunal evidence indicates less reliance on marine resources than Hoffman's model predicts. They present an "economic mosaic" model, which stresses local resource availability, the relative importance of terrestrial mammal hunting, the influence of other cultural variables (i.e., social, political, ideological) and features of the landscape on economic activity, and the regional importance of eels as a critical winter resource (Figure 64).

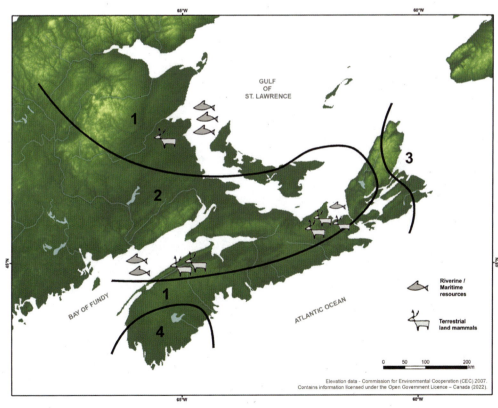

Figure 64: Nash and Miller economic mosaic model for the precontact Mi'kmaq (adapted from drawing in Nash and Miller 1987 by Bryn Tapper).

6: THE CLAY POT PEOPLE

In the 1980s, Stephen Davis (1986) presented an ecological model for precontact settlement and subsistence strategies in the St. Margaret's Bay area, along the Atlantic coast of Nova Scotia. His "contiguous habitat subsistence" model features four interacting habitats that provide access to

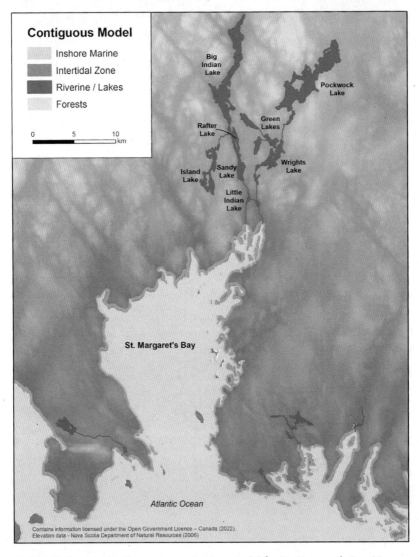

Figure 65: Stephen Davis contiguous habitat model for St. Margaret's Bay, Nova Scotia (adapted from drawing in Davis 1986 by Bryn Tapper).

inshore marine, intertidal, riverine/lacustrine, and forest ecological zones (Figure 65). Key resources include anadromous fish species, shellfish, cod, and seabird eggs in the warmer seasons, and seals, beaver, otter, and ungulates in the winter. The main residential camps are on the coast, with interior logistical camps for fish runs and hunting.

In the 1980s, Ronald Nash was working in southwestern Nova Scotia, in the Minas Basin area. Based on his fieldwork at the Melanson site, along the Gaspereau River, he proposes a "central place" model, which emphasizes local resource diversity (Nash et al. 1991). The Gaspereau River is presented as having the most favourable climate in the Minas Basin area. He identifies five aquatic and five terrestrial microenvironments, providing access to a wide variety of anadromous and marine fish species, waterbirds, shellfish, ungulates, bear, beaver, hare, and edible berries. Although not included in Nash's model, the river also provides access to an extensive system of interior lakes and runs close to the major source of White Rock quartzite, which is a dominant chipped stone raw material used on the system, along with cherts from nearby North Mountain.

For the most part, the models presented above were devised to make sense out of settlement and subsistence data for relatively small study areas. Important elements of the models are characteristics of the local landscape, site size and distribution, and the faunal record. Most of the models were developed before there was any substantial archaeobotanical record, and lithics were generally ignored (see Vignette 15). A more comprehensive model like Nash's economic mosaic model, which incorporates the entire region and focuses on regional rather than on local resource diversity, would include the following elements (adapted from Deal 2002).

1. The region is divided into five physiographic areas, beginning with the traditional territories. The Mi'kmaw territory is further divided into three areas, based on the three distinct coastal zones of the Gulf of St. Lawrence, the Atlantic coast, and the Bay of Fundy. Each of the zones has varying coastal features, tidal ranges, currents, and water temperatures, which affect local resource diversity. For example, Ronald Nash has pointed

out that seven important marine fish species of the Atlantic zone are scarce in the Bay of Fundy, and that shellfish are more abundant on the Atlantic coast. While seabird colonies are abundant on the Atlantic coast, the extensive marshlands of the Fundy coast attract more migrating birds.

2. While the Chiputneticook–St. Croix and Saint John waterways are important transportation routes, most travel in central and western New Brunswick was probably done in the interior, along shorter routes with portages linking the numerous lakes and small rivers. William Ganong recorded the extensive network of routes that existed at contact. By contrast, travel along the coast of the Gulf of St. Lawrence was more likely between interior and coast, due to the number of smaller, shorter river systems. Most of the recorded early travel routes for mainland Nova Scotia linked shorter rivers with interior lakes by portages, and thereby created coast-to-coast routes (e.g., Pentz 2008).

3. While many of the same plant species were available for fuel, construction, medicines, plant fibres, and edible fruits, some significant species were found in only one or two areas. This included groundnut, butternut, Canada plum, wild grape, and basswood. The presence of butternuts at Port Joli likely demonstrates a regional exchange of foodstuffs. Further, corn horticulture was possible only in a few favourable areas. Similarly, certain species of fauna are more closely associated with a specific area, such as oysters and walrus with the Gulf of St. Lawrence.

4. Unlike most faunal and floral resources, desirable lithics are often found in remote and difficult-to-access locations. Some regions are well supplied, while others must make do with a poor grade of materials, travel long distances to collect raw materials, or acquire them through exchange. More exotic materials, like Ramah and Mistassini cherts, likely were traded into the region.

We have seen that accumulated archaeological information has revealed the flaws in Hoffman's cyclical settlement and subsistence model for the precontact period in the Maritimes. A regional diversity model like the one outlined here provides a baseline against which we can estimate the relative resource richness of smaller study areas and allows us to put perceived local patterns of mobility and trade into a broader perspective. Eventually, we may even be able to develop a settlement and subsistence model that considers local resource variability over time. It is important to remember that Indigenous populations were sensitive to changing resource availability and adapted their movements and settlement systems accordingly.

Vignette 15: St. Croix Village

The St. Croix site is located along the southeastern bank of the St. Croix River, Hants County, Nova Scotia (Figure 66). It has yielded evidence of more than 3,000 years of occupation, making it one of the more significant archaeological sites in the region. This site, not to be confused with the St. Croix River bordering part of present-day New Brunswick and Maine, was a focus of investigation for the Minas Basin Archaeological Project from 1990 to 1993, which studied precontact resource exploitation and settlement patterns in the Minas Basin region. St. Croix was one of the first sites in the region to be sampled for paleoethnobotanical materials and remains a key site to our understanding of precontact plant use (Deal and Halwas 2008). The site was also featured in a thermoluminescence dating project, which has helped to refine the regional ceramic sequence (Godfrey-Smith et al. 1993).

The St. Croix site was first identified by John Erskine in 1964. It was revisited in 1989 during the second year of the Minas Basin Archaeological survey. The site was later the focus of two archaeological field schools: for Memorial University in 1990 and for Acadia University in 1993, during which a total of 33 m² were sampled. The river forms part of a traditional portage route connecting the Minas Basin area (and Bay of Fundy) with St. Margaret's Bay on the Atlantic coast. Much of the site has been disturbed by historic farming and construction activities, yet the area chosen for excavation has shown evidence of disturbance only along the eastern edge. Most of the material culture recovered dates to the Woodland period. The occupants of St. Croix relied heavily on stone tool raw materials from Scots Bay,

6: THE CLAY POT PEOPLE

Figure 66: Artist's conception of life at a Woodland period spring–summer campsite. From an original watercolour by Brittany Roberts, commissioned by Michael Deal, 2013.

but also made extensive use of quartzites of the White Rock Formation from the Gaspereau Valley. A few exotic materials also were recovered, including a projectile point made from a raw material quarried in the Mistassini area of Quebec (Figure 67).

The faunal assemblage consisted of 801 calcined bone fragments: including 81 large, 32 medium, and 3 small mammal specimens, one unidentified fish vertebra, and the right distal tibia of a fox (*Vulpes* sp.). The recovered plant remains consisted of 59 specimens representing 20 species, including pin cherry (*Prunus pensylvanica*), foxtail (*Seteria sp.*), and elderberry (*Sambucus canadensis*). The size and location of the site, along with the quantity and diversity of material culture collected, suggest that it was probably a small village, where groups collected to exploit anadromous fish runs in the spring and/or fall seasons.

In 1993, St. Croix became the focus of a ceramic dating project, in which sherds were collected for dating using the thermoluminescence (or TL)

6: THE CLAY POT PEOPLE

technique. This method is preferable to radiocarbon dating since it provides a date for the ceramic sherd itself. Dating of the ceramics was conducted by Dorothy Godfrey-Smith and two students at the Luminescence Laboratory at the Department of Earth Sciences, Dalhousie University. The laboratory analysis resulted in five TL dates, which provided, along with three radiocarbon

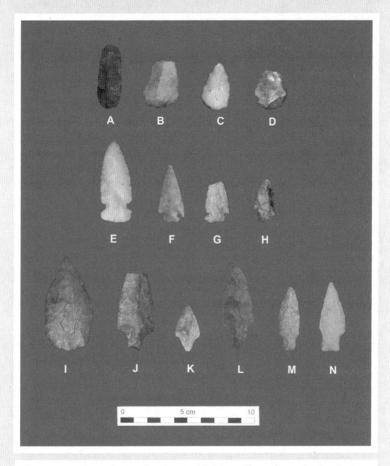

Figure 67: Selected Woodland period lithic artifacts from the St. Croix site excavations (1989–90, 1993, 2012): (A) side scraper, (B–C) end scrapers, (D) thumbnail scraper, (E) side-notched projectile point, (F–H) corner-notched projectile points, (I) biface, (J–K) contracting stem projectile points, and (L–N) straight to slightly expanding stem projectile points. Photographs by Michael Deal.

dates, a basic chronological framework against which we could interpret the cultural history of the Minas Basin area (Deal et al. 1994; Godfrey-Smith et al. 1997). A former owner of the property had amassed a small collection of Late Archaic stemmed projectile points from a field that runs behind the site to the northeast. What appears to be a Late Archaic drill was recovered from a Middle Woodland deposit at the site and is assumed to be either an heirloom or intrusive to the deposit. The presence of Archaic materials at the site is significant because few sites in the region have produced *in situ* Archaic deposits.

In 2012, Cameron Milner returned to the site as part of his MA research (2013). His objectives were to continue the original excavation to the northwest, along the riverbank, and to test heavily disturbed areas of the site to determine if any of the original deposits were intact. His work extended the known northwestern limit of the site another 60 m and he was able to identify a thin, undisturbed occupation layer below heavily impacted areas of the site. His work also expanded the collection of charred plant remains and increased the size of the Middle/Late Woodland ceramic and lithic assemblages.

Historic Lifeways Develop in the Maritime Peninsula

The role of Transitional Archaic technologies in the development of Indigenous cultural traditions in the Maritimes is still unclear, but it seems likely the Early Woodland manifestation in most of the region developed out of the local Late Archaic cultures. The Woodland was characterized by a more diverse hunting, gathering, and fishing economy that varied across the region in terms of kinds of resources and their relative productivity. The main addition to the local technology was pottery, which provided serving, storage, and cooking containers. Early vessels may have been used primarily for the processing and storage of fish for feasting and exchange, but by Middle Woodland times they served more for storage and cooking, like the wooden and brass containers in the historic period. New, smaller projectile points represent the introduction of a bow-and-arrow technology. Small scrapers may be associated with the adoption of birchbark technology, particularly the birchbark canoe.

The Early Woodland saw increased contact with Indigenous peoples to the west and the earliest rock art in the region. By 2,800 ^{14}C yrs BP, some areas of the region were adopting a local variant of Meadowood technology, large-scale storage practices, and a cremation burial tradition. This phenomenon is seen primarily in northeastern New Brunswick, the St. Croix drainage and adjacent parts of Maine, and southwestern Nova Scotia. These same people may have adopted a new mortuary pattern around 2,500 ^{14}C yrs BP that is associated with the Ohio Valley Adena Tradition. Adena mortuary goods, like tubular smoking pipes and exotic lithic tools, were traded into the area, and may represent the introduction of a new spiritual system by an itinerant priesthood. Local burials followed Adena practices but added several local elements and the use of local raw materials. These sites clustered in the Red Bank and Halifax-Dartmouth areas.

The Middle and Late Woodland periods flow almost seamlessly into the historic period. Shellfish productivity increased in areas like Passamaquoddy Bay and Port Joli Harbour, which allowed for year-round occupation at some sites during the Middle Woodland. Our best evidence for Woodland period dwellings, as well as for sweat lodges, also comes from these areas. Following the elaborate burial practices of the Early Archaic, burials became simple interments. People living along the Saint John River and east coast of New Brunswick may have experimented with horticulture and likely practised arboriculture favouring fruit and nut trees. Intraregional trade was probably common until the Europeans arrived and their world was altered forever.

7

THE PROPHECY

> *"When there were no people in this country but Indians [Mi'kmaq], and before they knew of any others, a young woman had a singular dream. She dreamed that a small island came floating in towards the land, with tall trees on it, and living beings and amongst others a young man dressed in rabbit-skin garments."* (As related by the Mi'kmaw storyteller Josiah Jeremy on September 26, 1869; cf. Rand 1890, 155.)

THIS IS ONE OF SEVERAL Wabanaki accounts of first contact with Europeans. As the story unfolds and the prophecy comes to pass, the island with tall trees becomes a ship with masts. The men on board are at first thought to be bears and the Mi'kmaq on shore grab their bows and arrows and spears to shoot them. The young man dressed in rabbit-skin garments becomes a priest wearing a white stole. According to Kolodny (2012, 8) the story is full of symbolism and hidden meaning. Bears and rabbits have special places in Mi'kmaw lore. The bear is hunted as food yet is a dangerous beast. The rabbit is a trickster who creates deception though his words and deeds. White is the colour of the east on the compass, so the priest is a trickster from the east bringing a new spiritual system and the men are powerful and dangerous bear-men. According to Kolodny (2012, 13), "Jeremy's story conflated into a single narrative a series of events that must have occurred in different places within Mi'kmaw territory over many years and involved many different personages." A common feature of Mi'kmaw storytelling is to build on a story each time it is retold (Whitehead 2006, 2). Therefore, Jeremy's story of the first arrival both foretold and told of all the European arrival moments to follow (Kolodny 2012, 15) and helps modern Mi'kmaq to make sense of what is happening in the present.

"First contact" happened many times, as European fishermen and explorers encountered different Indigenous peoples along the Atlantic coast

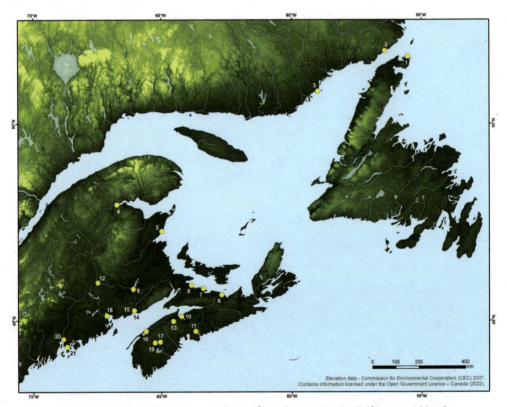

Figure 68: Selected Contact period sites from the Maritimes: 1. L'Anse aux Meadows, 2. Red Bay, 3. Havre Boulet and Mécatina, 4. Old Mission Point, 5. Tabusintac, 6. Hopps, 7. Oak Island, 8. Northport, 9. Jemseg, 10. Avonport, 11. Bedford Barrens, 12. Meductic, 13. Burnt Bone Beach, 14. Portland Point, 15. Ouigoudi (Navy Island), 16. Habitation (Port Royal), 17. McGowan Lake, 18. St. Croix Island, 19. Kejimkujik Lake sites, 20. Sandy Point, 21. Eggemoggin Reach.

7: THE PROPHECY

(Figure 68). Archaeologists refer to this period of sporadic Indigenous–European interaction as the "Contact period." As used here, it dates from the explorations of John Cabot to the establishment of the first long-term European settlement at Port Royal, Nova Scotia (ca. 1497–1605). Much of our understanding of the Contact period comes from ethnohistorical research. Early accounts of the Indigenous peoples of the region were generally biased and selective, depending on the social, spiritual, and political motivations of the narrators, and they should always be cited with caution. However, they do provide another way of thinking about past lifeways and should be included in the discussion. Based on ethnohistoric accounts, Patricia Nietfeld (1981) suggests that Contact period Mi'kmaq formed seasonally aggregated villages headed by leaders who were part family head and part chieftain, who organized feasts to reinvest any temporary surpluses. They had a stable form of social structure, midway between mobile hunter-gathers and sedentary people (Nietfeld 1981, 572; also see Miller 1983). Erickson (1978a, 131) also characterizes the Wolastoqiyik and Pesktomuhkatiyik as nascent chiefdoms at this time, but chiefs were formerly good hunters (and/or war leaders) who controlled their people through manipulation of supernatural powers.

Some researchers would extend the Contact period back to the time of Norse (Viking) exploration in the Atlantic region. The first Norse to set foot on Newfoundland soil are believed to be members of Leif Eriksson's expedition around AD 1000. If the Norse contacted Indigenous people in Newfoundland, as indicated in the sagas, then it was probably with the ancestors of the historic Beothuk (i.e., the Beaches or Little Passage archaeological cultures; Pastore 2000). The only confirmed Norse archaeological site in the region is a small staging site at L'Anse aux Meadows, near the tip of the Northern Peninsula of Newfoundland (Figure 69). This site was excavated first by Anne Stine and Helge Ingstad in the 1960s, and later by Birgitta Wallace of Parks Canada (A.S. Ingstad 1977; H. Ingstad 1969; Wallace 2000, 2006, 68). A new study sets a precise date for this site at AD 1021, based on high-precision, accelerator mass spectrometry (AMS) dating, in combination with distinctive features of the atmospheric ^{14}C record at that time (Kuitems et al. 2022, 388) and "sets a new point-of-reference for European cognisance of the Americas, and the earliest known year by which human migration had encircled the planet" (Kuitems et al. 2022, 390).

Birgitta Wallace (1991, 2018) believes that the "Vinland" of the Norse sagas refers to the entire Gulf of St. Lawrence area, including the east coast of New Brunswick, Prince Edward Island, and possibly eastern Nova Scotia. Evidence for this argument is based on the recovery of butternuts and pieces of eastern white cedar at L'Anse aux Meadows, both of which have a geographic growing limit of eastern New Brunswick. Wild grapes may also have been acquired from this area. A Norse coin recovered at the Goddard site in Maine may have been acquired through the existing Indigenous trading system, which extended as far north as northern Labrador (Bourque and Cox 1981; Cox 2000a, 2021, 57, 84–86). The coin was issued by King Olaf the Peaceful (1067–1093) and indicates that the Norse were still visiting the region several decades after Leif Eriksson's expedition (Gullbekk 2017). Contact with Indigenous populations appears to have

Figure 69: L'Anse aux Meadows National Historic Site, with insert of reconstructed Norse dwelling. Photograph courtesy of Bryn Tapper, with insert by Micheal Deal.

been sporadic and often antagonistic. Other than the Goddard site, their material culture has not turned up at archaeological sites on the Maritime Peninsula and they appear to have had little effect on traditional Indigenous lifeways.

The sixteenth century witnessed a continuous flow of traffic from Europe to catch fish along the shores of the North Atlantic, beginning with Breton and Norman fishermen from France and the Portuguese, who may have had a short-lived settlement (ca. 1525) on Cape Breton Island (i.e., the Fagundes Colony; Burton 2005, 104–44; Ganong 1964, 47ff.; Hoffman 1961, 35). At first, this was a wet fishery that did not require a land base. However, fishermen did come ashore for water and to hunt. With the switch to dry fishing and seasonal use of coastal areas for building stages to cut and dry fish, contact with Indigenous cultures increased. The introduction of European plants and animals probably began with the early migratory fishermen, so that by 1672 practically all economically important European species had been introduced to eastern North America (Saunders 1935).

Between 1530 and 1600, Basques from France and Spain began harvesting right and bowhead whales in the Strait of Belle Isle and established a seasonal site at Red Bay for rendering and barrelling oil (Tuck and Grenier 1989). Other major Basque sites at Havre Boulet and Mécatina, on the Quebec Lower North Shore, have yet to be fully explored. Excavation by William Fitzhugh at the Mécatina site has provided some information on this post-whaling occupation period, in the form of trade beads and Inuit soapstone vessels (Fitzhugh and Gallon 2002; also see Barkham 1980; Drouin 1988). By the 1580s, specially outfitted trading vessels (principally Basque and Norman) were making annual fur-trading trips to the region. Basque trade featured copper kettles, while Norman trade along the Atlantic seaboard featured a variety of copper ornamental objects (bells, bracelets, and rings), knives, hatchets, pots, pans, paternostri beads, hats, and cloth (Turgeon 1997, 2004). According to Bourque and Whitehead (1985; Bourque 2001, 119), by the early seventeenth century, enterprising

7: THE PROPHECY

Indigenous middlemen known as "Tarrantines" were trading European goods for furs along the coast of Maine using special canoes rigged with sails, called shallops (see Figure 70). The term "Tarrantine," which may have a Basque origin (Siebert 1973), has been equated with the English name for the people called Souriquois by the French, and who are now known as the Mi'kmaq. Prins and McBride (2007, 82, n. 91) believe that this term "does not just refer to the ancestors of Nova Scotia Mi'kmaq, but also to the Eastern Etchemins (ancestral to Maliseet [Wolastoqiyik] and Passamaquoddy [Peskotomuhkatiyik]." Panawahpskek writer Joseph Nicolar (1893, 129) may allude to Wabanaki infighting ("their own people making raids") that erupted between an alliance of the Mi'kmaq and Wolastoqiyik versus the Panawahpskek and their allies to the south. According to Alice Kolodny (2007, 64, 86), this was a dispute over access to European trade goods (sometimes known as the "Tarrantine Wars" of 1607–15; also see Bakker 2004, 80; Leowen 2016, 60; Prins and McBride 2007, 63–128).

Figure 70: Petroglyph of Mi'kmaw sailing vessel, McGowan Lake, Nova Scotia. Photograph courtesy Rob Ferguson, Parks Canada.

7: THE PROPHECY

Sustained contact with European fishermen and traders had dramatic long-term effects on the Indigenous population of the Maritimes. By 1550, some Mi'kmaw families, who normally wintered on the coast, were spending late winter and early spring inland to harvest furs and moving to the coast in the late spring and summer to trade with Europeans (Burley 1981). They traded furs and supplied meat and fish to Europeans for dried foods, like hardtack biscuits, and metal tools. Alcohol was also acquired, which led in some areas to social disintegration (Bailey 1969, 66ff.).

Population estimates for the time of contact vary greatly. We do know that there was a tremendous population decrease, primarily in coastal areas, due to the introduction of European diseases (especially smallpox). Ralph Pastore (1989) notes that the mortality rate among the Wolastoqiyik and Pesktomuhkatiyik for the first half of the seventeenth century was 67 per cent. Writing in the early seventeenth century, Pierre Biard (1959, 109) estimated the Mi'kmaw population ("Souriquoys") at 3,000 to 3,500 and the Wolastoqiyik and Peskotomuhkatiyik at 2,500. The first French census to include the Indigenous inhabitants of "Acadie" (i.e., modern Maritimes and part of northern Maine) was compiled by Joseph de Gargas, assistant to the Intendant at Port Royal, in 1687–88 (Morse 1935, 139–60). The census included 1,119 Indigenous people (277 men, 270 women, and 572 children) living in 229 wigwams in 22 villages. This is obviously a low estimate, and Gargas himself admitted that he had difficultly acquiring data and some areas are excluded (e.g., Prince Edward Island).

Early historic material culture is often recovered from archaeological sites but does not receive equal treatment to precontact materials in the final reports. Because they continued to use traditional campsites, single-component Contact period sites are rare in the Maritimes (e.g., Blair et al. 2017; Cox 2000b). A typical site is Burnt Bone Beach (BfDd-08) on Gaspereau Lake, Nova Scotia (Figure 71), where the Contact period is represented by a few trade beads and a copper tinkling cone, that is, a rolled piece of copper kettle used as a decoration on clothing (Laybolt 1999, 66–71). In fact, European material culture refashioned or repurposed by

7: THE PROPHECY

Indigenous peoples is often found at archaeological sites in the Northeast (Loren 2008, 23–27). The most distinctive sites of the Contact period are the burials. Archaeologists refer to a "Copper Kettle Burial Tradition," dating from the late 1500s to late 1600s. This tradition seems to be associated primarily with the Mi'kmaq, who occupied most of the coastal areas of the Maritimes and were heavily involved in the fur trade. However, Lescarbot (1928) described an elaborate burial on an island off the Maine coast, which included gifts of copper kettles and many other things (Figure 72). Bruce Bourque and Ruth Whitehead (1985) have even suggested that these were the burials of high-status traders (tarrantines). Copper kettle burials are known from at least 11 sites in the Maritimes, but sites have also been reported in Maine (Petersen et al. 2004; Whitehead 1987, 1991).

The best-known copper kettle burial site is the Hopps site in Pictou, Nova Scotia, where Harper (1957) reported a burial consisting of a layer of branches and twigs, followed by a layer of birchbark, on which bodies had

Figure 71: Aerial photograph of Burnt Bone Beach (BfDd-08), Gaspereau Lake, Nova Scotia, with insert of trade beads recovered at the site. Photographs by Michael Deal.

7: THE PROPHECY

been placed and covered with large, overturned kettles, and covered with another layer of birchbark and stones. These graves also included a cache of European trade goods, including glass beads, iron swords, knives, and daggers, along with a variety of fibre textile specimens. By this time, pottery and stone tools had been effectively replaced by European tools. Chemical analysis of 61 copper-based metals from the Hopps, Northport, and Avonport sites showed a chemical link between metals from Hopps and Northport, which indicated a common European source (Whitehead et al. 1998). The Avonport metals did not match samples from the other two sites.

Copper was already a valuable commodity and revered material in precontact times. Now, there was a reliable source in the form of copper kettles. According to seventeenth-century chronicler Nicolas Denys (1908, 441), "the kettle has always seemed to them, and seems still, the most

Figure 72: Small copper pot from BlCx-1 site, Northport, Nova Scotia. Originally published in Deal and Blair 1991, Figure 12.2. Courtesy of the Government of New Brunswick.

valuable article they attain from us." These vessels quickly replaced traditional earthenware containers, and once they were no longer useful for boiling liquids they could be converted into other uses (Martin 1975). Howey (2018, 51) notes that kettles were also readily incorporated in the traditional Mi'kmaw relational ontology and believed to possess their own animating spirits. As other-than-human relatives, kettles became central elements in elite Contact period burials. Some of these burial kettles were intentionally damaged ("killed") while others remained undamaged and inverted. According to Howey (2018, 62, 66), only upright kettles were useful as cooking pots, so those turned bottom up symbolically lost their European use and became suitable for a Mi'kmaw afterworld that was free from, but prepared for, colonial encroachment. In oral tradition, disturbed by the actions of the European missionaries, Kluskap overturned his European-made kettle and transformed it into an island to make it part of the Mi'kmaw landscape/homeland (Howey 2018, 66). Kluskap's action here would have had a different meaning in precontact times, as it could merely refer to the practice, in pottery-making cultures, of turning vessels bottom up when they are drying or no longer in use. By turning the inverted earthenware vessel into an island, Kluskap is returning it to the earth and creating a guidepost for travellers.

Port Royal Habitation and the Meeting of French and Indigenous Feasting Traditions

> *"I listened — and I heard the strokes of the first settler's ax on the first astonished trees, which would give him both his home and his heat."* (Buckler 1968, 23)

The first sustained contact between French and Indigenous peoples of the Maritimes occurred at Port Royal, Nova Scotia. In 1603, Pierre du Gua de Monts received royal patents giving him a monopoly on trade and colonization in the region. In 1605 he established the Habitation at Port Royal as a trading and colonizing settlement, after an attempt the previous year on St.

Croix Island had failed due to poor weather and loss of men due to scurvy (Pendery et al. 2012). The company included Jean de Biencourt de Poutrincourt of Picardy, the explorer Samuel de Champlain, and lawyer and supercargo Marc Lescarbot. Their primary goals were to consolidate the French hold on this region and to establish friendly relations with local Mi'kmaq.

The Habitation was situated on the north shore of the Annapolis Basin, about 16 km east of its entrance at Digby Gut and 11 km southwest of the modern town of Annapolis Royal (i.e., historic Port Royal). The population of the Habitation varied from 44 to 80 persons at any given time, and included two master builders, board sawyers, masons, stonecutters, blacksmiths, and locksmiths. The compound consisted of a group of buildings around a courtyard, like contemporary farms in northern France. It was fortified by two canon platforms and a palisade. It was originally constructed from the dismantled parts of the St. Croix buildings and expanded by Poutrincourt in 1607. The location of the original site was identified by historian William F. Ganong in 1911 and excavated by Boston architect Charles Coatsworth Pinkney over a period of 10 months in 1938–39 (Jefferys 1939; Kalman 1994, 31–33). Pinkney's report (1938), along with descriptions published by Champlain and Lescarbot, and research on surviving seventeenth-century structures in New France were used in a modern reconstruction of the fort by the Canadian government, under the direction of architect Kenneth Harris (1940; Figure 73).

The early settlers at the Port Royal Habitation relied heavily on the local Mi'kmaq to survive the cold Nova Scotian winters. In the fall of 1606, Champlain established a regimen of feasting at the Habitation that is known in English as the Order of Good Cheer (Powers 1991; Salter 1975). Both Champlain and Lescarbot stated that the main reason for instituting the Order was to prevent scurvy, which is caused by a lack of vitamin C in the diet. During the winter of 1604–05 at St. Croix, up to 36 of the 79 members of the expedition died of scurvy, including one minor noble (Pendery et al. 2012, 180). In 1605–06, 12 of the 45 men died of the same affliction at Port Royal. During the winter of feasting, scurvy was not a

7: THE PROPHECY

major threat. Champlain believed that agriculture must form the basis of the new French colonies and convinced DeMonts that they should plant gardens at St. Croix and, later, Port Royal (Saunders 1935, 390). The main contributors to the improved diet of the feasts were vegetables planted in these gardens in the summer and consumed in the winter, and cranberries, which were available all winter in the surrounding meadows (Thierry

Figure 73: Port Royal Habitation excavation 1938–39 by Charles Coatsworth Pinkney (A) and modern reconstruction (B). Photograph (A) from the archival collection of the Annapolis Heritage Society, photograph (B) by Michael Deal, 1990.

7: THE PROPHECY

2004, 137). The French also developed elaborate ceremonies for their feasts, which combined practices of their homeland with those of their Indigenous neighbours. French chronicles of this period allow us to explore these two rich traditions, and, along with available archaeological evidence, shed some light on the nature of precontact Mi'kmaw feasting.

Lescarbot (1928, 118) gave the best account of the ceremonies developed for the feasts, which were like the three services offered to the King of France, and symbolically transferred the prestige of the King to the New World (Thierry 2004, 140; Figure 74):

> There were 15 guests, each of whom in his turn, became steward and caterer of the day. At the dinner, the steward, with napkin on shoulder, staff of office in hand, and the collar of the order round his neck, led the van. The other guests in procession

Figure 74: C.W. Jeffrey's iconic vision of the Order of Good Cheer procession, with Mi'kmaw guests seated to the left. *The Picture Gallery of Canadian History* 1, 84 (1942).

followed, each bearing a dish. After grace in the evening, he resigned the insignia to his successor, and they drank to each other in a cup of wine. It was the steward's duty, to look to supplies, and he would go hunt or fish a day or two before his turn came and add some dainty to the ordinary fare. During the winter they had fowl and game in abundance, supplied by the Indians [Mi'kmaq] and by their own exertions. These feasts were often attended by Indians [Mi'kmaq] of all ages and both sexes, sometimes twenty or thirty being present. The Sagamore, or chief, Membertou, the greatest Sagamore of the land, and other chiefs, when there, were treated as guests and equals.

The French believed that the Mi'kmaq greatly appreciated their hospitality, especially since it was a mild winter, which made it more difficult to hunt with snowshoes and fish through the ice (Champlain 1922 (1), 447). A typical menu at the feast included fresh bread, pastries, vegetables, fruits, wine, and a variety of available meats, including duck, bustard, grey and white geese, partridge, lark, moose, caribou, beaver, otter, bear, rabbit, lynx, raccoon, and sturgeon.

Lescarbot (1928, 221-31) also devoted an entire chapter of his book on New France to Indigenous feasting, which he referred to by the Mi'kmaw word "tabagie." Feasts were held on any possible occasion when sufficient food was available, including feasts of health, farewell, hunting, peace, war, or thanksgiving, and at marriages and funerals (Denys 1908; LeClercq 1910; also Hoffman 1955, 678-79). To the French, Mi'kmaw feasts were rather plain, since they had no salt or spices for seasoning, no bread, and they drank only water, or seal grease or oil on special occasions. Feasts were normally attended by men only. The meat consumed at feasts was limited to a single species, so that beaver, moose, and bear were never found in the same meal. In winter, they served venison, but from spring through summer it was mostly fish. Lescarbot says that they ate all meats except wolf, and he notes that they often provided the French with beaver, sturgeon, and salmon. Shellfish were available year-round, but Lescarbot claimed that they did not eat mussels. They also collected eggs from Canada geese. Meat and fish were cooked as stews in large kettles and eaten with deep spoons from birchbark bowls. Lescarbot notes that they stretched their bellies as much as possible and ate until there was no more meat.

Feasts were accompanied by opening speeches and ended with dances and songs and more speeches in honour of the host and passing around a tobacco pipe of friendship. According to Nicolas Denys (1908, 410), the opening speeches usually included a recital of genealogies, sometimes dating back 20 generations. In the mid-eighteenth century, the Abbé Maillard (1758, 7–8) describes a closing speech in which the host is compared to a tree "whose large and strong roots afford nourishment to a number of small shrubs." The importance of traditional feasts among the Mi'kmaq continued into the late nineteenth century, when it often existed alongside Catholic ceremonies (e.g., Rand 1894, xxxi). In later times, games of prowess and games of chance were included in feasting events (Wallis and Wallis 1955). Feasting is also an integral part of Mi'kmaw oral tradition and appears in many of the Kluskap stories (Rand 1894).

Another seventeeth-century chronicler, Chrestien LeClercq, gives us the following account of a war feast:

> Crying "Ho, ho, ho!" three or four times, the men, carrying their dishes, entered the festive wigwam, sat down in the first vacant place, smoked some of the chief's tobacco, and were tossed some meat or offered it on a pointed stick. When all had eaten, two or three distinctive cries summoned the women, children, and the young boys who had not yet killed a moose, and any disqualified men, to receive the remains of the meat outside the wigwam. (LeClercq 1910, 290–92)

When we consider the foods and preparation techniques of French and Mi'kmaw feasts, it is important to stress that they came from two vastly different food traditions. The Mi'kmaq shared the broader Indigenous perspective, sometimes termed kincentric ecology, in which they viewed themselves as part of an extended ecological family and that survival in any environment depended upon respect for all living things within it (e.g., Sable and Francis 2012, 33–34; Salmon 2000). French explorers of this period considered foods to be either domestic or wild and the diversity in their diet was largely due to class differences. Since the early Middle Ages, the European nobility had established that wild game was its privilege (Lafrance and Desloges 1993, 24). The upper classes consumed an unusual amount of meat, while the diet of lower classes was primarily cereals and vegetable stews, along with dairy products and some meat and fish (Mennell 1985, 41). During the sixteenth and seventeenth centuries the French diet was influenced by Italian cuisine, which led to a new interest in salads and vegetables among the nobility (Dickenson 2008, 45). By the 1660s, the number of vegetable species mentioned in cookbooks doubled, including North American species such as pumpkins and squashes, potatoes, and kidney beans (Dickenson 2008, 46).

While the French were not particularly fond of the Mi'kmaw cuisine, they did experiment with preparing wild unfamiliar plant and animal foods in the French fashion (Dickenson 2008, 3). They learned of many new meats and developed a liking for lynx, raccoon, and bear, which they compared favourably to beef. The beaver's tail meat was considered a delicacy. Lescarbot witnessed a moose hunt, in which the Mi'kmaw hunters first roasted the meat, then made a delicious broth by efficiently producing a trough from tree wood and cooking the meat in the container of water by adding red hot rocks (1927, 270–71; Spiess 1981). The French preferred their moose cooked in pot pies with spicy sauces. They particularly liked the Mi'kmaw practice of making long orations after the meal and passing around a pipe, and they adopted both practices at their own feasts.

Food for the Order of Good Cheer came from three sources; provisions brought on board ship from France, cereals and vegetables grown at the Habitation gardens, and wild foods, either supplied by Mi'kmaq or by the men themselves (Powers 1991). Ship's provisions were limited to peas, beans, rice, prunes, raisins, dried cod, salt fish, olive oil, and butter, but they also brought hogs, hens, and pigeons (Lescarbot 1928, 96, 274). In 1606, they had 45 casks ("tuns") of wine, each equivalent to about 252 gallons, which accounted for a ration of 1½ pints per day for each person. They planted wheat, rye, barley, oats, beans, hemp, flax, turnip, radish, cabbage, and garden herbs in the autumn. Champlain (1922 (1), 371) had a summer home to the east of the Habitation where he planted gardens and created a small reservoir, which he stocked with fish for the feasts. The harvested grain meant that bread was plentiful all winter. Wild foods made up the bulk of the French feasts. In the winter, moose were hunted with guns by the French, but beaver was caught through the ice by the Mi'kmaq. Other wild game included otters, bear, and caribou. Seal was available in January. In March and April, spawning fish were available, including smelt, herring, sturgeon, and salmon. Eggs and waterfowl were also abundant in April. In May, cod and other fish were acquired, along with shellfish. According to Lescarbot (1928, 285) and Champlain (1922, 249), the men also collected sea scallops, cockles, sea urchins, clams, sea snails, crabs, and lobsters.

Edible local flora included beach peas from along the shore and Jerusalem artichoke, which became very popular in Europe. The Jerusalem artichoke (*Helianthus tuberosus*) is an ancient Wabanaki food staple, with a starchy underground tuber that can be roasted, baked, fried, stewed, or boiled (Wiseman and Tayler 2018, 147–50). Wild fruits were widely available, including gooseberries, raspberries, strawberries, and cranberries, which were gathered in the winter and made into marmalade to serve with meat dishes. The Jesuit missionary Pierre Biard, who lived at Port Royal from 1611 to 1613, mentioned that the Mi'kmaq shelled and ate acorns (1959, 3, 108). Lescarbot also drank maple syrup in the early spring, as shown to him by the Mi'kmaq. Additional information is provided by Champlain's 1612 map of New France, which included a decorative border with the plants of the region (Figures 75 and 76). Only a few of them are

7: THE PROPHECY

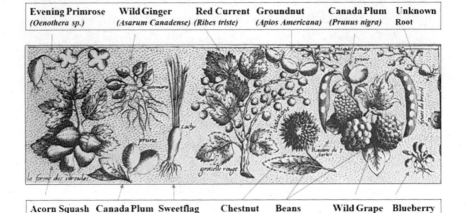

Figure 75: Botanical border (left side) from Samuel de Champlain's 1612 Map of New France. The original map is in the John Carter Brown Library, Providence, Rhode Island (Accession #: 0339a, File Name: 0339a-000, Call #: Cabinet Ca612 1).

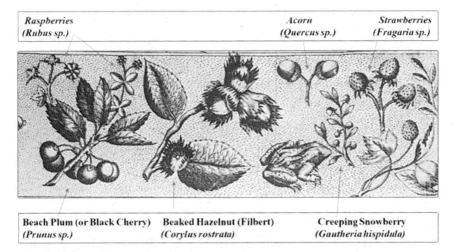

Figure 76: Botanical border (right side) from Samuel de Champlain's 1612 Map of New France. The original map is in the John Carter Brown Library, Providence, Rhode Island (Accession #: 0339a, File Name: 0339a-000, Call #: Cabinet Ca612 1).

labelled, but almost all have been identified from the drawings (see Dickenson 2009, 33–34; Ganong 1909). The upper figures in the panel on the left side of the map include evening primrose, wild ginger, a red currant bush, groundnut tubers, a Canadian plum, and an unidentified root plant. In the lower half appear acorn squash, two more Canadian plums, sweetflag, American chestnut, haricot beans, three bunches of grapes, and blueberries. All these species are known from the area around the Habitation, except for grapes, which are found in the Saint John River Valley of New Brunswick. The right panel includes various fruits and nuts, including raspberries, strawberries, black cherry, a creeping snowberry bush, beaked hazelnuts (filberts), and acorns. Again, all these species are available in Port Royal.

At the feasts, dishes were prepared by a cook and bread was provided by the stone carvers and masons, who were converted to bakers. The menu included hearty broths and meat pies of moose meat or turtledoves (Lescarbot 1928, 45, 97, 118). Other techniques used in seventeenth-century Acadia were described by Nicolas Denys (1908, 318, 349–59). A daily staple was soup made from boiled peas and salt pork, which is still popular today. Fish was boiled or roasted on a spit. Sturgeon was carved into slices and boiled four to five hours. Beaver was also roasted, and the heart, liver, and lungs were fried. Porpoise tripe was made into black pudding. Lobsters were boiled and served with sauces and tortoise was boiled and fricasseed. Deserts were limited to what could be done with dried raisins, prunes, and whatever berries were in season.

Unfortunately, Pinkney's excavation of the Habitation did not include the collection of faunal or floral evidence. The faunal assemblage from a single feature at DeMonts's 1604 site on St. Croix Island indicated a heavy Indigenous meat diet, including beaver, ducks, geese, grouse, turtle, cod, alewife, and sculpin (Pendery et al. 2012, 175–76). All the animals hunted and collected by the French for their feasts are well known from Late Woodland shell middens in the region (Erskine 1998. 90–92; Stewart 1989). Dogs had a special association with Mi'kmaw feasting, and according to

Nicolas Denys (1908, 430), serving dog meat to a guest was the highest form of compliment. Dog remains have been recovered from several precontact shell middens in the Mi'kmaw region (Erskine 1998, 51; Leonard 2017, 29; Munkirttick 2013; Stewart 1989, 121). Despite the taboo mentioned by Lescarbot, mussel is common in the nearby shell middens (Erskine 1998, 51).

Based on the ethnohistoric and ethnographic records, the current paleoethnobotanical record significantly under-represents the variety of species utilized by the precontact Mi'kmaq (Deal 2008a; Asch-Sidell 1999). The Mi'kmaq were known as avid traders in the early Contact period (Bourque and Whitehead 1985, 1994) and presumably in precontact times. Certain foodstuffs like Canada plums, butternuts, groundnut tubers, wild grapes, basswood, and tobacco had limited geographical ranges and were valuable trading commodities. For example, Lescarbot (1928, 229) noted the heavy use of tobacco by the Mi'kmaq, and not just at feasts. The likely source of the tobacco was from Indigenous peoples in New England and would have been acquired through trade. Two butternut fruits were recently found in a shell midden site at Port Joli (Deal et al. 2011). The butternut is not native to Nova Scotia but is common in New Brunswick along the Saint John and upper Miramichi River valleys and has been recovered from precontact sites in New Brunswick and the Gaspé area (Foulkes 1981; Trembley 1997; Varley 1999, 43). Experimental studies with the collection and processing of various nut species in the 1980s concluded that butternuts are not a reliable subsistence food due to the low-calorie yield per hour of work (Talalay et al. 1984). However, in the post-Contact period they were chosen for their desirable flavour and eaten raw or crushed and mixed with other foods (Speck and Dexter 1951).

The topic of feasting is rarely addressed in the archaeological literature for the region. However, the complex ceremonies associated with seventeenth-century Mi'kmaw feasting suggest that it was an entrenched activity that existed long before the French arrived and may have been more elaborate in precontact times. Because they were a mobile foraging society, it will be difficult to identify the archaeological evidence, but a few criteria can be suggested. Besides the examples of special foods mentioned above, it might be manifested in oversized, special-purpose wigwams, unusually large pottery cooking vessels, larger than normal hearths or roasting pits, bone dumps, prestige items for spiritual display, and smoking paraphernalia (see Hayden 2001, 40–41; Stokes 1991). Erickson (1978a, 123; Harper 1954, 27) mentions separate rectangular feasting lodges at the early seventeenth-century Wolastoqwey village of Ouigoudi, on Navy Island, at the mouth of the Saint John River. It is quite likely that the large pottery vessels holding 10 to 25 litres and large storage pits recorded at several sites in the Mi'kmaw region are related to feasting activities (Stapelfeldt 2009, 124; Suttie 2006, 70–80).

The descriptions left by Lescarbot and Champlain give us a clear picture of Mi'kmaw feasting in the first decade of the seventeenth century and what aspects of Mi'kmaw foodways were valued by the French and adopted for their own use. In their review of feasting studies, Brian Hayden and Suzanne Villeneuve indicate that feasting can take on varying roles, such as establishing group and gender identities, embedding memories, creating political power, accomplishing work, and developing prestige technologies (2001). The French at Port Royal had the practical incentive of warding off scurvy, but the feasts also fostered solidarity among the gentlemen and blurred class boundaries. It also mirrored the French regime in Europe and created strong and lasting ties with the Mi'kmaq. Mi'kmaw feasting upheld group solidarity in times of war and plenty, acknowledged the authority of the chief, enforced gender and social status, and honoured the ancestors. According to Hoffman (1955, 686) "it was the greatest honor for a Micmac [Mi'kmaw] man, and the goal of all his achievements, for him to receive honor and recognition in the solemn feasts of his nation."

Colonial Life after Port Royal

During the French colonial regime (1604–1713) traditional Indigenous culture was further eroded by the arrival of French missionaries, who introduced the Catholic religion and worked to cement relations with the

French settlers. Their support of the French in conflicts with the English resulted in poor treatment under the following English regime, which exerted pressure on Indigenous peoples to convert to Protestantism. The arrival of the Loyalists (i.e., Americans who remained loyal to Britain) after the American Revolution led to the establishment of three colonial jurisdictions in the Maritimes, each with a different view of Indigenous rights.

An important account of Indigenous life during the French Regime is provided by John Gyles (1875). Gyles was taken into captivity at the age of nine by a group of Wolastoqiyik during King William's War (1688–97). He was originally taken at Pemaquid, on the Penobscot River, in 1694, but spent most of the next six years living a seasonally mobile lifestyle along the Saint John River. He gives the following account of the perfect Wolastoqwey couple of his era:

> If parents have a daughter marriageable they seek a husband for her who is a good hunter. If she has been educated to make monoodah (Indian bags), birch dishes, to lace snow-shoes, make Indian shoes, string wampum belts, sew birch canoes, and boil the kettle, she is esteemed a lady of fine accomplishments. If the man sought out for husband has a gun and ammunition, a canoe, spear, and hatchet, a monoodah, a crooked knife, looking glass and paint, a pipe, tobacco, and knot-bowl to toss a kind of dice in, he is accounted a gentleman of a plentiful fortune. (Gyles 1875, 27)

Gyles's account was written less than a century after the first European attempt at settlement on St. Croix Island, New Brunswick, and two centuries after the first period of sustained European exploration and trade. Many of the material items mentioned in his description were introduced during the sixteenth century, including the metal kettle, gun and ammunition, metal hatchet, and looking glass. Long gone were the distinctive ceramic pots and stone arrowheads of the Late Woodland.

Postcontact Archaeology

Despite a long-standing interest in the petroglyphs at Kejimkujik Lake, in southwestern Nova Scotia (Mallery 1894, 37–42; Molyneaux 1984a, 1984b; Robinson 1977; Tapper 2020; Whitehead 1992), very little archaeological research has focused on postcontact (Contact and colonial) Indigenous sites. Many traditional campsites must have been abandoned after European contact as Indigenous populations dwindled. Early historic Indigenous villages, like Ouigoudi, at the mouth of the Saint John River (c. 1604–10), have not been precisely relocated by archaeologists (Harper 1954). Furthermore, the seventeenth-century European trading posts at Meductic and Jemseg, on the same river, have received only fleeting attention (Lee 1966; Smith 1982). Our best early postcontact site is the ill-fated du Monts fort on St. Croix Island (Pendery et al. 2012).

Indigenous people become more difficult to identify in the postcontact archaeological record. If we recover a European-made iron axe at an Indigenous site we assume that it was acquired and used by one of the site inhabitants (i.e., it becomes culturally and analytically no longer a European artifact, but an Indigenous one; Silliman 2010, 37). On the other hand, when Indigenous people live or work in colonial spaces (e.g., through mixed marriage or as live-in servants) they become lost archaeologically because archaeologists identify both the household material culture and architecture as European (Silliman 2010). Silliman (2010, 39) recommends that we rethink how we interpret ethnically mixed deposits, and especially when we can use written documentation to help interpret them.

A curious example dated from the early seventeenth century is the burial of a man dressed in armour found in 1899 at Eggemoggin Reach, Maine (Spiess 1982), along the major traffic route between Mount Desert Island and the Penobscot Bay and River (Prins and McBride 2007, 62). The burial included remnants of body armour and helmet, and a military-issued halberd and blunderbuss. The burial was dug into a precontact shell midden, so the deceased could have been either French or Indigenous.

A significant feature of the Contact period is the wide distribution of small, short, white cylindrical, marine-shell beads alongside manufactured European beads. Hamell (2011, 1) points out that marine-shell beads are known from prehistoric contexts in the Northeast, yet in combination with European glass beads they were often used for specific functions by Indigenous peoples and Europeans during the seventeenth century, commonly referred to as wampum (see Vignette 16). Even seventeenth-century chroniclers, like Lescarbot (1928, 332) and LeClercq (1910, 301), distinguished between wampum and beadwork. Lescarbot (1928, 98) reports that in 1606 Jean de Biencourt de Poutrincourt and Champlain left Port Royal for Chouacoet (Saco, Maine) where they entered an alliance with Chief Marchin, in which many gifts were given, including bracelets made with white and blue glass beads. This seems to be a clear example of using beadwork as wampum. Beads are found at sixteenth- and seventeenth-century Wabanaki sites, and especially burials, but not all of them can be considered as wampum.

Delmas (2016, 91–96) sees the evolution of the copper kettle burials in four phases, which exemplify the transition from precontact to postcontact periods in the Maritimes. Phase 1 (ca AD 1500–40) corresponds to the early Contact period and is characterized by shell beads, and European metal and glass objects are rare. Phase 2 (ca AD 1540–60) corresponds to the early trade of copper and iron objects and disc-shell beads of Indigenous or European origin. Phase 3 (ca AD 1580–1600) is characterized by the appearance of large copper kettles, large iron axes, knives, and shell and glass beads. The latter includes monochrome and polychrome blue glass beads and faïence (frit core) beads (Delmas 2016, 91). Phase 4 (ca AD 1600–30) is the period of French trade and early attempts at settlement in Acadia. White and blue beads (mostly mass-produced) are the most common and generally in tubular, oval, doughnut, or spherical forms. Using this sequence, five burial sites from the Maritime Peninsula can be roughly dated. The earliest is a Phase 2 site (pre-1580) at Oak Island, Nova Scotia, followed by Phase 3 sites at Northport and Pictou (Hopps site) in Nova Scotia and Sandy Point, Maine, and a Phase 4 site at Avonport, Nova Scotia (Delmas

2016, 92–95). The last site dates to the early Acadian settlement period at Port Royal (Whitehead 199, 78). The blue and white trade beads and tinkling cone from Burnt Bone Beach probably postdate the initial settlement of Port Royal.

Vignette 16: Wampum Use on the Maritime Peninsula

Boone (2012, 211) points out that histories can also be painted, knotted, and threaded. For the Wabanaki the wampum belt served as a kind of historical document during the years following European contact (ca. AD 1615–1800). Each belt is composed of white and purple shell beads woven together in broad strips, which conveyed the nature, structure, and content of the message and cued an oral recitation of the message (Boone 2012, 225–26). The belts included various symbolic forms, such as wigwams, humans, or geometric motifs, and the colours of the beads were an additional source of information. The wampum belt tradition was preceded by using strings of disc-shaped shell beads, which consisted of white beads made from whelk shells and purple beads made from quahog clam shells (Speck 1919, 6). In fact, the word "wampum" is a shortened version of the Narragansett Algonquian word *wampumpaegue* or *wampumpeake*, which means "string of white beads," and only white beads predate the Contact period (Loren 2008, 86). A string of beads could be used to invite a person to a meeting (or council), and wampum could be used for personal ornamentation (e.g., in bracelets, necklaces, sewn into garments, and inlaid into personal possessions (Bradley 2011, 26–27). Wampum was used in social exchanges, such as replying to a message, sealing an agreement, condoling a loss, and the more formal wampum belts were the Indigenous equivalent to European treaties (Bradley 2011, 27).

Becker (2013, 25) refers to the ca. 1620–1820 period as the time of wampum diplomacy, both between Indigenous peoples and between Indigenous peoples and Europeans. According to Walker (1984, 120), Wabanaki wampum strings dealt with concerns of the moment, while belts and collars invoked "enduring compacts, fixed contracts and permanent relationships." Although Indigenous alliances may date back to the early seventeenth century (Wiseman

2001, 77–81), few Wabanaki wampum belts have survived. One of the best-known belts, although it has only survived as a facsimile made following the specifications of Penobscot elder Newell Lyon (Speck 1915, 500; 1919, 37), is the Wabanaki Confederacy Belt, which signifies the alliance of the four eastern members. According to Speck (1919, 38; Figure 77):

> This was a somewhat broader belt with a black background, denoting former hostility among the tribes, lightened on the margins with white borders denoting the bonds of friendship that now surround them. . . . The four white triangles are tribal "wigwams," the Penobscot, Passamaquoddy, Malecite, and Micmac [Panawahpskek, Peskotomuhkatiyik, Wolastoqiyik, and Mi'kmaq]. In the center is the pipe, which is the symbol of the peace ceremony by which the allies are joined. Such a belt would serve very general purposes in the days of the confederacy. It was a reminder of the Confederacy to be carried by messengers from any council as a testimonial.

Wampum also appears in several of the surviving Wabanaki stories, such as the Mi'kmaw story "The Invisible Boy," "when the old man arrived, he brought a quantity of small, beautiful, variegated shells, out of which in former times wampum was manufactured, and for which, in these later times, glass beads are substituted." (As related by Mi'kmaw storyteller Susan Barss, Charlottetown, in May 1869; cf. Rand 1894, 103)

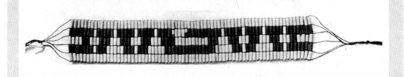

Figure 77: Wabanaki Confederacy wampum belt facsimile made following the specifications of Panawahpskek (Penobscot) elder Newell Lyon (Speck 1915, Plate 24b).

Precontact Period in Retrospect

Archaeology in the Maritimes has come a long way since the days of the "pioneer" naturalists, yet there are still huge gaps in our understanding of the precontact period. Rising sea levels have drowned many coastal sites and interior sites are impacted by farming, lumbering, mining, and the expansion of modern communities. Some periods are known almost exclusively from private collections and pedestrian surveys. Furthermore, information is often slow to circulate, with much of it consisting of the "grey" literature of government reports, conference papers, and student theses.

We have known since the 1960s that the first humans to explore and settle in the region were descended from the widely dispersed Clovis culture (known to archaeologists as the Palaeo or "Palaeoindian" peoples). The current evidence suggests that they arrived around 11,000 years ago after a long migration over many generations eastward below the Great Lakes and Champlain Sea and into northwestern New Brunswick. They eventually reached Chignecto Bay and possibly spread along the shoreline of southwestern Nova Scotia. Our best evidence for their presence and way of life comes from sites of the Debert/Belmont Complex. They were hunter-gatherers who specialized in caribou hunting, although fishing and sea mammal hunting were probably also practised. The Palaeo peoples were skilled flint knappers, with a thorough knowledge of the lithic resources in the areas they lived. It seems likely that these people were here to stay and represent the original Indigenous inhabitants for the Maritimes, and they are probably directly ancestral to the living populations in this region. Even though there were a few later migrations into the area, the migrant peoples were likely absorbed by the resident population. However, the migrants brought new ideas and traditions, which were adopted in modified form in some parts of the region. Surviving oral stories and historical anecdotes hint at these earlier times (Bourque 2001, 19; Sable and Francis 2012).

The next arrivals in the Maritime Peninsula, sometime after 10,000 years ago, were also Palaeo hunter-gatherers, but they had replaced the fluted projectile point technology with long thin lance-like points. They appear to have migrated down the St. Lawrence River from southern Ontario and Quebec and were probably the first inhabitants of the Gaspé Peninsula. Their relationship with the earlier Palaeo population is unclear; however, based on the distribution of the lanceolate projectile points, they did not penetrate south in any great numbers. They do show up in areas like Gaspereau Lake, but they may represent a limited adoption. It appears that the descendants of the original Palaeo settlers gradually spread out to occupy the rest of the Maritimes. They may have eluded archaeological discovery thus far because the landscape has changed so dramatically over time and many coastal sites are under water. This situation may change in the future as new technology is brought into archaeological research. They probably developed local tool forms, maybe from perishable materials, which are not comparable to those of better-known cultures in surrounding areas. Whether or not the small, triangular, fluted points from the Jones site date to the Late Palaeo period, it does make sense that people living on the Gulf of St. Lawrence shores would have developed a sea mammal hunting and fishing livelihood. The Archaic maritime subsistence pattern very likely has Palaeo roots.

We have many more archaeological sites to illustrate the Archaic period, although most of the Maritimes sites are disturbed. There is little evidence of an Early Archaic period like that identified in New England. It does appear that portions of the Maritimes that form the northern extension of the Gulf of Maine drainage area shared in the local Middle and Late Archaic cultural developments identified by Brian Robinson (1992, 2006). The Middle Archaic component at the Gaspereau Lake site is a classic example of the Gulf of Maine Archaic Tradition (ca. 9,500–6,000 ^{14}C yrs BP). However, we have yet to identify examples of Robinson's Morrow Point Burial Complex. These people made elegant woodworking tools but did not make recognizable stone projectile points. They were more marine-oriented than their ancestors, possibly using dugout canoes to exploit marine fish and sea mammals, although not all researchers are convinced

(Sanger 2009a, 25ff., 2009b, 2009c; Wright 1999, 586). People living to the east of the Saint John River drainage in New Brunswick and the Shubenacadie River drainage in Nova Scotia seem to have been more attuned to exploiting the rich marine life in the Gulf of St. Lawrence region.

The Moorehead Phase of the Late Archaic may also have local roots in Maine and spread to portions of the Maritimes. In Maine, the faunal evidence from the Turner Farm site shows a preference for swordfish and large cod, along with deer, moose, and beaver. These people had a very distinctive burial tradition that required copious amounts of powdered red ochre. Cow Point, on the Saint John River, is the easternmost expression of this tradition. Gaspereau Lake also showed evidence of a Moorehead Phase occupation, although the Nova Scotian collection shows a local flavour. It seems likely that there was an extensive trade going on with Archaic peoples in the north, with Ramah chert and red ochre moving south and possibly dugout canoes and slate bayonets moving north (Bourque 2012). This trade likely included perishable goods as well, like animal hides, bone and wood tools, and foodstuffs. In northern New Brunswick and Maine, a more interior-oriented hunting and fishing Archaic culture is recognized, which may have developed from the local Archaic culture, but with clear western influences. The large side-notched projectile points that are the hallmark of the Laurentian Tradition are common at several sites and are scattered throughout the remainder of the region. The technologies of the two peoples overlap in most areas. In eastern Nova Scotia and Cape Breton Island we appear to have a resident population that adopted tool forms from both traditions.

At the end of the Archaic period there was a movement of people from what is today New England into Maine. The exact timing and number of people are matters of debate. These people either pushed out or assimilated the Moorehead Phase population. They are found along the coast and interior of Maine and east to the St. Croix River system in New Brunswick and as far north as the Gaspé. They also crossed the Gulf of Maine to Nova Scotia and probably travelled up the Annapolis River as far as Gaspereau Lake and Minas Basin and south along the Mersey River drainage. Eventually they appear in Passamaquoddy Bay and may have travelled as far east as Prince Edward Island. These people were more diversified hunter-gatherers than the Moorehead people and used distinctive broad-bladed projectile point styles. They hunted deer, moose, bear, and seals, captured waterfowl, fished for cod, and collected shellfish. They also fished with weirs along the coast and took advantage of the spring anadromous fish runs on interior rivers. Exotic lithic sources from Maine found at the Boswell site indicate continued connection with coastal groups to the south. However, it seems that in eastern New Brunswick and Nova Scotia the Archaic population interacted more with Archaic peoples to the west, and eventually this led to major changes in the Maritimes that had relatively little effect on Maine.

In the Maritimes there may have been another movement of people and/or new ideas into the region at the beginning of the Woodland period, this time, from the west through northern New Brunswick. Major technological changes involved the spread of pottery-making and the beginning of bow-and-arrow hunting. There is also evidence of trade, both with the west and within the region, including lithics and foodstuffs. What developed was a local variant of the Meadowood culture, which is found throughout the region. Both habitation and burial sites are known, and distinctive Meadowood material culture includes projectile points and drills, cache blades, gorgets, atlatl weights, copper awls, and fabric-impressed pottery. It seems that areas such as Red Bank, New Brunswick, may have been the home of an elite group that controlled access to local resources for the purposes of trade to acquire prestige goods. The people in Red Bank would later adopt a new mortuary pattern and possibly belief system, with roots in the Adena area of the Ohio Valley. This was not likely a migration of people, but the acquisition of exotic materials associated with the Adena spiritual system. An extensive Adena-related burial mound was excavated at Red Bank during the 1970s and another was excavated at Whites Lake, near Halifax, in the 1980s. This phenomenon lasted less than

500 years. In the future, excavation of such burial sites will occur only under Indigenous supervision (see ANSMC 2016a).

The Middle Woodland period that followed began a pattern of settlement and subsistence that persisted until the arrival of the Europeans around AD 1500. The basic boundaries for the three historically known peoples may have been established at this time, although movement between areas may have been quite fluid. Various styles in pottery decoration and arrowheads appear, with considerable local variation. Trade was probably more intraregional in scale. Corn, bean, and squash horticulture was introduced in southern Maine. However, there is no archaeological evidence that this suite of crops had spread to the Maritimes. There is ethnohistoric evidence that some areas may have adopted corn and tobacco before the Europeans arrived, and groundnuts and plum may have been introduced earlier. As contact with Europeans intensified, major changes occurred in all aspects of Indigenous life, from political organization, spiritual life, and technology to diet. However, precontact Indigenous history remains alive through oral traditions, place names, art, and the material culture left behind by the ancestors.

The Maritimes still have relatively few archaeologists studying precontact archaeology compared with the rest of the country. However, a very committed base of academics and graduate students currently works there, as well as an active and engaged cultural resource management (CRM) community (e.g., Colwell-Pasch 2017; Glen 2016; Sanders 2014). Over the last decade, several important new projects have been undertaken. Some of these involve the restudy of previously explored sites using new approaches (e.g., Betts 2019; Rosenmeier et al. 2012), while others explore newly discovered sites (e.g., Deal et al. 2022; Kristmanson 2019). There have been steady improvements to the study of rock art, artifact dating, and sediment and residue analyses (e.g., Burchell and Harris 2018; Deal et al. 2019; Mudie and Lelièvre 2013; Pickard et al. 2011; Taché and Craig 2015; Tapper 2021; Tapper and Moro Albadia 2021; Tapper et al. 2020; Woolsey 2017). There is a continuing concern for the conservation of coastal sites, including submerged landscapes (e.g., Betts et al. 2018; Lacroix et al. 2014; Taylor 2020; Weatherbee et al. 2020). However, many challenges lie ahead, such as securing funding for research projects, timely publishing of results, and access to the archaeological grey literature. We continue to work on closing the gaps in the precontact timeline, and particularly the transitions from Palaeo to Early Archaic and the Archaic to Woodland.

Modern Indigenous concerns about archaeological methods and interpretations have a tremendous effect on current archaeological practice in this region. Indigenous organizations have become heavily involved in local archaeological practice and more young Indigenous archaeologists are being trained. The concerns of Indigenous communities over the treatment of burials and sacred landscapes are factored into archaeological projects and surviving oral traditions and artwork have gained a new importance for archaeological interpretation. The last decade has also witnessed a dramatic increase in collaborative projects between Indigenous communities and local governments and cultural resource management companies. This bodes well for future archaeological work in the Maritimes.

REFERENCES CITED

Abbe Museum. 2017. "Abbe Launches Archaeology Advisory Committee." https://www.abbemuseum.org/blog/2017/8/8/abbe-launches-archaeological-advisory-committee.

Abrams, M.D., and G.J. Nowacki. 2008. "Native Americans as Active and Passive Promoters of Mast and Fruit Trees in the Eastern USA." *The Holocene* 18, no. 7: 1123–37.

Adney, E.T. 1933. "Archaeological Plans of Prehistoric Campsites: Saint John River between Woodstock and Tobique." Manuscript on file at the New Brunswick Museum, Saint John.

Allen, P. 1981. *The Oxbow Site: Chronology and Prehistory in Northeastern New Brunswick*. New Brunswick Manuscripts in Archaeology. Fredericton, NB: Department of Historical and Cultural Resources.

Allen, P. 1989. "The Gerrish Site (CeDk-2): A Report on Preliminary Excavations." *Man in the Northeast* no. 37: 25–34.

Allen, P. 1991. *Metepenagiag: New Brunswick's Oldest Village*. Red Bank, NB: Red Bank Indian Band.

Allen, P. 1993. "Prehistory." In *Field Guide to the Quaternary Geology of Southwestern New Brunswick*, edited by A.A. Seaman, B.E. Broster, L.C. Cwynar, M. Lamouthe, R.F. Miller, and J.J. Thibault, 31–33. Fredericton: New Brunswick Department of Natural Resources and Energy, Mineral Resources, Open File Report 93-1.

Allen, P. 1996. "Maritime Regional Report." In *Statement of Principles for Ethical Conduct Pertaining to Aboriginal Peoples: A Report from the Aboriginal Heritage Committee*, edited by B. Nicholson, D. Pokotylo, and R. Williamson, 17–20. Ottawa: Canadian Archaeological Association and the Department of Communications.

REFERENCES CITED

Allen, P. 2005. *The Oxbow Site 1984: Metepenagiag Mi'kmaq First Nation, Miramichi, New Brunswick.* New Brunswick Manuscripts in Archaeology 39. Fredericton, NB: Archaeological Services, Heritage Branch, Culture and Sport Secretariat.

Allen, P., M. Nicholas, and F. Thériault. 2004. *Rocks Provincial Park: The 1994 Archaeological Survey and Historical Inventory.* New Brunswick Manuscripts in Archaeology 33E. Fredericton, NB: Archaeological Services, Heritage Branch, Culture and Sport Secretariat.

Allen, P., and G. Orechia. 1995. "Ashes to Ashes, Dust to Dust: Finally at Rest." Press statement prepared for the annual general meeting of the New Brunswick Museums Association, Fredericton, NB.

Ambrose, J. 1867. "Some Account of the Petrel — the Sea Serpent — and the Albicore — as Observed in St. Margaret's Bay, — Together with a Few Observations on a Beach-mound or Kitchen-midden, near French Village." *Proceedings of the Nova Scotian Institute of Science for 1863, 1864, 1865, 1866* 1: 34–43.

Anderson, A., and G. Hrynick. 2019. "A Reported Hafted Biface from Pennamaquan Lake, Washington County, Maine." *Maine Archaeological Society Bulletin* 59, no. 2: 1–8.

Anderson, T.W. 1980. "Holocene Vegetation and Climatic History of Prince Edward Island, Canada." *Canadian Journal of Earth Sciences* 17: 1152–65.

Anderson, T.W., R.W. Mathews, and C.E. Schweger. 1989. "Holocene Climatic Trends in Canada with Special Reference to the Hypsithermal Interval." In *Quaternary Geology of Canada and Greenland*, edited by R.J. Fulton, 481–539. Ottawa: Geological Survey of Canada, Geology of Canada No. 1.

Anderson, W.P., comp. 1919. *Micmac Place-Names in the Maritime Provinces and Gaspé Peninsula*, recorded by S.T. Rand. Ottawa: Surveyor General's Office.

Anonymous. 1959. "Summary of the Proceedings of the Conference on Archaeology in Nova Scotia Held at Citadel Hill in Halifax, October 31, 1959." MS on file, Nova Scotia Museum, Halifax.

Anonymous. 1970a. "Discover Ancient Indian Burial Area." *Daily Gleaner*, Aug. 12: 1–2.

Anonymous. 1970b. "Desecration Charged by Union, Indians Protest Excavation Work at Ancient Burial Grounds." *Daily Gleaner*, Aug. 14: 1.

Anonymous. 1970c. "Won't Demonstrate at Burial Ground." *Daily Gleaner*, Aug. 12: 1–2.

Anonymous. 1970d. "Says Archaeologists' Attitude Must Change." *Daily Gleaner*, Sept. 2: 17.

Anonymous. 1989. "Archaeologist Studies Relics from 'Nova Scotian Atlantis'." *Evening Telegram*, Jan. 14: 56.

Armstrong, N. 1991. "Sark Seeks Return of Ancient Bones." *The Guardian* (Charlottetown), May 1.

Aronson, S. 1997. "Aboriginal Land Rights." In *Aboriginal Issues Today: A Legal and Business Guide*, edited by S.B. Smart and M. Coyle, 32–52. North Vancouver: Self Counsel Press.

Asch Sidell, N. 1999. "Prehistoric Plant Use in Maine: Paleoindian to Contact Period." In *Current Paleoethnobotany*, edited by J.P. Hart, 191–223. Albany: New York State Museum Bulletin, Vol. 404.

Ash, M. 1985. "Daniel Wilson — The Man Who Invented Prehistory?" *Popular Archaeology* (May): 12–16.

Assembly of Nova Scotia Mi'kmaq Chiefs (ANSMC). 2015. "Culture, Heritage and Archaeology Strategic Plan." Truro, NS: Mi'kmaq Rights Initiative. http://mikmaqrights.com/wp-content/uploads/2014/01/2015-ANSMC-CHA-Strategic-Plan.pdf.

Assembly of Nova Scotia Mi'kmaq Chiefs (ANSMC). 2016a. "Principles of Mi'kmaw Ancestral Remains Protocols." Truro, NS: Mi'kmaq Rights Initiative. https://mikmaqrights.com/wp-content/uploads/2020/11/2016-Human-Remains-Protocols-The-Fundamental-Principle.pdf.

Assembly of Nova Scotia Mi'kmaq Chiefs (ANSMC). 2016b. "Statement of Principles Regarding Archaeological Resources." Truro, NS: Mi'kmaq Rights Initiative. http://mikmaqrights.com/wp-content/uploads/2014/01/2016-Sept-ANSMC-Statement-of-Archaeological-Principles.pdf.

Atalay, S. 2006. "Indigenous Archaeology as Decolonizing Practice." *American Indian Quarterly* 30: 280–311.

Augustine, M., C. Turnbull, P. Allen, and P. Ward. 2006. *"To Hold It in My Hand."* New Brunswick Manuscripts in Archaeology 43. Fredericton, NB: Archaeological Services, Heritage Branch, Department of Wellness, Culture and Sport.

Bailey, A.G. 1969. *The Conflict of European and Eastern Algonkian Cultures 1504–1700*. Toronto: University of Toronto Press.

Bailey, L.W. 1883. "Indian Relics from New Brunswick." *Science* 1: 245–46.

Bailey, L.W. 1887. "On the Relics of the Stone Age in New Brunswick." *Bulletin of the Natural History Society of New Brunswick* 5: 1–15.

Bailey, L.W. 1923. "The University Museum." *The Brunswickian* (Jan.–Feb.): 136–44.

Baird, S.F. 1882. "Notes on Certain Aboriginal Shell Mounds on the Coast of New

Brunswick and New England." *Proceedings of the United States National Museum* 4: 292–97.

Bakker, P. 2004. "Finding the Almouchiquois: Native American Families, Territories, and Land Sales in Southern Maine." *Ethnohistory* 51, no. 1: 73–100.

Barkham, S. 1980. "A Note on the Strait of Belle-Isle during the Period of Basque Contact with Indians and Inuit." *Études/Inuit/Studies* 4, nos. 1–2: 51–58.

Barr, S.M., and R.P. Raeside. 1998. "Petrology and Tectonic Implications of Silurian (?) Metavolcanic Rocks in the Clyburn Brook Area and on Ingonish Island, Northeastern Cape Breton Island, Nova Scotia." *Atlantic Geology* 34, no. 1: 27–37.

Bartlett, C.M. 2011. "Integrative Science/*Toqwa'tu'kl Kjijitaqnn*: The Story of Our Journey in Bringing Together Indigenous and Western Scientific Knowledges." In *Ta'n Wetapeksi'k: Understanding from Where We Come*, edited by T. Bernard, L.M. Rosenmeier, and S.L. Farrell, 179–86. Truro, NS: Eastern Woodland Print Communications.

Bartlett, C., M. Marshall, and A. Marshall. 2012. "Two-Eyed Seeing and Other Lessons Learned within a Co-Learning Journey of Bringing Together Indigenous and Mainstream Knowledges and Ways of Knowing." *Journal of Environmental Studies and Sciences* 2: 331–40.

Basso, K.H. 1996. *Wisdom Sits in Places: Landscapes and Language among the Western Apache*. Albuquerque: University of New Mexico Press.

Becker, M.J. 2013. "Wampum Bags and Containers from the Native Northeast." *Material Culture* 45, no. 1: 21–48.

Belcher, W.R. 1989. "Archaeology of the Knox Site, East Penobscot Bay, Maine." *Maine Archaeological Society Bulletin* 29, no. 1: 33–46.

Belcher, W.R., D. Sanger, and B.J. Bourque. 1994. "The Bradley Cemetery: A Moorehead Burial Tradition Site in Maine." *Canadian Journal of Archaeology* no. 18: 3–28.

Benmouyal, J. 1987. *Des Paléoindians aux Iroquoiens en Gaspésie: Six Mille and d'Histoire*. Quebec: Ministère des Affaires Culturelles, Dossiers 63.

Bernard, T., L.M. Rosenmeier, and S.L. Farrell, eds. 2011. *Ta'n Wetapeksi'k: Understanding from Where We Come*. Truro, NS: Eastern Woodland Print Communications.

Betts, M., ed. 2019. *Place-Making in the Pretty Harbour. The Archaeology of Port Joli, Nova Scotia*. Mercury Series. Ottawa: University of Ottawa Press.

Betts, M., S.E. Blair, and D.W. Black. 2012. "The Old Man and the Sea: Perspectivism,

Mortuary Symbolism and Human–Shark Relationships on the Maritime Peninsula." *American Antiquity* 77, no. 4: 621–45.

Betts, M., M. Burchell, and B.R. Schöne. 2017. "An Economic History of the Maritime Woodland Period in Port Joli, Nova Scotia." In *North American East Coast Shell Midden Research*, edited by M.W. Betts and M.G. Hrynick, 18–41. *Journal of the North Atlantic*, Special Volume 10.

Betts, M.W., and M.G. Hrynick. 2021. *The Archaeology of the Atlantic Northeast*. Toronto: University of Toronto Press.

Betts, M., M.G. Hrynick, and A. Pelletier-Michaud. 2018. "The Pierce-Embree Site: A Palaeoindian Findspot from Southwestern Nova Scotia." *Canadian Journal of Archaeology* 42, no. 2: 255–62.

Biard, P. 1959. *Relation of New France of its Lands, Nature of the Country and its Inhabitants*. In *The Jesuit Relations and Allied Documents, Volume III, Acadia 1611–1616*, edited by R.G. Thwaites, 26–283. New York: Pageant Books.

Binford, L.R. 1962. "Archaeology as Anthropology." *American Antiquity* 28: 217–25.

Binford, L.R. 1980. "Willow Smoke and Dogs' Tails: Hunter-Gatherer Settlement Systems and Archaeological Site Formation." *American Antiquity* 45: 4–20.

Bintliff, J.L. 1986. "Archaeology at the Interface: An Historical Perspective." In *Archaeology at the Interface: Studies in Archaeology's Relationships with History, Geography, Biology and Physical Science*, edited by J.L. Bintliff and C.F. Gaffney, 4–31. Oxford, UK: BAR International Series S300.

Bishop, J.C. 1983. "Phil's Beach: An Artifact Analysis and Comparative Study." *Nexus: The Canadian Student Journal of Anthropology* 3, nos. 1-2: 15–59.

Black, D. 1992. *Living Close to the Ledge: Prehistoric Human Ecology of the Bliss Islands, Quoddy Region, New Brunswick, Canada*. Occasional Papers in Northeastern Archaeology 6. Dundas, ON: Copetown Press.

Black, D. 1993. *What Images Return: A Study of the Stratigraphy and Seasonality of a Shell Midden in the Insular Quoddy Region, New Brunswick*. Manuscripts in Archaeology 27. Fredericton, NB: Archaeological Services, Department of Municipalities, Culture and Housing.

Black, D. 1995. "Pioneers of New Brunswick Archaeology: Spencer Fullerton Baird." *Fieldnotes: Newsletter of the New Brunswick Archeological Society* 2, no. 1: 5–9. http://www.unb.ca/fredericton/arts/departments/anthropology/pdfs/dwblack/baird.pdf.

Black, D.W. 1997. "A Native Artifact from the Ocean Floor near Indian Island." *Fieldnotes: Newsletter of the New Brunswick Archaeological Society* 3, no. 2: 5–7.

Black, D.W. 2000. "Rum Beach and the Susquehanna Tradition in the Quoddy Region, Charlotte County, NB." *Canadian Journal of Archaeology* 24: 89–106.

Black, D.W. 2004. "Ponapsqey: Stone Materials." In *Wolastoqiyik Ajemsweg: The People of the Beautiful River at Jemseg. Volume 2: Archaeological Results*, edited by S.E. Blair, 91–116. Fredericton, NB: Archaeological Services, Heritage Branch, Culture and Sport Secretariat.

Black, D. 2008. "Pioneers of New Brunswick Archaeology II: Abraham Gesner." http://www.unb.ca/fredericton/arts/departments/anthropology/pdfs/dw-black/gesner.pdf.

Black, D. 2009. "Pioneers of New Brunswick Archaeology III: Loring Woart Bailey." http://www.unb.ca/fredericton/arts/departments/anthropology/pdfs/dwblack/bailey.pdf.

Black, D.W. 2011. "Background, Discussion and Recommendations for Extending the Analysis of Lithic Materials Used by Palaeoindians at the Debert and Belmont Sites." In *Ta'n Wetapeksi'k: Understanding from Where We Come*, edited by T. Bernard, L.M. Rosenmeier, and S.L. Farrell, 111–28. Truro, NS: Eastern Woodland Print Communications.

Black, D.W. 2013. "'Some Clams in Those Days': Shell Midden Archaeology on the Bliss Islands." In *Underground New Brunswick: Stories of Archaeology*, edited by P. Erickson and J. Fowler, 27–36. Halifax: Nimbus Publishing.

Black, D.W. 2017. "Archaeological Sea Mammal Remains from the Maritime Provinces of Canada." In *North American East Coast Shell Midden Research*, edited by M.W. Betts and M.G. Hrynick, 70–89. *Journal of the North Atlantic*, Special Volume 10.

Black, D.W. 2018. "'. . . gathering pebbles on a boundless shore . . .': The Rum Beach Site and Intertidal Archaeology in the Canadian Quoddy Region." University of New Brunswick Libraries, Scholar Research Repository. https://unbscholar.lib.unb.ca/islandora/object/unbscholar%3A9409.

Black, D.W. 2022. "Far Northeastern Flaked-Lithic Material Acquisition and Exchange: Looking Through the Bliss Islands Lens." In *The Far Northeast: 3000 BP to Contact*, edited by K.R. Holyoke and M.G. Hrynick, 79–122. Mercury Series, Archaeological Paper 181. Ottawa: Canadian Museum of History and University of Ottawa Press.

Black, D.W., J.E. Reading, and H.G. Savage. 1998. "Archaeological Records of the Extinct Sea Mink, *Mustela macrodon* (Carnivora: Mustelidae), from Canada." *Canadian Field-Naturalist* 112, no. 1: 45–49.

Black, D.W., and R.H. Whitehead. 1988. "Prehistoric Shellfish Preservation and Storage on the Northeast Coast." *North American Archaeologist* 9, no. 1: 17–30.

Black, D.W., and L.A. Wilson. 1999. "The Washademoak Lake Chert Source, Queens County, New Brunswick, Canada." *Archaeology of Eastern North America* 27: 81–108.

Blair, C., and D.B. Black. 1991. "The Northeast Point Site: A Single Component Occupation without Middens, on the Bliss Islands." Paper presented at the annual meeting of the Canadian Archaeological Association, St. John's.

Blair, S.E., ed. 2004a. *Wolastoqiyik Ajemseg: The People of the Beautiful River at Jemseg. Volume 2: Archaeological Results*. New Brunswick Manuscripts in Archaeology 36E. Fredericton, NB: Archaeological Services, Heritage Branch, Culture and Sport Secretariat.

Blair, S.E. 2004b. "Ancient Wolastoq'kew Landscapes: Settlement and Technology in the Lower Saint John River Valley, Canada." PhD diss., University of Toronto.

Blair, S.E. 2010. "Missing the Boat in Lithic Procurement: Watercraft and the Bulk Procurement of Tool-stone on the Maritime Peninsula." *Journal of Anthropological Archaeology* 29: 33–46.

Blair, S., M. Horne, A.K. Patton, and W.J. Webb. 2017. "Birch Cove and the Protohistoric Period of the Northern Quoddy Region, New Brunswick, Canada." In *North American East Coast Shell Midden Research*, edited by M.W. Betts and M.G. Hrynick, 59–69. *Journal of the North Atlantic*, Special Volume 10.

Blair, S., T. Jarratt, and P. Ward. 2014. "Weaving Together Two Ways of Knowing: Archaeological Organic Artifact Analysis and Indigenous Textile Arts." *North American Archaeologist* 35, no. 4: 295–302.

Blair, S.E., and K. Perley. 2013. "The People of the Beautiful River at Jemseg." In *Underground New Brunswick: Stories of Archaeology*, edited by P. Erickson and J. Fowler, 17–26. Halifax: Nimbus Publishing.

Blair, S.E., and M.P. Rooney. 2022. "Cultural Patterning through the Early Maritime Woodland in the Far Northeast: A Perspective from the Archaeological Landscape of Metepenagiag, Mi'kmaqi." In *The Far Northeast: 3000 BP to Contact*, edited by K.R. Holyoke and M.G. Hrynick, 123–74. Mercury Series, Archaeological Paper 181. Ottawa: Canadian Museum of History and University of Ottawa Press.

Blair, S.E., and P. Ward. 2013. "The Metepenagiag Complex." In *Underground New Brunswick: Stories of Archaeology*, edited by P. Erickson and J. Fowler, 7–16. Halifax: Nimbus Publishing.

Bleakney, J.S., and D. Davis. 1983. "Discovery of an Undisturbed Bed of 3800 Year Old Oysters (*Crassostrea virginia*) in Minas Basin." *Proceedings of the Nova Scotia Institute of Science* 33: 1–6.

Boardman, S.K. 1903. *The Naturalist of the Saint Croix: A Memoir of George A. Boardman*. Bangor, ME: Charles H. Glass.

Bock, P.K. 1978. "Micmac." In *Handbook of North American Indians, Volume 15, Northeast*, edited by B.G. Trigger, 109–22. Washington, DC: Smithsonian Institution.

Bonnichsen, R., ed. 1981. *Archaeological Research at Munsungun Lake: 1981 Preliminary Technical Report of Activities*. Munsungun Lake Paper No.7. Orono: Institute for Quaternary Studies and the Center for the Study of Early Man, University of Maine.

Bonnichsen, R., D. Keenlyside, and K. Turnmire. 1991. "Paleoindian Patterns in Maine and the Maritimes: An Overview." In *Prehistory of the Maritime Provinces: Past and Present Research*, edited by M. Deal and S. Blair, 1–28. Fredericton, NB: Council of Maritime Premiers.

Boone, E.H. 2012. "Presidential Lecture: Discourse and Authority in Histories Painted, Knotted, and Threaded." *Ethnohistory* 59, no. 2: 211–23.

Bordon, C.E. 1952. "A Uniform Site Designation Scheme for Canada." *Anthropology of British Columbia* 3: 44–48.

Borns, H.W., Jr. 1966. "The Geography of Paleo-Indian Occupation in Nova Scotia." *Quaternaria* no. 8: 49–57.

Borstel, C.L. 1982. *Archaeological Investigations at the Young Site, Alton, Maine*. Occasional Publications in Maine Archaeology 2. Augusta, ME: Maine Historic Preservation Commission.

Boudreau, J. 2008. *A New England Typology of Native American Projectile Points*. New Bedford, MA: Alphagraphics.

Bourgeois, V.G.J. 1999. "A Regional Precontact Ceramic Sequence for the Saint John River Valley." MA thesis, University of New Brunswick.

Bourque, B.J. 1975. "Comments on the Late Archaic Populations of Central Maine: The View from Turner Farm." *Arctic Anthropology* 12, no. 2: 35–45.

Bourque, B.J. 1992. *Prehistory of the Central Maine Coast*. New York: Garland.

Bourque, B.J. 1994. "Evidence for Prehistoric Exchange on the Maritime Peninsula." In *Prehistoric Exchange Systems in North America*, edited by J.E. Ericson and T.G. Baugh, 23–46. New York: Plenum Press.

Bourque, B.J. 1995. *Diversity and Complexity in Prehistoric Maritime Societies: A Gulf of Maine Perspective*. New York: Plenum Press.

Bourque, B.J. 2001. *Twelve Thousand Years: American Indians in Maine.* Lincoln: University of Nebraska Press.

Bourque, B.J. 2002. "Marine Shell Midden Archaeology (1860–1910) and the Influence of Adolphe von Morlot." In *New Perspectives on the Origins of Americanist Archaeology*, edited by D.L. Browman and S. Williams, 148–63. Tuscaloosa: University of Alabama Press.

Bourque, B.J. 2012. *The Swordfish Hunters: The History and Ecology of an Ancient American Sea People.* Piermont, NH: Bunker Hill Publishing.

Bourque, B.J., and S.L. Cox. 1981. "The Maine State Museum Investigation of the Goddard Site." *Man in the Northeast* no. 22: 3–27.

Bourque, B.J., S.L. Cox, and R.A. Lewis. 2006. "The Archaic Period of the Merrymeeting Bay Region, South Central Maine." In *The Archaic of the Far Northeast*, edited by D. Sanger and M.A.P. Renouf, 307–40. Orono: University of Maine Press.

Bourque, B.J., B. Johnson, and R.S. Steneck. 2008. "Possible Prehistoric Fishing Effects on Coastal Marine Food Webs in the Gulf of Maine." In *Human Impacts on Ancient Marine Ecosystems: A Global Perspective*, edited by J. Erlandson and T. Ricks, 164–86. Berkeley: University of California Press.

Bourque, B.J., and H.W. Krueger. 1994. "Dietary Reconstruction from Human Bone Isotopes for Five New England Coastal Populations." *Paleonutrition: The Diet and Health of Prehistoric Americans*, edited by K.D. Sobolik, 195–209. Carbondale, IL: Southern Illinois University Center for Archaeological Investigations.

Bourque, B.J., and R.H. Whitehead. 1985. "Tarrentines and the Introduction of European Trade Goods in the Gulf of St. Lawrence." *Ethnohistory* 32, no. 4: 327–41.

Bourque, B.J., and R.H. Whitehead. 1994. "Trade and Alliances in the Contact Period." In *American Beginnings: Exploration, Culture, and Cartography in the Land of Norumbega*, edited by E.W. Baker, E.A. Churchill, R.S. D'Abate, K. Jones, V.A. Konrad, and H.E. Prins, 131–47. Lincoln: University of Nebraska Press.

Bradley, B.A. 1995. "Clovis Ivory and Bone Tools." In *Le Travail et L'Usage de L'Ivoire au Paleolithique Suprieur*, edited by J. Hahn, M. Menu, Y. Taborin, P. Walter, and F. Widemann. Ravello, Italy: Actes de la Table Ronde, Centro Universitario Europeo per i Beni Culturali.

Bradley, J.W. 2011. "Re-Visiting Wampum and Other Seventeenth-Century Shell Games." *Archaeology of Eastern North America* 39: 25–51.

Bradley, J.W. 2014. "Glass Beads from Champlain's *Habitation* on Saint Croix Island, Maine, 1604–1613." *Journal of the Society of Bead Researchers* 26: 47–63.

Bradley, J.W., A. Spiess, R. Boisvert, and J. Boudreau. 2010. "What's the Point? Modal Forms and Attributes of Paleoindian Bifaces and the New England–Maritimes Region." *Archaeology of Eastern North America* 36: 119–72.

Brewster, G., S.A. Davis, M. Frappier, R.J. Mott, and R.R. Stea. 1996. "Preliminary Report on the Debert/Belmont Palaeo-Indian Project." In *Archaeology in Nova Scotia 1991, Curatorial Report Number 81*, edited by S. Powell, 81–88. Halifax: Nova Scotia Museum.

Brennan, L.A. 1974. "The Lower Hudson: A Decade of Shell Middens." *Archaeology of Eastern North America* 2, no. 1: 81–93.

Brigham, M., N. Bartone, J. Reed, and E.R. Cowie. 2001. "Introduction to the Archaeological Phase III Excavations at NTOLONAPEMK, the Eastern Surplus Company Superfund Site, 96.02." *Bulletin of the Maine State Archaeological Society* 41, no. 2: 27–39.

Brigham, M.S., E.R. Cowie, R.N. Bartone, S.R. Scharoun, R.A. Cyr, and J.A. Reed. 2006. "The Archaeology of N'Tolonapemk (96.02 ME) 'Our Ancestor's Place': Phase III Data Recovery at the Eastern Surplus Company Superfund Site, Meddybemps, Washington County, Maine." In Vol. II. A report prepared for the U.S. Environmental Protection Agency through Tetra Tech NUS, Inc. by the Archaeology Research Center, Department of Social Sciences and Business, University of Maine at Farmington, Farmington.

Brooks, L.T., and C.M. Brooks. 2010. "The Reciprocity Principle and Traditional Ecological Knowledge: Understanding the Significance of Indigenous Protest on the Presumpscot River." *International Journal of Critical Indigenous Studies* 3, no. 2: 11–28.

Bryan, K. 1950. *Flint Quarries — The Sources of Tools and, at the same time, the Factories of the American Indian*. Cambridge, MA: Harvard University, Peabody Museum Papers 17(3).

Brzezicki, A.B. 2015. "Getting a Handle on Ground Stone: A Technological Analysis of the Ground Stone Axes, Adzes, and Gouges in the George Frederick Clarke Collection." MA thesis, University of New Brunswick.

Buchanan, S. 1999. "The Archaeology of Mi'kmaq Heritage on Prince Edward Island." *Encounters* 2, no. 1: 15, 17.

Buchanan, S. 2011. "Something New on the Horizon: The 'Tusket Tradition' and the Middle Woodland Milieu of Prince Edward Island and the Southern Gulf of St. Lawrence." Paper presented at the annual meeting of the Canadian Archaeological Association, Halifax.

Buckler, E. 1968. *Oxbells and Fireflies*. Toronto: McClelland & Stewart.

Bunker, V. 1992. "Stratified Components of the Gulf of Maine Tradition at the Eddy Site, Amoskeag Falls." In *Early Holocene Occupation in Northern New England*, edited by B. Robinson, J. Petersen, and A. Robinson, 135–48. Occasional Papers in Maine Archaeology 9. Augusta: Maine Historic Preservation Commission.

Burchell, M., and A. Harris. 2018. "Stable Isotope Research in Canadian Archaeology: The Next 50 Years." *Canadian Journal of Archaeology* 42, no. 1: 115–23.

Burke, A.L. 2000. "Lithic Procurement and the Ceramic Period Occupation of the Interior of the Maritime Peninsula." PhD diss., State University of New York, Albany.

Burke, A.L. 2003. "Archetypal Landscapes and Seascapes: Coastal versus Interior in the Archaeology of the Maritime Peninsula." *Northeast Anthropology* 66: 41–55.

Burke, A.L. 2006. "Stone Tool Raw Materials and Sources of the Archaic Period in the Northeast." In *The Archaic of the Far Northeast*, edited by D. Sanger and M.A.P. Renouf, 409–36. Orono: University of Maine Press.

Burke, A.L. 2022. "A Chronological and Typological Framework for Bifacial Stone Tools in the Maritime Peninsula during the Ceramic Period." In *The Far Northeast: 3000 BP to Contact*, edited by K.R. Holyoke and M.G. Hrynick, 175–218. Mercury Series, Archaeological Paper 181. Ottawa: Canadian Museum of History and University of Ottawa Press.

Burley, D. 1981. "Proto-Historic Ecological Effects of the Fur Trade on Micmac Culture in Northeastern New Brunswick." *Ethnohistory* 28: 203–16.

Burley, D. 1983. "Cultural Complexity and Evolutions in the Development of Coastal Adaptations among the Micmac and Coast Salish." In *The Evolution of Maritime Cultures on the Northeast and Northwest Coasts of North America*, edited by R.J. Nash, 157–72. Burnaby, BC: Simon Fraser University, Department of Archaeology, Occasional Publication 11.

Burton, E. 2005. "Portuguese Interest in Settlement in Sixteenth-Century Northeastern North America: A Historiographical Reassessment." MA thesis, Saint Mary's University.

Byers, D.S. 1959. "The Eastern Archaic: Some Problems and Hypotheses." *American Antiquity* 24: 233–57.

Byers, D.S. 1960. Report to John M. Kemper, Clerk of the Board of Trustees, Phillips Academy. Annual Report 1959, Robert S. Peabody Foundation for Archaeology, Phillips Academy, Andover, MA.

Byers, D.S. 1966. "The Debert Archaeological Project: The Position of Debert with Respect to the Paleo-Indian Tradition." *Quaternaria* no. 8: 33–47.

Byers, D.S. 1979. *The Nevin Shellheap: Burials and Observations*. Papers for the Robert S. Peabody Foundation for Archaeology 9, Andover, MA.

Byers, D.S., Faye Cooper-Cole, and W.C. McKern. 1943. "Report on the First Archaeological Conference on the Woodland Pattern." *American Antiquity* 8: 393–400.

Cameron, H.L. 1954. "New Maps of Historic Sites in Nova Scotia." *Transactions of the Royal Society of Canada* (Third Series, Section 2) 48: 59–64.

Cameron, H.L. 1956. "Nova Scotia Historic Sites." *Transactions of the Royal Society of Canada* (Third Series, Section 2) 50: 1–7.

Cameron, H.L. 1958. "History from the Air." *Photogrammetric Engineering* 24, no. 3: 366–75.

Campbell, J.A. 2016. "*Mu Awsami Keji'kewe'k L'nuk Mi'kma'ki*: New Perspectives on the Transitional Archaic Period in Southwestern Nova Scotia." MA thesis, Memorial University of Newfoundland.

Canadian Archaeological Association (CAA). 2022. "Principles of Ethical Conduct." https://canadianarchaeology.com/caa/about/ethics/principles-ethical-conduct.

Canadian Museum of Civilization (CMC). 1992. "Policy: Human Remains." Ottawa: Canadian Museum of Civilization.

Chalifoux, É. 1999. "Late Paleoindian Occupation in a Coastal Environment: A Perspective from La Martre, Gaspé Peninsula, Quebec." *Northeast Anthropology* no. 57: 69–79.

Chalifoux, É., and A. Burke. 1995. "L'Occupation Préhistorique du Témiscouata (est du Québec), un Lieu de Portage entre Deux Grandes Voies de Circulation." In *Archéologies Québécoises. Paléo Québec* no. 23, edited by A.M. Balac, C. Chapdelaine, N. Clermont, and F. Duguay, 237–70. Montreal: Recherches Amérindiennes au Québec.

Champlain, S. de. 1922. *The Works of Samuel de Champlain. Volume 1. 1599–1607*. Translated and edited by H.H. Langton and W.F. Ganong. Toronto: The Champlain Society.

Chapdelaine, C., and S. Bourget. 1992. "Premier Regard sur un Site Paléoindian Récent à Rimouski (DcEd-1)." *Récherches Amérindiennes au Québec* 22, no. 1: 17–32.

Childe, V.G. 1925. *The Dawn of European Civilization*. London: Kegan Paul.

Christenson, A.L. 2011. "Who Were the Professional North American Archaeologists of 1900? Clues from the Work of Warren K. Moorehead." *Bulletin of the History of Archaeology* 21, no. 1: 4–22.

Christianson, D. 1985. "Archaeology and Lake Rossignol." *Mersey Quarterly* (Winter): 8–9.

Christianson, D.J. 1991. "Report on the Chamber's Fluted Point Preform." In *Archaeology in Nova Scotia 1987 and 1988*, edited by S.A. Davis, C. Lindsay, R. Ogilvie, and B. Preston, 7–12. Halifax: Nova Scotia Museum Curatorial Report 69.

Christie Boyle, F. 1986. *Archaeological Reconnaissance of Ste. Anne's Point, Fredericton, York County, New Brunswick*. Fredericton, NB: Department of Tourism, Recreation, and Heritage, Manuscripts in Archaeology 12E.

Clark, J.G.D. 1954. *Excavations at Star Carr*. Cambridge: Cambridge University Press.

Clarke, D.L. 1968. *Analytical Archaeology*. London: Methuen.

Clarke, G.F. 1974. *Someone before Us: Our Maritime Indians*, 3rd ed. Fredericton, NB: Unipress.

Clermont, N. 1978. "Le Sylvicole Initial." In *Images de la Préhistoire du Québec*, edited by C. Chapdelaine. *Récherches Amérindiennes au Québec* 7, nos. 1–2: 31–54.

Colwell-Pasch, C. 2017. "A Case Study in Enhanced Landscape Testing Projects: Phase II of the Glenwood Project." Paper presented at the annual meeting of the Canadian Archaeological Association, Gatineau, QC.

Connolly, J. 1977. "Archaeology in Nova Scotia and New Brunswick between 1863 and 1914 and Its Relationship to the Development of North American Archaeology." *Man in the Northeast* no. 13: 3–34.

Cotter, J.L., comp. 1962. "Notes and News — Northeast." *American Antiquity* 27, no. 3: 454–56.

Cox, S.L. 1991. "Site 95.20 and the Vergennes Phase in Maine." *Archaeology of Eastern North America* 19: 135–61.

Cox, S.L. 2000a. "A Norse Penny from Maine." In *Vikings: The North Atlantic Saga*, edited by W.W. Fitzhugh and E.I. Ward, 206–07. Washington, DC: Smithsonian Institution Press.

Cox, S.L. 2000b. "An Early Contact Native Site on the Upper St. Croix River." *Maine Archaeological Society Bulletin* 40, no. 2: 1–10.

Cox, S.L. 2021. *Goddard: A Prehistoric Village Site on Blue Hill Bay, Maine*. Occasional Publications in Maine Archaeology 16. Augusta: Maine Historic Preservation Commission.

Cox, S.L., and D. Kopec. 1988. "Archaeological Excavations at the Watson Site, Frenchman's Bay." *Maine Archaeological Society Bulletin* 28, no. 1: 38–45.

Crabtree, D. 1967. "Notes on Experiments in Flintknapping: 3. The Flint Knappers Raw Materials." *Tebiwa* 10: 8–25.

Crader, C. 1998. "Prehistoric Use of Beaver in Coastal Maine (U.S.A.)." *Anthropozoologica* nos. 25–26: 225–36.

Crawford, G.W., and D.G. Smith. 2003. "Paleoethnobotany in the Northeast." In *People and Plants in Ancient Eastern North America*, edited by P.E. Minnis, 172–257. Washington, DC: Smithsonian Books.

Creese, J.L. 2011. "Algonquian Rock Art and the Landscape of Power." *Journal of Social Archaeology* 11, no. 1: 3–20.

Crock, J.G., J.B. Petersen, and R. Anderson. 1993. "Scalloping for Artifacts: A Biface and Plummet from Eastern Blue Hill Bay, Maine." *Archaeology of Eastern North America* 21: 179–92.

Crosby, D.G. 1962. *Wolfville Map-Area, N.S. (21 H1)*. Ottawa: Geological Survey of Canada, Memoir 325.

Crotts, A. 1984. "Pattern and Variation on Prehistoric Lithic Resource Exploitation in Passamaquoddy Bay, Charlotte County, New Brunswick." MSc thesis, University of Maine.

Curran, M.L. 1996. "Paleoindians in the Northeast: The Problem of Dating Fluted Point Sites." *Review of Archaeology* 17, no. 1: 2–5.

Cybulski, J.S., N.S. Ossenberg, and W.D. Wade. 1979. "Statement on the Excavation, Treatment, Analysis and Disposition of Human Skeletal Remains from Archaeological Sites in Canada." *Canadian Review of Physical Anthropology* 1, no. 1: 32–36.

Daigle, J.J., N. Michelle, D.J. Ranco, and M.R. Emery. 2019. "Traditional Lifeways and Storytelling: Tools for Adaptation and Resilience to Ecosystem Change." *Human Ecology* 47, no. 2: 777–84. DOI: 10.1007/s10745-019-00113-8.

Davis, R.B., and G.L. Jacobson, Jr. 1985. "Late Glacial and Early Holocene Landscapes in Northern New England and Adjacent Areas of Canada." *Quaternary Research* 23: 341–68.

Davis, S.A. 1977. "Buried Heritage." *Mersey Quarterly* 64: 7–9.

Davis, S.A. 1978. *Teacher's Cove: A Prehistoric Site on Passamaquoddy Bay*. New Brunswick Archaeology 1. Fredericton, NB: New Brunswick Historical Resources Administration.

Davis, S.A. 1980. "Coastal Erosion, Neglect, Disinterest Threatening Maritime Archaeology and Resources." In *Proceedings of the 1980 Conference on the Future of Archaeology in the Maritime Provinces*, edited by D.M. Shimabuku, 6–17. Halifax: Saint Mary's University, Occasional Papers in Anthropology 8.

Davis, S.A. 1982. "A Late Archaic Cache/Burial from New Brunswick." *Man in the Northeast* 24: 135–46.

Davis, S.A. 1983. "Rising Sea Levels Threaten Archaeological Sites." *Canadian Geographical Journal* 103, no. 2: 40–46.

Davis, S.A. 1986. "Man, Molluscs and Mammals: A Study of Land Use and Resources in the Late Holocene of the Maritime Provinces of Canada." PhD diss., Wolfson College, Oxford University.

Davis, S.A. 1991a. "Excavations at Whites Lake, 1987." In *Archaeology in Nova Scotia 1987–1988*, edited by S.A. Davis, C. Lindsay, B. Ogilvie, and B. Preston, 57–67. Halifax: Nova Scotia Museum, Curatorial Report 69.

Davis, S.A. 1991b. "Two Concentrations of Palaeo Indian Occupation in the Far Northeast." *Revista de Arqueología Americana, Revue d'Archéologie Américaine* 3: 31–56.

Davis, S.A. 1991c. "Yarmouth County Survey." In *Archaeology in Nova Scotia, 1987–1988*, edited by S.A. Davis, C. Lindsay, R. Ogilvie, and B. Preston, 69–88. Halifax: Nova Scotia Museum, Curatorial Report 69.

Davis, S.A. 1991d. "The Ceramic Period of Nova Scotia." In *Prehistory of the Maritime Provinces: Past and Present Research*, edited by M. Deal and S. Blair, 85–100. Fredericton, NB: Council of Maritime Premiers.

Davis, S.A. 1998. "History of Archaeology in Nova Scotia." In *Bringing Back the Past: Historical Perspectives on Canadian Archaeology*, edited by P.J. Smith and D. Mitchell, 153–62. Hull, Quebec: Canadian Museum of Civilization, Archaeological Survey of Canada, Mercury Series No. 158.

Davis, S.A. 2011. "*Mi'kmakik Teloltipnik L'nuk—Saqiwe'k L'nuk*: How Ancient People Lived in Mi'kma'ki." In *Ta'n Wetapeksi'k: Understanding from Where We Come*, edited by T. Bernard, L.M. Rosenmeier, and S.L. Farrell, 11–22. Truro, NS: Eastern Woodland Print Communications.

Davis, S.A., and D. Christianson. 1988. "Three Palaeo-Indian Specimens from Nova Scotia." *Canadian Journal of Archaeology* 12: 190–96.

Dawson, J.W. 1878. *Acadian Geology: The Geological Structure, Organic Remains, and Mineral Resources of Nova Scotia, New Brunswick, and Prince Edward Island*, 3rd ed., with supplement. London: Macmillan.

Deal, M. 1984a. "The Archaeological Significance of the Chiputneticook–St. Croix Drainage System." MS on file. Fredericton, NB: Archaeological Services.

Deal, M. 1984b. "Diggity (BjDu-17): A Ceramic Period Site on Spednic Lake, Southwestern New Brunswick." MS on file. Fredericton, NB: Archaeological Services, Department of Municipalities, Culture and Housing.

Deal, M. 1986. "Late Archaic and Ceramic Period Utilization of the Mud Lake Stream Site, Southwestern New Brunswick." *Man in the Northeast* no. 32: 67–94.

Deal, M. 1988. "Western Minas Basin Project 1988: Preliminary Report." MS on file, Halifax: Nova Scotia Museum.

Deal, M. 1990. "Preliminary Report on the Macroplant Remains from the Melanson Site, Kings County, Nova Scotia." In *Melanson: A Large Micmac Village in King's County, Nova Scotia*, edited by R.J. Nash and F.L. Stewart, 177–86. Halifax: Nova Scotia Museum, Curatorial Report 67.

Deal, M. 1996. "Western North Shore Survey 1991: Archaeology of Tatamagouche Bay and Vicinity." *Nova Scotia Museum, Curatorial Report* 81: 27–52.

Deal, M. 2002. "Aboriginal Land and Resource Use in New Brunswick during the Late Prehistoric and Early Historic Period." In *Northeast Subsistence-Settlement Change A.D. 700–1300*, edited by J.P. Hart and C.B. Rieth, 321–44. Albany: New York State Museum Bulletin 496.

Deal, M. 2008a. "Paleoethnobotanical Research in the Maritime Provinces." *North Atlantic Prehistory* 1: 1–23.

Deal, M. 2008b. "Abandonment Patterning at Archaeological Settlements." In *Archaeological Concepts for the Study of the Cultural Past*, edited by A. Sullivan, 141–57. Salt Lake City: University of Utah Press.

Deal, M. 2013. "Boswell Site Archaeological Project 2012." *Archaeology in Nova Scotia: 2012 News* 4: 24–35.

Deal, M. 2016. *The Collection of Ages: Precontact Archaeology of the Maritime Provinces*. St. John's: Printing Services, Memorial University.

Deal, M. 2017. "The Role of the Direct Historical Approach in North American Ethnoarchaeology: A Northern Perspective." *Ethnoarchaeology* 9, no. 1: 1–23.

Deal, M., and S. Blair, eds. 1991. *Prehistoric Archaeology in the Maritime Provinces: Past and Present Research*. Fredericton, NB: Council of Maritime Premiers, Reports in Archaeology 8.

Deal, M., and A. Butt. 1991. "Preliminary Report on the 1990 Archaeological Fieldwork at the Prehistoric St. Croix Site, Hants County, Nova Scotia." MS on file. Halifax: Nova Scotia Museum.

Deal, M., J. Campbell, and B. Tapper. 2022. "Archaeology and the Meanderings of the Annapolis River: A View from the Boswell Site." *Canadian Journal of Archaeology* 46, no. 1: 52–99.

Deal, M., J. Corkum, D. Kemp, J. McClair, S. McIlquham, A. Murchison, and B. Wells. 1987. "Archaeological Investigations at the Low Terrace Site (BaDg2), Indian Gardens, Queen's County, Nova Scotia." *Nova Scotia Museum, Curatorial Report* 63: 149–228.

Deal, M., G. Best, C. Cullingworth, J. Grant, M. Lawton, K. Osmond, M. Renganthan, and T. Schell. 1994. "Preliminary Report on the 1993 Excavations at the St. Croix Site, Hants County, Nova Scotia." MS on file. Halifax: Nova Scotia Museum.

Deal, M., T. Farrell, L. Hartery, A. Harris, and M. Sanders. 2019. "Ceramic Use by the Middle and Late Woodland Foragers of the Maritime Provinces." In *Circumpolar Ceramics: A New Research Paradigm for Hunter-Gatherer Technology*, edited by K. Gibbs and P. Jordan, 168–92. Cambridge: Cambridge University Press.

Deal, M., and S. Halwas. 2008. "Late Prehistoric Plant Use in the Minas Basin Area, Nova Scotia." In *Current Paleoethnobotany in the Northeast II*, edited by J.P. Hart, 171–80. New York State Museum Bulletin 512. Albany: University of the State of New York, and State Education Department.

Deal, M., S. Halwas, C. Loder, and M. Betts. 2011. "Recent Paleoethnobotanical Research at Western Nova Scotia Shell Midden Sites."*Archaeology in Nova Scotia: 2010 News* 2: 30–40.

Deal, M., J. Morton, and E. Foulkes. 1991. "The Role of Ceramics among the Prehistoric Hunter-gatherers of the Maine–Maritime Region: A View from the New Brunswick Interior." In *Prehistoric Archaeology in the Maritime Provinces: Past and Present Research*, edited by M. Deal and S. Blair, 171–96. Reports in Archaeology 8. Fredericton, NB: Council of Maritime Premiers.

Deal, M., and D. Rutherford. 2001. "The Distribution and Diversity of Nova Scotian Archaic Sites and Materials: A Re-examination." In *Archaeology in Nova Scotia 1992, 1993, and 1994*, edited by S. Powell, 142–73. Halifax: Nova Scotia Museum, Curatorial Reports 95.

Deal, M., D. Rutherford, B. Murphy, and S. Buchanan. 2006. "Rethinking the Archaic Sequence for the Maritime Provinces." In *The Archaic of the Far Northeast*, edited by D. Sanger and M.A.P. Renouf, 253–83. Orono: University of Maine Press.

Décima, E.B., and D.F. Dincauze. 1998. "The Boston Back Bay Fish Weirs." In *Hidden Dimensions: The Cultural Significance of Wetland Archaeology*, edited by K. Bernick, 157–74. Pacific Rim Archaeology and Wetland Archaeology Research Project (WARP), Occasional Paper No. 11. Vancouver: University of British Columbia Press.

Delmas, V. 2016. "Beads and Trade Routes: Tracing Sixteenth-Century Beads around the Gulf and into the Saint Lawrence Valley." In *Contact in the 16th Century: Networks among Fishers, Foragers, and Farmers*, edited by B. Loewen and C. Chapdelaine, 77–115. Mercury Series Archaeology Paper 176. Ottawa: Canadian Museum of History and University of Ottawa Press.

Densmore, H. 1984. "Indian Remains Returned to Nova Scotia Micmacs." *Chronicle Herald*, July 26.

Denys, N. 1908. *Description & Natural History of the Coasts of North America (Acadia)*. (1672). Translated and edited by W.F. Ganong. Publications of the Champlain Society 2. Toronto: Champlain Society.

DesBrisay, M.B. 1879. "Nova Scotia Archaeology: Ancient Pottery." *Proceedings and Transactions of the Nova Scotian Institute of Science* 7: 218.

Dickason, O.P. 1997. *The Myth of the Savage and the Beginnings of French Colonialism in the Americas*. Calgary: University of Alberta Press.

Dickason, O.P. 1998. "Art and Amerindian Worldviews." In *Earth, Water, Air and Fire. Studies in Canadian Ethnohistory*, edited by D.T. McNab, 21–31. Waterloo, ON: Wilfrid Laurier University Press.

Dickenson, V. 2008. "Cartier, Champlain, and the Fruits of the New World: Botanical Exchange in the 16th and 17th Centuries." *Scientia Canadensis: Canadian Journal of the History of Science, Technology and Medicine* 31, no. 1: 14–56.

Dickenson, V. 2009. "Curiosity in Edibility: The Taste of New France." In *What's to Eat? Entrées in Canadian Food History*, edited by Nathalie Cooke, 21–54. Montreal and Kingston: McGill-Queen's University Press.

Dincauze, D.F. 1993. "Antecedents and Ancestors at Last." Review of *Early Holocene Occupation in Northern New England*, edited by B. Robinson and J. Petersen. *Review of Archaeology* 14, no. 2: 12–22.

Dincauze, D.F. 1996. "Large Paleoindian Sites in the Northeast: Pioneers' Marshalling Camps?" *Bulletin of the Massachusetts Archaeological Society* 57, no. 1: 3–17.

Dincauze, D.F., and V. Jacobson. 2001. "The Birds of Summer: Lakeside Routes into Late Pleistocene New England." *Canadian Journal of Archaeology* 25: 121–26.

Donovan, K. 2009. "Precontact and Settlement: Ingonish and Northern Cape Breton from the Paleo Indians to the 18th century." *Nashwaak Review* (St. Thomas University, Fredericton) 22–23 (Spring–Summer): 330–87.

Doran, G.H., ed. 2002. *Windover: Multidisciplinary Investigations of an Early Archaic Florida Cemetery*. Gainesville: University Press of Florida.

Dostal, J., and C. Dupuy. 1984. "Geochemistry of the North Mountain Basalts (Nova Scotia, Canada)." *Chemical Geology* 45: 245–61.

Doyle, R.G. 1995. "Analysis of Lithic Artifacts: The Identification, Petrologic Description, and Statistical Analysis of Lithic Artifacts Recovered from the

Turner Farm Site." In *Diversity and Complexity in Prehistoric Maritime Societies: A Gulf of Maine Perspective,* edited by B.J. Bourque, Appendix 6, 297–316. New York: Plenum.

Doyle, R.G., Jr., N.D. Hamilton, J.B. Petersen, and D. Sanger. 1985. "Late Paleo-Indian Remains from Maine and Their Correlations in Northeastern Prehistory." *Archaeology of Eastern North America* 13: 1–33.

Drewett, P.L. 2000. "Step Trenching." In *Archaeological Method and Theory: An Encyclopedia,* edited by Linda Ellis, 594. New York: Garland.

Drouin, P. 1988. "Les baleiniers basques à l'Île Nue de Mingan." *Archeological Journal of Canada* 12: 1–15.

Dumais, P. 1978. "La Bas Saint-Laurent." In Images de la Préhistoire du Québec, comp. by C. Chapdelaine. *Recherches Amérindiennes au Québec* nos. 1–2: 63–74.

Dumais, P. 2000. "The La Martre and Mitis Late Paleoindian Sites: A Reflection on the Peopling of Southeastern Quebec." *Archaeology of Eastern North America* 28: 81–112.

Dumais, P., J. Poirier, and G. Rousseau. 1993. "Squatec (ClEe-9), a Late Pleistocene/Early Holocene Site in Southeastern Quebec, Canada." *Current Research in the Pleistocene* 10: 14–18.

Dunbar, J.S., and D.D. Webb. 1996. "Bone and Ivory Tools from Submerged Paleoindian Sites in Florida." In *The Paleoindian and Early Archaic Southeast,* edited by D.G. Anderson and K.E. Sassaman, 331–53. Tuscaloosa: University of Alabama Press.

Dunlop, A. 1986. "George Patterson: A Pictou Historian." *Collections of the Royal Nova Scotia Historical Society* 42: 81–92.

Duns, D.D. 1880. "On Stone Implements from Nova Scotia and Canada, and on the Use of Copper Implements by the Aborigines of Nova Scotia." *Proceedings of the Society of Antiquaries of Scotland, New Series* 3: 176–80.

Edwards, R.L., and K.O. Emery. 1977. "Man on the Continental Shelf." In *Amerinds and Their Paleoenvironments in Northeast North America. Annals of the New York Academy of Sciences* 288: 245–56.

Eldridge, S. 2007. "Archaeology at the Stanley Site, Monhegan Island, Maine: Implications for Modeling Late Archaic Coastal Adaptations." *Maine Archaeology Society Bulletin* 47, no. 2: 1–20.

Ellis, C. 2004. "Understanding 'Clovis' Fluted Point Variability in the Northeast: A Perspective from the Debert Site, Nova Scotia." *Canadian Journal of Archaeology* 28, no. 2: 205–53.

Ellis, C. 2011. "Lithic/Stone Technology at the Debert Site." In *Ta'n Wetapeksi'k: Understanding from Where We Come*, edited by T. Bernard, L.M. Rosenmeier, and S.L. Farrell, 99–110. Truro, NS: Eastern Woodland Print Communications.

Erickson, P.A. 1978. "Prehistoric Human Remains from Bear River, Nova Scotia." *Man in the Northeast* nos. 15/16: 138–46.

Erickson, P.A. 1985. "Native Skeletons from Nova Scotia." *Teaching Anthropology Newsletter* (Saint Mary's University, Halifax) 7: 9–13.

Erickson, V.O. 1978a. "Maliseet-Passamaquoddy." In *Handbook of North American Indians, Volume 15, Northeast*, edited by B.G. Trigger, 123–36. Washington, DC: Smithsonian Institution.

Erickson, V.O. 1978b. "The Micmac *Buoin*, Three Centuries of Cultural and Semantic Change." *Man in the Northeast* nos. 15–16: 3–41.

Ericson, J.E. 1984. "Toward the Analysis of Lithic Production Systems." In *Prehistoric Quarries and Lithic Production*, edited by J.E. Ericson and B.A. Purdy, 1–9. Cambridge: Cambridge University Press.

Erskine, J.S. 1958. "Micmac Notes 1958." MS on file. Halifax: Nova Scotia Museum.

Erskine, J.S. 1959. "Micmac Notes 1959." MS on file. Halifax: Nova Scotia Museum.

Erskine, J.S. 1960. "Shell-heap Archaeology of Southwestern Nova Scotia." *Nova Scotia Institute of Science, Proceedings* 24, part 4: 339–75.

Erskine, J.S. 1961. *Micmac Notes 1960*. Halifax: Nova Scotia Museum, Occasional Paper 1.

Erskine, J. S. 1962. *Micmac Notes 1962*. Halifax: Nova Scotia Museum, Occasional Paper 2.

Erskine, J.S. 1964. "Debert Site, Colchester County." MS on file. Halifax: Nova Scotia Museum.

Erskine, J.S. 1966. "Birds of Yesterday." *Nova Scotia Bird Society Newsletter* 8, no. 3: 27–29.

Erskine, J.S. 1975. *The French Period in Nova Scotia A.D. 1500–1700 and Present Remains: A Historical, Archaeological and Botanical Survey*. Halifax: Mount Saint Vincent University Press.

Erskine, J.S. 1998. *Memoirs on the Prehistory of Nova Scotia, 1957–1967*, edited by M. Deal. Halifax: Nova Scotia Museum, Special Report.

Erwin, J., A. Crompton, and M. Bolli. 2018. "Sabbath Point (DeBd-08) Unmanned Aerial Vehicle (UAV) Mapping Project." *Provincial Archaeology Office, Annual Review 2017*. 16: 54–60.

Fader, G. 2005. "Marine Archaeology Offshore Digby Neck, Bay of Fundy." Unpublished MS, prepared by Atlantic Marine Geological Consulting Ltd, Halifax.

https://www.novascotia.ca/nse/ea/whitespointquarry/09.Reference.Documents/14.Fader.Marine.Archaeology.pdf.

Fagan, B.M. 2006. *Archaeology: A Brief Introduction*, 9th ed. Hoboken, NJ: Pearson Education.

Farnell, R., G.P. Hare, E. Blake, V. Bowyer, C. Schweger, S. Greer, and R. Gotthardt. 2004. "Multidisciplinary Investigations of Alpine Ice Patches in Southwest Yukon, Canada: Paleoenvironmental and Paleobiological Investigations." *Arctic* 57, no. 3: 247–59.

Feest, C. 1995. "The Collecting of American Indian Artifacts in Europe, 1493–1750." In *America in European Consciousness, 1493–1750*, edited by K.O. Kupperman, 324–60. Chapel Hill: University of North Carolina Press.

Ferguson, A.M. 2004. *Guide to Heritage Resource Impact Assessment in New Brunswick*. New Brunswick Manuscripts in Archaeology 35. Fredericton, NB: Culture and Sports Secretariat, Government of New Brunswick.

Ferguson, A., and C.J. Turnbull. 1980. "Ministers Island Seawall: An Experiment in Archaeological Site Preservation." In *Proceedings of the 1980 Conference on the Future of Archaeology in the Maritime Provinces*, edited by D.M. Shimabuku, 88–94. Halifax: Saint Mary's University, Occasional Papers in Anthropology 8.

Ferguson, R.S.O. 1986. "Archaeological Sites in the Kejimkujik National Park, Nova Scotia." MS on file, Environment Canada, Parks Canada, Halifax.

Ferguson, S.A., comp. 1983. *Geological Map of the Hantsport Area Nova Scotia*. Halifax: Nova Scotia Department of Mines and Energy, Map 83-1.

Fergusson, C.B. 1963. "Nova Scotian Institute of Science." *Bulletin of the Public Archives of Nova Scotia* 18.

Fewkes, J.W. 1896. "A Prehistoric Shell Heap on Prince Edward Island." *American Antiquarian and Oriental Journal* 18: 30–33.

Fiedel, S.J. 1991. "Correlating Archaeology and Linguistics: The Algonquian Case." *Man in the Northeast* 41: 9–32.

Fitzhugh, W.W., and M. Gallon. 2002. *The Gateways Project 2002: Surveys and Excavations from Petit Mécatina to Belles Amours*. Report submitted to the Ministry of Culture and Communications, Government of Québec, Québec City.

Fladmark, K.R. 1978. *A Guide to Basic Archaeological Field Procedures*. Burnaby, BC: Department of Archaeology, Simon Fraser University, Publication 4.

Ford, R.I., ed. 1978. *The Nature and Status of Ethnobotany*. Ann Arbor: Museum of Anthropology, University of Michigan, Anthropological Papers 67.

Foreman, C.T. 1943. *Indians Abroad 1493–1938*. Norman: University of Oklahoma Press.

Foulkes, E.B. 1981. "Fulton Island. A Stratified Site in the Saint John River Valley of New Brunswick." MA thesis, Trent University.

Foulkes, E., G. Sandström, and R.J. Dale. 1984. "Tabular Comparison of Prov./Terr. Heritage Legislation." Report prepared for NOGAP Programme, Archaeological Survey of Canada. Ottawa: Canadian Museum of Civilization.

Fowler, J. 1870. "On Shell Heaps in New Brunswick." *Annual Report of the Smithsonian Institution* 25: 389.

Fowler, W.S. 1966a. "Cache of Engraved Pebbles from New Brunswick." *Bulletin of the Massachusetts Archaeology Society* 28, no. 1: 15–17.

Fowler, W.S. 1966b. "Ceremonial and Domestic Products of Aboriginal New England." *Bulletin of the Massachusetts Archaeological Society* 27, nos. 3–4.

Francis, D.A., and R.M. Leavitt. 2008. *A Passamaquoddy-Maliseet Dictionary*. Orono: University of Maine Press.

Ganong, W.F. 1899. "A Monograph of Historic Sites in the Province of New Brunswick." *Transactions of the Royal Society of Canada*, No. III, Section II: 213–57.

Ganong, W.F. 1901. "Note 32, the Physiographic Origin of Our Portage Routes." *Bulletin of the New Brunswick Natural History Society* 19: 313–14.

Ganong, W.F. 1904a. "Upon Aboriginal Pictographs Reported from New Brunswick." *Bulletin of the Natural History Society of New Brunswick* 22: 175–77.

Ganong, W.F. 1904b. "A Monograph of the Origins of Settlements in the Province of New Brunswick — Contributions to the History of New Brunswick." *Royal Society of Canada, Transactions, Section II* 10: 3–185.

Ganong, W.F. 1909. "The Identity of the Animals and Plants Mentioned by the Early Voyagers to Eastern Canada and Newfoundland." *Transactions of the Royal Society of Canada* 3: 197–242.

Ganong, W.F. 1913a. "Supplement to Note 125 — The Ancient Indian Portage Route from Gaspereau to Cains River." *Bulletin of the Natural History Society of New Brunswick* 30: 429–34.

Ganong, W.F. 1913b. "Supplement to Note 126 — The Ancient Indian Portages from Salmon River to Richibucto." *Bulletin of the Natural History Society of New Brunswick* 30: 444–49.

Ganong W.F. 1914. "Supplement to Note 131 — The Ancient Portage Route from the Washademoak to Adjacent Waters." *Bulletin of the Natural History Society of New Brunswick* 31: 23–34.

Ganong, W.F. 1964. *Crucial Maps in the Early Cartography and Place-Nomenclature of the Atlantic Coast of Canada*, with an Introduction, Commentary, and Map Notes by T.E. Layng. Royal Society of Canada Special Publications. Toronto:

University of Toronto Press.

Garlie, T.N. 1992. "An Ethnohistorical and Archaeological Review Regarding Aboriginal Mortuary Remains Reported from Nova Scotia and New Brunswick and the Potential for Future Research." BA Honours thesis, Memorial University of Newfoundland.

Gaulton, B., B. Tapper, D. Williams, and D. Teasdale. 2019. "The Upper Island Cove Petroglyphs: An Algonquian Enigma." *Canadian Journal of Archaeology* 43, no. 2: 123–61.

Gesner, A. 1836. *Remarks on the Geology and Mineralogy of Nova Scotia*. Halifax: Gossip & Coade.

Gesner, A. 1839. *First Report on the Geological Survey of the Province of New Brunswick*. Saint John, NB.

Gesner, A. 1847. "Report of the Geological Survey of Prince Edward Island." *Journal of the House of Assembly of Prince Edward Island*. Appendix D: 1–22. Charlottetown: John Ings.

Gesner's Museum of Natural History (GMNH). 1842. *Synopsis of the Contents of Gesner's Museum of Natural History at Saint John, N.B. Opened on the Fifth Day of April, 1842*. Saint John, NB: H. Chubb.

Gilpin, E. 1898. "President's Address." *Proceedings of the Nova Scotia Institute of Science* 9, no. 4: xcv–xcix.

Gilpin, J.P. 1874. "On the Stone Age in Nova Scotia." *Proceedings and Transactions of the Nova Scotian Institute of Science* 3: 220–31.

Girouard, M.L. 2012. "The Original Meaning and Intent of the Maine Indian Land Claims: Penobscot Perspectives." MA thesis, University of Maine. https://digitalcommons.library.umaine.edu/etd/1715.

Glen, C. 2016. "Tusket Falls." *Archaeology in Nova Scotia: 2013/14 News* 5: 18–23. Halifax: Nova Scotia Museum.

Gloade, G. 2008. "Mi'kmawey Debert Cultural Centre: Cultural Memory Timeline Embedded in the Mi'kmaq Legends of Kluskap." In *Preserving Aboriginal Heritage, Technical and Traditional Approaches,* edited by Carole Dignard, Kate Helwig, Janet Mason, Kathy Nanowin, and Thomas Stone, 245–51. Ottawa: Canadian Conservation Institute.

Gloade, G. 2020. "*L'mu'juiktuk* Cape d'Or." https://www.mikmaweydebert.ca/ancestors-live-here/cape-dor/.

Godfrey-Smith, D.I., M. Deal, and I. Kunelius. 1997. "Thermoluminescence Dating at the St. Croix Site: Chronology Building in Southwestern Nova Scotia." *Geoarchaeology* 12, no. 3: 251–73.

Goodwin, W.L 1892. "Notes on an Old Indian Encampment." *Canadian Record of Science* 5: 284–85.

Gordon, J. 1993. *Construction and Reconstruction of a Mi'kmaq Sixteenth Century Cedar Bark Bag.* Halifax: Nova Scotia Museum, Curatorial Report 76.

Gordon, J. 1995. *Mi'kmaq Textiles: Sewn-Matting, BkCp-1 Site, Pictou, Nova Scotia.* Halifax: Nova Scotia Museum, Curatorial Report 80.

Gordon, J. 1997. *Mi'kmaq Textiles: Rush and Other Fibres, BkCp-1 Site, Pictou, Nova Scotia.* Halifax: Nova Scotia Museum, Curatorial Report 82.

Gorham, R.P. 1928. "Record of a Brass Tub Indian Burial, Red Bank, Northumberland Co., New Brunswick." MS on file. Fredericton, NB: Provincial Archives of New Brunswick.

Gorham, R.P. 1943. "The History of Plum Culture in New Brunswick." *Acadian Naturalist* no. 2: 59–69.

Gossip, W. 1867. "On the Occurrence of Kjoekkenmoedding on the Shores of Nova Scotia." *Proceedings and Transactions of the Nova Scotian Institute of Science* 1, no. 2: 94–99.

Gramly, R.M. 1980. "Raw Material: Source Areas and 'Curated' Tool Assemblages." *American Antiquity* 45, no. 4: 823–33.

Gramly, R.M. 1982. "The Vail Site: A Palaeo Indian Encampment in Maine." *Bulletin of the Buffalo Society of Natural Sciences* 30.

Gramly, R.M. 1999. *The Lamb Site: A Pioneering Clovis Encampment.* Buffalo, NY: Persimmon Press.

Gramly, R.M., and R.E. Funk. 1990. "What Is Known and Not Known about the Human Occupation of the Northeastern United States Until 10,000 BP." *Archaeology of Eastern North America* 18: 5–31.

Gullason, L., R. Tremblay, C. Carlson, E. Yellowhorn, J.-L. Pilon, and M. Deal. 2008. "Indigenous European Contact in Canada." In *América: Contacto e Independencia*, edited by M.C.M. Scatamacchia and F.E. Solano, 164–95. Madrid: Instituto Geográfico Nacional.

Gullbekk, S.H. 2017. "The Norse Penny Reconsidered: The Goddard Coin — Hoax or Genuine?" *Journal of the North Atlantic* 33: 1–8.

Hadlock, W.S. 1947. "The Significance of Certain Textiles found at Redbank, New Brunswick, in Relation to the History of the Culture Area." *Acadian Naturalist* 2, no. 8: 49–62.

Hall, J. 2015. "Maliseet Cultivation and Climatic Resilience on the Wəlastəkw/Saint John River during the Little Ice Age." *Acadiensis* 44, no. 2: 3–25.

Halwas, S.J. 2006. "Where the Wild Things Grow: A Paleoethnobotanical Study of

Late Woodland Plant Use at Clam Cove, Nova Scotia." MA thesis, Memorial University of Newfoundland.

Hamell, G.R. 2011. "Wampum Facts from the Other Side of the Fire." Paper prepared for the 11th Annual Algonquian Peoples Seminar, New York State Museum, Albany. https://www.academia.edu/37275178/HAMELL_GEORGE_R_ms_2011_WAMPUM_FACTS_FROM_THE_OTHER_SIDE_OF_THE_FIRE_doc.

Hammer, J. 1976. "Identification and Distribution of Some Lithic Raw Materials from New York State." *Man in the Northeast* no. 11: 39–62.

Hammon, D.J. 1984. "A Ceramic Period Coastal Adaptation in Holt's Point, New Brunswick." MA thesis, University of New Brunswick.

Hamilton, W.D., and W.A. Spray. 1977. "Extracts from Mr. Perley's First Report Respecting the Indians on the Saint John." In *Source Materials relating to the New Brunswick Indian*, compiled and edited by W.D. Hamilton and W.A. Spray, 83–88. Fredericton, NB: Hamray Books.

Hanley, J., A. Terekhova, P. Drake, K. Cottreau-Robins, R. Lewis, and B. Boucher. 2022. "Geochemical Provenance of Copper in Precontact Artifacts on the Maritime Peninsula, Eastern Canada: Determining Source Using Laser Ablation-Inductively Coupled Plasma-Mass Spectrometry." In *The Far Northeast: 3000 BP to Contact*, edited by K.R. Holyoke and M.G. Hrynick, 219–58. Mercury Series, Archaeological Paper 181. Ottawa: Canadian Museum of History and University of Ottawa Press.

Hare, P.G., S.A. Greer, R. Gotthardt, R. Farnell, V. Bowyer, C. Schweger, and D. Strand. 2004. "Ethnographic and Archaeological Investigations of Alpine Ice Patches in Southwest Yukon, Canada." *Arctic* 57, no. 30: 260–72.

Harper, J.R. 1954. "Ouigoudi: The Indian Village at the Mouth of the St. John: 1604–1616." In *Champlain and the St. John 1604–1954*, edited by G. MacBeath, 27–29. Saint John: New Brunswick Historical Society.

Harper, J.R. 1956. *Portland Point: Crossroads of New Brunswick History. Preliminary Report of the 1955 Excavation*. Saint John: New Brunswick Museum, Historical Studies 9.

Harper, J.R. 1957. "Two Seventeenth Century Copper-kettle Burials." *Anthropologica* 4: 11–36.

Harris, K.D. 1940. "Restoration of the Habitation of Port Royal, Lower Granville, Nova Scotia." *Journal of the Royal Architectural Institute of Canada* 17, no. 7: 111–16.

Harris, M. 1968. *The Rise of Anthropological Theory*. New York: Crowell.

Harris, M. 1979. *Cultural Materialism: The Struggle for a Science of Culture*. New York: Random House.

Haviland, W.A., and M.W. Power. 1994. *The Original Vermonters: Native Inhabitants, Past and Present*. Hanover, VT: University of Vermont.

Hayden, B. 2001. "Fabulous Feasts: A Prolegomenon to the Importance of Feasting." In *Feasts: Archaeological and Ethnographic Perspectives on Food, Politics, and Power*, edited by M. Dietler and B. Hayden, 23–64. Washington, DC: Smithsonian Institution Press.

Hayden, B., and S. Villeneuve. 2011. "A Century of Feasting Studies." *Annual Reviews of Anthropology* 4: 433–49.

Hayward, P. 1973. *Early Man in Nova Scotia*. Halifax: Nova Scotia Museum.

Heckenberger, M.J., J.B. Petersen, and L.A. Basa. 1990a. "Early Woodland Period Ritual Use of Personal Adornment at the Boucher Site." *Annals of the Carnegie Museum* 59, no. 3: 173–217.

Heckenberger, M.J., J.B. Petersen, L.A. Basa, E.R. Cowie, A.E. Spiess, and R.E. Stuckenrath. 1990b. "Early Woodland Period Mortuary Ceremonialism in the Far Northeast: A View from the Boucher Cemetery." *Archaeology of Eastern North America* 18: 109–44.

Hedden, M. 1985. "Sexuality in Maine Petroglyphs: Comments on the Cover Design." *Maine Archaeological Society Bulletin* 25, no. 1: 3–6.

Hedden, M. 2004. "Passamaquoddy Shamanism and Rock-Art in Machias Bay, Maine." In *The Rock-Art of Eastern North America: Capturing Images and Insight*, edited by C. Diaz-Granados and J.R. Duncan, 319–43. Tuscaloosa: University of Alabama Press.

Hedden, M. 2022. "Petroglyphs at Site 61.72, Washington County, Maine: A Visionary Tradition of Mi'kmaq Medicine-men?" *Maine State Archaeology Society* 62, nos. 1 & 2: 1–21.

Hoffman, B.G. 1955. "Historical Ethnography of the Micmacs of the 16th and 17th Centuries." PhD diss., University of California, Berkeley.

Hoffman, B.G. 1961. *Cabot to Cartier: Sources for a Historical Ethnography of Northeastern North America 1497–1550*. Toronto: University of Toronto Press.

Holmes, W.H. 1914. "Areas of American Culture Characterization Tentatively Outlined as an Aid in the Study of the Antiquities." *American Anthropologist* 16: 413–46.

Holmes, W.H. 1919. *Handbook of Aboriginal American Antiquities, Part 1, Introducton: The Lithics Industries.* Washington, DC: Smithsonian Institution, Bureau of American Ethnology, Bulletin 60.

Holyoke, K.R., and M.G. Hrynick. 2022. "Continental Thoughts, (Maritime) Peninsular Perspective." In *The Far Northeast: 3000 BP to Contact*, edited by K.R. Holyoke and M.G. Hrynick, 1–22. Mercury Series, Archaeological Paper 181. Ottawa: Canadian Museum of History and University of Ottawa Press.

Honeyman, D. 1879. "Nova Scotia Archaeology: Ancient Pottery." *Proceedings and Transactions of the Nova Scotian Institute of Science* 7: 217–18.

Hornborg, A.-C. 2006. "Visiting the Six Worlds: Shamanistic Journeys in Canadian Mi'kmaq Cosmology." *Journal of American Folklore* 119, no. 473: 312–36.

Howey, M.C.L. 2018. "Dead Kettles and Indigenous Afterworlds in Early Colonial Encounters in the Maritimes." In *Relational Identities and Other-than-Human Agency in Archaeology*, edited by E. Harrison-Buck and J.A. Hendon, 51–71. Boulder: University Press of Colorado.

Hoyle, B.G., D.C. Fisher, H.W. Borns, Jr., L.L. Churchill-Dickson, C.C. Dorion, and T.K. Weddle. 2004. "Late Pleistocene Mammoth Remains from Coastal Maine, U.S.A." *Quaternary Research* 61: 277–88.

Hrynick, M.G. 2011. "Woodland Period Domestic Architecture on the Coast of the Maritime Provinces: A Case Study from Port Joli Harbour." MA thesis, University of New Brunswick.

Hrynick, M.G., and M.W. Betts. 2014. "Identifying Ritual Structures in the Archaeological Record: A Maritime Woodland Period Sweathouse from Nova Scotia, Canada." *Journal of Anthropological Archaeology* 35: 92–105.

Hrynick, M.G., and M.W. Betts. 2017. "Relational Approach to Hunter-Gatherer Architecture and Gendered Use of Space at Port Joli, Nova Scotia." In *North American East Coast Shell Midden Research*, edited by M.W. Betts and M.G. Hrynick, 1–17. *Journal of the North Atlantic*, Special Volume 10.

Hrynick, M.G., and M.W. Betts. 2019. "Architectural Features." In *Place-Making in the Pretty Harbour: The Archaeology of Port Joli, Nova Scotia*, edited by M.W. Betts, 129–59. Mercury Series. Ottawa: University of Ottawa Press.

Hrynick, M.G., and M.W. Betts. 2022. "'And we showered with a thousand praises the woman who had been the fire's guardian': Ancestral Wabanaki Gender and Place-making in the Woodland Period." In *The Far Northeast: 3000 BP to Contact*, edited by K.R. Holyoke and M.G. Hrynick, 259–84. Mercury Series, Archaeological Paper 181. Ottawa: Canadian Museum of History and University of Ottawa Press.

Hrynick, M.G., M.W. Betts, and D.W. Black. 2012. "A Late Maritime Woodland Period Dwelling from Nova Scotia's South Shore: Evidence for Patterned Use of Domestic Space." *Archaeology of Eastern North America* 40: 1–25.

Hrynick, M.G., and D.W. Black. 2016. "Cultural Continuity in Maritime Woodland Period Domestic Architecture in the Quoddy Region." *Canadian Journal of Archaeology* 40: 23–67.

Hudgell, G.-J., M.S. Brigham, R.N. Bartone, and E.R. Cowie. 2013. "The Grand Lake Outlet Site: An Early Paleoindian Encampment on the St. Croix River, Maine/New Brunswick Border." *Maine Archaeological Society Bulletin* 53, no. 1: 27–58.

Hume, B.D. 2011. "Evolutionisms: Lewis Henry Morgan, Time, and the Question of Sociocultural Evolutionary Theory." *Histories of Anthropology Annual* 7: 91–126.

Ingstad, A.S. 1977. *The Discovery of a Norse Settlement in America: Excavations at L'Anse aux Meadows, Newfoundland, 1961–1968.* Oslo: Norwegian University Press.

Ingstad, H. 1969. *Westward to Vinland: The Discovery of Pre-Columbian Norse House-Sites in North America.* New York: St. Martin's Press.

Jackson, L.J. 1987. "Ontario Paleoindians and Proboscidians: A Review." *Current Research in the Pleistocene* 4: 109–12.

Jalbert, C.L. 2001. "A Lesson in Stone: Examining Patterns of Lithic Resource Use and Craft-learning in the Minas Basin Region of Nova Scotia." MA thesis, Memorial University of Newfoundland.

Jamal, M. 2006. "Treaty Interpretation after *R. v. Marshal*; *R. v. Bernard*." *Supreme Court Law Review: Osgoode's Annual Constitutional Cases Conference* 34: 443–63.

Jarratt, T.L. 2013. "The Augustine Mound Copper Sub-Assemblage: Beyond the Bead." MA thesis, University of New Brunswick.

Jeandron, J. 1996. "Portland Point Revisited." B.A. Honours thesis, University of New Brunswick.

Jeandron, J. 1997. "The Washademoak Chert Source." In *JCAP Preliminary Technical Report*, edited by S.E. Blair, 2: 4–59. Fredericton: Archaeological Services, New Brunswick Department of Municipalities, Culture and Housing.

Jefferys, C.W. 1939. "The Reconstruction of the Port Royal Habitation of 1605–1613." *Canadian Historical Review* 20, no. 4: 369–77.

Jefferys, C.W. 1942. *The Picture Gallery of Canadian History, Volume 1, Discovery to 1763.* Illustrations drawn and collected by C.W. Jefferys, assisted by T.W. McLean, 84. Toronto: Ryerson Press.

Jenness, D. 1941. "William John Wintemberg 1876–1941." *American Antiquity* 7, no. 1: 64–66.

Jerkic, S.M. 1988. "Human Remains from the Skora Site: A Report on the Skeletal Remains Excavated." MS on file, Department of Archaeology, Memorial University of Newfoundland.

Jerkic, S.M. 1992. "Preliminary Report on Skeletal Material from Prince Edward Island." MS on file, Department of Archaeology, Memorial University of Newfoundland.

Johnson, M. 2019. *Archaeological Theory: An Introduction*, 3rd ed. London: Wiley Blackwell.

Johnson, L.M., and E.S. Hunn. 2010. "Introduction." In *Landscape Ethnoecology: Concepts of Biotic and Physical Space*, edited by L.M. Johnson and E.S. Hunn, 1–14. New York: Berghahn.

Jones, J.M. 1864. "Recent Discoveries of Kjökkenmöddlings." *Anthropological Review and Journal of the Anthropological Society of London* 2: 223–26.

Julien, D.M., T. Bernard, and L.M. Rosenmeier. 2008. "Paleo Is Not Our Word: Protecting and Growing a Mi'kmaw Place." In *Archaeologies of Placemaking: Monuments, Memories, and Engagement in Native North America*, edited by P.E. Rubertone, 35–57. Walnut Creek, CA: Left Coast Press.

Kain, S.W. 1894. "Appendix A. Thirty-second Report of the Council of the Natural History Society of New Brunswick." *Bulletin of the Natural History Society of New Brunswick* 2: 63–68.

Kain, S.W. 1901. "Notes on the Archaeology of New Brunswick." *Bulletin of the Natural History Society of New Brunswick* no. 19: 287–99.

Kain, S.W. 1905. "Prehistoric Times in New Brunswick." *Bulletin of the Natural History Society of New Brunswick* 5: 152–56.

Kalman, H. 1994. *The Concise History of Canadian Architecture*. Oxford: Oxford University Press.

Keenlyside, D.L. 1980a. "Prince Edward Island Archaeological Research 1980." In *Archaeological Resources in the Maritimes 1980*, edited by C.J. Turnbull, 62–99. Fredericton, NB: Council of Maritime Premiers, Reports in Archaeology No. 5, Archaeology Branch, Historical Resources Administration.

Keenlyside, D.L. 1980b. "1978." In *Archaeological Survey of Canada Annual Reviews, 1977–1979*, edited by R.J.M. Marois, 14–16. Mercury Series, Archaeological Paper 95. Ottawa: National Museums of Canada.

Keenlyside, D.L. 1984a. "Ulus and Spearpoints: Two Archaeological Finds from Prince Edward Island." *The Island Magazine* 16 (Fall/Winter): 25–27.

Keenlyside, D.L. 1984b. *The Prehistory of the Maritimes*. Canada's Visual History, Vol. 65. Ottawa: National Museum of Man and National Film Board of Canada.

Keenlyside, D.L. 1985a. "Late-Palaeo-Indian Evidence from the Southern Gulf of St. Lawrence." *Archaeology of Eastern North America* 13: 79–92.

Keenlyside, D.L. 1985b. "La Période Paleoindienne sur L'Ile du Prince Edouard." *Recherches Amérindiennes au Québec* 15: 119–26.

Keenlyside, D.L. 1990. *An Archaeological Survey of the Upper Reaches of the Tracadie River Estuary, New Brunswick.* Fredericton: New Brunswick Archaeology 26, Municipalities, Culture and Housing.

Keenlyside, D.L. 1991. "Paleoindian Occupations of the Maritimes Region of Canada." In *Clovis: Origins and Adaptations*, edited by R. Bonnichsen and K. Turnmire, 163–73. Orono, ME: Center for the Study of the First Americans.

Keenlyside, D.L. 1999. "Glimpses of Atlantic Canada's Past." *Los Modos de Vida Marítimos en Norte y Mesoamérica: El Estado de la Cuestión. Revista de Arqueología Americana* no. 16: 49–76.

Keenlyside, D.L. 2001. "Walrus: An Oft-Forgotten Resource in Precontact Atlantic Canada." Paper presented at the annual meeting of the Canadian Archaeological Association, Ottawa.

Keenlyside, D.L. 2006. "New Finds from the Island's Offshore." *Island Magazine* 59: 10–12.

Keenlyside, D.L. 2011. "Observations on Debert and the Late Palaeo/Early Archaic Transition." In *Ta'n Wetapeksi'k: Understanding from Where We Come*, edited by T. Bernard, L.M. Rosenmeier, and S.L. Farrell, 145–56. Truro, NS: Eastern Woodland Print Communications.

Keenlyside, D.L., and C. Andreasen. 2009. "Indigenous Fishing in Northeast North America." In *A History of the North Atlantic Fisheries. Volume 1: From Early Times to the Mid-Nineteenth Century,* edited by D.J. Starkey, J.T. Thór, and I. Heidbrink, 372–86. Bremen, Germany: German Maritime Studies 6, Hauschild.

Keenlyside, D., and H. Kristmanson. 2016. "The Palaeo-Environment and the Peopling of Prince Edward Island: An Archaeological Perspective." In *Time and a Place: An Environmental History of Prince Edward Island*, edited by E. MacDonald, J. MacFadyen, and I. Novaczek, 59–81. Montreal: McGill-Queen's University Press/Island Studies Press.

Kehoe, A.B. 2002. "Europe's Prehistoric Dawn Reproduced: Daniel Wilson's Magisterial Archaeology." In *New Perspectives on the Origins of Americanist Archaeology*, edited by D.L. Browman and S. Williams, 133–47. Tuscaloosa: University of Alabama Press.

Kelley, J.T., D. Belknap, and S. Claesson. 2010. "Drowned Coastal Deposits with Associated Archaeological Remains from a Sea-Level 'Slowstand': Northwestern Gulf of Maine, USA." *Geology* 38, no. 8: 695–98.

Kelly, R.L. 1983. "Hunter-Gatherer Mobility Strategies." *Journal of Anthropological Research* 39: 277–306.

Kelly, R.L. 1992. "Mobility/Sedentism; Concepts, Archaeological Measures and Effects." *Annual Review of Anthropology* 21: 43–66.

Kelly, R.L. 2007. *The Foraging Spectrum: Diversity in Hunter-Gatherer Lifeways.* New York: Percheron Press.

Key, A.F. 1973. *Beyond Four Walls: The Origins and Development of Canadian Museums.* Toronto: McClelland & Stewart.

Kidder, A.V. 1924. *An Introduction to the Study of Southwestern Archaeology: With a Preliminary Account of the Excavations at Pecos.* Papers of the Southwestern Expedition 1. New Haven, CT: Department of Archaeology, Phillips Academy.

King, S.J. 2011. "Conservation Controversy: *Sparrow, Marshall,* and the Mi'kmaq of Esgenoôpetitj." *International Indigenous Policy Journal* 2, no. 4: Article 4 (14 pages).

King, S.J. 2014. *Fishing in Contested Waters: Place and Community in Burnt Church/Esgenoôpetitj.* Toronto: University of Toronto Press.

Kinsella, L. 2013. "The Bannerstone: A Prehistoric Prey-Specific Artifact Designed for Use in the Eastern Woodlands of North America." *Ethnoarchaeology* 5, no. 1: 24–55.

Klein, G. de Vries. 1962. "Triassic Sedimentation, Maritime Provinces, Canada." *Geological Society of America, Bulletin* 73: 1127–46.

Knoll, M.K., and B.B. Huckell. 2019. *SAA Guidelines for Preparing Legacy Archaeology Collections.* https://www.saa.org/quick-nav/saa-media-room/saa-news/2019/02/08/saa-releases-guidelines-for-preparing-legacy-archaeological-collections-for-curation.

Kolodny, A. 2007. Introduction to Joseph Nicolar's 1893 *The Life and Traditions of the Red Man.* Durham, NC: Duke University Press.

Kolodny, A. 2012. "'The Coming of the White Man': Native American First Contact Stories in the Literature Classroom." *Studies in American Indian Literatures* 24, no. 4: 1–20.

Kolodny, A. 2021. "Competing Narratives of Ancestry in Donald Trump's America and the Imperatives for Scholarly Intervention." In *Decolonizing Prehistory, Deep Time and Indigenous Knowledges in North America*, edited by G. Mackenthun and C. Mucher. Tucson: University of Arizona Press. https://torl.biblioboard.com/viewer/8fe5ddc8-e7fc-4358-9168-bfa2e38e8e26.

Kristmanson, H. 1992. "The Ceramic Sequence for Southwestern Nova Scotia: A Refinement of the Petersen/Sanger Model." MA thesis, Memorial University of Newfoundland.

Kristmanson, H. 1997. "The Micmac and New Brunswick Archaeology: Working with the Fort Folly Band." In *At a Crossroads: Archaeology and First Peoples in Canada*, edited by G.P. Nicholas and T.D. Andrews, 24: 19–32. Burnaby, BC: Archaeology Press, Simon Fraser University.

Kristmanson, H. 2008. "Taking Archaeology to Court: The Use of Archaeological Knowledge in Aboriginal Rights and Title Litigation." PhD diss., University of Manchester.

Kristmanson, H. 2010. "Prince Edward Island Archaeology Update 2010." MS on file, Provincial Archaeologist's Office, Aboriginal Affairs Secretariat, Province of Prince Edward Island.

Kristmanson, H. 2019. "Pitawelkek: A 2000-Year-Old Archaeological Site in Malpeque Bay." *Island Magazine* (Fall): 2–14.

Kristmanson, H., and M. Deal. 1993. "The Identification and Interpretation of Finishing Marks on Prehistoric Nova Scotian Ceramics." *Canadian Journal of Archaeology* 17: 74–84.

Kuitems, M., B.L. Wallace, C. Lindsay, A. Scifol, P. Doeve, K. Jenkins, S. Lindauer, P. Erdil, P. M. Ledger, V. Forbes, C. Vermeeren, R. Friedrich, and M.W. Dee. 2022. "Evidence for European Presence in the Americas in AD 1021." *Nature* 601: 388–91. https://doi-org.qe2a-proxy.mun.ca/10.1038/s41586-021-03972-8.

Kupperman, K.O. 2000. *Indians and English: Facing Off in Early America*. Ithaca, NY: Cornell University Press.

Lackowicz, R. 1991. "Plant Use amongst the Recent and Prehistoric Aboriginal Populations of Acadia: a General Overview, Synthesis and Critique." BA Honours essay, Memorial University of Newfoundland.

Lacroix, D., T. Bell, J. Shaw, and K. Westley. 2014. "Submerged Archaeological Landscapes and the Recording of Precontact History: Examples from Atlantic Canada." In *Prehistoric Archaeology of the Continental Shelf: A Global Review*, edited by A. Evans, J. Flatman, and N.C. Flemming, 37–52. New York: Springer.

Lafrance, M., and Y. Desloges. 1993. "Game as Food in New France." In *New England's Creatures: 1400–1900*, edited by P. Benes, 24–44. *The Dublin Seminar for New England Folklife* 18. Boston: Boston University.

Laliberté, M. 1992. "Des Paléoindiens dans la Région de Québec: Quelques Évidences Tirées des Researches de 1990 à Saint-Romuald." *Archéologiques* 5–6: 46–51.

Laroque, C. 2013. "The History Mystery of the Val-Comeau Canoe." In *Underground New Brunswick: Stories of Archaeology*, edited by P. Erickson and J. Fowler, 47–54. Halifax: Nimbus Publishing.

Lavine, M.A. 1996. "Accommodating Age: Radiocarbon Results and Fluted Point Sites in Northeastern North America." *Archaeology of Eastern North America* 16: 33–64.

Laybolt, A.D. 1999. "Prehistoric Settlement and Subsistence Patterns at Gaspereau Lake, Kings County, Nova Scotia." MA thesis, Memorial University of Newfoundland.

LeClercq, C. 1910. *New Relation of Gaspesia, with the Customs and Religion of the Gaspesian Indians*. (1691). Translated and edited by W.F. Ganong. Publications of the Champlain Society 5. Toronto: Champlain Society.

Lee, D.E. 1966. "Meductic Indian Village." In *Miscellaneous Historical Reports on Sites in the Atlantic Provinces*. National Historic Parks and Sites Branch, Manuscript Report 107: 95–106. Ottawa: Parks Canada.

Lee, M. 1999. "Incised Designs on Stone, Ceramic, Bone, and Wood Artifacts from the Atlantic Region: A Comparative Study." Honours essay, Memorial University of Newfoundland.

Leechman, D. 1942. "Obituary: Harlan Ingersoll Smith (1972–1940)." *Canadian Field-Naturalist* 56, no. 7: 114.

Leland, C.G. 1884. *The Algonquin Legends of New England*. Boston: Houghton, Mifflin and Company.

Lelièvre, M. 2012. "'Ajiwsin (You move from one place to another)': Mobility, Emplacement and Politics in (Post-)colonial Nova Scotia." PhD diss., University of Chicago.

Lelièvre, M.A. 2017a. *Unsettling Mobility: Mediating Mi'kmaw Sovereignty in Post-contact Nova Scotia*. Tucson: University of Arizona Press.

Lelièvre, M.A. 2017b. "Constructing a Sacred Chronology: How the Nova Scotian Institute of Science Made the Mi'kmaq a People Without Prehistory." *Ethnohistory* 64, no. 3: 401–26.

Lelièvre, M. 2017c. "Temporal Changes in Marine Shellfish? A Preliminary Archaeological Perspective from the Northumberland Strait." In *North American East Coast Shell Midden Research*, edited by M.W. Betts and M.G. Hrynick, 42–58. *Journal of the North Atlantic*, Special Volume 10.

Lelièvre, M.A., A. Abram, C. Martin, and M. Moran. 2022. "All Our Relations: Re-Animating the Mi'kmaw Landscape on Nova Scotia's Chignecto Peninsula." In *The Far Northeast: 3000 BP to Contact*, edited by K.R. Holyoke and

M.G. Hrynick, 285–314. Mercury Series, Archaeological Paper 181. Ottawa: Canadian Museum of History and University of Ottawa Press.

Lelièvre, M.A., C. Martin, A. Abram, and M. Moran. 2020. "Bridging Indigenous Studies and Archaeology through Relationality? Collaborative Research on the Chignecto Peninsula, Mi'kma'ki." *American Indian Quarterly* 44, no. 2: 171–95.

Lenik, E.J. 2002. *Picture Rocks: American Indian Rock Art in the Northeast Woodlands*. Hanover, NH: University Press of New England.

Lenik, E.J. 2012. "The Thunderbird Motif in Northeastern Indian Art." *Archaeology of Eastern North America* 40: 163–85.

Leonard, K. 1995. "Woodland or Ceramic Period: A Theoretical Problem." *Northeast Anthropology* 50: 19–30.

Leonard, K. 1996. "Mi'kmaq Culture during the Late Woodland and Early Historic Period." PhD diss., University of Toronto.

Leonard, K. 2002. "Jedaick (Shediac, NB): A Nexus through Time." Unpublished report prepared for the Shediac Bay Watershed Association. Archaeoconsulting, Shediac Bridge.

Leonard, K. 2005. "First Nations Archaeology at the Enclosure, Miramichi, NB." Unpublished report submitted to Archaeological Services, Heritage Branch Culture and Sport Secretariat. Fredericton: New Brunswick Department of Education.

Leonard, K. 2017. "Why *Waltes* Was a Woman's Game." In *Prehistoric Games of North American Indians: Subarctic to Mesoamerica*, edited by Barbara Voorhies, 19–33. Salt Lake City: University of Utah Press.

Lescarbot, M. 1928. *Nova Francia: A Description of Acadia, 1606*, translated by P. Erondelle. London: George Routledge & Sons.

Levine, M.A. 1999. "Native Copper in the Northeast: An Overview of Potential Sources Available to Indigenous Peoples." In *The Archaeological Northeast*, edited by M.A. Lavine, K.E. Sassaman, and M.S. Nassaney, 183–89. Westport, CT: Bergin and Garvey.

Levine, M.A. 2007. "Determining the Provenance of Native Copper Artifacts from Northeastern North America: Evidence from Instrumental Neutron Activation Analysis." *Journal of Archeological Science* 24: 572–87.

Lewis, G.M. 2008. "Maps, Mapmaking, and Map Use by Native North Americans." In *Encyclopaedia of the History of Science, Technology, and Medicine in Non-Western Cultures*, edited by H. Selin, 51–182. Dordrecht: Springer.

Lewis, R. 2006a. "Mi'kmaq Rights and Title Claim: A Review of the Precontact Archaeological Factor." *Mi'kmaq Maliseet Nation News* (June): 16–17.

Lewis, R. 2006b. "Precontact Fish Weirs: A Case Study from Southwestern Nova Scotia." MA thesis, Memorial University of Newfoundland.

Lewis, R., and T. Sable. 2014. "The Mi'kmaq: T'an Mi'kmaqik Telo'ltipni'k Mi'kma'kik — How the People Lived in Mi'kma'kik. In *Native Peoples: The Canadian Experience*, 4th ed., edited by C.R. Wilson and C. Fletcher, chap. 15. Toronto: Oxford University Press.

Libby, W.F. 1955. *Radiocarbon Dating*, 2nd ed. Chicago: University of Chicago Press.

Lippert, D. 1997. "In Front of the Mirror: Native Americans and Academic Archaeology." In *Native Americans and Archaeologists: Stepping Stones to Common Ground*, edited by N. Swidler. Walnut Creek, CA: Altamira Press.

Loewen, B. 2016. "Intertwined Enigmas: Basques and Saint Lawrence Iroquoians in the Sixteenth Century." In *Contact in the 16th Century: Networks among Fishers, Foragers, and Farmers*, edited by B. Loewen and C. Chapdelaine, 57–75. Mercury Series Archaeology Paper 176. Ottawa: Canadian Museum of History and University of Ottawa Press.

Loren, D.D. 2008. *In Contact: Bodies and Spaces in the Sixteenth- and Seventeenth-Century Eastern Woodlands.* New York: Altamira.

Loring, S. 1980. "Paleo-Indian Hunter and the Champlain Sea: A Presumed Association." *Man in the Northeast* 19: 15–41.

Loring, S. 1988. "Review of 'The Carson Site'." *Maine Archaeological Society Bulletin* 28: 48–54.

Lothrop, J.C., D.L. Lowery, A.E. Spiess, and C.J. Ellis. 2016. "Early Human Settlement of Northeastern North America." *PaleoAmerica* 2, no. 3: 192–251.

Lothrop, J.C., P.E. Newby, A.E. Spiess, and J.W. Bradley. 2011. "Paleoindians and the Younger Dryas in the New England–Maritimes Region." *Quaternary International* 242: 546–69.

Lucas, G. 2005. *The Archaeology of Time*. New York: Routledge.

Luedtke, B.E. 1979. "The Identification of Sources of Chert Artifacts." *American Antiquity* 44, no. 4: 744–57.

Lyman, R.L., and M.J. O'Brien. 2001. "The Direct Historic Approach, Analogical Reasoning, and Theory in Americanist Archaeology." *Journal of Archaeological Method and Theory* 8, no. 4: 303–42.

MacCarthy, M. 2003. "Mobility, Migration and Projectile Point Diversity in the Late Paleoindian Period of the Far Northeast." MA thesis, Memorial University of Newfoundland.

REFERENCES CITED

MacDonald, G.F. 1965. Letter to J.S. Erskine, Oct. 29, 1965, Concerning the Excavation of a Site on Gaspereau Lake, Nova Scotia. Ottawa: National Museum of Canada, Human History Branch.

MacDonald, G.F. 1966. "The Technology and Settlement Pattern of a Paleo-Indian Site at Debert, Nova Scotia." *Quaternaria* 8: 59–80.

MacDonald, G.F. 1968. *Debert: a Palaeo-Indian Site in Central Nova Scotia*. Anthropology Papers, No. 16. Ottawa: National Museum of Canada.

MacDonald, G.F. 1971. "A Review of Research on Paleo-Indian in Eastern North America, 1960–1970." *Arctic Anthropology* 8, no. 2: 32–41.

MacDonald, G.F. 1982. "Foreword." In *The Vail Site: A Palaeo-Indian Encampment in Maine*, by R.M. Gramly, x–xi. Buffalo, NY: Bulletin of the Buffalo Society of Natural Sciences 30.

MacDonald, G.F. 2011. "The Debert Site: A Retrospective." In *Ta'n Wetapeksi'k: Understanding from Where We Come*, edited by T. Bernard, L.M. Rosenmeier, and S.L. Farrell, 7–10. Truro, NS: Eastern Woodland Print Communications.

MacDonald, M. 2020. "The Dispute over Nova Scotia's Indigenous Lobster Fishery, Explained." *National Observer*, Oct. 20. https://www.nationalobserver.com/2020/10/20/news/nova-scotia-indigenous-lobster-fishery-dispute-explained.

MacDonald, S.L. 1994. "Exploring Patterns of Lithic Material Use in the Insular Quoddy Region, Charlotte County, New Brunswick." MA thesis, University of New Brunswick.

MacInnes, D. 2021. "Pre-European Population Dynamics on the Maritime Peninsula." *Archaeology of Eastern North America* no. 49: 133–55.

Mack, K.E., D. Sanger, and A.R. Kelley. 2002. "The Bob Site: A Multicomponent Archaic and Ceramic Period Site on Pushaw Stream, Maine." Occasional Publications in *Maine Archaeology* Number 12. Augusta: Maine Archaeological Society and Maine State Preservation Commission.

Mackie, Q. 1995. "Prehistory in a Multicultural State: A Commentary on the Development of Canadian Archaeology." In *Theory in Archaeology: A World Perspective*, edited by P.J. Ucko, 178–96. London: Routledge.

MacKinnon, C. 2003a. "The Beausejour Plummets." *The White Fence* no. 22 (Mar.). http://heritage.tantramar.com/WFNewsletter_22.html.

MacKinnon, C. 2003b. "Visitors to Our Shores: The Susquehanna Tradition." *The White Fence* no. 23 (Nov.). https://tantramarheritage.ca/2003/11/white-fence-23/.

MacKinnon, C., and D. Colpitts. 2006. "The Black Island Knife: A Proto-historic (c. A.D. 1500–1600) Copper Artifact from the Missaguash Marsh." *The White Fence* no. 31 (Nov.). https://tantramarheritage.ca/2006/02/white-fence-31/.

MacNeish, R.S. 1979. "Obituary: Douglas Swain Byers 1903–1978."*American Antiquity* 44, no. 4: 708–10.

Maillard, A.S.P. (Abbé). 1758. *An Account of the Customs and Manners of the Micmaki and Maricheets Savage Nation, Now Dependent on the Government of Cape Breton*. London: S. Hooper and A. Morley.

Mallery, G. 1894. *Picture-Writing of the American Indians*. Extract from the Tenth Annual Report of the Bureau of Ethnology. Washington, DC: Government Printing Office.

Mann, A.E. 2021. "Dietary Change among *Canis familiaris* during the Late Ceramic Period on the Maine-Maritime Peninsula: A Case Study from the Holmes Point West Site (ME 62-8), Machias Bay, Maine." Master's thesis, University of Maine.

Maritime Committee on Archaeological Cooperation (MCAC). 1978. *The Teaching of Archaeology in Maritime Universities*. A report submitted to the Maritime Provinces Higher Education Commission. Fredericton, NB: Council of Maritime Premiers, Fredericton.

Marois, R.J.M. 1979. "Identification du Bord sur les Vases en Ceramique sans Parement en Prehistorie (Canada)." Paper presented at the 45th International Congress of Americanists, Vancouver.

Martijn, C. 1989. "A Micmac Domain of Islands." In *Actes du Vigtième Congrès des Algonquinistes*, edited by W. Cowan, 209–31. Ottawa: Carleton University Press.

Matthew, G.F. 1884. "Discoveries at a Village of the Stone Age at Bocabec, N.B." *Bulletin of the Natural History Society of New Brunswick* 3: 6–29.

Matthew, G.F. 1896. "Report on the Summer Camp at French Lake." *Bulletin of the Natural History Society of New Brunswick* 13: 84–88.

Matthew, G.F. 1900. "A Quarry and Workshop of the Stone Age in New Brunswick." *Proceedings of the Royal Society of Canada* 6: 61–69.

Matthew, G.F., and S.W. Kain. 1905. "An Earthenware Pot of the Stone Age Found at Maquapit Lake." *Bulletin of the Natural History Society of New Brunswick* 23: 345–54.

Maymon, J.H., and C.E. Bolian. 1992. "The Wadleigh Falls Site: An Early and Middle Archaic Period Site in Southeastern New Hampshire." In *Early Holocene Occupation in Northern New England*, edited by B. Robinson, J. Petersen, and

A. Robinson, 117–34. Occasional Papers in Maine Archaeology 9. Augusta: Maine Historic Preservation Commission.

McCaffrey, M.T. 1986. "La Prehistoire de la Madeleine: Bilan Preliminaire." In *Les Micmacs et la Mer*, edited by C.A. Martijn, 99–162. Montreal: Recherches Amerindiennes au Québec.

McCaffrey, M. 2016. "Maritimes Walrus and Their Hunters on the Îles de la Madeleine, Québec." *Arctic Studies Center Newsletter* 23: 49–52. Washington, DC: National Museum of Natural History, Smithsonian Institution.

McEachen, P.J. 1996. "The Meadowood Early Woodland Manifestation in the Maritimes: A Preliminary Interpretation." MA thesis, Memorial University of Newfoundland.

McEachen, P. 2004. "Pihcesis: A Brief Look at the Meadowood in the Maritime Provinces." In *Wolastoqiyik Ajemsweg: The People of the Beautiful River at Jemseg. Vol. 2: Archaeological Results*, edited by S.E. Blair, 245–50. Fredericton, NB: Archaeological Services, Heritage Branch, Culture and Sport Secretariat.

McEachen, P., P. Allen, P. Julig, and D.G.F. Long. 1999. "The Tozer Site Revisited: Implications for the Early Woodland Period in New Brunswick." *Canadian Journal of Archaeology* 22, no. 2: 157–66.

McGhee, R. 1977. "Who Owns Prehistory? The Bering Land Bridge Dilemma." *Canadian Journal of Archaeology* 13: 13–20.

McIntosh, W. 1909. "Aboriginal Pottery of New Brunswick." *Bulletin of the Natural History Society of New Brunswick* 6, no. 27: 110–20.

McIntosh, W. 1911. "Archaeology. Report of Council." *Bulletin of the Natural History Society of New Brunswick* 29: 363–66.

McIntosh, W. 1913. "Archaeology. Report of Council." *Bulletin of the Natural History Society of New Brunswick* 30: 486–87.

McIntosh, W. 1914. "Chipped and Flaked Implements from New Brunswick." *Bulletin of the Natural History Society of New Brunswick* 7, no. 31: 39–48.

McNeill, J. 1960. Letter from Jane McNeill, Nova Scotia Museum of Science, to Dr. William J. Mayer-Oakes. MS on file. Halifax: Nova Scotia Museum.

McTavish, L., and J. Dickison. 2007. "William MacIntosh, Natural History and the Professionalization of the New Brunswick Museum, 1898–1940." *Acadiensis* 36, no. 2: 72–90.

Mennell, S. 1985. *All Manners of Food: Eating and Taste in England and France from the Middle Ages to the Present*. New York: Blackwell.

Mi'kmaw Atlas. 2019. "Ta'n Weji-sqalia'tiek Mi'kmaw Place Names." http://mikmawplacenames.ca/about/.

Miller, P. 1887. "Notice of Three Micmac Flint Arrowheads from Merigomish Harbour on the Northern Coast of Nova Scotia." *Proceedings of the Society of Antiquarians of Scotland* 9: 212–14.

Miller, R.F., and D.N. Buhay. 2007. "Gesner's Museum of Natural History, an Early Canadian Geological Collection." *Geoscience Canada* 34, no. 1: 37–48.

Miller, V.P. 1983. "Social and Political Complexity on the East Coast: The Micmac Case." In *The Evolution of Maritime Cultures on the Northeast and the Northwest Coasts of America*, edited by R.J. Nash, 41–55. Department of Archaeology, Publication 11. Burnaby, BC: Simon Fraser University.

Milner, C. 2013. "Stratigraphic Integrity and Disturbance at the Woodland Period St. Croix Village Site (BfDa-1), Hants County, Nova Scotia." MA thesis, Memorial University of Newfoundland.

Molyneaux, B.L. 1980. "Landscape Images: Rock Paintings in the Canadian Shield." *Rotunda* 13, no. 3: 6–11.

Molyneaux, B.L. 1984a. *An Analysis and Interpretation of the Micmac Petroglyphs of Kejimkujik National Park*, Vols. 1–3. Halifax: Parks Canada.

Molyneaux, B.L. 1984b. "The McGowan Lake Petroglyph Recording Project, Queens County, Nova Scotia, 1983." MS on file. Halifax: Nova Scotia Museum.

Molyneaux, B.L. 1989. "Concepts of Humans and Animals in Post-Contact Micmac Rock Art." In *Animals into Art*, edited by H. Morphy, 193–214. Boston: Unwin Hyman.

Monahan, V. 1990. "Copper Technology in the Maritimes: An Examination of Indigenous Copper Working in the Maritime Provinces during the Protohistoric Period." BA Honours thesis, Saint Mary's University.

Monckton, S.G. 2000. "Meadows Flotation Sample Components." MS on file. Dartmouth, NS: Jacques Whitford.

Monckton, S.G. 2004. "Preliminary Report on the Plant Materials." In *Wolastoqiyik Ajemseg: The People of the Beautiful River at Jemseg. Vol. 2: Archaeological Results*, edited by S. Blair, 123–25. New Brunswick Manuscripts in Archaeology 36E. Fredericton, NB: Archaeological Services, Heritage Branch, Culture and Sport Secretariat.

Moorehead, W.K. 1922. *A Report on the Archaeology of Maine*. Andover, ME: The Andover Press.

Morgan, L.H. 1877. *Ancient Society*. New York: Holt.

Morin, E. 2020. "Revisiting Bone Grease Rendering in Highly Fragmented Assemblages."*American Antiquity* 85, no. 3: 535–53.

Morlot, A. von. 1861. "General Views on Archaeology." *Annual Report of the Smithsonian Institution for 1860*, 284–343.

Morlot, A. von. 1863. "An Introductory Lecture to the Study of High Antiquity, Delivered at the Academy of Lausanne, Switzerland, on the 29th of November 1860." *Annual Report of the Smithsonian Institution for 1863*, 303–15.

Morrill, P., and W.P. Hinckley. 1959. *Maine Mines and Minerals, Vol. 2, Eastern Maine*. East Winthrop, ME: Winthrop Mineral Shop.

Morrill, P., and W.P. Hinckley. 1981. *Maine Mines and Minerals, Vol. 1, Western Maine*. East Winthrop, ME: Winthrop Mineral Shop.

Mosher, J., and A. Spiess. 2004. "An Archaic Site at Mattamiscontis on the Penobscot River." *Maine Archaeological Society Bulletin* 44, no. 2: 1–35.

Mournier, R.A. 2003. *Looking Beneath the Surface: The Story of Archaeology in New Jersey*. New Brunswick, NJ: Rutgers University Press.

Mudie, P.J., and M.A. Lelièvre. 2013. "Palynological Study of a Mi'kmaw Shell Midden, Northeast Nova Scotia, Canada." *Journal of Archaeological Science* 40: 2161–75.

Munkittrick, J. 2013. "Faunal Analysis of Canid Bones from Sam Orr's Pond Site (BgDs-15), Quoddy Region, New Brunswick." Honours essay, University of New Brunswick.

Murphy, B.M. 1998. "Researching the Early Holocene of the Maritime Provinces." MA thesis, Memorial University of Newfoundland.

Murphy, B.M., and D.W. Black. 1996. "Zooarchaeology in the Canadian Maritimes." *Canadian Zooarchaeology* 9 (Spring): 2–20.

Nash, R.J. 1978. "Prehistory and Cultural Ecology — Cape Breton, Nova Scotia." In *Papers from the Fourth Annual Congress of the Canadian Ethnology Society*, edited by R.J. Pearson, 131–55. Ottawa: Canadian Ethnology Service Paper 40.

Nash, R.J. 1986. "Mi'kmaq: Economics and Evolution." *Curatorial Report* 57, no. 1: 1–104. Halifax: Nova Scotia Museum.

Nash, R. 1997. "Archetypal Landscapes and the Interpretation of Meaning." *Cambridge Archaeological Journal* 7, no. 1: 57–69.

Nash, R.J., and V.P. Miller. 1987. "Model Building and the Case of the Micmac Economy." *Man in the Northeast* no. 34: 41–56.

Nash, R.J, and F.L. Stewart. 1990. "Melanson: A Large Micmac Village in Kings County, Nova Scotia." *Curatorial Report* 67. Halifax: Nova Scotia Museum.

Nash, R.J., F.L. Stewart, and M. Deal. 1991. "Melanson: A Central Place in Southwestern Nova Scotia." In *Prehistoric Archaeology in the Maritime Provinces:*

Past and Present Research, edited by M. Deal and S. Blair, 213–20. Reports in Archaeology 8. Fredericton, NB: Council of Maritime Premiers.

Newby, P., J. Bradley, A. Spiess, B. Shuman, and P. Leduc. 2005. "A Paleoindian Response to Younger Dryas Climate Change." *Quaternary Science Reviews* 24: 141–54.

Newcomer, M.H. 1971. "Some Quantitative Experiments in Handaxe Manufacture." *World Archaeology* 3: 85–94.

Newsom, B.D. 2017. "Potters on the Penobscot: An Archaeological Case Study Exploring Human Agency, Identity, and Technological Choice." PhD diss., University of Massachusetts.

Newsom, B.D. 2022. "Variation amid Homogeneity: An Examination of Early Ceramic-Period Technologies from the Penobscot River Valley in Maine." In *The Far Northeast: 3000 BP to Contact*, edited by K.R. Holyoke and M.G. Hrynick, 315–44. Mercury Series, Archaeological Paper 181. Ottawa: Canadian Museum of History and University of Ottawa Press.

Newsom, B., N.D. Lolar, and I. St. John. 2021. "In Conversation with the Ancestors: Indigenizing Archaeological Narratives at Acadia National Park, Maine." *Genealogy* 5, no. 4: 1–10.

Nicholson, B., D. Pokotylo, and R. Williamson, eds. 1996. *Statement of Principles for Ethical Conduct Pertaining to Aboriginal Peoples: A Report from the Aboriginal Heritage Committee*. Ottawa: Canadian Archaeological Association and the Department of Communications.

Nicolar, J. 1893 (1979). *The Life and Traditions of the Red Man*. Bangor, ME: C.H. Glass. (Reprinted Fredericton, NB: Saint Annes Point Press).

Nietfeld, P.K.L. 1981. "Determinants of Aboriginal Micmac Political Structure." PhD diss., University of New Mexico.

Nilsson, S. 1868. *The Primitive Inhabitants of Scandinavia. An Essay on Comparative Ethnography, and a Contribution to the History of the Development of Mankind: Containing a Description of the Implements, Dwellings, Tombs, and Mode of Living of the Savages in the North of Europe during the Stone Age*, 3rd ed. Edited with an introduction by J. Lubbock. London: Longmans, Green and Co.

Noble, W.C. 1973. "Canada." In *The Development of North American Archaeology*, edited by J.E. Fitting, 49–83. Garden City, NY: Anchor Press/Doubleday.

O'Grady, M.A. 1993. "In the Footsteps of Jesse Walter Fewkes: Early Archaeology at Rustico Island." *Island Magazine* 33 (Spring/Summer): 10–16.

Pastore, R.T. 1989. "Native History in the Atlantic Region during the Colonial Period." *Acadiensis* 20, no. 1: 200–25.

Pastore, R.T. 2000. "Recent Indian Peoples and the Norse." In *Full Circle: First Contact. Vikings and Skraelings in Newfoundland and Labrador*, edited by K.E. McAleese, 43-47. St. John's: Newfoundland Museum.

Patterson, G. 1877. *History of the County of Pictou, Nova Scotia*. Montreal: Dawson Bros.

Patterson, G. 1883. "Antiquities of Nova Scotia." *Annual Report of the Smithsonian Institution*, 673-77.

Patterson, G. 1890. "The Stone Age in Nova Scotia, as Illustrated by a Collection of Relics Presented to Dalhousie College." *Proceedings and Transactions of the Nova Scotian Institute of Science* 7: 231-53.

Patterson, S. 2009. "Eighteenth-Century Treaties: The Mi'kmaq, Maliseet, and Passamaquoddy Experience." *Native Studies Review* 18, no. 1: 25-52.

Patrik, L.E. 1985. "Is There an Archaeological Record?" *Advances in Archaeological Method and Theory* 8: 27-62.

Patton, A.K., S.E. Blair, and W.J. Webb. 2022. "Later Late Maritime Woodland Settlement in Peskotomuhkatihkuk: Re-Envisioning Chronology, Shellfishing, and Site Formation at the Cusp of Contact." In *The Far Northeast: 3000 BP to Contact*, edited by K.R. Holyoke and M.G. Hrynick, 345-81. Mercury Series, Archaeological Paper 181. Ottawa: Canadian Museum of History and University of Ottawa Press.

Paul, S. 2016. "What is the MACA?" *Resource and Development Newsletter (Kingsclear First Nation)* 5: 2. http://kingsclear.ca/assets/resource-development-coordinator-notices/2016/RDCC_April_2016.pdf.

Pawling, M.A., and J.B. Mitchell. 2008. "Maine Indian Claims Settlement Act of 1980." In *Treaties with American Indians: An Encyclopedia of Rights, Conflicts, and Sovereignty*, Vol. 3, edited by D.L. Fixico, 716-18. Santa Barbara, CA: ABC CLIO.

Pearson, R. 1962. "Two Traditions in Northastern North America." Paper presented at the annual meeting of the Society for American Archaeology, Tucson.

Pearson, R. 1966. "Some Recent Archaeological Discoveries from Prince Edward Island." *Anthropologica* New Series 8, no. 1: 101-09.

Pelletier, B.G., and B.S. Robinson. 2005. "Tundra, Ice and a Pleistocene Cape on the Gulf of Maine: A Case of Paleoindian Transhumance." *Archaeology of Eastern North America* 33: 163-76.

Pendery, S., S. Noël, and A. Spiess. 2012. "Diet and Nutrition." In *Saint Croix Island, Maine: History, Archaeology, and Interpretation*, edited by S. Pendery, 171-84. Augusta: Maine Historic Preservation Commission and the Maine Archaeology Society.

Penobscot Nation and University of Maine. 2018. "Memorandum of Understanding between the Penobscot Nation and the University of Maine Systems, University of Maine at Orono." http://umaine.edu/nativeamericanprograms/wp-content/uploads/sites/320/2018/05/Penobscot-Nation-UMaine-MOU.pdf.

Pentz, B.C. 2008. "A River Runs Through It: An Archaeological Survey of the Upper Mersey River and Allains River in Southwest Nova Scotia." MA thesis, Memorial University of Newfoundland.

Pentz, B.C. 2013. "An Inventory of Private Collections from Southwest Nova Scotia." Report submitted to the Nova Scotia Museum, Halifax.

Peskotomuhkati Nation at Skutik (PNS). 2020. "Peskotomuhkati Persistence." https://qonaskamkuk.com/peskotomuhkati-nation/peskotomuhkati-persistence/.

Petersen, J.B. 1985. "Ceramic Analysis in the Northeast: Resume and Prospect." In *Ceramic Analysis in the Northeast: Contributions to Methodology and Culture History*, edited by J.B. Petersen, 5–25. Occasional Publications in Northeastern Anthropology 9, no. 2.

Petersen, J.B. 1991. "Archaeological Testing at the Sharrow Site: A Deeply Stratified Early to Late Holocene Cultural Sequence in Central Maine." *Occasional Publications in Maine Archaeology* 8. Augusta: Maine Archaeology Society and the Maine Historic Preservation Commission.

Petersen, J.B. 1996. "The Study of Native Fibre Industries from Eastern North America: Resume and Prospect." In *A Most Indispensable Art: Native Fiber Industries from Eastern North America*, edited by J.B. Petersen, 1–29. Knoxville: University of Tennessee Press.

Petersen, J.B., R.N. Barone, and B.J. Cox. 2000. "The Varney Farm Site and the Late Paleoindian Period in Northeastern North America." *Archaeology of Eastern North America* 28: 113–40.

Petersen, J.B., M. Blustain, and J.W. Bradley. 2004. "'Mawooshen' Revisited: Two Native American Contact Period Sites on the Central Maine Coast." *Archaeology of Eastern North America*: 1–71.

Petersen, J.B., and D.E. Putnam. 1992. "Early Holocene Occupation in the Central Gulf of Maine Region." In *Early Holocene Occupation in Northern New England*, edited by B. Robinson, J. Petersen, and A. Robinson, 13–62. Occasional Papers in Maine Archaeology 9. Augusta: Maine Historic Preservation Commission.

Petersen, J.B., B.S. Robinson, D.F. Belknap, J. Stark, and L.K. Kaplan. 1994. "An Archaic and Woodland Period Fish Weir Complex in Central Maine." *Archaeology of Eastern North America* 22: 197–222.

Petersen, J.B., and D. Sanger. 1991. "An Aboriginal Ceramic Sequence for Maine and the Maritime Provinces." In *Prehistory of the Maritime Provinces: Past and Present Research*, edited by M. Deal and S. Blair, 113-70. Fredericton, NB: Council of Maritime Premiers, Reports in Archaeology 8.

Phillips, R.B. 2011. *Museum Pieces: Toward the Indigenization of Canadian Museums*. Montreal and Kingston: McGill-Queen's University Press.

Pickard, F.D., A. Robichaud, and C.P. Laroque. 2011. "Using Dendrochronology to Date the Val Comeau Canoe, New Brunswick and Developing an Eastern White Pine Chronology for the Canadian Maritimes." *Dendrochronologia* 29: 3-8.

Pielou, E.C. 1991. *After the Ice Age: The Return of Life to Glaciated North America*. Chicago: University of Chicago Press.

Piers, H. 1890. "Aboriginal Remains in Nova Scotia." *Proceedings and Transactions of the Nova Scotian Institute of Science* 7: 276-90.

Piers, H. 1895. "Relics of the Stone Age in Nova Scotia." *Proceedings and Transactions of the Nova Scotian Institute of Science* 9: 26-58.

Piers, H. 1911. "Provincial Museum and Science Library." *Report of the Department of Mines 1910, Province of Nova Scotia*, 194-220. Halifax: King's Printer.

Piers, H. 1915a. "A Brief Historical Account of the Nova Scotian Institute of Science, and the Events Leading up to Its Formation; the Biographical Sketches of Its Deceased Presidents and Other Prominent Members." *Proceedings and Transactions of the Nova Scotian Institute of Science, 1910-1914*, 8: liii-cix.

Pike, K.-A. 2013. "Bearing Identity: A Biocultural Analysis of Human Remains from Old Mission Point (ClDq-1), New Brunswick." MA thesis, Memorial University of Newfoundland.

Pinkney, C.C. 1938. "Habitation of Port Royal, Acadia, New France, Lower Granville, Nova Scotia: Skeleton Report to Accompany Plans and Profiles Derived from Research Excavations." Report submitted to the Associates of Port Royal, Boston, Massachusetts, in collaboration with the Department of Mines and Resources, Ottawa.

Plourde, M. 2006. "The Cap de Bon-Désir Site: A New Regional Variation of the Gulf of Maine Archaic Tradition." In *The Archaic of the Far Northeast*, edited by D. Sanger and M.A.P. Renouf, 139-59. Orono: University of Maine Press.

Pollock, S.G., N.D. Hamilton, and R. Bonnishen. 1999. "Chert from the Munsungun Lake Formation (Maine) in Palaeoamerican Archaeological Sites in Northeastern North America: Recognition of Its Occurrence and Distribution." *Journal of Archaeological Science* 26: 269-93.

Pottie, E. 2019. "Ancient Burial Grounds along the Bras d'Or Lake under Threat." *Chronicle Herald*, Jan. 13. https://www.thechronicleherald.ca/lifestyles/ancient-burial-grounds-along-the-bras-dor-lake-under-threat-275422/.

Powell, S., C.E. Garza, and A. Hendricks. 1982. "Ethics and Ownership of the Past: The Reburial and Repatriation Controversy." In *Archaeological Method and Theory*, edited by M.B. Schiffer, Vol. 5, 1–42. Tucson: University of Arizona Press.

Powers, J.M. 1991. "L'Ordre de Bon Temps: Good Cheer as the Answer." In *Oxford Symposium on Food & Cookery, 1990: Feasting and Fasting: Proceedings*, edited by H. Walker, 164–72. London: Prospect Books.

Preston, B. 1974. "An Archaeological Survey of the Shubenacadie River System, 1970." Halifax: Nova Scotia Museum, Curatorial Report no. 18.

Preston, B. 1975. "An Archaeological Survey of Reported Acadian Sites in the Annapolis Valley and Minas Basin Areas 1971." Halifax: Nova Scotia Museum, Curatorial Report no. 20.

Preston, B. 1991. "The Management of Nova Scotia's Archaeological Resources." In *Prehistoric Archaeology in the Maritime Provinces: Past and Present Research*, edited by M. Deal and S. Blair, 259–66. Reports in Archaeology no. 8. Fredericton, NB: Council of Maritime Premiers.

Price, F., and A. Spiess. 2007. "A New Submerged Prehistoric Site and Other Fisherman's Reports near Mount Desert Island." *Maine Archaeological Society Bulletin* 47, no. 2: 21–35.

Prins, H.E.L. 1986. "Micmacs and Maliseets in the St. Lawrence River Valley." In *Actes du Dix-Septième Congrès des Algonquinistes*, edited by W. Cowan, 263–78. Ottawa: Carleton University Press.

Prins, H.E.L. 1994. "Children of Gluskap: Wabanaki Indians on the Eve of the European Invasion." In *American Beginnings: Exploration, Culture, and Cartography in the Land of Norumbega*, edited by E.W. Baker, E.A. Churchill, R. D'Abate, K.L. Jones, V.A. Conrad, and H.E.L. Prins, 95–117, 325–33. Lincoln: University of Nebraska Press.

Prins, H.E.L. 1996. *The Mi'kmaq: Resistance, Accommodation, and Cultural Survival*. New York: Harcourt Brace.

Prins, H.E.L, and B. McBride. 2007. "Asticou's Island Domain: Wabanaki Peoples at Mount Desert Island 1500–2000." *Acadia National Park Ethnographic Overview and Assessment*, Vol. 1. Bar Harbor, ME, and Boston: Abbe Museum and Northeast Region Ethnography Program, National Park Service.

Purdy, B.A. 1984. "Quarry Studies: Technological and Chronological Significance." In *Prehistoric Quarries and Lithic Production*, edited by J.E. Ericson and B.A.

Purdy, 119–27. Cambridge: Cambridge University Press.

Quinn, D.B. 1981. *Sources for the Ethnography of Northeastern North America to 1611*. Ottawa: National Museum of Man, Mercury Series, Canadian Ethnology Service no. 76.

Raghavan, M., et al. 2015. "Genomic Evidence for the Pleistocene and Recent Population History of Native Americans." *Science* 349, no. 6350: 841–51.

Rand, S.T. 1890. "The Coming of the White Man Revealed: Dream of the White Robe and Floating Island." *American Antiquarian and Oriental Journal* 12, no. 3: 155–56.

Rand, S.T. 1894. *Legends of the Micmacs*. Wellesley Philological Publications. New York: Longmans, Green and Co.

Rau, C. 1865. "Artificial Shell-Deposits in New Jersey." *Annual Report of the Smithsonian Institution for 1864*, 370–74.

Ray, R.B., comp. 1977. *The Indians of Maine and the Atlantic Provinces: A Bibliographical Guide*. Portland: Maine Historical Society.

Ritchie, D., and R.A. Gould. 1985. "Back to the Source: A Preliminary Account of the Massachusetts Hill Quarry Complex." In *Stone Tool Analysis*, edited by M.G. Plew, J.C. Woods, and M.G. Pavesic, 35–53. Albuquerque: University of New Mexico Press.

Ritchie, W.A. 1955. "Recent Discoveries Suggesting an Early Woodland Burial Cult in the North East." *New York State Museum and Science Service Circulars*, no. 40. Albany: University of the State of New York.

Ritchie, W.A. 1980. *The Archaeology of New York State*, rev. ed. New York: Harbor Hill.

Ritchie, W.A. 1985. "Fifty Years of Archaeology in the Northeastern United States: A Retrospect." *American Antiquity* 50, no. 2: 412–20.

Ritchie, W.A., and D.W. Dragoo. 1959. "The Eastern Dispersal of Adena." *American Antiquity* 25: 43–50.

Robinson, B. 1992. "Early and Middle Archaic Period Occupation in the Gulf of Maine Region: Mortuary and Technological Patterning." In *Early Holocene Occupation in Northern New England*, edited by B. Robinson, J. Petersen, and A. Robinson, 63–116. *Occasional Papers in Maine Archaeology* no. 9. Augusta: Maine Historic Preservation Commission.

Robinson, B. 1996a. "Projectile Points and Other Diagnostic Things and Culture Boundaries in the Gulf of Maine Region." *Maine Archaeological Society Bulletin* 36, no. 2: 1–24.

Robinson, B. 1996b. "A Regional Analysis of the Moorehead Tradition: 8,500–

3,700 B.P." *Archaeology of Eastern North America* 24: 95–148.

Robinson, B. 2006. "Burial Ritual, Technology, and Cultural Landscape in the Far Northeast: 8600–3700 B.P." In *The Archaic of the Far Northeast*, edited by D. Sanger and M.A.P. Renouf, 341–81. Orono: University of Maine Press.

Robinson, B.S., and A.S. Heller. 2017. "Maritime Culture Patterns and Animal Symbolism in Eastern Maine." In *North American East Coast Shell Midden Research*, edited by M.W. Betts and M.G. Hrynick, 90–104. *Journal of the North Atlantic*, Special Vol. 10.

Robinson, B., and J.B. Petersen. 1992. "Early Holocene Occupation in the Central Gulf of Maine Region." In *Early Holocene Occupation in Northern New England*, edited by B. Robinson, J. Petersen, and A. Robinson, 1–12. *Occasional Papers in Maine Archaeology* 9. Augusta: Maine Historic Preservation Commission.

Robinson, F. 2012. "Between the Mountains and the Sea: An Exploration of the Champlain Sea and Paleoindian Land Use in the Champlain Basin." In *Late Pleistocene Archaeology and Ecology in the Far Northeast*, edited by C. Chapdelaine, 191–217. College Station: Texas A&M University Press.

Robinson, M. 1977. *Rock Drawings of the Micmac Indians*. Halifax: Nova Scotia Museum.

Robinson, M. 2014. "Animal Personhood in Mi'kmaq Perspective." *Societies* 4, no. 4: 672–88.

Rojo, A. 1987. "Excavated Fish Vertebrae as Predictors in Bioarchaeological Research." *North American Archaeologist* 8, no. 3: 209–26.

Rosenmeier, L. 2010. "Towards an Archaeology of Descent: Spatial Practice and Communities of Shared Experience in Mi'kma'ki." PhD diss., Brown University.

Rosenmeier, L.M., S. Buchanan, R. Stea, and G. Brewster. 2012. "New Sites and Lingering Questions at the Debert and Belmont Sites, Nova Scotia." In *Late Pleistocene Archaeology and Ecology in the Far Northeast*, edited by C. Chapdelaine, 113–34. College Station: Texas A&M University Press.

Rouse, I. 1958. "The Inference of Migrations from Anthropological Evidence." In *Migration in New World Culture History*, edited by R.H. Thompson, 63–68. *University of Arizona Social Science Bulletin* 27.

Rowley-Conwy, P. 2006. "The Concept of Prehistory and the Invention of the Terms 'Prehistoric' and 'Prehistorian': The Scandinavian Origin, 1833–1850." *European Journal of Archaeology* 9, no. 1: 103–30.

Rutherford, D.E. 1989. "The Archaic/Ceramic Period Transition in New Brunswick and Maine: An Analysis of Stemmed Biface Morphology." MA thesis, Memorial University of Newfoundland.

Rutherford, D.E. 1990a. "Continuity of Moorehead Phase Populations in New Brunswick and Maine." In *Proceedings of the 1990 Algonquian Conference*, St. John's, 329-36.

Rutherford, D.E. 1990b. "Reconsidering the Middlesex Burial Phase in the Maine Maritimes Region." *Canadian Journal of Archaeology* 14: 169-81.

Rutherford, D.E., and Robert K. Stevens. 1991. "Geochemical and Physical Analysis of Metachert from the Ramah Group, Northern Labrador." Paper presented at the annual meeting of the Canadian Archaeological Association, St. John's.

Sabina, A.P. 1965. *Rock and Mineral Collecting in Canada*, Vol. 3: *New Brunswick, Nova Scotia, Prince Edward Island, and Newfoundland*. Geological Survey of Canada, Miscellaneous Report 8. Ottawa: Department of Mines and Technical Surveys.

Sable, T. 2011. "Legends as Maps." In *Ta'n Wetapeksi'k: Understanding from Where We Come*, edited by T. Bernard, L.M. Rosenmeier, and S.L. Farrell, 157-71. Truro, NS: Eastern Woodland Print Communications.

Sable, T., and B. Francis. 2012. *The Language of the Land, Mi'kma'ki*. Sydney, NS: Cape Breton University Press.

Salmon, E. 2000. "Kincentric Ecology: Indigenous Perceptions of the Human-Nature Relationship." *Ecological Adaptations* 10, no. 5: 1327-32.

Salter, M.A. 1975. "L'Ordre de Bon Temp." *Nova Scotia Historical Quarterly* 5, no. 2: 143-54.

Sanders, M. 2014. "End of Dyke Site Mitigation 2012: Final Report." Report submitted to Nova Scotia Power Incorporated. Halifax: CRM Group.

Sanders, M., W.B. Stewart, and D. Kelman. 2009. "Lane's Mills Dam Archaeological Testing, 2008, Gaspereau Lake Reservoir, Kings County, Nova Scotia." Report submitted to Nova Scotia Power Incorporated. Halifax: CRM Group.

Sanger, D. 1971. "Prehistory of Passamaquoddy Bay: A Summary." *Maine Archaeological Society Bulletin* 11, no. 2: 14-19.

Sanger, D. 1973a. *Cow Point: An Archaic Cemetery in New Brunswick*. Archaeological Survey of Canada, Mercury Series 12. Ottawa: National Museum of Man.

Sanger, D. 1973b. "Recent Meetings on Maine-Maritimes Archaeology: A Synthesis." *Man in the Northeast* 7: 128-29.

Sanger, D. 1975. "Cultural Change as an Adaptive Process in the Maine-Maritimes Region." *Arctic Anthropology* 12, no. 2: 60-75.

Sanger, D. 1976. "The Earliest Settlements: 9000 B.C. to A.D. 1600." In *Maine Forms of Architecture*, edited by D. Thompson, 3-14. Waterville, ME: Colby College Museum of Art.

Sanger, D. 1979a. "Who Were the Red Paints?" In *Discovering Maine's Archaeological Heritage*, edited by D. Sanger, 67–82. Augusta: Maine Historic Preservation Commission.

Sanger, D. 1979b. "Some Thoughts on the Scarcity of Archaeological Sites in Maine between 10,000 and 5,000 years ago." In *Discovering Maine's Archaeological Heritage*, edited by D. Sanger, 23–34. Augusta: Maine Historic Preservation Commission.

Sanger, D. 1979c. "An Introduction to the Prehistory and Paleo-Environments of the Maine–Maritime Provinces Area." In *Discovering Maine's Archaeological Heritage*, edited by D. Sanger, 11–22. Augusta: Maine Historic Preservation Commission.

Sanger, D. 1982. "Changing Views of Aboriginal Settlement and Seasonality in the Gulf of Maine." *Canadian Journal of Anthropology* 2: 195–203.

Sanger, D. 1986. "An Introduction to the Prehistory of the Passamaquoddy Bay Region." *American Review of Canadian Studies* 16, no. 2: 139–59.

Sanger, D. 1987. *The Carson Site and the Late Ceramic Period in Passamaquoddy Bay, New Brunswick*. Mercury Series, Archaeological Survey of Canada Paper 135. Ottawa: Canadian Museum of Civilization.

Sanger, D. 1991a. "Five Thousand Years of Contact between Maine and Nova Scotia." *Maine Archaeological Society Bulletin* 31, no. 2: 55–61.

Sanger, D. 1991b. "Cow Point Revisited." In *Prehistory of the Maritime Provinces: Past and Present Research*, edited by M. Deal and S. Blair, 73–88. Fredericton, NB: Council of Maritime Premiers.

Sanger, D. 1996a. "Gilman Falls Site: Implications for the Early and Middle Archaic of the Maritime Peninsula." *Canadian Journal of Archaeology* 20: 7–28.

Sanger, D., 1996b. "Testing the Models: Hunter-gatherer Use of Space in the Gulf of Maine, USA." *World Archaeology* 27, no. 3: 512–26.

Sanger D. 1996c. "An Analysis of Seasonal Transhumance Models for Pre-European State of Maine." In *Contributions to the Archaeology of Northeastern North America: A Special Issue of the Review of Archaeology*, edited by B. Robinson, 54–58. Salem, MA: Peabody Essex Museum.

Sanger, D. 2000. "'Red Paint People' and Other Myths of Maine Archaeology." *Maine History* 39: 3.

Sanger, D. 2005. "Pre-European Dawnland: Archaeology of the Maritime Peninsula." In *New England and the Maritime Provinces: Connections and Comparisons*, edited by S.J. Hornsby and J.G. Reid, 15–31, 318–29. Montreal and Kingston: McGill–Queen's University Press.

Sanger, D. 2006. "An Introduction to the Archaic of the Maritime Peninsula: The View from Central Maine." In *The Archaic of the Far Northeast*, edited by D. Sanger and M.A.P. Renouf, 221-52. Orono: University of Maine Press.

Sanger, D. 2008. "Discerning Regional Variation: The Terminal Archaic Period in the Quoddy Region of the Maritime Peninsula." *Canadian Journal of Archaeology* 32, no. 1: 1-42.

Sanger, D. 2009a. "Foraging for Swordfish (*Xiphias gladius*) in the Gulf of Maine." In *Painting the Past with a Broad Brush. Papers in Honour of James Valliere Wright*, edited by D.L. Keenlyside and J.-L. Pilon. Mercury Series Archaeology Paper 170, Hull, PQ: Canadian Museum of Civilization.

Sanger, D. 2009b. "Late Archaic Period Swordfish Hunting: An Ethnoarchaeological Approach." *Maine Archaeological Society Bulletin* 49, no. 1: 7-22.

Sanger, D. 2009c. "Canoes, Dugouts, and Gouges: Is There Any Logical Connection?" *Maine Archaeological Society Bulletin* 49, no. 2: 17-34.

Sanger, D. 2010. "Semi-Subterranean Houses in the Ceramic Period along the Coast of Maine." *Maine Archaeological Society Bulletin* 50, no. 2: 23-45.

Sanger, D. 2012. "Appendix A2: Native Occupations on Saint Croix Island." In *Saint Croix Island, Maine: History, Archaeology, and Interpretation*, edited by S. Pendery, 247-68. Occasional Publication in Archaeology no. 14. Augusta: Maine Historic Preservation Commission and Maine Archaeological Society.

Sanger, D., W.R. Belcher, and D.C. Kellogg. 1992. "Early Holocene Occupation at the Blackman Stream Site, Central Maine." In *Early Holocene Occupation in Northern New England*, edited by B.S. Robinson, J.B. Petersen, and A.K. Robinson, 149-61. Augusta: Occasional Publications in Maine Archaeology no. 9.

Sanger, D., and D.F. Belknap. 1987. "Human Responses to Changing Marine Environments in the Gulf of Maine." In *Man and the Mid-Holocene Climatic Optimum*, edited by N.A. McCinnon and G.S.L. Stewart, 245-61. *Proceedings of the 17th Annual Chacmool Conference*. University of Calgary.

Sanger, D., R.B. Davis, R.G. MacKay, and H.W. Borns. 1977. "The Hirundo Archaeological Project — An Interdisciplinary Approach to Central Maine Prehistory." In *Amerinds and Their Paleoenvironments in Northeastern North America*, edited by W.S. Newman and B. Salwen, 457-71. *Annals of the New York Academy of Sciences* no. 288.

Sanger, D., and S.A. Davis. 1991. "Preliminary Report on the Bain Site and the Chegoggin Archaeological Project." In *Prehistory of the Maritime Provinces: Past and Present Research*, edited by M. Deal and S. Blair, 59-71. Fredericton, NB: Council of Maritime Premiers.

Sanger, D., A.R. Kelley, and H. Almquist. 2003. "Geoarchaeological and Cultural Interpretation in the Lower Penobscot Valley, Maine." In *Proceedings of a Symposium held at the New York Natural History Conference VI*, edited by D.L. Cremeens and J.P. Hart, 135–50. Albany: New York State Museum Bulletin 497.

Sanger, D., and R.G. MacKay. 1973. "The Hirundo Archaeological Project — Preliminary Report." *Man in the Northeast* no. 6: 21–29.

Sanger, D., and B. Newson. 2000. "Middle Archaic in the Lower Piscataquis River, and Its Relationship to Laurentian Tradition in Central Maine." *Maine Archaeological Society Bulletin* 40, no. 1: 1–22.

Sanger, D., M.A. Pawling, and D.G. Soctomah. 2006. "Passamaquoddy Homeland and Language: The Importance of Place." In *Cross-cultural Collaboration: Native Peoples and Archaeologists in the Northeastern United States*, edited by J. Kerber, 314–28. Lincoln: University of Nebraska Press.

Sanger, D., and M.A.P. Renouf, eds. 2006. *The Archaic of the Far Northeast*. Orono: University of Maine Press.

Sanger, D., and M.J. Sanger. 1986. "Boom and Bust on the River: The Story of the Damariscotta Oyster Shell Heaps." *Archaeology of Eastern North America* 14: 65–78.

Sassaman, K.E. 1999. "A Southeastern Perspective on Soapstone Vessel Technology in the Northeast." In *The Archaeological Northeast*, edited by M.A. Lavine, K.E. Sassaman, and M.S. Nassaney, 75–95. Westport, CT: Bergin and Garvey.

Saunders, R.M. 1935. "First Introduction of European Plants and Animals in Canada." *Canadian Historical Review* 16: 388–406.

Schiffer, M.B. 1987. *Formation Processes of the Archaeological Record*. Albuquerque: University of New Mexico Press.

Scott, W.B., and M.G. Scott. 1988. *Atlantic Fishes of Canada*. Toronto: University of Toronto Press.

Shaw, J., C.L. Amos, D.A. Greenberg, C.T. O'Reilly, D. Russell Parrott, and E. Patton. 2010. "Catastrophic Tidal Expansion in the Bay of Fundy, Canada." *Canadian Journal of Earth Sciences* 47: 1079–91.

Shaw, L.C., 1988. "A Biocultural Evaluation of the Skeletal Population from the Nevin Site, Blue Hill, Maine." *Archaeology of Eastern North America* 16: 55–77.

Sheldon, H.L. 1988. "The Late Prehistory of Nova Scotia as Viewed from the Brown Site." *Curatorial Report* no. 61. Halifax: Nova Scotia Museum.

Siebert, F.T., Jr. 1973. "The Identity of the Tarrantines, with an Etymology." *Studies in Linguistics* 23: 69–77.

Silliman, S. 2010. "Indigenous Traces in Colonial Spaces: Archaeologies of Ambiguity, Origin, and Practice." *Journal of Social Archaeology* 10, no. 1: 28-58.

Simonsen, B.O. 1978. "Attrition of Coastal Archaeological Resources in the Maritime Provinces of Canada; Part I." *Reports in Archaeology* no. 2. Fredericton, NB: Council of Maritime Premiers.

Simonsen, B.O. 1979. "Attrition of Coastal Archaeological Resources in the Maritime Provinces of Canada; Part II." *Reports in Archaeology* no. 3. Fredericton, NB: Council of Maritime Premiers.

Smith, A.C. 1886. "On Pre-historic Remains and on an Internment of the Early French Period at Tabusintac." *Bulletin of the New Brunswick Natural History Society* 5: 14-19.

Smith, B.L. 1948. "An Analysis of the Maine Cemetery Complex." *Bulletin of the Massachusetts Archaeological Society* 9, nos. 2-3.

Smith, C. 2020. "The Passamaquoddy People Could Be Close to Gaining Recognition in Canada." *CBC News*. https://www.cbc.ca/news/canada/new-brunswick/treaty-indiginous-first-nation-recognition-hunting-fishing-rights-border-st-croix-maine-1.5478601.

Smith, H.I. 1917. "Archaeological Studies in Northern Nova Scotia." *Proceedings of the Nineteenth International Congress of Americanists*, 35-36.

Smith, H.I. 1929. "The Archaeology of Merigomish Harbour, Nova Scotia." In *Some Shell-Heaps in Nova Scotia*, edited by H.I. Smith and W.J. Wintemberg, 1-104, 130-70. Bulletin of the National Museum of Canada no. 47.

Smith, H.I., and W.J. Wintemberg. 1929. *Some Shell-Heaps in Nova Scotia*. Bulletin of the National Museum of Canada no. 47.

Smith, N.N. 1982. "Meductic Reassessed 1981." *Papers of the Thirteenth Algonquian Conference*, edited by W. Cowan, 201-09. Ottawa: Carleton University Press.

Smith, N.N., and W. Walker. 1997. "The Changing Role of Shamans and Their Magic in the Validation and Maintenance of Wabanaki Culture." *Papers of the 28th Algonquian Conference, 1996*, Winnipeg, 365-71.

Snow, D. 1977. "Rock Art and the Power of Shamans." *Natural History* 86, no. 2: 42-49.

Snow, D.R. 1980. *The Prehistory of New England*. New York: Academic Press.

Snow, H.E. 1994. "Archaeological Investigations at Kerr Point (BjCo-15) Merigomish Harbour, Nova Scotia: Excavation of a 'Shell Heap.'" Honours thesis, St. Francis Xavier University.

Soctomah, D. 2005. *A Visit to Our Ancestors Place: Meddybemps — N'tolonapemk Village*. Princeton, ME: Passamaquoddy Tribal Historic Preservation Office.

Soctomah, D., E.R. Cowie, and A. Spiess, guest curators. 2012. *N'tolonapemk: Our Relatives' Place*. Exhibit. Bar Harbor, ME: Abbe Museum.

Speck, F.G. 1915. "The Eastern Algonkian Wabanaki Confederacy." *American Anthropologist* New Series 17, no. 3: 492–508.

Speck, F.G. 1919. "Penobscot Shamanism." *Memoirs of the American Anthropological Association* 6: 239–88.

Speck, F.G. 1922. "Beothuk and Micmac." *Indian Notes and Monographs*. Heye Foundation. New York: Museum of the American Indian.

Speck, F.G. 1924. "Micmac Slate Image." *Indian Notes and Monographs* 1: 153–54. Heye Foundation. New York: Museum of American Indian.

Speck, F.G. 1940. *Penobscot Man: The Life History of a Forest Tribe in Maine*. Philadelphia: University of Pennsylvania Press.

Speck, F.G., and R.W. Dexter. 1951. "Utilization of Animals and Plants by the Micmac Indians of New Brunswick." *Journal of the Washington Academy of Sciences* 41: 250–59.

Speck, F.G., and R.W. Dexter. 1952. "Utilization of Animals and Plants by the Malecite Indians of New Brunswick." *Journal of the Washington Academy of Sciences* 42: 1–7.

Spiess, A.E. 1981. "Progress in Prehistoric Technology: Advances in Cooking Practices." *Maine Archaeological Society Bulletin* 21, no. 1: 8–13.

Spiess, A.E. 1982. "A Skeleton in Armour: An Unknown Chapter in Maine Archaeology." *Maine Archaeological Society Bulletin* 22, no. 1: 17–24.

Spiess, A.E. 1992. "Archaic Period Subsistence in New England and the Maritime Provinces." In *Early Holocene Occupation of Northern New England*, edited by B.S. Robinson, J.B. Petersen, and A.K. Robinson, 163–85. Occasional Papers in Maine Archaeology no. 9. Augusta: Maine Historic Preservation Commission.

Spiess, A.E. 1996. "Two Isolated Paleoindian Artifacts from Maine." *Archaeology of Eastern North America* 16: 65–74.

Spiess, A.E. 2017. "People of the Clam: Shellfish and Diet in Coastal Maine Late Archaic and Ceramic Period Sites." In *North American East Coast Shell Midden Research*, edited by M.W. Betts and M.G. Hrynick, 105–12. *Journal of the North Atlantic*, Special Volume no. 10.

Spiess, A.E., B.J. Bourque, and R.M. Gramly. 1983a. "Early and Middle Archaic Site Distribution in Western Maine." *North American Archaeologist* 4, no. 3: 225–43.

Spiess, A.E., B.J. Bourque, and S.L. Cox. 1983b. "Cultural Complexity in Maritime Cultures: Evidence from Penobscot Bay, Maine." In *The Evolution of Maritime Cultures on the Northeast and Northwest Coasts of America*, edited by R.

Nash, 91–108. Department of Archaeology. Burnaby: Simon Fraser University.

Spiess, A., and L. Cranmer 2001. "Native American Occupations at Pemaquid: Review and Results." *Maine Archaeological Society Bulletin* 41, no. 2: 1–25.

Spiess, A.E., M.L. Curran, and J.R. Grimes. 1985. "Caribou (*Rangifer tarandus L.*) Bones from New England Paleoindian Sites." *North American Archaeologist* 6, no. 2: 145–59.

Spiess, A.E., and M. Hedden. 2000. "Susquehanna Tradition Activity Areas at the Waterville-Winslow Bridge." *Maine Archaeological Society Bulletin* 40, no. 1: 23–54.

Spiess, A., and J. Mosher. 2006. "Archaic Period Hunting and Fishing around the Gulf of Maine." In *The Archaic of the Far Northeast*, edited by D. Sanger and M.A.P. Renouf, 383–408. Orono: University of Maine Press.

Spiess, A.E., and J.B. Petersen. 2000. "End of the Susquehanna Tradition, Circa 3000 B.P., in Maine." Paper presented at the annual meeting of the Canadian Archaeological Association, Ottawa.

Spiess, A.E., and D. Wilson. 1987. *Michaud: A Palaeo Indian Site in the New England Maritimes Region*. Occasional Publications in Maine Archaeology no. 6. Augusta: Maine Historic Preservation Commission and the Maine Archaeological Society.

Spiess, A.E., and D. Wilson. 1989. "Paleoindian Lithic Distribution in the New England Maritimes Region." In *Eastern Paleoindian Lithic Resource Use*, edited by C.J. Ellis and J.C. Lothrop, 75–97. Boulder, CO: Westview Press.

Spiess, A., D. Wilson, and J. Bradley. 1998. "Paleoindian Occupation in the New England–Maritime Region: Beyond Cultural Ecology." *Archaeology of Eastern North America* 26: 201–64.

Spooner, I., H. White, S. Principato, S. Stolze, and N. Hill. 2014. "Records of Late Holocene Moisture Regime from Wetlands in Nova Scotia, Canada." *Geological Society of America Abstracts with Programs* 46, no. 2: 88.

Squires, W.A. 1945. *The History and Development of the New Brunswick Museum (1842–1945)*. Administrative Series no. 2. Saint John, NB: Publications of the New Brunswick Museum.

St. Amand, F., T. Childs, E.J. Reitz, S. Heller, B. Newsom, T.C. Rick, D. Sandweiss, and R. Wheeler. 2020. "Leveraging Legacy Archaeological Collections as Proxies for Climate and Environmental Research." *Proceedings of the National Academy of Sciences* 117, no. 15: 8287–94.

Stapelfeldt, K. 2009. "A Form and Function Study of Precontact Pottery from

Atlantic Canada." MA thesis, Memorial University of Newfoundland.

Stea, R.R. 2011. "Geology and Palaeoenvironmental Reconstruction of the Debert-Belmont Site." In *Ta'n Wetapeksi'k: Understanding from Where We Come*, edited by T. Bernard, L.M. Rosenmeier, and S.L. Farrell, 55–73. Truro, NS: Eastern Woodland Print Communications.

Stea, R.R., and R.J. Mott. 1998. "Deglaciation of Nova Scotia: Stratigraphy and Chronology of Lake Sediment Cores and Buried Organic Sections." *Géographie de Physique et Quaternaire* 52: 3–21.

Steeves, P.F. 2015. "Decolonizing Indigenous Histories: Pleistocene Archaeology Sites of the Western Hemisphere." PhD diss., State University of New York, Binghamton.

Steward, J.H. 1955. *Theory of Culture Change*. Urbana: University of Illinois Press.

Stewart, F.L. 1989. "Seasonal Movements of Indians in Acadia as Evidenced by Historical Documents and Vertebrate Faunal Remains from Archaeological Sites." *Man in the Northeast* no. 38: 55–77.

Stewart, F.L. 2009. "Abenaki Dietary Change and Continuity during the Contact-Period in Maine." In *Painting the Past with a Broad Brush. Papers in Honour of James Valliere Wright*, edited by D.L. Keenlyside and J.-L. Pilon, 37–64. Mercury Series Archaeology Paper 170. Hull, PQ: Canadian Museum of Civilization.

Stewart, K.D. 1984. *Oyster*. Underworld World Series. Ottawa: Fisheries and Oceans Canada.

Stoddard, T. 1950. "Northeastern Archaeological Survey: Second Annual Report." MS on file at the Robert S. Peabody Foundation for Archaeology, Phillips Academy, Andover, MA.

Stoddard, T., and R.H. Dyson, Jr. 1956. "Exploratory Excavations at the Graham Site in Eastern New Brunswick." MS on file at the Robert S. Peabody Foundation for Archaeology, Phillips Academy, Andover, MA.

Stokes, P. 1991. "Feasts in the Archaeological Record." In *Oxford Symposium on Food & Cookery 1990, Proceedings*, edited by H. Walker, 198–201. London: Prospect Books.

Storck, P.L., and A.E. Spiess. 1994. "The Significance of New Faunal Identifications Attributed to an Early Paleoindian (Gainey Complex) Occupation at the Udora Site, Ontario, Canada." *American Antiquity* 59, no. 1: 121–42.

Stright, M.J. 1990. "Archaeological Sites on the North American Continental Shelf." *Geological Society of America, Centennial Special* 4: 439–65.

Struiver, M., and H.W. Borns, Jr. 1975. "Late Quaternary Marine Invasion of Maine: Its Chronology and Associated Crustal Movement." *Geographical Society of America Bulletin* 86: 99–104.

Stuckenrath, R., Jr. 1966. "The Debert Archaeological Project, Nova Scotia: Radiocarbon Dating." *Quaternaria* no. 8: 75–80.

Suttie, B.D. 2005. "Archaic Period Archaeological Research in the Interior of Southwestern New Brunswick." MA thesis, University of New Brunswick.

Suttie, B.D. 2006. "Mejipkei and Taboogul Mejipkei: Fit Features on the Miramichi." MS on file, Archaeological Services Unit, Fredericton, NB.

Suttie, B.D. 2007. "A Contribution to the Archaic Period in Southwestern New Brunswick." *Occasional Papers in Northeastern Archaeology* no. 16. St. John's: Copetown Press.

Suttie, B.D. 2010. "The Bristol/Shiktehawk Site — A Historical Background Study and Analysis of the George Frederick Clarke Cache." MS on file, Archaeological Services, Fredericton, NB.

Suttie, B.D. 2013. "Fortuitous Finds and the Archaic Period in Southwestern New Brunswick." In *Underground New Brunswick: Stories of Archaeology*, edited by P. Erickson and J. Fowler, 1–6. Halifax: Nimbus Publishing.

Suttie, B.D. 2014a. "Internal Research Activity Report: Stable Isotope Signatures derived from Encrustations on Low Fired Precontact Ceramic and Steatite Vessel Fragments from New Brunswick." MS on file, Archaeological Services, Fredericton.

Suttie, B.D. 2014b. "Late Paleoindian Projectile Point from Southeastern New Brunswick." *Field Notes: Newsletter of the New Brunswick Archaeological Society* 8, no. 1: 9.

Suttie, B.D., and M.A. Nicholas 2012. "Final Technical Report on 2011 Test Excavations at BgDq-39, BgDq-40, BgD-4 and BgDq-38 in the Vicinity of Pennfield, NB." MS on file, Archaeological Services, Fredericton, NB.

Suttie, B.D., M.A. Nicholas, J. Jeandron, G. Aylesworth, A. Brzezicki, and A. Hamilton. 2013. "Recent Research on Four Sites Spanning 13,000 years from Southwestern New Brunswick, Canada." *Canadian Archaeological Association Newsletter* 31, no. 1: 69–77.

Taché, K. 2005. "Explaining Vinette 1 Pottery Variability: The View from the Batsican Site, Quebec." *Canadian Journal of Archaeology* 29, no. 2: 165–233.

Taché, K. 2011a. *Structure and Regional Diversity of the Meadowood Interaction Sphere*. Museum of Anthropology, Memoir 48. Ann Arbor: University of Michigan.

Taché, K. 2011b. "New Perspectives on Meadowood Trade Items." *American Antiquity* 76, no. 1: 41–79.

Taché, K., and O.E. Craig. 2015. "Cooperative Harvesting of Aquatic Resources and the Beginning of Pottery Production in Northeastern North America." *Antiquity* 89: 177–90.

Taché, K., D. White, and S. Seelen. 2008. "Potential Functions of Vinette 1 Pottery: Complementary Use of Archaeological and Pyrolysis GC/MC Data." *Archaeology of Eastern North America* 36: 63–90.

Talalay, L., D.R. Keller, and P.J. Munson. 1984. "Hickory Nuts, Walnuts, Butternuts, and Hazelnuts: Observations and Experiments Relevant to Their Aboriginal Exploitation in Eastern North America." In *Experiments and Observations of Aboriginal Wild Plant Utilization in Eastern North America*, edited by P.J. Munson, 338–59. Indiana Historical Society, Prehistory Research Series 6, no. 2.

Tapper, B. 2020. "Exploring Relationality: Perspectives on the Research Narratives of the Rock Art of the Algonquian-Speaking Peoples of Central and Eastern Canada." *Journal of Archaeological Method and Theory* 27: 723–44. doi: 10.1007/s10816-020-09467-6.

Tapper, B. 2021. "*Kwipek, Mi'kma'ki: Pemiaq Aqq Pilua'sik Ta'n Tel Amalilitu'n Kuntewiktuk* / Continuity and Change in Mi'kmaw Petroglyphs at Bedford, Nova Scotia, Canada." In *Ontologies of Rock Art: Images, Relational Approaches and Indigenous Knowledge*, edited by O. Moro Abadía and M. Porr, 374–94. New York: Routledge.

Tapper, B., and O. Moro Abadia. 2021. "Interpreting Scenes in the Rock Art of the Canadian Maritimes." In *Making Scenes: Global Perspectives on Scenes in Rock Art*, edited by I. Davidson and A. Nowell, 295–309. New York: Berghahn Books.

Tapper, B., O. Moro Abadia, and D. Zawadzka. 2020. "Representations and Meaning in Rock Art: The Case of Algonquian Rock Images." *World Archaeology* 52, no. 3: 458–71. doi: 10.1080/00438243.2021.1897660.

Taylor, C.A. 2020. "Paleogeography, Sea-Level Change and the Peopling of the Maritimes: An Archaeological Perspective." PhD diss., Dalhousie University.

Thierry, É. 2004. "A Creation of Champlain's The Order of Good Cheer." In *Champlain: The Birth of French America*, edited by R. Litalien and D. Vaugeois, translated by K. Roth, 135–42. Montreal and Kingston: McGill-Queen's University Press.

Thompson, J.P. 1974. "Stratigraphy and Geochemistry of the Scots Bay Formation, Nova Scotia." MSc thesis, Acadia University.

Tremblay, R. 1997. "Présence du Noyer cendré dans l'estuaire du Saint-Laurent durant la préhistoire." *Récherches Amérindiennes au Québec* 27, nos. 3-4: 99-106.

Trigger, B.G., ed. 1986. *Native Shell Mounds of North America: Early Studies*. New York: Garland.

Trigger, B.G. 1989. *A History of Archaeological Thought*. Cambridge: Cambridge University Press.

Tuck, J.A. 1975. "The Northeastern Maritime Continuum: 8000 Years of Cultural Development in the Far Northeast." *Arctic Anthropology* 12, no. 2: 139-47.

Tuck, J.A. 1978a. "Archaic Burial Ceremonialism in the 'Far Northeast'." In *Essays in Northeastern Anthropology in Memory of Marion E. White*, edited by W. Engelbrecht and D. Grayson, 67-77. Occasional Publications in Northeastern Anthropology no. 5.

Tuck, J.A. 1978b. "Regional Cultural Developments 3000 B.C. to 300 B.C." In *Handbook of North American Indians, Northeast*, Vol. 15, edited by B.C. Trigger, 28-43. Washington, DC: Smithsonian Institution.

Tuck, J.A. 1984. *Maritime Provinces Prehistory*. Ottawa: National Museums of Canada.

Tuck, J.A. 1991. "The Archaic Period in the Maritime Provinces." In *Prehistoric Archaeology in the Maritime Provinces: Past and Present Research*, edited by M. Deal and S. Blair, 29-57. Reports in Archaeology no. 8. Fredericton, NB: Council of Maritime Premiers.

Tuck, J.A., and R. Grenier. 1989. *Red Bay, Labrador: World Whaling Capital A.D. 1550-1600*. St. John's: Atlantic Archaeology.

Turgeon, L. 1998. "French Fishers, Fur Traders, and Amerindians during the Sixteenth Century: History and Archaeology." *William and Mary Quarterly* 55, no. 4: 585-610.

Turgeon, L. 2004. "The French in New England before Champlain." In *Champlain: The Birth of French America*, edited by R. Litalien and D. Vaugeois, translated by K. Roth, 98-112. Montreal and Kingston: McGill-Queen's University Press.

Turnbull, C.J. 1974a. "Old Mission Point 1973: Report for an Archaeological Survey of Canada Salvage Contract." MS on file, Archaeological Survey of Canada. Ottawa: National Museum of Man.

Turnbull, C.J. 1974b. "The Second Fluted Point from New Brunswick." *Man in the Northeast* 7: 109-10.

Turnbull, C.J. 1976. "The Augustine Site: A Mound from the Maritimes." *Archaeology of Eastern North America* 4: 50–62.

Turnbull, C.J. 1977. *The State of Archaeology in the Maritimes*. Reports in Archaeology no. 1. Fredericton, NB: Council of Maritime Premiers.

Turnbull, C.J. 1978. "2,000-Year-Old Indian Heritage Revealed: The Augustine Burial Mound." *New Brunswick* 3, nos. 2–3: 16–23.

Turnbull, C.J. 1988a. "Reflections on a Ground Slate Bayonet Fragment from the Tantramar Marsh, Upper Bay of Fundy." *Canadian Journal of Archaeology* 12: 87–107.

Turnbull, C.J. 1988b. "The McKinlay Collection: Another Middlesex Tradition Component from Red Bank, Northumberland County, New Brunswick." *New Brunswick Manuscripts in Archaeology* no. 17. Fredericton, NB: Archaeology Branch, Department of Tourism, Recreation and Heritage.

Turnbull, C.J. 2003. "Foreword: The Road to Jemseg." In *Wolastoqiyik Ajemseg: The People of the Beautiful River at Jemseg*. Vol. 1: *Important Stories and Spoken Histories*, edited by K. Perley and S. Blair, ix–xi. New Brunswick Manuscripts in Archaeology 36E. Fredericton, NB: Archaeological Services, Heritage Branch, Culture and Sport Secretariat.

Turnbull, C.J., and P. Allen. 1978. "More Paleo-Indian Points from New Brunswick." *Man in the Northeast* nos. 15–16: 147–53.

Turnbull, C.J., and P. Allen. 1988. "Review of *Maritime Provinces Prehistory* by James A. Tuck." *Canadian Journal of Archaeology* 12: 250–60.

Turnbull, C.J., and D.W. Black. 1988. "The Slate Ulu from White Horse Island." In *Bliss Revisited: Preliminary Accounts of the Bliss Islands Archaeology Project, Phase II*, edited by D.W. Black, 73–79. Manuscripts in Archaeology 24E. Fredericton: New Brunswick Department of Tourism, Recreation and Heritage.

Tuross, N., M.L. Fogel, L. Newsom, and G.H. Doran. 1994. "Subsistence in the Florida Archaic: The Stable-Isotope and Archaeobotanical Evidence from the Windover Site." *American Antiquity* 59, no. 2: 288–303.

Tyzzer, E.E. 1943. "Animal Tooth Implements from Shell Heaps of Maine." *American Antiquity* 8: 354–62.

Union of Nova Scotia Indians (UNSI). 2000. "Everyone Welcome to Join Mi'kmaq Treaty Day Celebrations Sept. 30th and Oct. 1st." News release. http://www.unsi.ns.ca/treatyday99.html.

University of Maine at Farmington, Archaeology Research Center (UMF/ARC). 2002. *N'tolonapemk: An Ancient Native American Village on Meddybemps Lake, Maine*. Pamphlet produced by the University of Maine at Farmington

Archaeology Research Center. Bangor, ME: United States Environmental Protection Agency and the Maine Historic Preservation Commission.

Varley, C. 1999. "Atlantic Region." *Canadian Archaeological Association Newsletter* 19, no. 1: 43–51.

Wake, W. 1995. "Prince Edward Island's Early Natural History Society." *The Island Magazine* 37 (Spring/Summer): 27–33.

Walker, W. 1996. "Wabanaki 'Little People' and Passamaquoddy Social Control." *Papers of the 27th Algonquian Conference, 1995*, University of Manitoba, Winnipeg, 353–61.

Wallace, B.L. 1989. "Selective Exploitation of Shellfish at Rustico Island, Prince Edward Island." Paper presented at the annual meeting of the Canadian Archaeological Society, Fredericton, NB.

Wallace, B.L. 1991. "L'Anse aux Meadows: Gateway to Vinland." *Acta Archaeologica* 61: 166–97.

Wallace, B.L. 2000. "The Viking Settlement at L'Anse aux Meadows." In *Vikings: The North Atlantic Saga*, edited by W.W. Fitzhugh and E.I. Ward, 208–16. Washington, DC: Smithsonian Institution Press.

Wallace, B.L. 2006. *Westward Vikings: The Saga of L'Anse aux Meadows*. St. John's: Historic Sites Association of Newfoundland and Labrador.

Wallace, B.L. 2018. "Finding Vinland." *Canada's History* (Feb./Mar.): 20–29.

Wallis, W.D., and R.S. Wallis. 1955. *The Micmac Indians of Eastern Canada*. Minneapolis: University of Minnesota Press.

Warman, C. 1986. Untitled Report on Macroplant Remains from Five Sites on the Bliss Islands, Letang Harbour, N.B.: BgDq-4; BgDq-6; BgDq-7; BgDr-60; BgDr-62. MS on file, Department of Archaeology, Memorial University of Newfoundland.

Watson, L.W. 1899a. "The Natural History and Antiquarian Society of Prince Edward Island." *Bulletin of the Natural History Society of New Brunswick* 17: 180–81.

Watson, L.W. 1899b. "The Natural History and Antiquarian Society of Prince Edward Island." *Bulletin of the Natural History Society of New Brunswick* 18: 261–62.

Weatherbee, W., D. van Proosdij, and J. Fowler. 2020. "Microfossils, Remote Sensing, and GIS for Proxy-dating Coastal Archaeological Sites and Landscapes: A Case from Minas Basin, Bay of Fundy, Canada." MS on file, Permit A2020NS068. Halifax: Nova Scotia Museum.

Webster, J.C. 1945. "Introduction." In *The History and Development of the New Brunswick Museum (1842–1945)*, by W.A. Squires, 4–6. Administrative Series no. 2. Saint John: Publications of the New Brunswick Museum.

Wells, B. 1987. "Botanical Remains." In *Archaeological Investigations at the Low Terrace Site (BaDg-2) Indian Gardens, Queen's County, Nova Scotia*, edited by M. Deal, J. Corkum, D. Kemp, J. McClair, S. McIlquham, A. Murchison, and B. Wells, 166–73. Curatorial Report 63: 149–228. Halifax: Nova Scotia Museum.

Whitehead, R.H. 1987. *Plant Fibre Textiles from the Hopps Site: BkCp-1*. Curatorial Report no. 59. Halifax: Nova Scotia Museum.

Whitehead, R.H. 1991. "The Protohistoric Period in the Maritime Provinces." In *Prehistory of the Maritime Provinces: Past and Present Research*, edited by M. Deal and S. Blair, 227–258. Fredericton, NB: Council of Maritime Premiers.

Whitehead, R.H. 1992. "A New Micmac Petroglyph Site." *The Occasional* 13, no. 1: 7–12.

Whitehead, R.H. 1993. *Nova Scotia: The Protohistoric Period (1500–1630)*. Curatorial Report no. 75. Halifax: Nova Scotia Museum.

Whitehead, R.H. 2006. *Stories from the Six Worlds: Micmac Legends*. Halifax: Nimbus Publishing.

Whitehead, R.H., L.A. Pavlish, R.M. Farquhar, and R.G.B. Hancock. 1998. "Analysis of Copper-based Metals from Three Mi'kmaq Sites in Nova Scotia." *North American Archaeologist* 19, no. 4: 279–92.

Will, R. 2012. "Site 117.39: A Probable Middle Archaic Chipped Stone Tool Workshop and Cache Location, Rockwood, Maine." *Maine Archaeological Society* 52, no. 2: 27–56.

Will, R. 2017. "The North Wind Site (7.11)." *Maine Archaeological Society* 57, no. 1: 3–20.

Willey, G.R., and P. Phillips. 1958. *Method and Theory in American Archaeology*. Chicago: University of Chicago Press.

Williamson, J. 2019. "Photogrammetric Surveys in the Exploits River Valley." *Provincial Archaeology Office Annual Review 2019*. 18: 227–33.

Willoughby, C.C. 1935. *Antiquities of the New England Indians*. Peabody Museum of American Archaeology and Ethnology. Cambridge, MA: Harvard University Press.

Wilson, D. 1851. *The Archaeology and Prehistoric Annals of Scotland*. London: Macmillan.

Wilson, D. 1855. "Hints for the Formation of a Canadian Collection of Ancient Crania." *Canadian Journal* 3, no. 15: 345–47.

Wilson, D. 1862. *Prehistoric Man: Researches into the Origin of Civilization in the Old and New Worlds*. London: Macmillan.

Wintemberg, W.J. 1913. Untitled document: Ground Stone Points: Quebec, Ungave, New Brunswick, Nova Scotia, Cape Breton, Prince Edward Island and Newfoundland. 1. QC. 2. NB. Archives, Archaeological Documents, Box 62, File 5. Ottawa: Canadian Museum of Civilization.

Wintemberg, W.J. 1914. "Archaeological Work on the Atlantic Coast, 1913." *Summary Report of the Geological Survey of Canada, Department of Mines for the Calendrical Year of 1913*. Anthropological Division, Sessional Paper no. 26: 385–86. Ottawa: Geological Survey of Canada.

Wintemberg, W.J. 1937. "Artifacts from Presumed Ancient Graves in Eastern New Brunswick." *Transactions of the Royal Society of Canada*, Section II: 205–09.

Wintemberg, W.J. 1942. "The Geographic Distribution of Aboriginal Pottery in Canada." *American Antiquity* 8: 129–41.

Wintemberg, W.J. 1943. "The Geographical Distribution of Aboriginal Pottery in Canada." *Minnesota Archaeologist* 9: 46–58. (Reprint of *American Antiquity* paper with editorial comments).

Wiseman, F.M. 2001. *The Voice of the Dawn: An Autohistory of the Abenaki Nation*. Hanover, NH: University Press of New England.

Wiseman, F.M. 2006. *Reclaiming the Ancestors. Decolonizing a Taken Prehistory of the Far Northeast*. Hanover, NH: University Press of New England.

Wiseman, F.M., and R. Tayler. 2018. *Seven Sisters. Ancient Seeds and Food Systems of the Wabanaki People and the Chesapeake Bay Region*. Scarborough, ON: Earth Haven Learning Centre.

Wolff, C.B., and T.M. Urban. 2014. "Beneath the Surface: A Geophysical Survey of the Multicomponent Stock Cove Site (CkAl-3) of Southeastern Newfoundland." *North Atlantic Archaeology* 3: 125–33.

Woolsey, C.A. 2013. "'For My Indian Friends': The George Frederick Clarke Collection and Its Place in New Brunswick's Archaeological History." In *Underground New Brunswick: Stories of Archaeology*, edited by P. Erickson and J. Fowler, 37–46. Halifax: Nimbus Publishing.

Woolsey, C.A. 2017. "A Historical Approach to Shifting Technologies of Ceramic Manufacture at Gaspereau Lake, Kings County, Nova Scotia." PhD diss., McMaster University.

Woolsey, C.A. 2018. "Shifting Priorities Apparent in Middle and Late Woodland Ceramics from Nova Scotia." *North American Archaeologist* 39, no. 4: 260–91.

Woolsey, C.A. 2020. "A Direct-Dated Ceramic AMS Sequence from the Gaspereau Lake Reservoir Site Complex, Maine-Maritimes Region, Northeastern North America." *Radiocarbon*: 1–19. DOI:10.1017/RDC.2019.149.

Woolsey, C. 2022. "The Changing Role of Ceramics during the Woodland Period in the Far Northeast: Evidence from Some Large Ceramic Assemblages in New Brunswick and Nova Scotia. In *The Far Northeast: 3000 BP to Contact*, edited by K.R. Holyoke and M.G. Hrynick, 285–314. Mercury Series, Archaeological Paper no. 181. Ottawa: Canadian Museum of History and University of Ottawa Press.

Worsaae, J.J.A. 1849. *The Primeval Antiquities of Denmark*. Translated by W.J. Thoms. London: Parker.

Wright, J.V. 1985. "The Development of Prehistory in Canada, 1935–1985." *American Antiquity* 50, no. 2: 421–33.

Wright, J.V. 1995. *A History of the Native People of Canada. Vol. 1 (10,000–1000 B.C.)*. Ottawa: Canadian Museum of Civilization.

Wright, J.V. 1999. *A History of the Native People of Canada. Vol. 2 (1000 B.C.–A.D. 500)*. Ottawa: Canadian Museum of Civilization.

Wyman, J. 1868. "An Account of Some Kjoekkenmoeddings, or Shell-Heaps, in Maine and Massachusetts." *American Naturalist* 1: 561–84.

Younging, G. 2018. *Elements of Indigenous Style: A Guide for Writing by and about Indigenous Peoples*. Edmonton: Brush Education.

Zawadzka, D. 2019. "Rock Art and Animism in the Canadian Shield." *Time and Mind* 12, no. 2: 79–94.

INDEX

(Page numbers in italics denote figures.)

Abbe Museum (Maine), 4, 13
Adena, *see* Middlesex Early Woodland
adze, *see* ground stone adzes
Algonquian-speaking peoples: in the Maritimes, 2; rock art tradition, 211–12; origin of word wampum, 271
Allen, P., 83, 116, 121, 145, 164, 189, 203; repatriation of human remains, 17; collaboration, 59; Oxbow site, *202*, 236
Amherst Shore site, *98*, 114, 116
archaeological cultures, 68, 72–73, 75, 94, 145, 164, 249
archaeological record, 5, 7, 12, 63–65, 68, 74, 95, 137, 145, 173, 181, 216, 269; defined, 63–64
archaeological sites: defined, xvii; as cultural property, 7; Indigenous stewardship, 10–11; mitigation, 12; monitoring and protection of, 12, 51, 55, 60; threats of destruction, 68, 272; classification of, 89
archaeology: and Indigenous history, 1–2; stages of research in the Maritimes, 24; graduate programs, 24, 57
Archaic Period, *28*; scarcity of early sites, 129–31; physical setting, 131–34; Archaic to Woodland transition, 171–80; summary, 181–83; *see also* Early/Middle Archaic peoples; Late Archaic peoples; individual sites from Figure 28
art (Indigenous), 84–85; *see also* incised decoration; petroglyphs; textiles
artifact: defined, xvii
assemblage: concept, 75
Assembly of Nova Scotia Mi'kmaq Chiefs (Maw-lukutijik Saqmaq), 11
Atalay, S.: *Indigenous Archaeology*, 5
atlatl, *see* spear thrower
attribute analysis: for lithics and ceramics, 113
Augustine Mound site, 12, *52*, *186*, 195–203, 214
avocational archaeologists, 49, 51, 58, 60, 92, 117, 194, 200
Avonport site, 158, *248*, 255, 270–71
axe, *see* ground stone axes

INDEX

Bailey, L.W. (naturalist period), 25, 40, 59, 71–72, 86

Bain site, *130*, 152

Baird, S.F. (naturalist period), 38–39, 60, 86

Basin Head site, *98*, 121

baskets (basketry), 36, 93, 188, 195, 203, 208, 236; *see also* textiles

Basques, 251–52

Bay of Fundy, 239–41; tidal activity, 132; coastal erosion, 10, *23*; productivity, 130, 218; travel route, 159; lithic sources, 29, 37, 86, 220–21, 227, 236; copper sources, 196–97, 219; absence of oysters in Woodland, 53; drowned sites in, 58, 133

bayonets (slate), *143*, 150, 153–54, *154*, 156, 159–60, *160*, *161*, 162–63; with textile impressions, *151*; in Archaic trade, 182, 275

Bear River site, 16, *130*, *186*, 199, 228

Beausejour Beach site, *130*, *155*, 156–58, 165, 168

beaver (*Castor canadensis*): Palaeo, 106, 108, 126; Archaic, 137–38, 147, 150, 182; Woodland, 32, 42, 44, 188, 192, 199, 203, 216, 239; Contact, 36, 260–65; as clothing, 188; taboos relating to, 80; *see also* fur trade

beaver, extinct giant (*Castoroides ohioensis*), 79, 81, 84, 132

Bedford Barrens (Kwipek) site, 212, *248*

Betts, M., 145, 166; collaboration, 15; shell midden studies, 75, 82, 91, 277–78; Pierce-Embree site, 99, 117; Port Joli site, 70, 75, 90, 209–10, 213, 219, 234; shark teeth in cosmology, 200

Biard, P. (seventeenth-century chronicler), 84, 228, 253, 263

bifaces (projectile point preforms or knives): Palaeo, 117–18, *118*, 123; Archaic, 137, 140, 145, *146*, 147, 156, 167, 170, *170*, 177, 179; Woodland, 44, 189, 191–93, 196, 198, 200, 202–03, 208, 226, 231, *243*; from underwater sites, 132–33

Big Clearwater site, *130*, 149

bipolar core technique: Palaeo, 112; Woodland, 226

birchbark: construction, 208, 244; canoes, 85, 153, 166, 244, 268

birdstones (spear thrower weights), 189, 192, 194–95; *see also* spear throwers

Black, D.: zooarchaeology, 5, 57, 70, 75, 91–92, 167, 216–19; shell midden studies, 71, 89, 91, 93, 158, 208, 234; lithic studies, 29, 39, 132–34, 180, 220, 227, 231; Rum Beach site, 173–74

black bear (*Ursus americana*): Archaic, 137, 148, 165, 168, 182; Woodland, 32, 42, 45, 199, 216, 239; Contact, 260–63; in cosmology, 247; bear grease and dreams, 50; in "The Prophecy" story, 247

Blackman Stream site, *98*, 134, 137

Blair, S., 57, 227, 253; collaboration, 6, 12; Saint John River, 174, 180; Jemseg site, 12, 189; Metepenagiag complex, 195

block-end tubular (smoking) pipes,

198–203, *201*, 245
boating technology, 234
Bob site, 185, *186*
Bocabec site, 18, 39, *41*, 42–43, *43*, 53, *186*
bone, tooth, and antler technology:
  Palaeo, 97, 112–13, 126; Archaic,
  135–36, 139–40, 145, 150, *154*, 159,
  166–68; Woodland, 44–45, 53, *59*,
  192, 199, 217, *217*, 242; Contact,
  267; extraction of bone grease, 82;
  cut marks on bone, 92
Bonnichsen, R.D., 108, 116–17, 121
Bordon site designation system, 55
Boswell site, 15, 64, *130*, 149, 163, 169–75, *170–72*, 180, 183, 276
Boucher site, *186*, *187*, 198–99, 203
Bourque, B.J., 10, 31, 108, 139, 144, 273;
  Moorehead phase, 145–49, 151–53,
  159–61; Transitional Archaic, 163–67; Turner Farm site, 153–54, 156,
  167, 185; precontact trade, 152–53,
  275; Contact trade, 250–51, 254,
  266
bow-and-arrow technology, 26, 29, 31,
  37, 81, 247, 269, 277; introduction,
  244, 276
Boyleston Fish Weir site, *130*, 166
broadpoints (or broadspears), 163
Bull Brook site, *98*, 108–09, 113
burial traditions: Early/Middle Archaic, 139, 155, 181; Late Archaic, 47,
  144–46, 151–53, 158–63, 182, 275;
  Transitional Archaic, 163–67, 182–83; Meadowood (Early Woodland), 13, 17, 49, 189, 191–94, 197–98, 245, 276; Middlesex (Adena),
  16, 26, 37, 195–203, 214, 245, 276;
Middle/Late Woodland, 16, 34, 94,
  209, 215, 245; Contact, 26, 33, 40,
  49, 51, 92–93, 214–15, 254, 256, 270
Burke, A.L.: lithic studies, 77, 79, 170,
  188–89, 207–08, 220–21, 236
Burnt Bone Beach site, *248*, 253–54,
  254, 271
butternut (*Juglans cinerea*): Woodland,
  188, 213, 240, 266; Contact, 250,
  266
Byers, D.S. (early professional period),
  30, 50–51, 60, 73–74, 137, 151; Debert site, 52–53, 110; Niven site, 159
Cabot, J. (European explorer), 249
cache blades (Early Woodland), 189,
  191, *191*, 194–96, 200; purpose of,
  189
caches (of artifacts): Archaic, 156, 165;
  Woodland, 57, 192; Contact, 36,
  255; *see also* cache blades
cal BP (calibrated radiocarbon dates
  before present): defined, 76
Campbell, J.A.: Boswell site, 163, 169,
  171, *171*
Canadian Archaeological Association
  (CAA), 56, 60; ethical principles,
  6–7, 59
Canadian Archaeological Radiocarbon
  Database (CARD), 77
Canal Beach site, *130*, 163, 167–68
Canavoy site, *130*, 176, *186*
canoes, 80, 82, 87, 139; Archaic, 152,
  166, 170; dugout, 152–53, 166, 170,
  274–75; birchbark, 42, 85, 153, 166,
  208, 214, 234, 268, 275; portage
  routes, 87, 138; on *wikhikons*, 85;
  in rock art, 211; in cosmology, 212

Cap-de-Bon-Désir site, *130*, 140
Cape d'Or site, *186*, 196–97, 219, 223, 227, 231
Cape Spear site, *98*, 113, 121
caribou (*Rangifer tarandus L.*), 80; Palaeo, 101, 105–10, 126–27, 273; Archaic, 150; Woodland, 116; Contact, 260–63; bone grease and marrow from, 82
ceramic (or pottery) technology, 49, *67*, 185; adoption, 185, 187; no longer used, 268; *see also* individual decorative styles Ceramic Period, *see* Woodland Period
Ceramic Period (CP) chronology (Petersen and Sanger), 54, 75, 77–78, 210
ceramic residues, 44, 70, 187, 206
Champlain, S. de (seventeenth-century chronicler), 256–70
Champlain Sea, 104, 106, 123, 126, 273
chert: relationship between quartz-based lithics, 222–23; lithic source areas, 227–31; *see also* lithic technology
chipped and ground adze blades (celts): Adena (Middlesex), 170, 188, 198, 200–02, 219
Citadel Hill conference (1959), 51, 60
clam, soft-shell (*Mya arenaria L.*): in shell middens, 14, 31, 42–45, 132, 144, 153, 158, 164, 218–19; clam-processing, 210, 219; as protein source, 158, 219; Contact, 263
Clam Cove site, *94*, *186*, *207*, 223, 226
Clarke, G.F. (avocational archaeologist), 49, 60, 92, 149, 169, 192, 200

climate: reconstruction of past, 1, 69, 126, 131, 164, 239; change over time, 24, 68, 79; effect on archaeological fieldwork, 24
Clovis (Palaeo) people, 75, 107, 126
coastal sites: erosion of, 10, 12, 16, *23*, 39, 53, 68, 173; surveys of, 58, 75, 232; submergence of, 126, 129, 131, 134, 169, 273, 274, 277; *see also* underwater sites
cod, Atlantic (*Gadus morhua*): Archaic, 150, 154, 164–65, 182; Woodland, 42, 218, 234–35, 239; Contact, 263, 265, 276; line sinkers in cod-fishing, 156; tomcod (*Microgadus tomcod*), 104
collaboration (between archaeologists and Indigenous peoples), xix, 5–6, 12–15, 59, 61, 112, 278
collections (of Indigenous artifacts): private, 9, 26, 33, 36–40, 48–49, 64, 99, 110, 116, 119, 122, 124, 140, 150, 169, 189, 199, 244, 273; and the establishment of museums in the Maritimes, 26–29, 49, 51, 53–55
colonialism: colonialist attitude in archaeology, xvii; impact on Indigenous peoples, 233, 247–48, 253
comparative ethnography, 72
complex, 145; defined, 76; site, 99, 110–12, 190, *190*, 273; fish weir, 166, 192; lithic (projectile point), 134, 136, 163; burial, 139, 198, 274
Confederacy of Mainland Mi'kmaq, 14, 81, 112
Contact Period: the prophecy, 247–48; nature of contact, 248–49; Norse,

250–51; French, Basques, and Portuguese, 251–56; French and Mi'kmaw feasting traditions, 256–67; colonial period, 267–72; *see also* sites from Figure 68
contiguous habitat model, 238, *238*
copper: sources, 37, 67, 189, 196–97, 219–20, *228*, 231; native copper industry, 197; awls, 189, 191, *191*, 194, 219, 276; kettles, 26, *72*, 82, 219, 251, 254–55, 270; knives, 34, 219; beads, 45, 47, 67, 167, 176, 196, 199–203, 251, 270; tinkling cones, 253, 271
"Copper Kettle Burial Tradition" (Contact Period), 254; examples, 26, 40, 92, 254, 270
cord-wrapped stick pottery decoration, 44, 204, *205*
corn (*Zea mays*), 210, 215–16, 240, 277
Council of Maritime Premiers, 56
Cow Point site, 16, *130*, *141*, 153, 159–60, *160*, *161*, 162–63, 275
cryptocrystalline lithics, 221–22, *222*, 231
cultural ecology, 74
cultural resource management (CRM), 61, 69, 112, 277–78
culture (Indigenous), xix, 19, 83, 87, 179, 231, 267; concept, 8, 11; archaeological culture, 68, 72, 75, 164
culture area, 72–73
culture change: models of, 70, 75
culture history, 68, 73–74, 77, 244
"dates as data" approach, 77
Davidson Cove site, 19, 23, *186*, 221, 224–27, *225*, 230
Davis, S.A., 56–59, 87, 89, 160, 165, 167,

185; coastal erosion studies, 58, 75; Belmont site, 99, *111*, 110–17, 120, 126; Bain site, 152; Tusket Falls, 169–70; Rafter Lake, 193; Skora site, 16, 200–01; contiguous habitat model, 238, *238*
Debert/Belmont complex, 99, 110–12, 273
Debert/Belmont sites, 52, 52–53, 60, 74, *98*, 98–99, 105–17, *111*, 126, 223, 227, 273
deer, whitetailed (*Odocoileus virginianus*): Palaeo, 105; Archaic, 135, 137, 147–48, 150, 153, 164–65, 182; Woodland, 42, 53, 82, 216, 234; Contact, 276
Deer Island sites, *130*, 133–34, 165, 167
dendrochronology (tree-ring dating), 76, 153
dentate stamped pottery decoration, 44, 204, *205*
Denys, N. (seventeenth-century chronicler), 80, 84, 255, 260–61, 265–66
Dickason, M.B.: Indigenous studies, 21, 79, 84, 95
Diggity site, 93, *130*, 177, *204*
Dincauze, D.F.: Palaeo studies, 106–07; Transitional Archaic, 165, 177–78; Neville site, 134, 137; Boyleston Fish Weir site, 166
direct historical approach, 87, 231
disease, 15, 159; introduction by Europeans, 233, 253
DNA analysis, 17
dog (*Canis familiaris*): hunting, 80, 216–17; burials, 153, 192, 199; and feasting, 197, 216–17, 265–66

domesticates: animals, 262–63; plants, 251, 262–63

drill: Palaeo, 112, 123; Archaic, 163, 166–69, *170*, 177, 182, 244; Woodland, 189, 191, 276

dugout canoe, 150, 152–53, 166, 274–75

dwellings (structures), 89–90; Palaeo, 110; Archaic, 138, 153, 166, 183; Woodland, 32, 41–44, 54, 65, 193, 208–09, 234, 245; colonial period, 50; gendered spaces, 209

Early/Middle Archaic peoples: Maine and New England, 134–36; Gulf of Maine Archaic Tradition, 136–39; Maritimes, 139–44; *see also* individual sites from Figure 28

Early Palaeo peoples: Clovis connection, 107; society, 107–08, settlement and subsistence, 108–09; projectile point styles, 113–22; *see also* individual sites from Figure 21

Early Professional Period, 24, 45–52, *46*

Early Woodland peoples: Meadowood, 189–97; Middlesex (Adena), 198–202; *see also* individual sub-periods and sites from Figure 47

Eddington Bend site, *186*, 233

eel (*Anguilla rostrata*), 91, 218; rights and title, 8; Archaic, 138, 181; Woodland, 188, 192, 206, 237; postcontact, 84

eel weir sites, *130*, 169, *186*, 192, 196

Eggemoggin Reach site, *248*, 269

Embden site, *186*, 212

endblades (Dorset Palaeoeskimo), 123, 125

end scraper: Archaic, 169, *193*; Woodland, 226, 231, *243*; *see also* scrapers; side scrapers

environmental change: and technology, 71, 94, 136; and human behaviour, 73; and settlement and mobility, 87, 106, 164; and shellfish exploitation, 209–10

Environmental Protection Agency (US), 13

Eqpahak (formerly Savage) Island site, xvii, 40, *186*

Erskine, J.S. (avocational archaeologist), 55, 60, 110, 116, 119, 149, 207, 241; site surveys, 52–53; shell midden studies, 51, 92, 218, 265–66; Port Joli site, 51, 210; Bear River site, 16; Gaspereau Lake site, 117, 142–43, 168

E'se'get Archaeological Project, 15

Esker site, *98*, 119

Etchemin, 252

ethnohistoric record (evidence), 3, 18, 87, 209–10, 230–31, 249, 266, 277

Europeans, 54; early contact with, 1–2, 21, 74, 83–84, 87–89, 211, 231–33, 247–51, 269; trade with, 67, 217–19, 235, 252–53, 269–71; introduction of diseases, 253–56; foodways and feasting, 256–67

exchange (trade), 67, 86; Palaeo, 110, 122, 127; Archaic, 152–53, 173–74; Woodland, 187–89, 194–99, 212, 215, 220, 230, 236, 240, 244; Contact, 67, 89, 218–19, 232–35, 240–41, 245, 251–56, 266, 271, 275–77

fabric-impressed pottery, 44, 54, 185, 192, 214, 252–53, 276; *see also*

Vinette 1

family units: Palaeo, 106-07, 110, 122, 126-27; Woodland, 219, 230-36, 253; Contact, 249

feasting: in oral traditions, 83, 261; pottery and, 83, 187-88, 244, 267; caches and, 194; dogs and, 197, 216-17; lodges for, 267; comparison of French and Mi'kmaw, 252, 257-67

fishing: Palaeo, 122, 273; Archaic, 134, 142, 147-48, 151-56, 164-65, 178, 182-83, 274-75; Woodland, 194-97, 211, 218, 235; Contact, 244, 251; Indigenous rights and, 8

fishing technology: fishhooks, 135, *154*, 199; barbed points, 29, 36, 150, *154*, 159, 192, *217*; leister point, 217, *217*; fishing club, 156; net (netting), 80, 106, 148; net sinkers, 134, 147, 156; weirs, 150, 192

flaked (chipped) stone technology, 37, 48, 97, 112, 117, 120-21, 124, 140, 142, 226

fluted projectile point technology, 97, 99, 105-09, *111*, 112-23, *115*, 126-27, 274

Forest City site, *98*, 117

Forks site, *186*, 200

Frostfish Cove site, 30-31, *32*, *186*

Fulton Island site, 93, 174, *186*, 200, 206, 213

fur trade, 89, 232, 235, 254

Ganong, W.F. (historian), 27, 218, 251, 257, 265; settlement patterning, 40, 86-87; portage routes, 40, 87, 200, 240; place names, 83

gardening: Woodland, 90; Contact, 215, 258, 262-63

gaspereau, alewife (*Alosa pseudoharengus*): Palaeo, 108; Archaic, 132, 138, 144, 148, 177, 181-82; Woodland, 192, 194, 197, 206, 218; Contact, 265

Gaspereau Lake site, 117, *130*, 142-43, *143*, 168

Geganisg site, Ingonish (Gegonish) Island, *98*, 108, 114, 119, 121, 122, 124, *186*

gender studies, 74, 86, 209, 267

Geographic Information Systems (GIS), 69

Geological Survey of Canada, 131; Archaeology Division, 46

Georges Bank, 100-01, 132

Gerrish site, *130*, 145-46, *146*

Gesner, A. (naturalist), 25, *25*, 29, 59, 227

Gesner's Museum of Natural History (GMNH), 25-27, 37, 49

"Ghost Hunter" story, 82

Gilman Falls sites, *130*, 137, 139

Gilpin, J.P. (naturalist period), 30, 72

glaciation (glaciers): glacial maximum, 22, 100, *100*; glacial till, 121, 127; refugia, 101; Palaeo, 109; ice patches, 109, 126; Wabanaki stories of deglaciation, 19, 21, 101-04

Goddard site, *186*, 231; Norse coin from, 250-51

Goldthwait Sea (ancestral Gulf of St. Lawrence), *100*, 101, 104, 124

gorget (neck ornament), 38, 189, *191*, 191-92, *193*, 194-203, 276

Gramly, R.M.: Palaeo studies, 108, 224,

230; Lambe site, 106, 116; Vail site, 109, 116
Great Diamond Island site, 185, *186*
"Great Glacier" stories, 19, 101–04
"Great Hiatus," 75, 131
grey literature in archaeology, 273, 278
groundnut (*Apios americana*): Woodland, 188, 210, 215, 240; Contact, 266, 277
ground slate bayonets, 150, 154, 156, 162, 182, 275; narrow-bladed, *143*, 151, *151*, 153, *154*, 159, *160*, *161*, 162–63; broad-bladed, *154*, 159–60, *161*, 162–63; swordfish bills, 153
ground slate projectile points, 133, 145, 147–48, 150, 154, *154*, 159, 162
ground stone adzes (celts): adze, 65, *141*; Middle Archaic 139; Moorehead phase, 153, proto-Laurentian, 147; Transitional Archaic, 168, 200–01; Adena (Middlesex), 198, 202; Woodland, 47; underwater finds, 132–33
ground stone axes (celts): defined, 29, 44–45, 65; hafting, 137–38; grooved, 163, 165; fully grooved, 168, 177; ¾ grooved, 169, *169*; Transitional Archaic 165, 182; Adena, 200
ground stone celts (undifferentiated adze or axe): 45, 137, 139, *143*, 162, 165, 168, *170*, 188–89, 192, 194, 200, 203
ground stone gouges, 26, 133, 138, 147, 153, 159; full-channelled gouge, 132, 134, 137, 139–42, *141*, *143*, 147, 181; shallow-grooved gouge, 141, *141*, 148, 153, *154*, 162, 170; adze/gouge combination, *141*
ground stone plummets, 132–33, 137, 147–48, 153, 156–57, 182; pre-plummets, 142, *143*; grooved (or knobbed), 132, *141*, *143*, *154*, *155*, *157*, 159, 162, 177, 214; as line sinker, 156
ground stone rods, 137–42, *143*, 148; use of, 138; quarry, 140
ground stone technology, 66, 134, 136–37, 150, 162, 173, 181; hafting, 137–38
Gulf of Maine, 130, 150, 154, 164, 166, 181–82, 274–75; tidal activity, 132
Gulf of Maine Archaic, 136–39, 142, 147, 181, 274
Gulf of St. Lawrence, 101, 121, 127, 152, 155, 181–82, 218–19, 239–40, 250, 275
Habitation (Port Royal), 54, *248*, 256–57, *258*, 262–63, 265
Harper, J.R. (early professional period), 51, 267, 269; Portland Point site, 50–51, 93, *157*, 158–59, 168, 214; Hopps site, 51, 93, 154
harpoon, 42, 44; barbed (or serrated) harpoon head, *35*, 36, 150, *154*, 159, 161, *161*; toggling harpoon head, 45, 150, *154*; foreshaft, *154*, 159
Havre Boulet site, *248*, 251
hearth (fireplace) feature, 70, 91; Palaeo, 110; Archaic, 142, 148–49, 153, 168, 175; Woodland, 42, 44, 193
Hedden, M.: rock art studies, 206, 212
Hedden site, *98*, 109
Hirundo site, *130*, 148, 177
Historic Sites Protection Act (1976), 56
history (Indigenous), 3, 76–86, 126–27,

INDEX

277; versus Western, xix, 1, 5, 13–14, 18, 72, 95
Hoffman, B.G. (ethnohistorian), 251, 260, 267; seasonal round subsistence model, 87–88, *88*, 231–32, 237, 246
Hogan-Mullin site, *98*, 119, 191
Holocene Epoch, 122, 129–30, 136–37
Holt's Point site, *186*; incised pebbles, 50, *160*, 204
Hopps site, 51, 93, 214, *248*, 254–55, 270
horizon: concept, 73, 152; defined, 75
horticulture, 210, 212, 215–16, 235, 240, 245, 277
Howe site, *186*, 191
Hrynick, M.G., 188; settlement pattern studies, 90, 208–09; Port Joli, 209
human remains, 16–18, 29; excavation and analysis of, 15–18, 34, 65, 72; ethical issues related to excavation and analysis, 7, 11, 15, 59; repatriation and reburial of, 7, 17, 202
hunter-gatherers (foragers), 3; mobility, 86, 152, 218, 241; settlement and subsistence patterns, 86–90; Palaeo, 106–09, 122, 126, 274; Archaic, 133, 135, 275; Woodland, 230, 236; Contact, 249
ice patches, *see* glaciation
incised decoration: on figurine, 50, *50*; on pebbles, 50, *160*, 204; on bone, 159, 167; on bayonets, 59, *160*, *161*, 162–63
Indian: use of term, xvii
Indian Gardens site, 93, 119, *130*, *141*, 150, *161*, 169
Indigenous archaeology, 5, 13, 74, 278

Indigenous peoples: on Maritime Peninsula today, 1–17; collaboration with archaeologists, xix–xx, 5–6, 12–15, 61, 278; ethnic affiliation with past peoples, 6, 36, 203–04; Contact population estimates, 253; *see also* history; oral traditions
Indigenous rights and title, 8–10
interior sites: survival of faunal remains at, 70, 91, 166; scarcity in early Holocene, 131; deeply stratified, 64, 70, 76, 129, 136, 141, 171, 173, *202*; dwellings at, 209; nut trees exploitation at, 182; pottery production at, 233; disturbance of, 273
"The Invisible Boy" story, 272
iron axes (European), 26, 268, 270
Jemseg site, 3, 12, 40, 94, 174, 185, *186*, 189, 192, 214, 216, *248*, 269
Jones site, *98*, 99, 121, 123–25, *125*, 274
Keenlyside, D.L.: Palaeo studies, 58, 99, 108–09, 113, 120–24, 132; on the importance of walrus hunting, 14, 108, 123, 155–56, 218; Jones site, 99; Tracadie sites, 236
Kejimkujik Lake (rock art) sites, 206, 211–12, *248*, 269
kincentric ecology, 262
Kingsclear site, *98*, 114, *115*, 116
Kluskap ("Gluskabe," or "Glooscap"): described, 80–81, 212; as teacher, 80; in stories, 81–82, 256; and feasting, 261
"Kluskap and the Giant Beaver" stories, 79, 81, 84, 132
Knox site, 185, *186*

INDEX

Kolodny, A.: Indigenous studies, 9–10, 252; concerning "The Prophecy" story, 247–48

Kristmanson, H.: Indigenous rights and title, 10; collaboration with Indigenous communities, 10–11, 14; ceramic studies, 78, 186–87; Pitawelkek site, 14

Lambe site, 106, 116

language: acceptable Indigenous terms, xvii–xviii; and cultural memory, xix; as part of Indigenous title, 8, 11

L'Anse Amour site, *130*, 155

L'Anse aux Meadows (Norse) site, *248*, 249–50, *250*

Late Archaic peoples: characteristics, 144–45; interior, 146–50; coastal, 150–63; Transitional (Terminal) origins, 163–66; early Transitional, 166–73; late Transitional, 173–76; transition to Woodland, 179–80; *see also* individual sites from Figure 28

Late Palaeo peoples: origins, 122; settlement and subsistence, 122–23; *see also* individual sites from Figure 21

Laurentian Archaic Tradition, 146–49, 181–82

leadership: Palaeo, 126; Woodland, 195, 230, 276; Contact, 249

LeClercq, C. (seventeenth-century chronicler), 80, 84, 209, 260–61, 270

Lelièvre, M. A.: collaboration, 6, 15; settlement patterning studies, 53, 209; Qospemk (Neville Lake) site, 175

Leonard, K.: paleoethnobotany, 210, 213–16, 219; Skull Island, 34, 84, 94, *186*, 215; on copper industry, 196–97

Lescarbot, M. (seventeenth-century chronicler): on shamans, 84; on Maine copper kettle burial, 254; on feasting, 257–67; on wampum, 270

Lewis, R., *32*, *94*; on appreciation of Indigenous knowledge and experience, xix; on language as key to cultural memory, xix; collaboration, xx, 6; Mi'kmaw historic timeline, 3; fish weirs, 188

lithic sources, 37, 40, 44, 52, 170, 173, 208, 219–31, *228*, *229*; quarries, 64, 110, 127; workshop sites, 23, 37, 224–26, *225*

lithic technology: terminology, 65, *66*; quartz-based, *222*; workmanship decline in late Woodland, 210

looting of sites: prevention of, 6

MacDonald, G.F.: Palaeo studies, 99, 107, 116–17; Debert site, 52–53, 110, 112, 227

Machias Bay rock art sites, 212

MacKinnon, C. (avocational archaeologist): Beausejour Beach site, 156–58, 165, 168, 219

Magdalen Islands sites, 2, *98*, 99, 101, 105, 122, 125, 131–32, 155, 221

Maliseet, *see* Wolastoqiyik

Maliseet [Wolastoqwey] Advisory Committee on archaeology, 12–13, 61

marine effigy plummets, *155*, *157*, 157–59

marine mammal hunting: Palaeo, 106, 108, 123, 274; Archaic, 133, 140, 151,

153–56, 167, 182; Woodland, 14, 127, 187, 216–18, 234, 240; Contact, 260, 263

Maritime Archaic Tradition, 123, 145, 151–52, 179, 182

Maritime Peninsula: defined, 2

"Maritime Triangle" projectile points, 121

marshalling areas, 106–07

Mason site, *186*, 199

Mattawamkeag site, *186*, 231

Matthew, G.F. (naturalist), 25, 27, 59, 92, 208, 227; Bocabec site, 18, 41–44, *43*, 53–54

McCleod-Leslie, H. (Mi'kmaq Rights Initiative), 12–13, 15

McEachen, P.J.: Meadowood studies, 180, 189, 191–94

McGowan Lake site, *248*, 252

McKinlay site, 198, 200–03

Meadowood (Early Woodland), 176, 180, 188–97, 204, 245, 276; habitation, 190–94; technology, 189, 245; burial practices, 191, 197–98

Meadowood Interaction Sphere, 188, 195

Mécatina site, *248*, 251

Medford site, *98*, 114, 116

Meductic site, 22, 48, 92, 140, 215, *248*, 269

Melanson site, 93, *98*, 114, *115*, 119, *169*, *186*, 209, 230, 239

Merigomish Harbour sites, 33–36, *35*, 38, 46, *47*, 53, 92, *186*, 217

Merrymakedge site (Kejimkujik Lake), *186*, 193

Metepenagiag (Red Bank) site complex, 190, *190*, 200, 203, 245, 276; collaborative work, 12, 16; large-scale storage, 195–96; copper kettle burial, 49, 93; textiles, 93, 214

Michaud site, *98*, 99, 108–09

middens, *see* shell middens

Middle/Late Woodland peoples: characteristics, 203–04; pottery (ceramics), 204–07; subsistence, 209–10, 213–19; rock art, 211–12; plant use, 213–16; animal use, 216–19; lithics, 219–31; settlement and subsistence models, 231–41; *see also* individual sites from Figure 47

Middlesex Early Woodland: linked to Ohio Valley Adena Tradition, 198; trade network, 199; burial practices, 164, 198; Augustine burial mound, 196, 202–03; McKinlay site, 203

Mi'kmaq (Micmac): people, 2–3; archaeological timeline, 3; collaborations with archaeologists and government agencies, 7, 10–11, 14–16, 112; rights and title, 8; modern plant use, 44; precontact period, 237, 266; Contact, 88, 215–17, 237, 247–49, 252, 257–63, 266

Mi'kmaq Rights Initiative, 11, 15

Mi'kmaw Atlas, 14

Mill Lake Bluff site, *130*, 140

Minas Basin Archaeological Project, 242

Ministers Island site, 10, *11*, *186*, 199–200

Modern Professional Period, 24, 52–59

Molyneau, B.L.: rock art research, 211–12, 269

Moorehead, W.K. (early professional period): "Red Paint" research, 47–48, *48*, 73, 144, 158, 162
Moorehead Burial Tradition, 75, 145, 153, 159, 182
Moorehead Phase, 145, 152–53, 159, 165, 179, 275
moose (*Alces alces*): Palaeo, 105; Archaic, 148, 150, 153, 159, 165, 182, 216, 276; Woodland, 32, 42, 53, 134, 216; Late Woodland, 234; Contact, 260–65; taboos, 79–80; bone grease, 82; in art 84
mosaic subsistence model, 237, *237*, 239
Mud Lake Stream site, 19, 93, *130*, 167, 174, *176–78*, 176–78, 180, 183, 185, *186*, 192, *193*, 197, 206, *217*
Munsungun Lake sites, *98*, 108–09, 122, 208, 220–21, 236
Murphy, B.M.: zooarchaeology, 5, 70, 75, 91; reanalysis of Gaspereau Lake site, 120, 140, 168
museums (Maritime provinces), 17, 26–29; Gesner's Museum, 25; Garden of the Gulf Museum (PEI), 141; New Brunswick Museum, 25, 27, 49–50, 53, 55; Nova Scotia Museum, 14–15, 55–59, 93, 223
mussel, blue (*Mytilus edulis* L.): Woodland, 31, 219, 266; Contact, 261; modern, 144
Nash, R.J., 57; settlement and subsistence studies, 53, 79, 89–90, 144, 189, 209, 218, 221, 227, 237; Melanson site, 119, 239
National Preservation Act (US, 1966), 13

Natural History Society (NB), 26–27, 30, 39, 41, 48–49
Natural History Society (PEI), 45
naturalist period, 24–45
nets (netting): bird hunting, 105; fishing, 156, 165; *see also* textiles
Neville site (New Hampshire), *130*, 134, 137
Nevin site, *130*, 151, 159
New Horton Creek site, *98*, 114, 116
New London Bay site, *98*, 121
Newsom, B., xvii, 16; Indigenous archaeology, 5, 82; ceramic studies, 185, 187, 232–33
Nicholas site, *98*, 110
Norse (Viking), 249–50; *see also* L'Anse aux Meadows
Northeastern Coastal Pattern, 90
Northport burial site, 93, 215, *248*, 255, *255*, 270
Northumberland Strait, 46, 58, 121, 124, 132, 157, 210
Northumbria, 104
Nova Scotian Institute of Science, 28, 30, 37-38
Oak Island site, *248*, 270
Ochre (red): Archaic, 139, 144–45, 153, 167–68, 177, 181–82; Woodland, 191–92, 194, 199–200, 275
Odaswanokh (Little Narrows) site, *98*, 120
Ohio Valley: and roots of Early Woodland Adena, 198, 245, 276
Old Mission Point site, 17, 201, *248*
oral traditions, xvii–xviii, 1, 5, 21, 59, 71, 84, 132, 158, 211–12, 256, 261, 277–78; defined, 79

"Order of Good Cheer," 19, 257, 259, *259*, 262
Orwell site, *186*, 198–99
Ouigoudi site, *248*, 267, 269
Oxbow site, 12, *186*, 195, *202*, 203, 236
oyster (*Crassostrea virginica*): Archaic, 132, 144, 158; Woodland, 14, 36, 45, 53, 142, 219, 240; in oral tradition, 158
Palaeo ("Paleoindian") period: 3–4, *98*; characteristics, 97–99; physical environment, 100–05; migrations, 106–07; summary, 123–27; *see also* Early Palaeo peoples; Late Palaeo peoples
"Palaeomarine" adaptation, 123
paleoethnobotany (archaeobotany), 69, *94*
palynology, 69, 129
Parks Canada, 14, 54
Passadumkeag River sites, *130*, 139
Passamaquoddy, *see* Peskotomuhkati
Patterson, G. (naturalist period), 32–38, *34*, 51, 53, 60, 72; work at Merigomish, 33–34
Peabody (Robert S.) Museum, 30, 50, 60, 110, 159
Pennfield site, *98*, 167–68
Pentz, B., 169; portage routes, 240
Peskotomuhkati (Passamaquoddy) people: identified, 2–3; archaeological timeline, 4; collaborations with archaeologists and government agencies, 235; Contact, 253, 272; postcontact, 84, 101–04, 211, 252
Petersen, J.B., 76, 129, 154; ceramic studies, 54, 75, 77–78, 210, 215, 232; Varney Farm site, 12; Sharrow site, 137, 142
petroglyphs (rock art): tradition, 29, 40, 211–212, 245, 277; Maine, 204, 206, 212; New Brunswick, 206; Nova Scotia, 206, 211–12, 269; Embden site, 212; Machias Bay sites, 204, 212; Kejimkujik Lake, 206, 211–12, 269; McGowan, 252
phase: concept, 73; defined, 75; Palaeo, 97; Moorehead, 145, 152–53, 159, 165, 179, 275; Vergennes, 146–47, 149; Transitional Archaic, 163; copper kettle, 276
Pierce-Embree site, *98*, 117
Piers, H. (early professional period), 24, *28*, 28–29, 32–33, 72
Pirate Cove site, *98*, 117, *118*
Pitawelkek site, 14, *186*
place names (Indigenous), 5, 83, 277; Study of, 13-14, 35, 40, 64, 69, 83–84
plum, Canada (*Prunus nigra*): Woodland, 92, 210, 213, 215, 240; Contact, 215, 265, 277; and site locations, 64
Point Deroche site, *98*, 115, 121
Port au Choix site, *130*, 156
Port Joli site, 15, 51, 70, *186*, 209–13, 219, 234, 240, 245, 266
Portland Point site, 50–51, 93, *130*, *157*, 159, 168, 174, 185, 214, *248*
Port Medway site, 19, *186*, 194
Port Royal, *see* Habitation
postcontact archaeology, 269-70
post-processual archaeology, 74
pottery, *see* ceramic technology

Preston, B., 55, 200; cultural resource management, 58
Prins, H.E.L.: Indigenous studies, 2, 85, 218, 252, 269
processual archaeology, 73–74
projectile points: attributes, styles, and boundaries, 2, 22, 188, 207–08; Early Palaeo, *111*, 112–20, *115*, 117; Late Palaeo, *115*, 120–25; Early/Middle Archaic, 134–35, 139, *143*; Gulf of Maine Archaic, 136–38; Late Archaic, *141*, *143*, 145, 148–53; Transitional Archaic, 163, 165–69, *170*, 173–76, *177*, 179–83, 276; Early Woodland, 77, 189, 191–94, *193*, 198, 201–03, *243*; Middle/Late Woodland, *207*, 207–08, 225, *243*, 244
"The Prophecy" story, 247-48
protohistoric, *see* Contact Period
provenience, 31, 110
pseudo-scallop shell pottery decoration, 44, 204, *204*
Quaco Head site, *98*, 114, *115*, 116
quahog, or hard-shell clam (*Mercenaria mercenaria*): Woodland, 31, 36, 219; Contact, 271
quarry sites (lithic quarrying), 19, 33, 40, 64, 86, 108, 110, 119, 124, 221, 224–27, 230; *see also* lithic sources
Quoddy region (NB), 173–74, 180, 183, 208, 231–34
radiocarbon dating technique, 18, 22, 73, 76–78; with stratigraphic analysis, 70, 172–73
Rafter Lake site, 150, 185, *186*, 193
Ramah metacherts: Archaic, 153, 176, 182, 275; Woodland, 29, 176, 220,
231, 236, 240
Rand, S.T.: compiler of Mi'kmaw stories, xviii, 80–82, 85, 132, 247, 261, 272
Red Bank, *see* Metepenagiag site complex
Red Bay site, *248*, 251
"Red Paint People," 73, 144; burials, 47, 144, 162–63; *see also* Moorehead phase
repatriation: and reburial of human remains, 7, 15–17; artifact collections, 7; material culture in foreign museums, 7
residues (on pottery), 14, 44; and stable isotope analysis, 70, 187, 206
Rimouski site, *98*, 123–24
Robinson, B., 2, 106, 147, 216; Bull Brook site, 109; Gulf of Maine Archaic tradition, 136–37, 142, 145, 274; burial tradition, 139
Robinson's Island site, *130*, 176
rock art, *see* petroglyphs
Ruisseau-des-Caps site, *130*, 167
Rum Beach site, *130*, 173–74
Rustico sites, 29, 45, 47, *130*, 176
Rutherford, D.E.: lithic studies, 139, 142, 149–50, 154, 162, 165, 179, 198, 203, 220
Sable, T.: Indigenous studies, 2, 79, 81–84, 87, 228, 262, 273
salmon, Atlantic (*Salmo salar*), 91; Palaeo, 108; Archaic, 132, 148–49; Woodland, 192, 194, 218; Contact, 261, 263
Sanders, M., 169; cultural resource management, 277
Sandy Point site, *248*, 270

Sanger, D.R., 24; collaboration, 13-14, 83; Archaic research, 75, 129-31, 136, 141, 147-48, 152-54, 158-59, 161, 164, 166, 170-74, 179-80, 274; "Red Paint People," 73, 144-45; settlement patterning studies, 88-89, 208, 232-35; shell midden studies, 32, 50, 200, 217-19; Blackman Stream site, 134, 137; Gilman Falls site, 139; Cow Point site, 159, 162-63

Savage Harbour sites, *98*, *115*, 121, 150, 176

scallop (*Phocapecten magellanicus*): Woodland, 31, 42; Contact, 263; artifacts recovered by modern dragging, 58, 132, 142, 157-58

scrapers (unifacial tools), *66*; Palaeo, *111*, 123-24; Archaic, 136, 138, 140, 142, 166, 174, 183; Woodland, 44, 188, 191-92, 203, 226, 244; *see also* end scraper; side scrapers

sea level change, 58, 65, 104, 129, 131-33, 181, 209, 273

seals (various species): Palaeo, 104, 106, 108, 123; Archaic, 140, 150, 153, 165, 182, 276; Woodland, 14, 187, 217, 234, 239; Contact, 260, 263

seriation technique, 73, 75, 77, 97; defined, 72

shallops, 252

shamanism, 84, 127, 153, 198, 200, 211-12

shark (various species): Archaic, 153; Woodland, 42, 200; spiritual power of shark teeth, 200

Sharrow site, *130*, 137, 142

shell beads: Woodland, 199; Contact, 270-71

shellfish exploitation, 91, 182, 188, 240, 245, 276; Maine coast, 158, 165, 181, 218; Passamaquoddy Bay, 42, 92, 218, 233-34; Minas Basin, 144; Merigomish Harbour, 36, 209; Port Joli Harbour, 210, 219, 234-35; Gulf of St. Lawrence, 237, 239; Contact, 261, 263; *see also* clam; oyster; quahog; scallop; shell middens

shell middens: in Maritimes, 21, 51, 64; nature of, 31; destruction of, 39, 46, 53; preservation of organics in, 70, 91-92, 217, 265-66; Danish *kjoekkenmoeddinger*, 29, 31; Pitawelkek, 14; Rustico, 29, 45, 47; Frostfish Cove, *6*, 30, *58*; Merigomish, 33, 36-38, 53, 209; Clam Cove, *20*, 223, 226; Quoddy Region, 38-39, 50, 88, 218; Phil's Beach (Bocabec), 41; Ministers Island, *10*, 200; Port Joli, 51, 70, 209, 266; Penobscot Bay, 232, 269

side scrapers (unifacial tool), *66*; Palaeo, 112; Woodland, *193*, *243*; *see also* scrapers; end scrapers

Skora (White's Lake) site, *186*, 198-200

Skull Island site (Shediac), 16, 34, 84, 94, *186*, 214-15

Smith, H.I., 46, *46*, 60; with Peabody Museum, 30; Merigomish sites, 36, *47*, 51, 53, 92

Smithsonian Institution, Washington, 29-30, 38

soapstone (steatite): pipe, 34; bowls, 26, 163-65, 168, 173-74, *175*, 251

Soctomah, D.: Indigenous studies, 4,

101–04; N'tolonapemk site, 138, 148
soils (sediments): acidity and organic preservation, 24, 34, 68, 70, 91; superposition (soil layering), 31–32; stratigraphic analysis, 39, 70, 76, 134, 172, 225; sampling, 22, 277; coring, 209; chemical analysis, 34
Souriquois, 252
"Southern Gulf" projectile points, 121
spear throwers (atlatls): described, 135; Archaic, 135, 139; Early Woodland, 276
Special Places Protection Act (NS, 1989), 56
Speck, F.R. (early professional period): Indigenous studies, 44, 49–50, 85, 93, 228, 230, 232, 236, 266, 271–72
Spiess, A.E.: zooarchaeology, 108, 137, 154, 156, 158, 165–66; Palaeo, 99, 113, 116–19; Archaic, 132–36, 147, 150, 163, 173; Contact, 210, 262, 269; Michaud site, 108–10
spirituality, 5–6, 14, 67–68, 79–84, 90, 144, 162, 183, 189, 198, 245–49, 267, 276–77; leaders, 17, 108, 127, 212
stable isotope analysis, 70
Stanley site, *130*, 153–54
Stark (projectile point style), 134–36, 139
St. Croix Island (NB), 174, *186*, 257–58, 265, 269
St. Croix River (NB), 9, 58, 138, 158, 165, 167, 174, 180, 192, 197, 215, 235, 240, 245, 275
St. Croix site (NS), 19, 78, 185, *186*, 194, 226, 241–43, *243*
Steele's Island site, *130*, 150
Stewart, F.L., 57; zooarchaeology, 88, 92, 158, 218, 265–66; Melanson site, 90, 209
"Stone Age," 37; Three Age System, 72
stratigraphy (stratigraphic analysis), 70–76, 148, 160, 168, *172*, *202*; defined, 39; deeply stratified sites, 64, 76, 90, 136, 171–73
sturgeon (*Acipenser* sp.): Archaic, 150; Woodland, 195, 218; Contact, 260–65
subsistence patterns (patterning), 65; defined, 67; Palaeo, 108; Archaic, 140, 147, 150, 154, 165, 182, 274; Woodland, 212, 233–37; Contact, 87
Sunkhaze Ridge site, *130*, 139
superposition (soil layering): and chronology, 31
Susquehanna peoples, *see* Transitional Archaic
Suttie, B.D.: Palaeo, 99, 115, 121; Archaic, 75, 139–40, 163, 168, 175; Woodland, 195, 200, 206, 267; Canal Beach site, 163, 167–68
Swanton site, *186*, 198–99
sweathouses (sweat lodges), 90, 209, 245
swordfish (*Xiphias gladius*): Archaic, 148–54, 164, 182, 275; swordfish bill (*rostrum*) harpoon foreshaft, *154*, 159
Tabusintac site, 40, *248*
Taché, K.: ceramics and residue studies, 70, 82, 185, 187–89, 277; Meadowood Interaction Sphere, 188, 195
Tapper, B.: rock art studies, 206, 211–12, 269, 277
Tarrantines: origin, 252; link to copper

kettle burials, 154; "Tarrantine Wars," 252

Teacher's Cove site, *130*, 167, 174

technology (precontact): defined, 65; through invention, 71; technological tradition, 75

temper (in ceramic paste), 44, 187, 210

terminology, xvii–xviii, *66*, *67*

textiles (matting, bags, cordage): Archaic, *151*, 151; Woodland, 188, 199–200, 202, 214–15; Contact, 36, 92–93, 232, 255, 268

thermoluminescence (TL) dating technique, 78, 241–43

tobacco (*Nicotiana rustica*) and smoking, 80, 216, 261, 266, 268, 277

Tozer site, *186*, 191, *191*, 196

Tracadie sites, *98*, 122, *186*, 236

trade, *see* exchange

tradition (technological): concept, 75, 108, 144, 159; defined, 75; Clovis, 107; Northeastern Palaeo, 108; Gulf of Maine Archaic, 136–42, 181, 274; Moorehead, 182; Moorehead burial, 145, 182, 275; Maritime Archaic, 145, 151; Laurentian, 146–48, 181, 275; Hathaway burial, 146–47; small stemmed point, 152; dugout canoe, 153; Transitional Archaic (Susquehanna), 163–64, 179, 182; Northeastern Susquehanna, 165; Middlesex, 199; Ohio Valley Adena, 245

traditional knowledge, xvii–xviii, 5, 91

Transitional Archaic: origin, 163–66; Early, 166–73; Late, 173–76; Susquehanna people, 163–66, 176, 179, 182, 189; burial tradition, 167; technology, 166–71, 173, 182; lifeways, 165–66, 174; Archaic-Woodland transition, 170–80

Truth and Reconciliation Commission of Canada: Calls to Action, 7

Tuck, J., 57, 110, 152, 203; "Great Hiatus" during early Holocene, 75, 129, 135; "Northeastern Maritime Continuum," 130; Maritime Archaic Tradition, 145, 151, 158, 162; Transitional Archaic, 163, 165–66, 179; Basques, 252

Turnbull, C.J., 54–55, 116, 120–21; stewardship of archaeological sites, 10; Archaic, 132–33, 160, 164; Red Bank research, 12, 16, 93, 189, 196, 198, 201–03, 214; Old Mission Point, 17

Turner Farm site, *130*, 153–56, *154*, 165–67, 176, 183–87, 275

Tusket Falls sites, *130*, 169–70

two-eyed seeing (research method), 5–6

ulu (thin, semicircular knife), 133, *133*, 139, 140–42, *141*, 145, 147, 156, 181–82; defined, 132

unifacial tools, *see* scrapers; side scrapers; end scrapers

Vail site, *98*, 99, 109, 116–17, 126

Varney Farm site, *98*, 99, 120–25

village sites: as a settlement type, 65, 85, 218, 233; precontact, 9, 12–13, 39, 42–44, 119, 194, 231, 235, 239, 241–44; Contact, 249, 253, 267, 269

Vinette I pottery style, 185, *187*, 187–94, 199, 214–15

Wabanaki Confederacy, 3, 272, *272*
Wabanaki peoples, 3, 13, 16, 252, 263; oral traditions, 79-80, 132, 211-12, 247; mapmaking, 85; wampum, 270-72
Wallace, B.L., 54; Norse studies, 249-50
Walrus (*Odobenus rosmarus A.*): Palaeo, 106, 108, 123; Archaic, 133, 155-56, 182; Woodland, 14, 218, 240; ivory tools, 38, 45; baculum fishing club, *155*, 156
wampum, 268, 270-72
Washademoak chert, 208, 220, 227, *229*
Watson site, *186*, 231
whale (various species): in Champlain Sea, 104, 106; Woodland bone tools, 38, 217; Basques harvest of, 251
Whitehead, R.: Indigenous studies, 67, 158, 212, 219, 248, 251-52, 254-55, 266, 269, 271; textiles, 93, 151, 214
wigwams: Woodland, 54, 206, 214; Contact, 84, 253, 261, 267, 271-72; post-contact, 5, 49; in oral traditions, 101-04
wikhikons, 85, *85*
Willoughby, C.C. (early professional period), 30, 144, 160, 199
Wilson, D. (naturalist period), 71-72, 92
Wilson site, *186*, 191

Windover site (Florida), 135
Windsor sites, 29, *98*, 115, *115*, 120
Wintemberg, W.J. (early professional period), 46-47, *46*, 49, 53, 60, 74, 119, 162, 191; Merigomish Harbour, 36; Eisenhauer shell midden site, 46, 92
"A Wizard Carries Off Glooscap's Housekeeper" story, 81-82
Wolastoqiyik, Wolastoqwey (or Maliseet), 33, 47, 49, 93, 129, 220; identified, 2; archaeological timeline, 4; collaboration with archaeologists and government agencies, 12-13; links to past populations, 180, 203, 206, 235; Contact, 249, 252-53, 267-68, 272; growing corn and storage, 196, 210, 215
Woodland Period, *186*; characteristics, 185-89; summary, 244-45; *see also* Early Woodland peoples; Middle/Late Woodland peoples; individual sites from Figure 47
woodworking, 44, 65, 112, 134, 138, 150, 153, 274
Woolsey, C.A.: ceramic studies, 78, 185, 188, 210, 277; George Clark Collection, 49
Younger Dryas event, 105-06, 109, 113
Zooarchaeology, 70, 92